Cells at Work!

はたらく細胞

01

AKANE SHIMIZU

CONTENTS

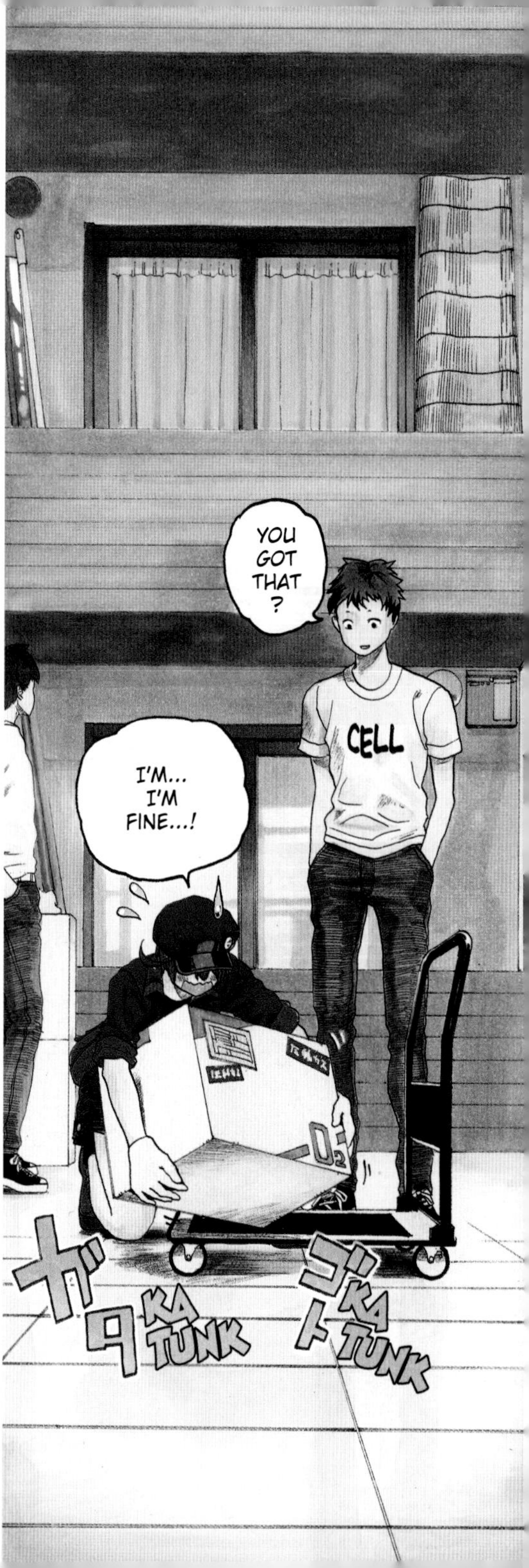

YOU GOT THAT ?
CELL
I'M... I'M FINE...!
O_2
ゴト KA TUNK
ガタ KA TUNK

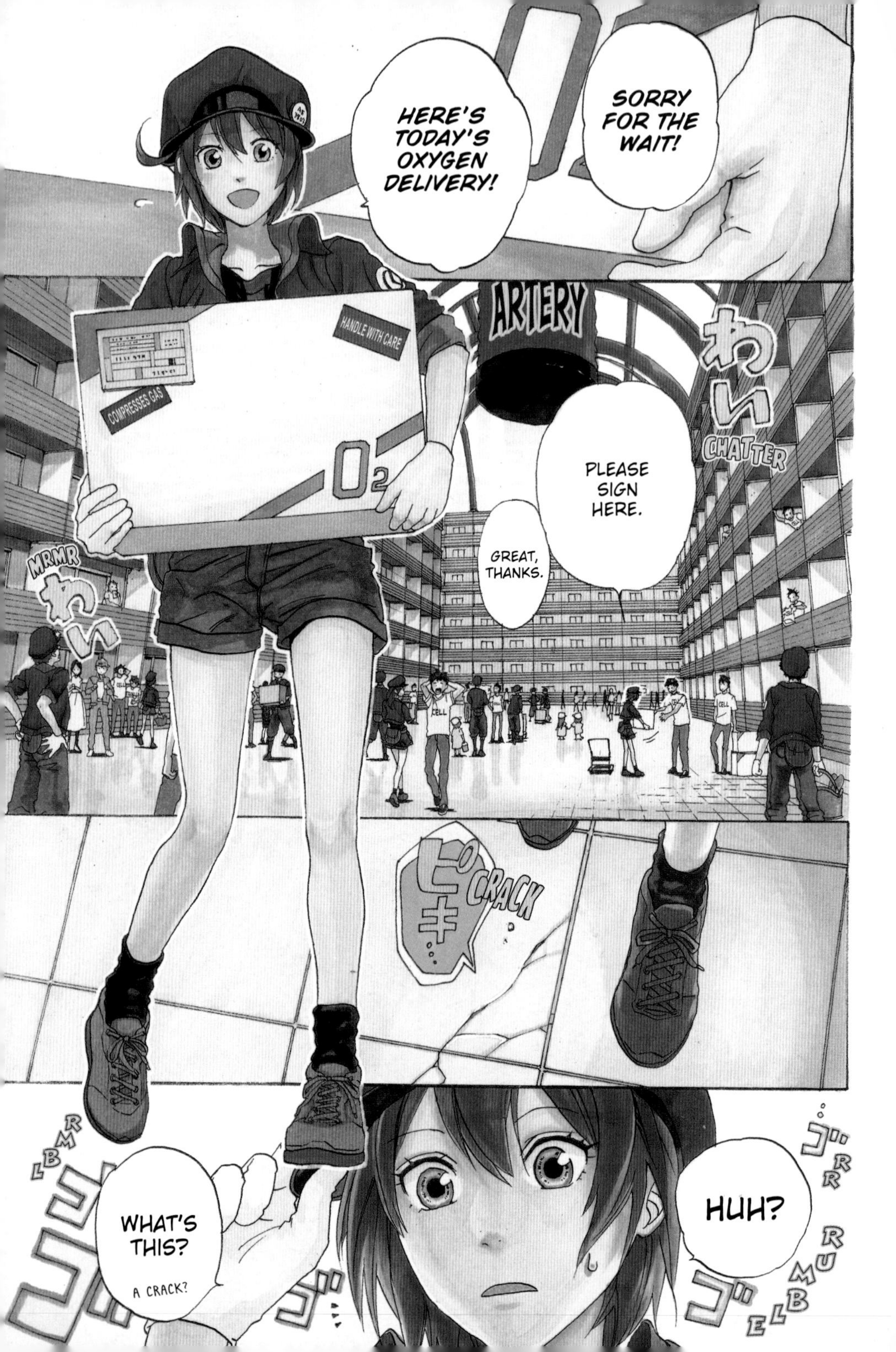
SORRY FOR THE WAIT!
HERE'S TODAY'S OXYGEN DELIVERY!
ARTERY
わい
CHATTER
PLEASE SIGN HERE.
GREAT, THANKS.
HANDLE WITH CARE
COMPRESSES GAS
O_2
MRMR
わい
ピキ
CRACK
ゴゴ
RUMBLE
HUH?
WHAT'S THIS?
A CRACK?
ゴゴ
RMBL

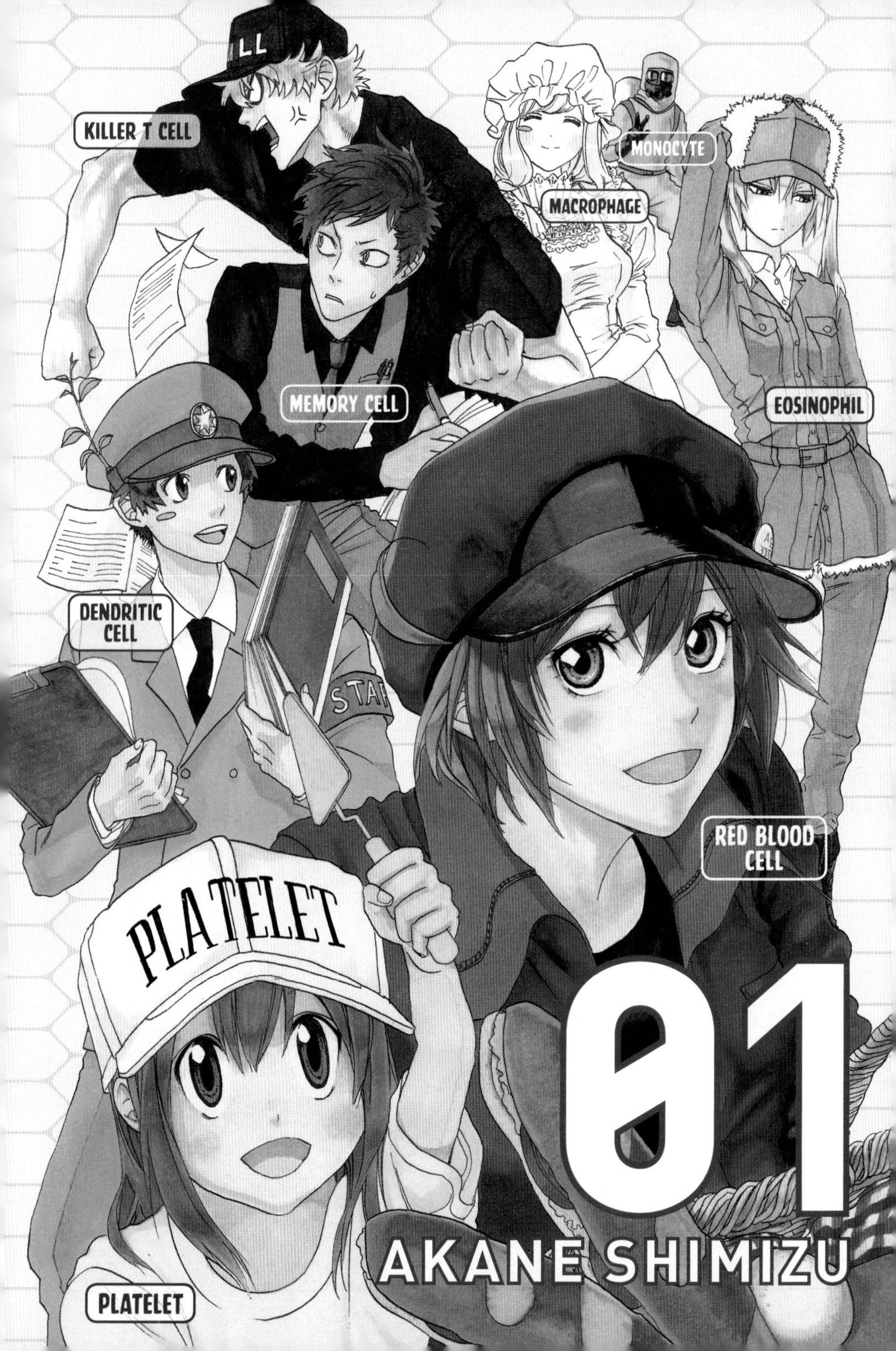
KILLER T CELL
MONOCYTE
MACROPHAGE
MEMORY CELL
EOSINOPHIL
DENDRITIC CELL
RED BLOOD CELL
PLATELET
01
AKANE SHIMIZU
PLATELET

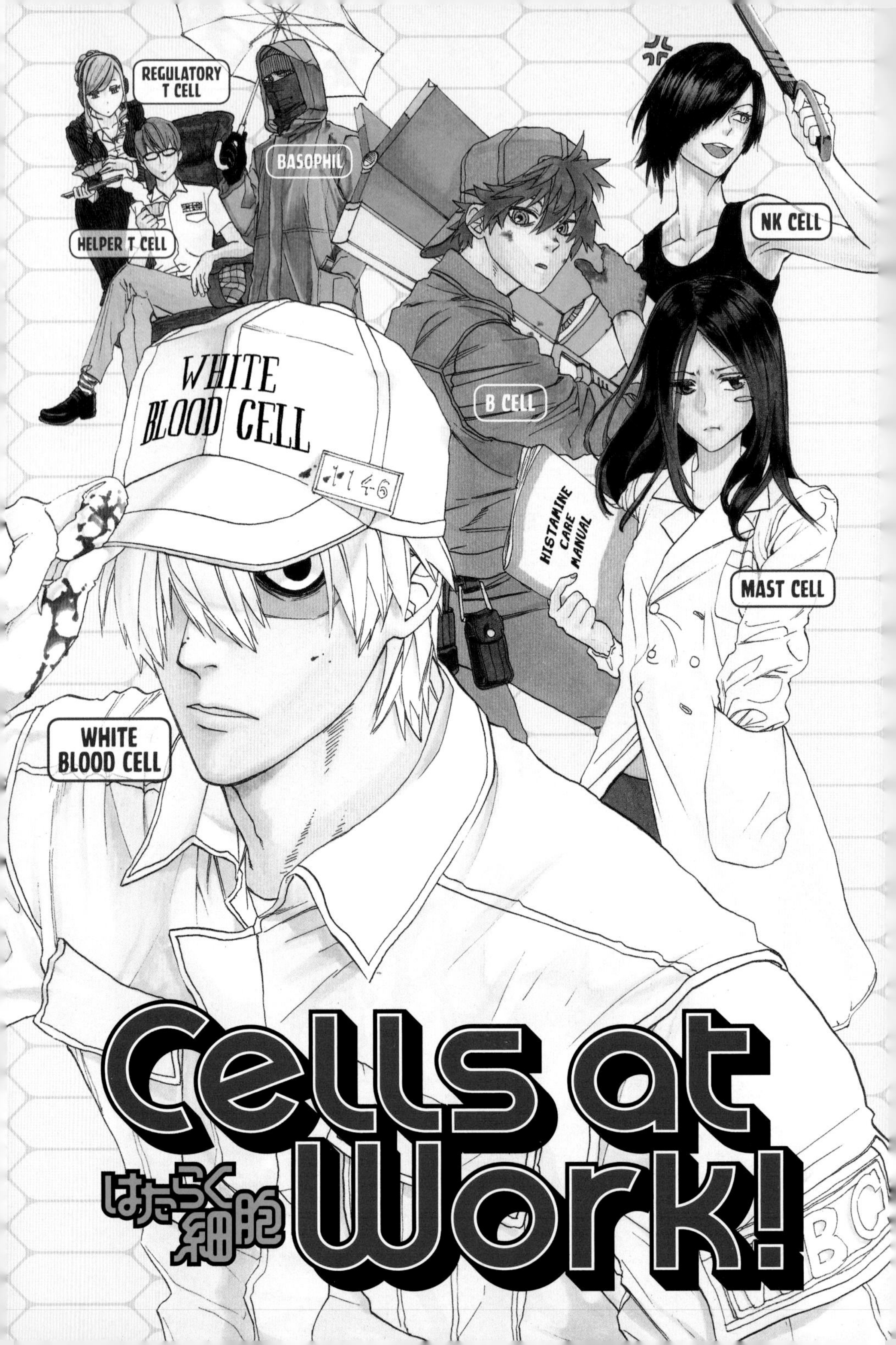
NK CELL
REGULATORY T CELL
BASOPHIL
HELPER T CELL
B CELL
WHITE BLOOD CELL
1146
HISTAMINE CARE MANUAL
MAST CELL
WHITE BLOOD CELL
Cells at Work!
はたらく細胞

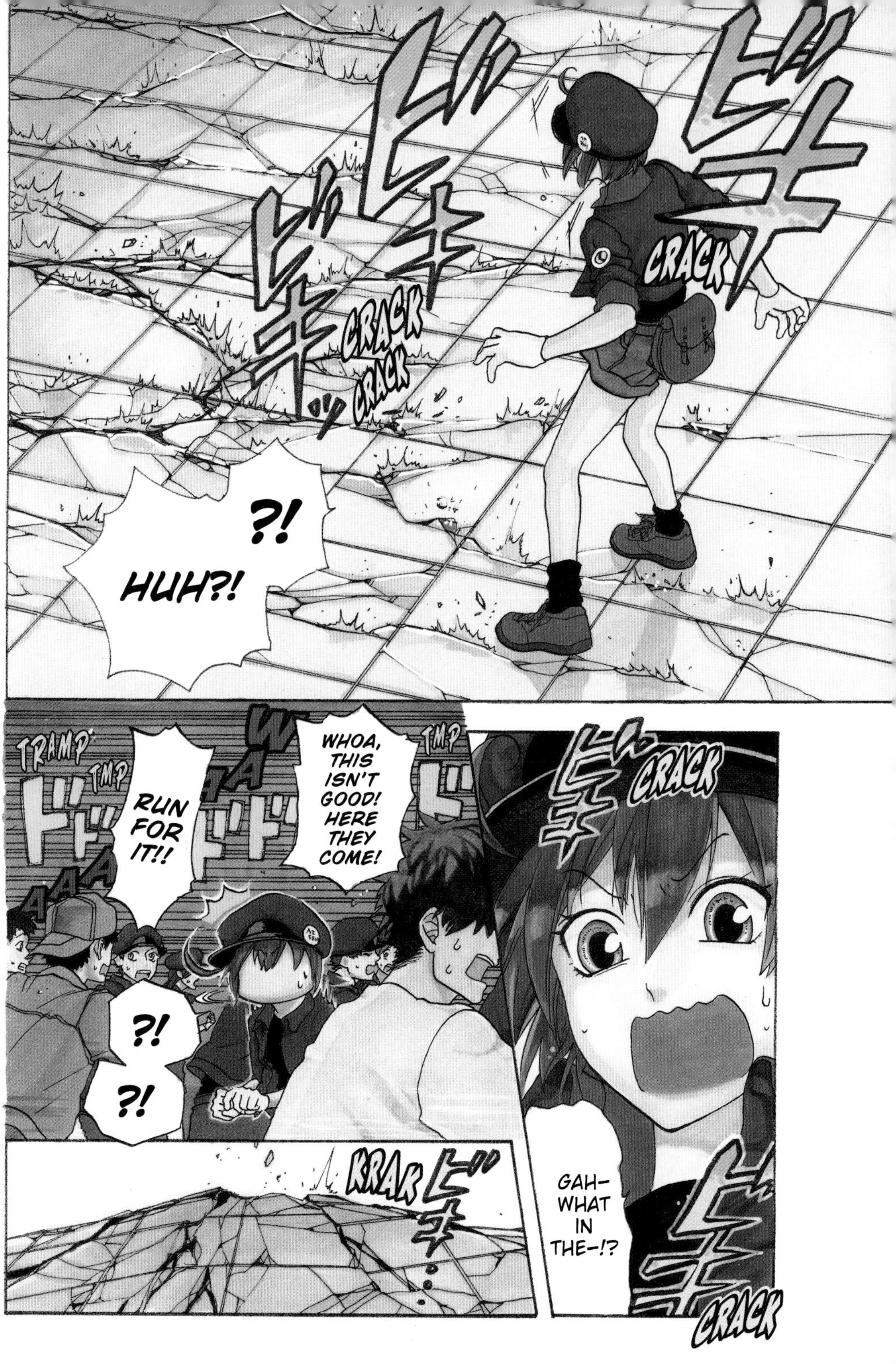
ビキ
CRACK
ビキビキ
CRACK
CRACK
?!
HUH?!
ビキ
CRACK
GAH—WHAT IN THE—!?
ビキ
CRACK
TMP
WHOA, THIS ISN'T GOOD! HERE THEY COME!
WAAA
RUN FOR IT!!
TRAMP
TMP
?!
?!
KRAK

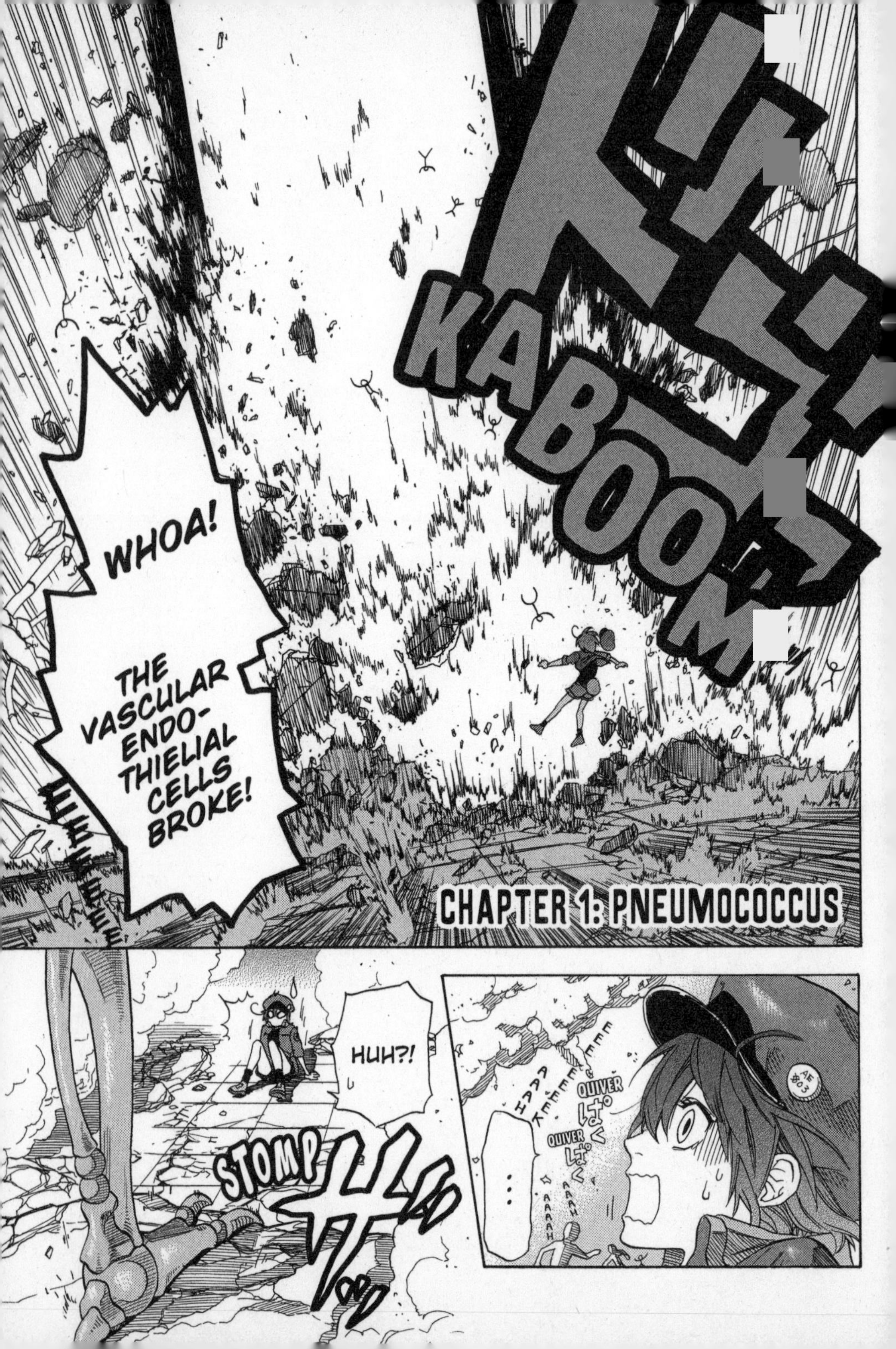
KABOOM
WHOA!
THE VASCULAR ENDO-THIELIAL CELLS BROKE!
EEEEEEEE
CHAPTER 1: PNEUMOCOCCUS
EEEEEEEE
AAAAH
QUIVER ぱく
QUIVER ぱく
AAAAH
...
HUH?!
STOMP

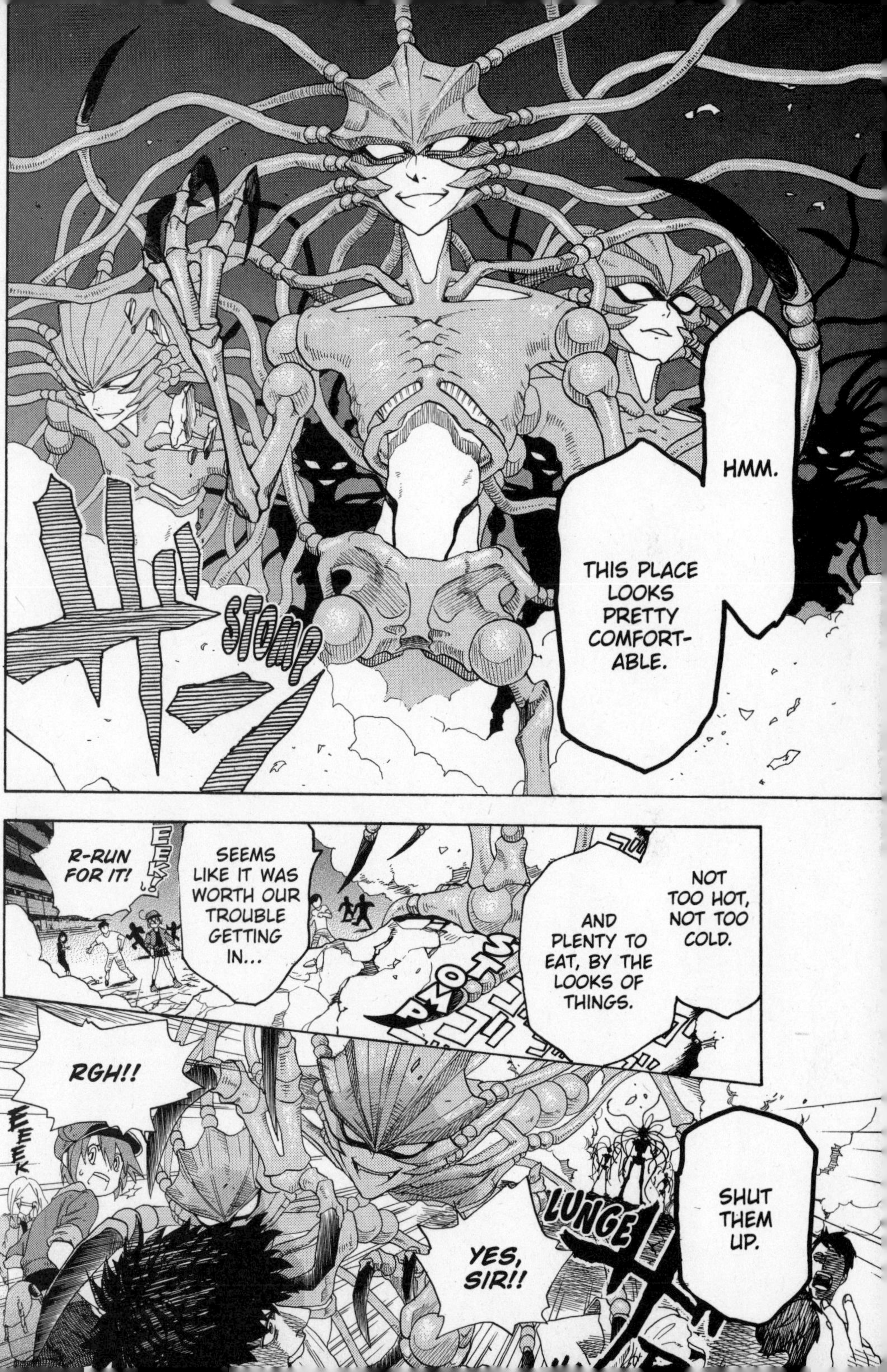
HMM.
THIS PLACE LOOKS PRETTY COMFORTABLE.
STOMP
NOT TOO HOT, NOT TOO COLD.
AND PLENTY TO EAT, BY THE LOOKS OF THINGS.
STOMP
SEEMS LIKE IT WAS WORTH OUR TROUBLE GETTING IN...
EEK!
R-RUN FOR IT!
SHUT THEM UP.
LUNGE
YES, SIR!!
RGH!!
EEEK

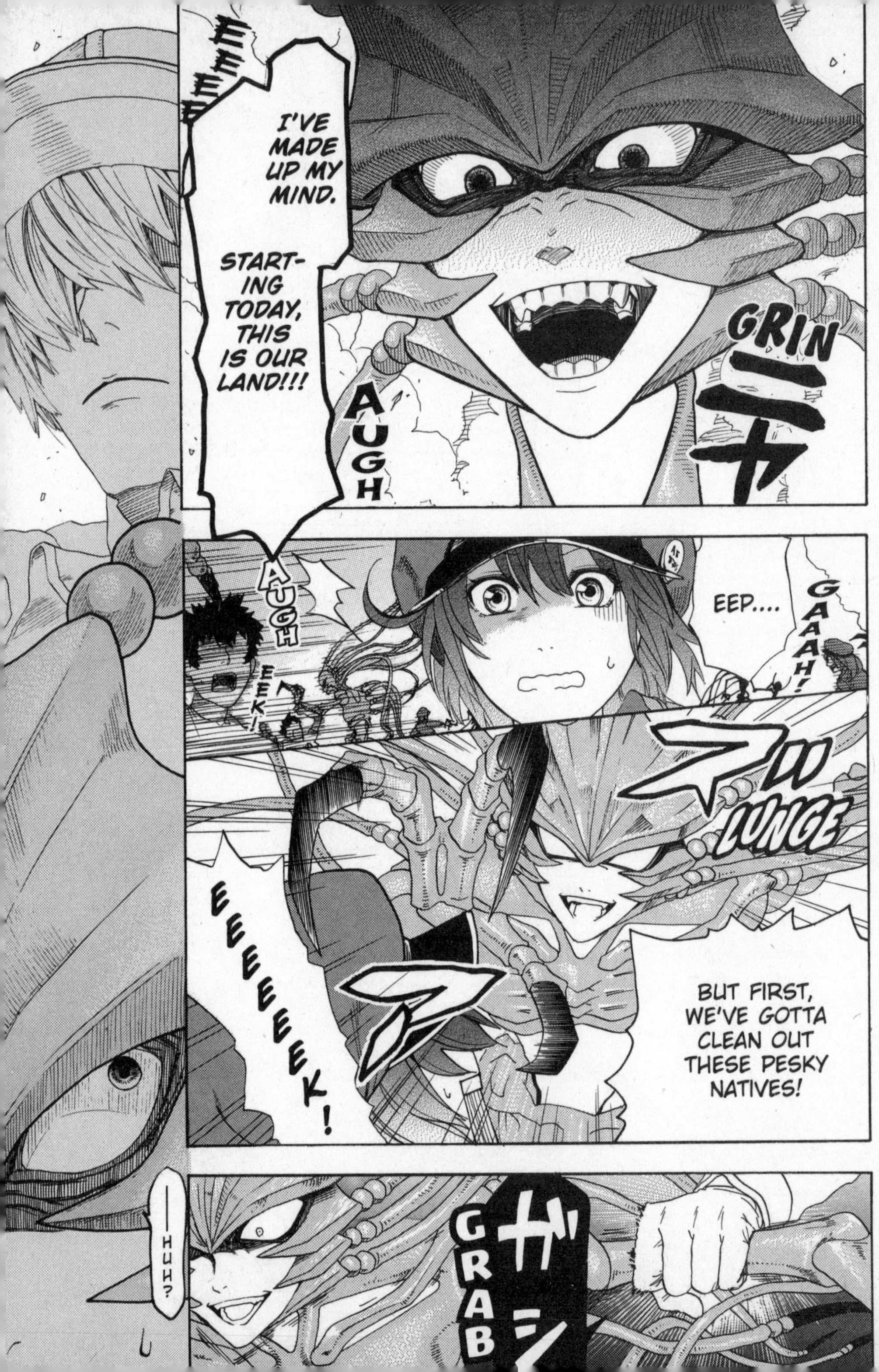
EEEE
I'VE MADE UP MY MIND.
STARTING TODAY, THIS IS OUR LAND!!!
GRIN
AUGH
GAAAH!
EEP....
AUGH
EEEK!
LUNGE
BUT FIRST, WE'VE GOTTA CLEAN OUT THESE PESKY NATIVES!
EEEEEEEK!
GRAB
—HUH?

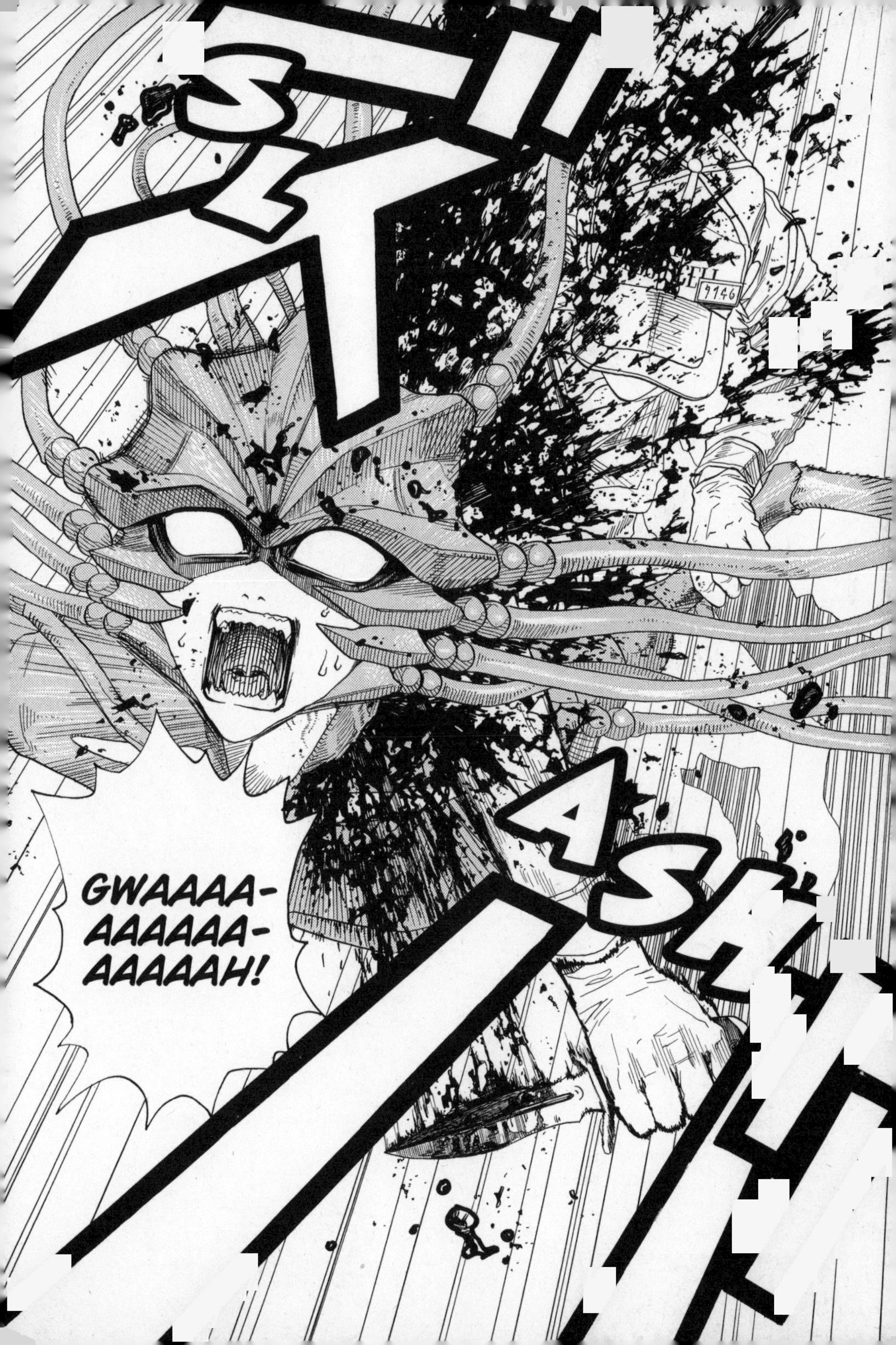
GWAAAA-AAAAAA-AAAAAH!

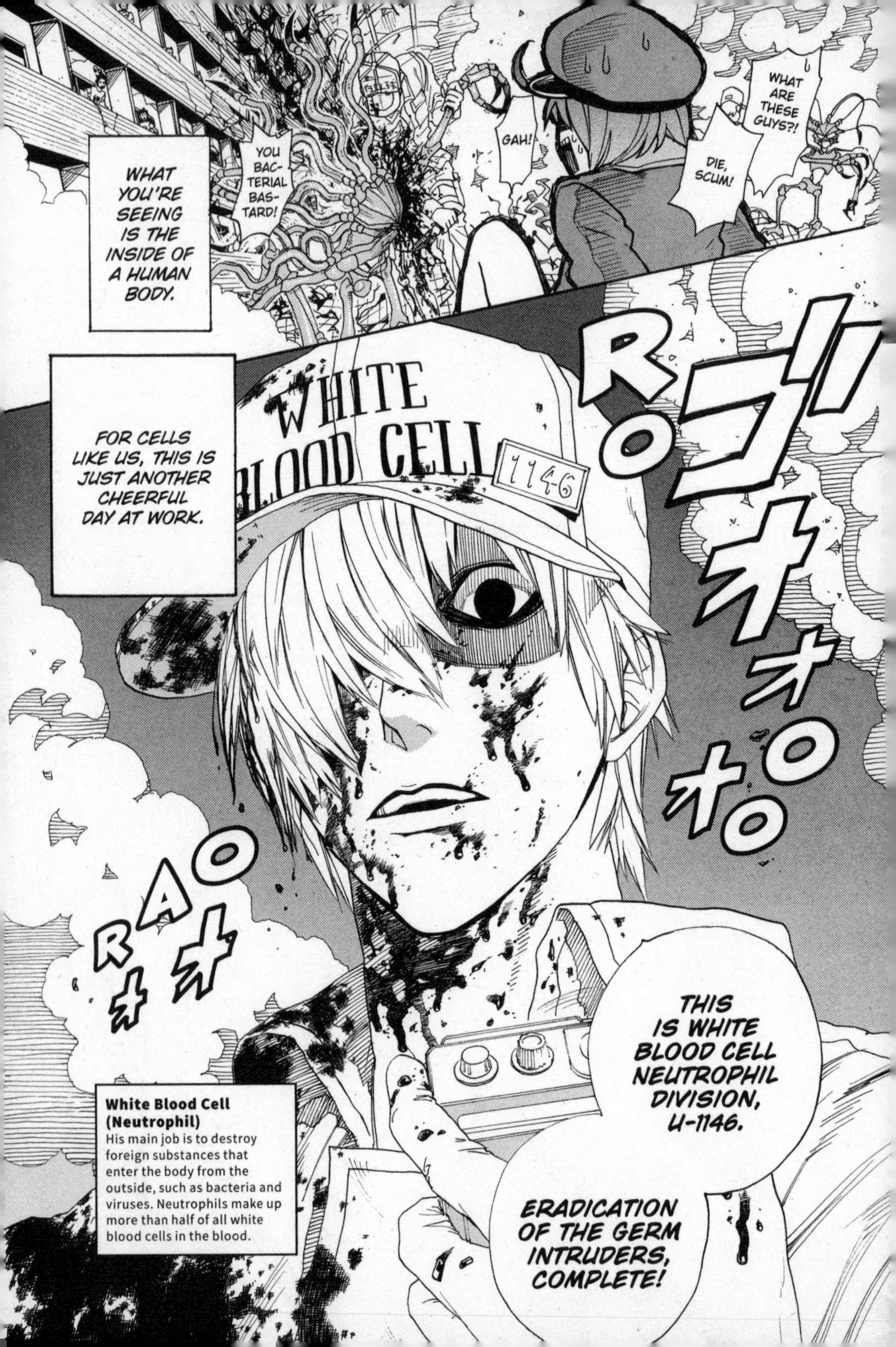
WHAT ARE THESE GUYS?!
DIE, SCUM!
GAH!
YOU BACTERIAL BASTARD!
WHAT YOU'RE SEEING IS THE INSIDE OF A HUMAN BODY.
ROOO
ゴオオオオ
FOR CELLS LIKE US, THIS IS JUST ANOTHER CHEERFUL DAY AT WORK.
WHITE BLOOD CELL
1146
THIS IS WHITE BLOOD CELL NEUTROPHIL DIVISION, U-1146.
ERADICATION OF THE GERM INTRUDERS, COMPLETE!
RAO
オオ
White Blood Cell (Neutrophil)
His main job is to destroy foreign substances that enter the body from the outside, such as bacteria and viruses. Neutrophils make up more than half of all white blood cells in the blood.

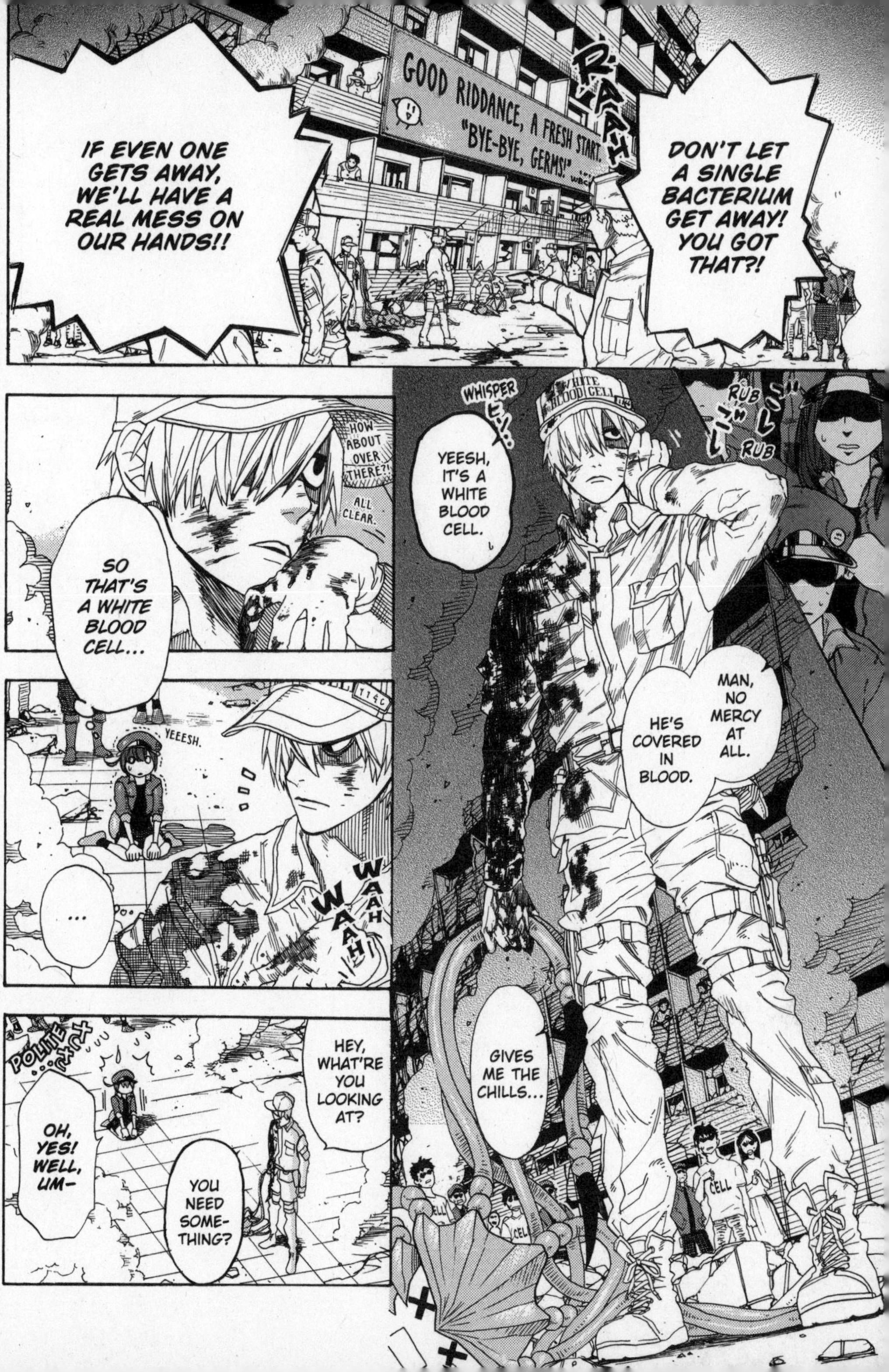
DON'T LET A SINGLE BACTERIUM GET AWAY! YOU GOT THAT?!
RAP!
GOOD RIDDANCE, A FRESH START. "BYE-BYE, GERMS!"
IF EVEN ONE GETS AWAY, WE'LL HAVE A REAL MESS ON OUR HANDS!!
RUB RUB
WHITE BLOOD CELL
WHISPER
YEESH, IT'S A WHITE BLOOD CELL.
MAN, NO MERCY AT ALL.
HE'S COVERED IN BLOOD.
GIVES ME THE CHILLS...
HOW ABOUT OVER THERE?!
ALL CLEAR.
SO THAT'S A WHITE BLOOD CELL...
YEEESH.
WAAAH
WAAAH
...
HEY, WHAT'RE YOU LOOKING AT?
YOU NEED SOMETHING?
POLITE
OH, YES! WELL, UM-

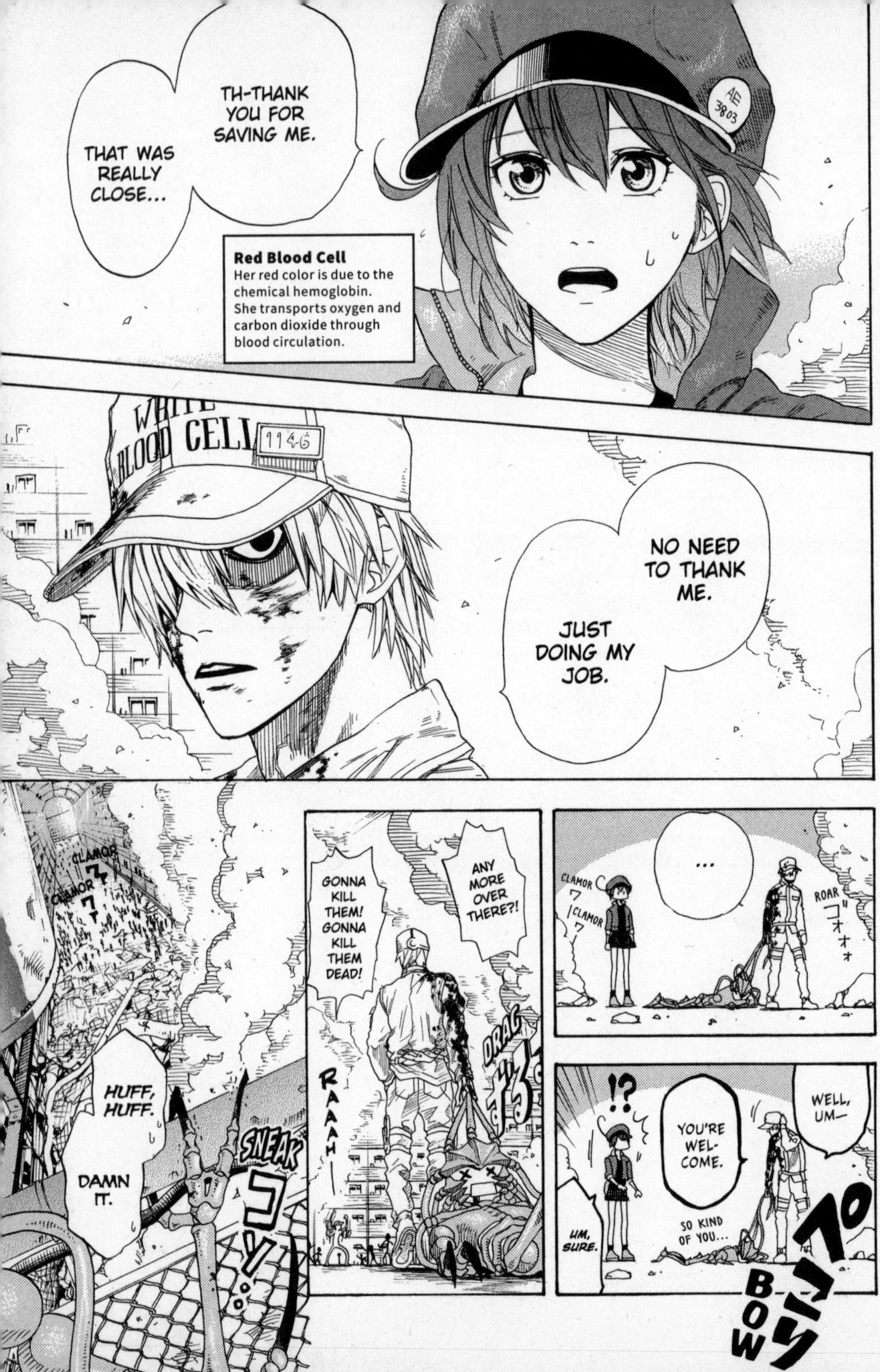
TH-THANK YOU FOR SAVING ME.
THAT WAS REALLY CLOSE...
Red Blood Cell
Her red color is due to the chemical hemoglobin. She transports oxygen and carbon dioxide through blood circulation.
AE 3803
WHITE BLOOD CELL 1146
NO NEED TO THANK ME.
JUST DOING MY JOB.
...
ROAR
CLAMOR
CLAMOR
WELL, UM—
YOU'RE WEL-COME.
!?
SO KIND OF YOU...
UM, SURE.
BOW
ANY MORE OVER THERE?!
GONNA KILL THEM! GONNA KILL THEM DEAD!
DRAG
RAAAH
CLAMOR
CLAMOR
HUFF, HUFF.
DAMN IT.
SNEAK

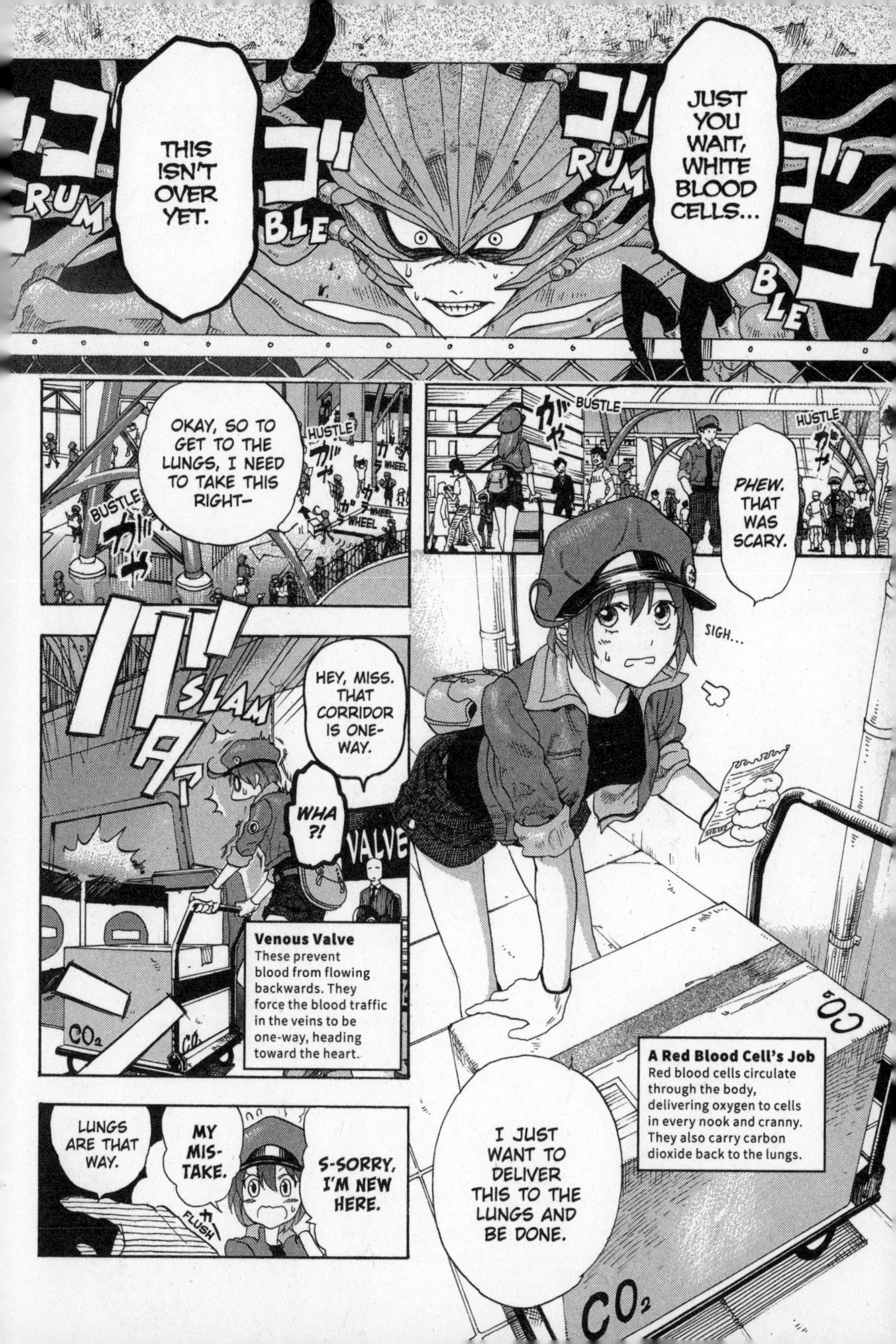
JUST YOU WAIT, WHITE BLOOD CELLS...
RUMBLE
THIS ISN'T OVER YET.
RUMBLE
BUSTLE
HUSTLE
PHEW. THAT WAS SCARY.
HUSTLE
WHEEL
WHEEL
WHEEL
BUSTLE
OKAY, SO TO GET TO THE LUNGS, I NEED TO TAKE THIS RIGHT–
SIGH...
I JUST WANT TO DELIVER THIS TO THE LUNGS AND BE DONE.
A Red Blood Cell's Job
Red blood cells circulate through the body, delivering oxygen to cells in every nook and cranny. They also carry carbon dioxide back to the lungs.
SLAM
HEY, MISS. THAT CORRIDOR IS ONE-WAY.
WHA?!
VALVE
Venous Valve
These prevent blood from flowing backwards. They force the blood traffic in the veins to be one-way, heading toward the heart.
S-SORRY, I'M NEW HERE.
MY MIS-TAKE.
FLUSH
LUNGS ARE THAT WAY.

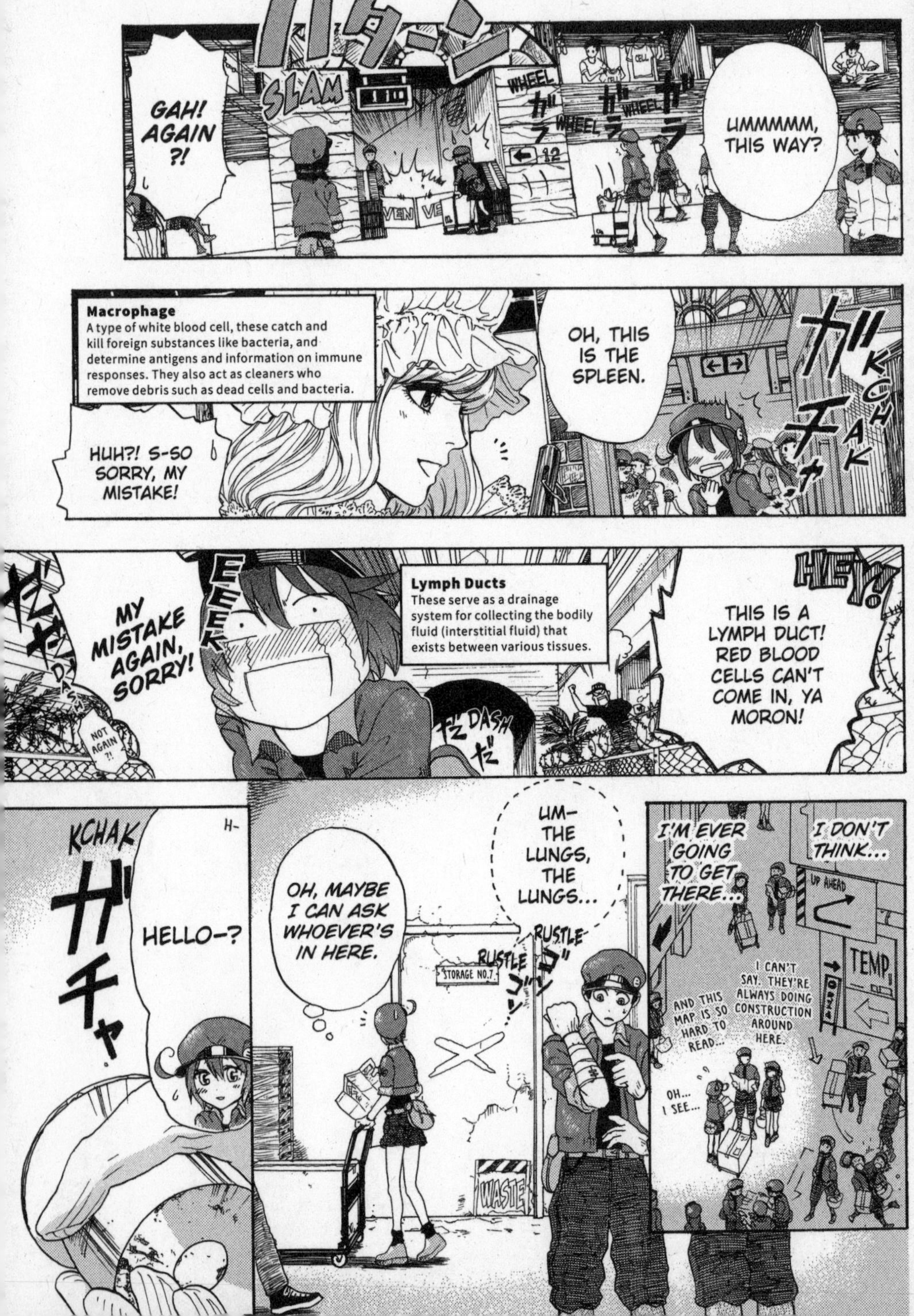
UMMMMM, THIS WAY?
CELL
WHEEL
WHEEL
WHEEL
12
SLAM
VEN
GAH! AGAIN?!
KCHAK
OH, THIS IS THE SPLEEN.
Macrophage
A type of white blood cell, these catch and kill foreign substances like bacteria, and determine antigens and information on immune responses. They also act as cleaners who remove debris such as dead cells and bacteria.
HUH?! S-SO SORRY, MY MISTAKE!
HEY!
THIS IS A LYMPH DUCT! RED BLOOD CELLS CAN'T COME IN, YA MORON!
DASH
Lymph Ducts
These serve as a drainage system for collecting the bodily fluid (interstitial fluid) that exists between various tissues.
EEEEK
MY MISTAKE AGAIN, SORRY!
DASH
NOT AGAIN?!
I DON'T THINK...
I'M EVER GOING TO GET THERE...
UP AHEAD
TEMP
I CAN'T SAY. THEY'RE ALWAYS DOING CONSTRUCTION AROUND HERE.
AND THIS MAP IS SO HARD TO READ...
OH... I SEE...
UM— THE LUNGS, THE LUNGS...
RUSTLE
RUSTLE
OH, MAYBE I CAN ASK WHOEVER'S IN HERE.
STORAGE NO.7
WASTE
KCHAK
H-
HELLO-?

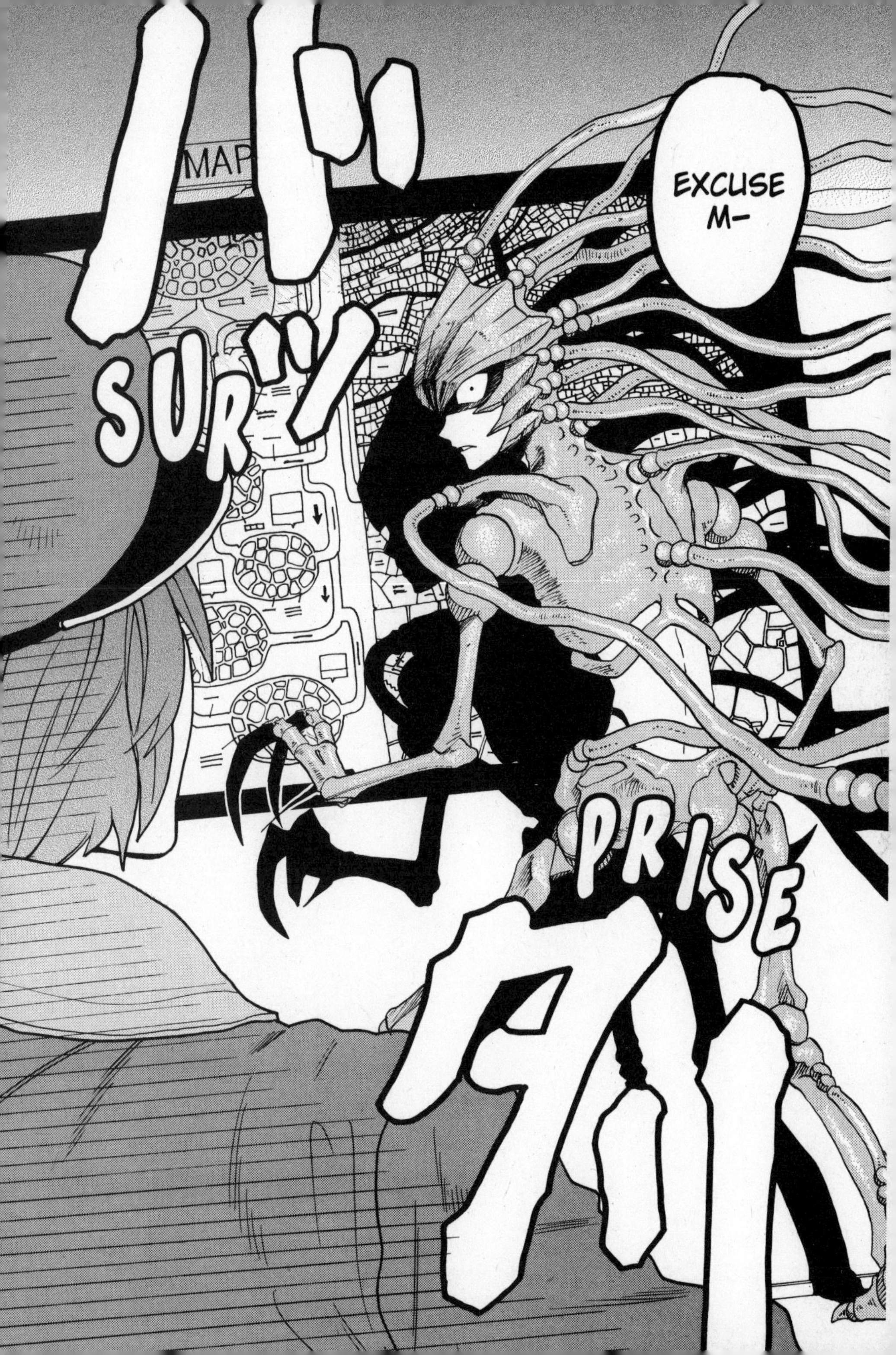
EXCUSE M-
SURPRISE
MAP

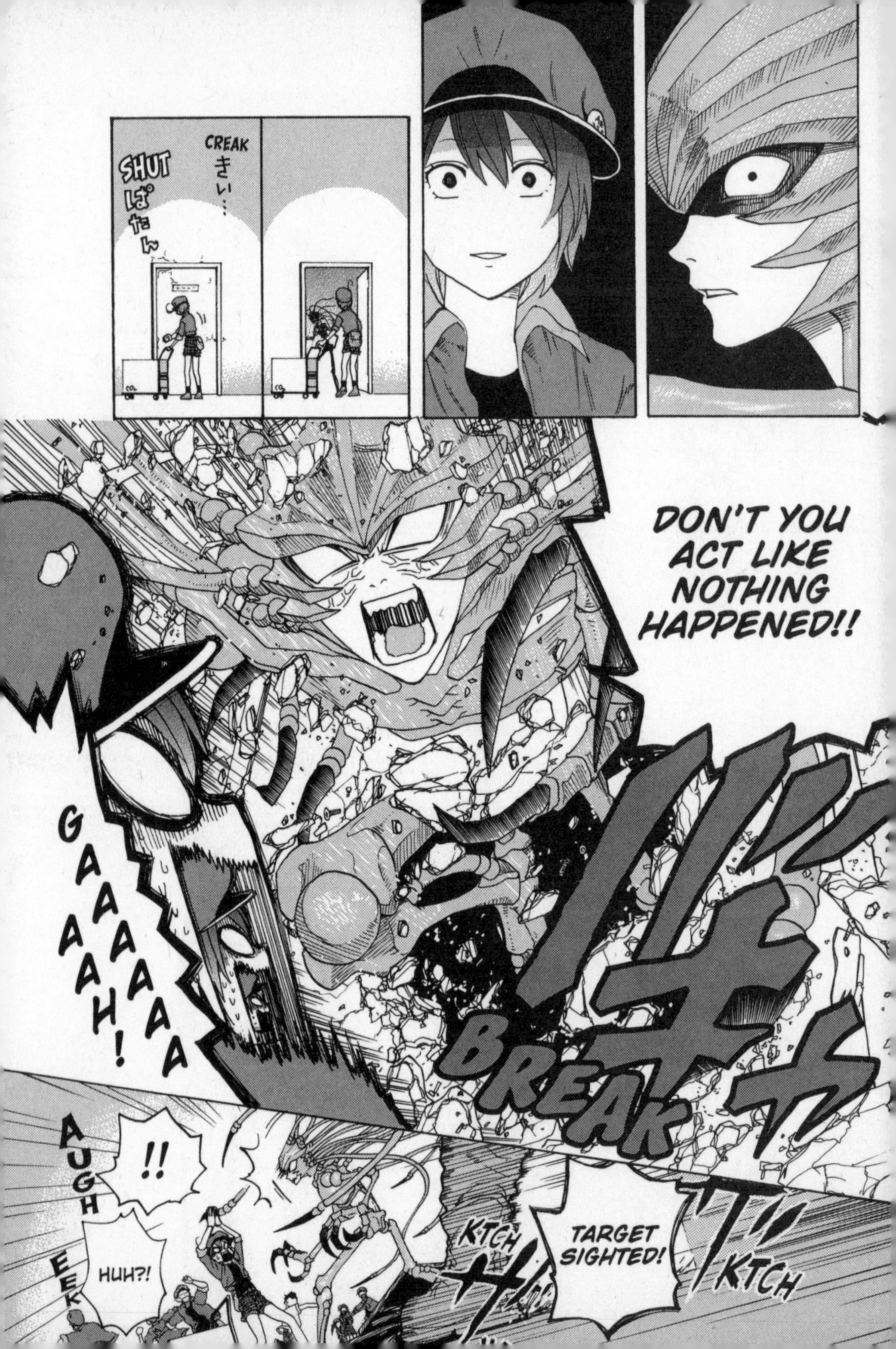
CREAK
きぃ…
SHUT
ぱたん
DON'T YOU ACT LIKE NOTHING HAPPENED!!
GAAAAAAAAAAH!
BREAK
KTCH
TARGET SIGHTED!
KTCH
!!
HUH?!
AUGH
EEK

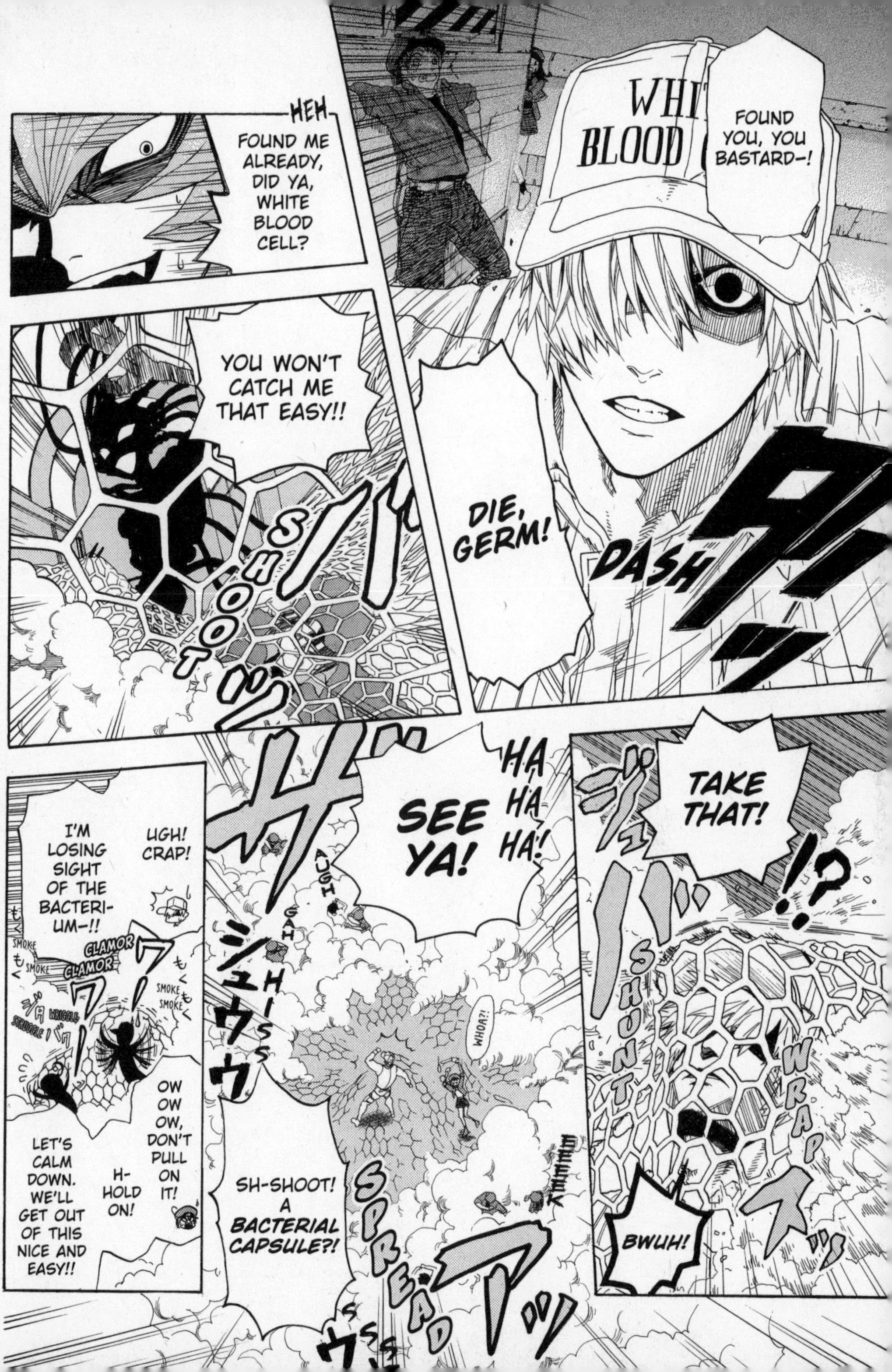
FOUND YOU, YOU BASTARD–!
DIE, GERM!
DASH
HEH
FOUND ME ALREADY, DID YA, WHITE BLOOD CELL?
YOU WON'T CATCH ME THAT EASY!!
SHOOOT
TAKE THAT!
!?
SHUNT
WRAP
BWUH!
HA HA HA!
SEE YA!
AUGH
GAH
HISS
WHOA?!
SH-SHOOT! A BACTERIAL CAPSULE?!
SPREAD
UGH! CRAP!
I'M LOSING SIGHT OF THE BACTERI-UM–!!
CLAMOR CLAMOR
SMOKE SMOKE
SMOKE SMOKE
WRIGGLE STRUGGLE
OW OW OW, DON'T PULL ON IT!
H-HOLD ON!
LET'S CALM DOWN. WE'LL GET OUT OF THIS NICE AND EASY!!

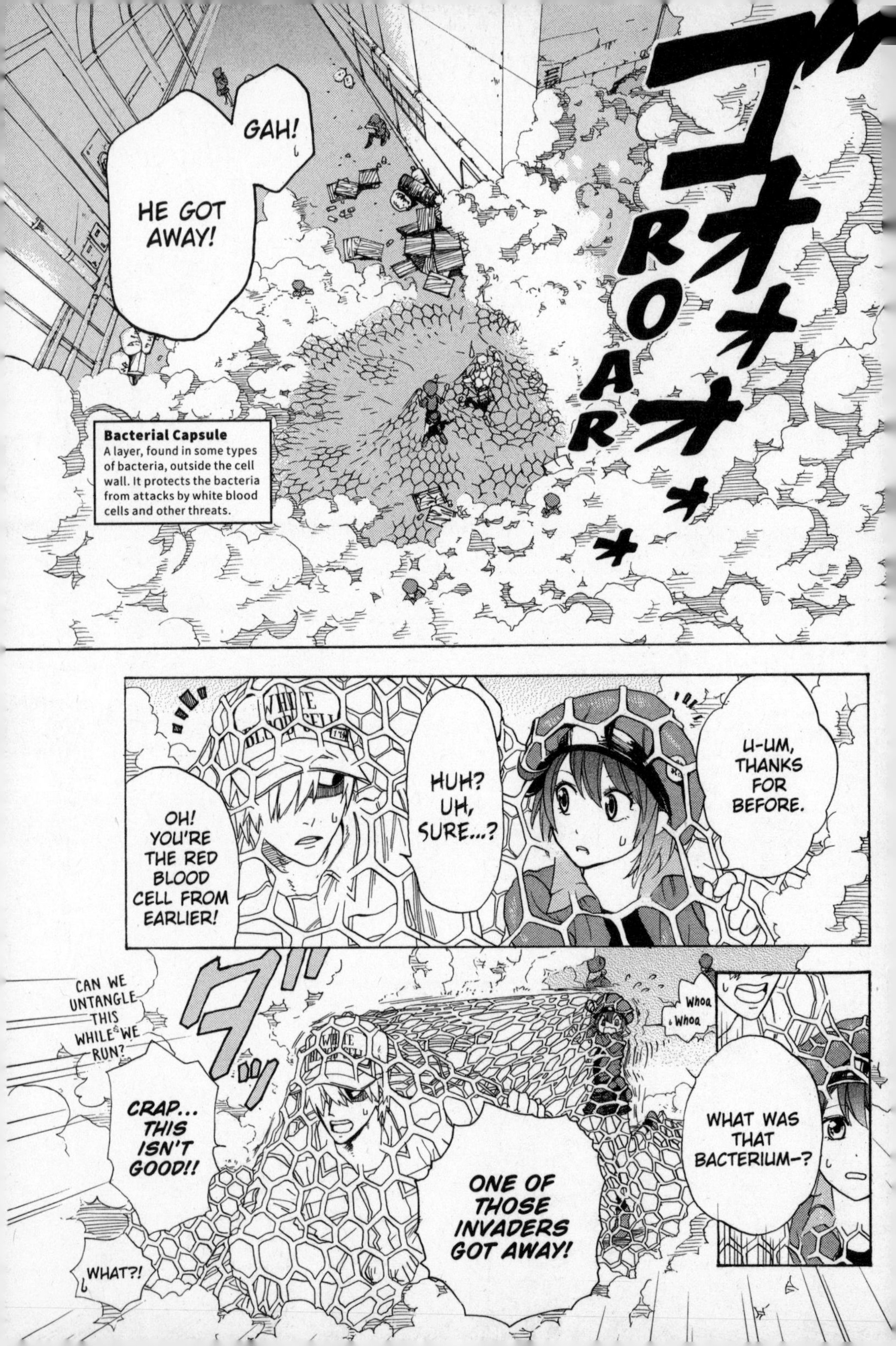
ROAR
GAH!
HE GOT AWAY!
Bacterial Capsule
A layer, found in some types of bacteria, outside the cell wall. It protects the bacteria from attacks by white blood cells and other threats.
U-UM, THANKS FOR BEFORE.
HUH? UH, SURE...?
OH! YOU'RE THE RED BLOOD CELL FROM EARLIER!
Whoa
Whoa
WHAT WAS THAT BACTERIUM-?
ONE OF THOSE INVADERS GOT AWAY!
CRAP... THIS ISN'T GOOD!!
CAN WE UNTANGLE THIS WHILE WE RUN?
WHAT?!

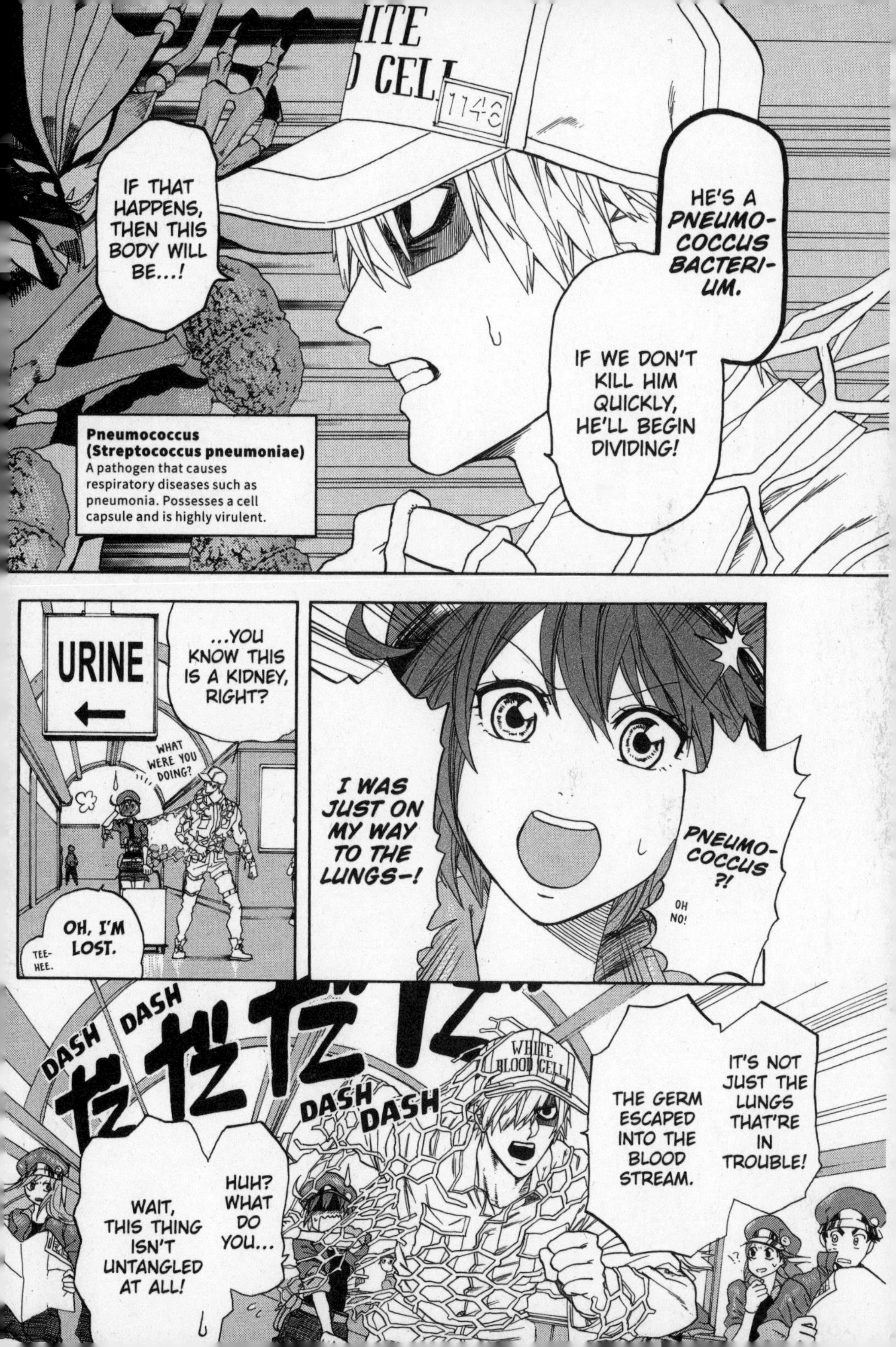
WHITE BLOOD CELL 1146
HE'S A PNEUMOCOCCUS BACTERIUM.
IF WE DON'T KILL HIM QUICKLY, HE'LL BEGIN DIVIDING!
IF THAT HAPPENS, THEN THIS BODY WILL BE...!
Pneumococcus (Streptococcus pneumoniae)
A pathogen that causes respiratory diseases such as pneumonia. Possesses a cell capsule and is highly virulent.
PNEUMOCOCCUS?!
OH NO!
I WAS JUST ON MY WAY TO THE LUNGS-!
...YOU KNOW THIS IS A KIDNEY, RIGHT?
URINE
WHAT WERE YOU DOING?
OH, I'M LOST.
TEE-HEE.
IT'S NOT JUST THE LUNGS THAT'RE IN TROUBLE!
THE GERM ESCAPED INTO THE BLOOD STREAM.
WHITE BLOOD CELL
DASH DASH
DASH DASH
HUH? WHAT DO YOU...
WAIT, THIS THING ISN'T UNTANGLED AT ALL!

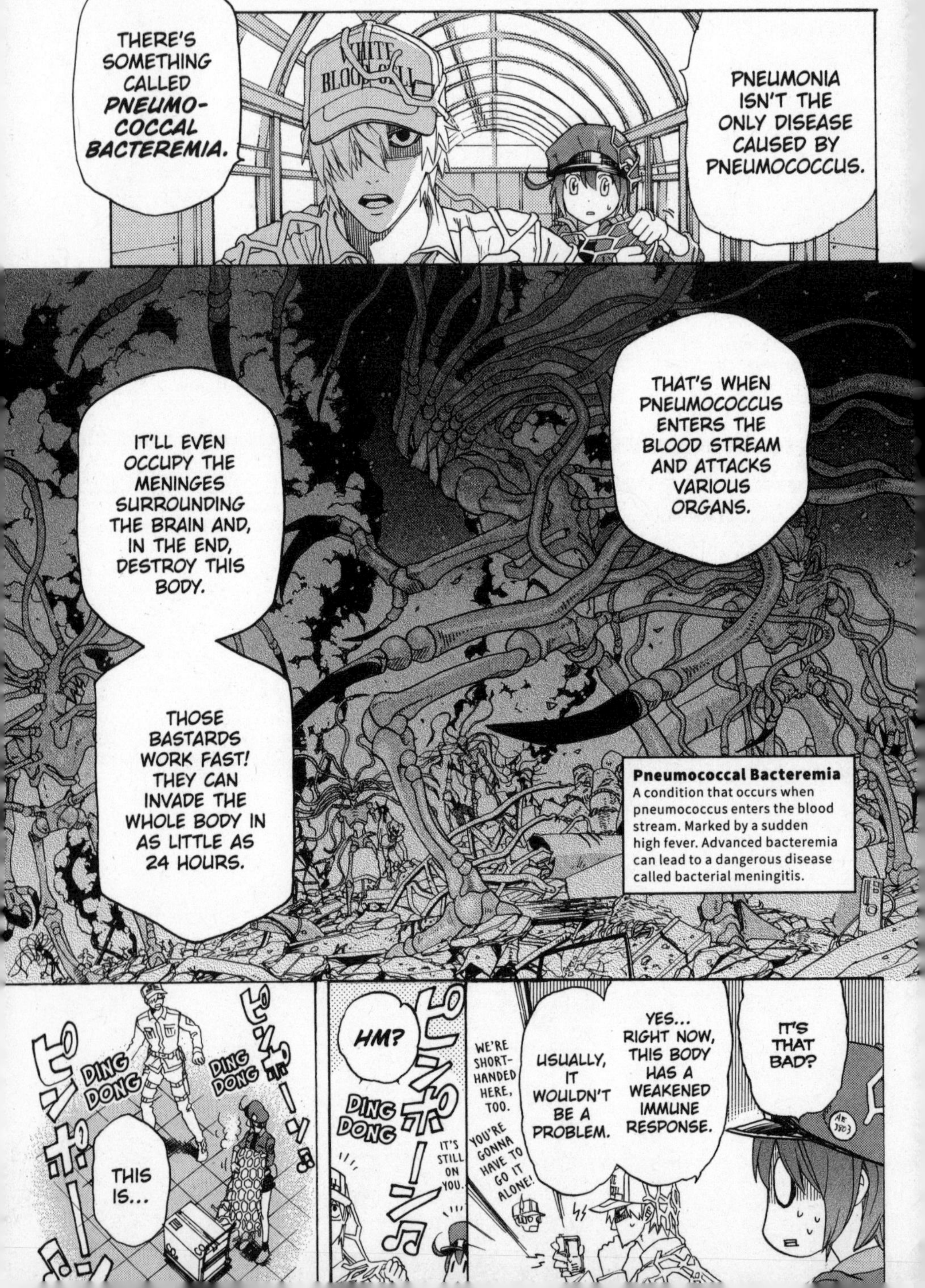
PNEUMONIA ISN'T THE ONLY DISEASE CAUSED BY PNEUMOCOCCUS.
THERE'S SOMETHING CALLED PNEUMOCOCCAL BACTEREMIA.
THAT'S WHEN PNEUMOCOCCUS ENTERS THE BLOOD STREAM AND ATTACKS VARIOUS ORGANS.
IT'LL EVEN OCCUPY THE MENINGES SURROUNDING THE BRAIN AND, IN THE END, DESTROY THIS BODY.
THOSE BASTARDS WORK FAST! THEY CAN INVADE THE WHOLE BODY IN AS LITTLE AS 24 HOURS.
Pneumococcal Bacteremia
A condition that occurs when pneumococcus enters the blood stream. Marked by a sudden high fever. Advanced bacteremia can lead to a dangerous disease called bacterial meningitis.
IT'S THAT BAD?
YES... RIGHT NOW, THIS BODY HAS A WEAKENED IMMUNE RESPONSE.
USUALLY, IT WOULDN'T BE A PROBLEM.
WE'RE SHORT-HANDED HERE, TOO.
YOU'RE GONNA HAVE TO GO IT ALONE!
HM?
DING DONG
IT'S STILL ON YOU.
DING DONG
DING DONG
THIS IS...

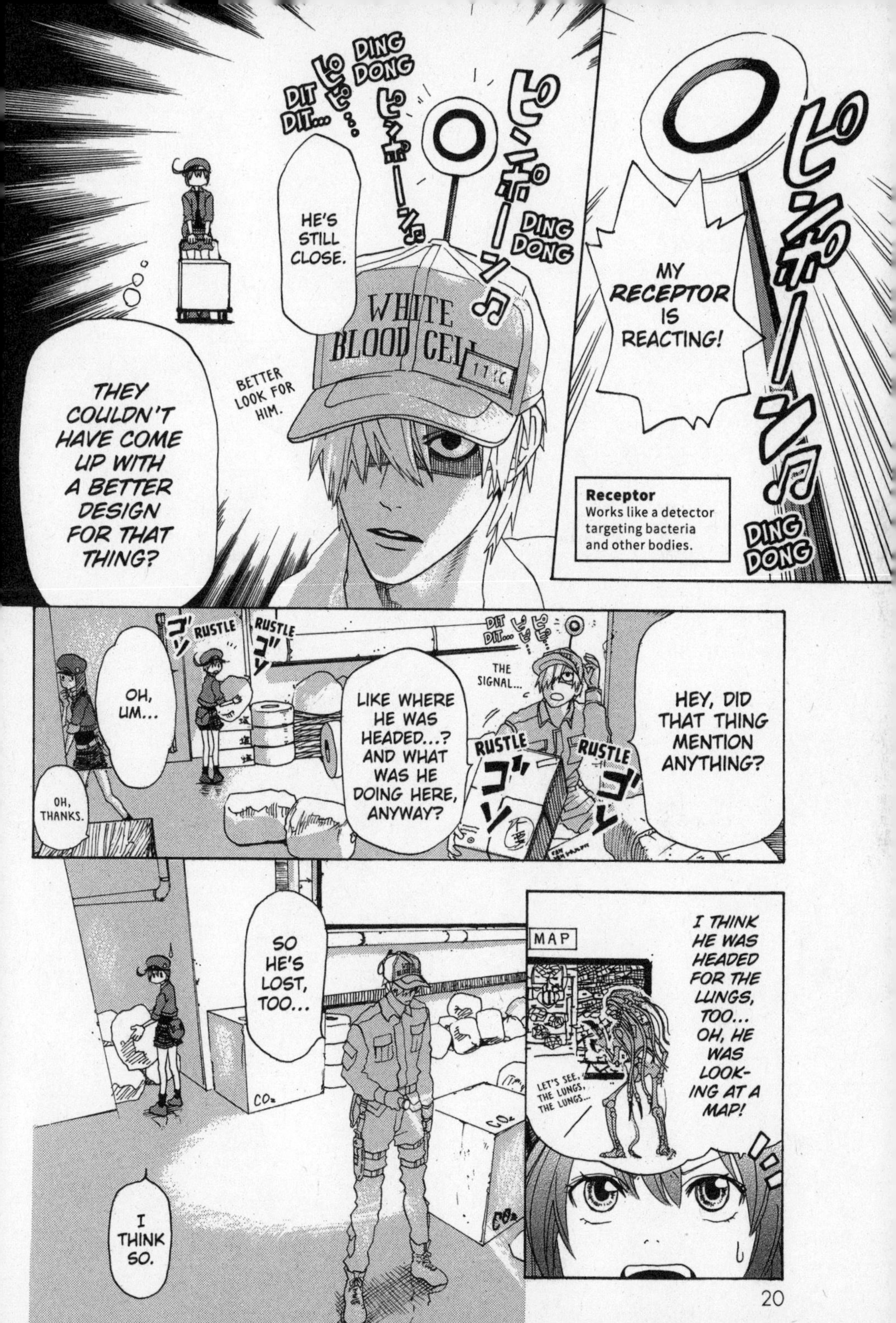
DING DONG
MY RECEPTOR IS REACTING!
Receptor
Works like a detector targeting bacteria and other bodies.
DING DONG
DING DONG
DIT DIT...
DING DONG
HE'S STILL CLOSE.
BETTER LOOK FOR HIM.
THEY COULDN'T HAVE COME UP WITH A BETTER DESIGN FOR THAT THING?
HEY, DID THAT THING MENTION ANYTHING?
DIT DIT...
THE SIGNAL...
RUSTLE
RUSTLE
LIKE WHERE HE WAS HEADED...? AND WHAT WAS HE DOING HERE, ANYWAY?
RUSTLE
RUSTLE
OH, UM...
OH, THANKS.
I THINK HE WAS HEADED FOR THE LUNGS, TOO... OH, HE WAS LOOKING AT A MAP!
MAP
LET'S SEE, THE LUNGS, THE LUNGS...
SO HE'S LOST, TOO...
I THINK SO.

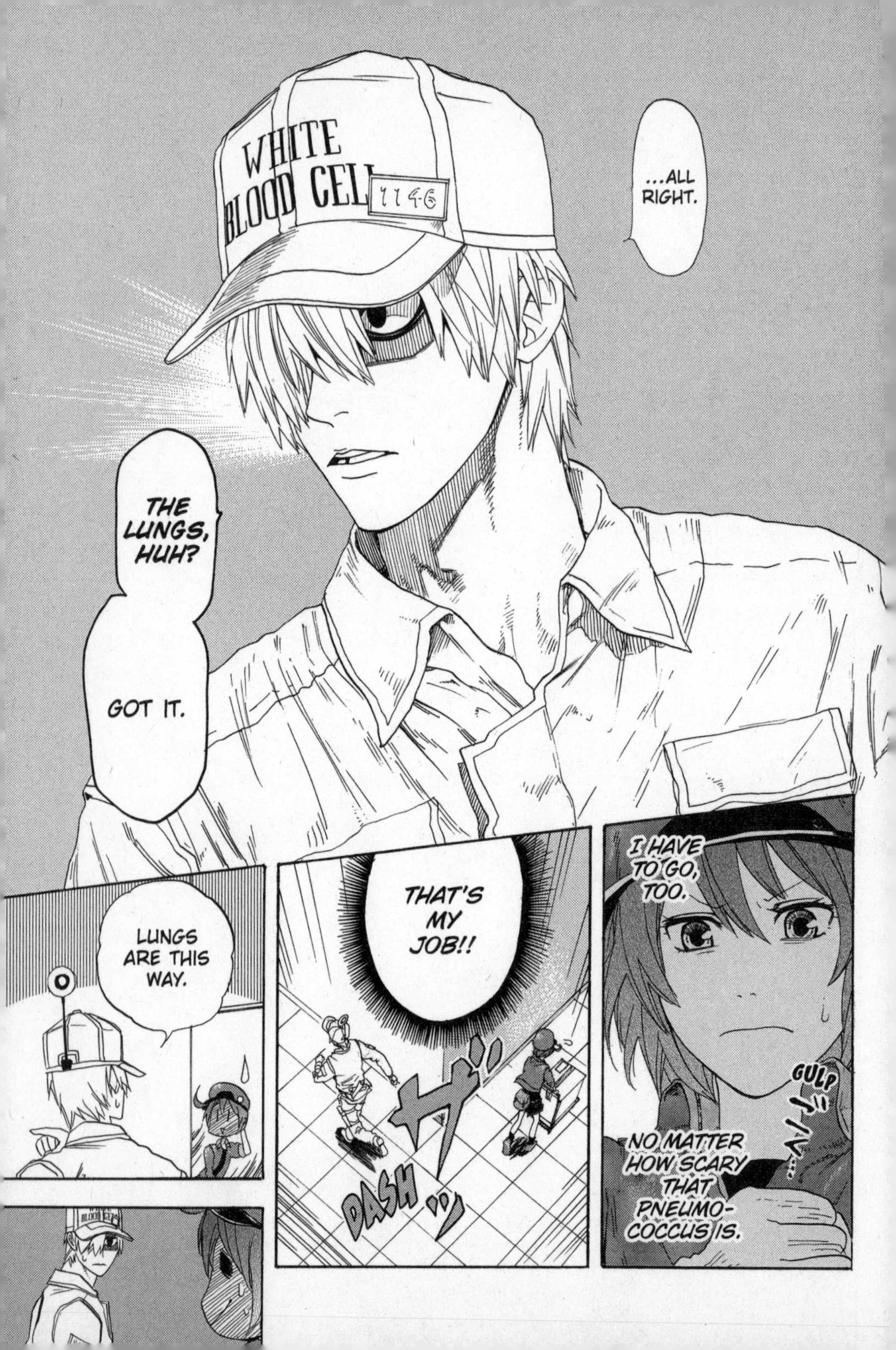
WHITE BLOOD CELL
1146
...ALL RIGHT.
THE LUNGS, HUH?
GOT IT.
I HAVE TO GO, TOO.
GULP
NO MATTER HOW SCARY THAT PNEUMO-COCCUS IS.
THAT'S MY JOB!!
DASH
LUNGS ARE THIS WAY.

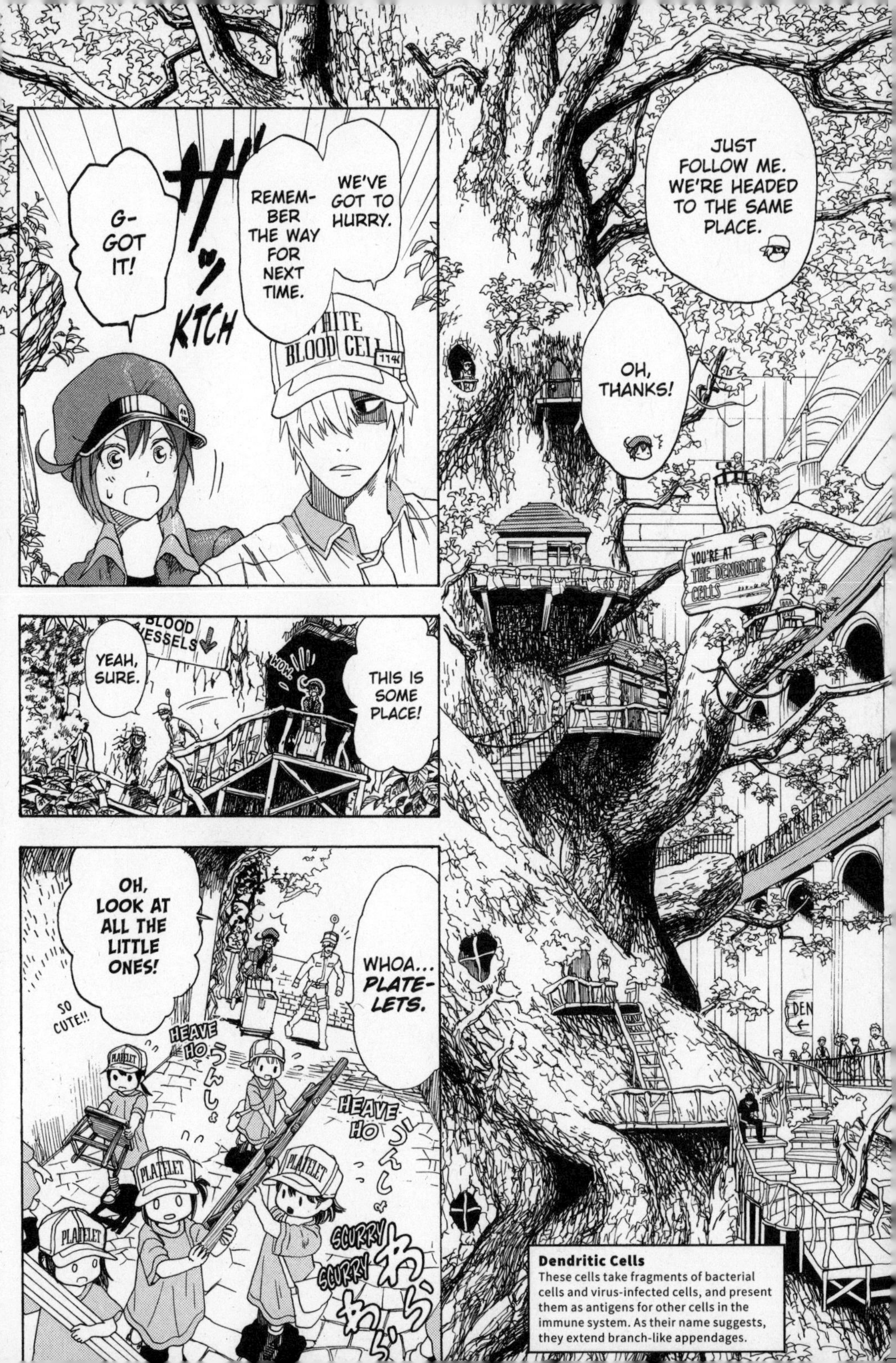
JUST FOLLOW ME. WE'RE HEADED TO THE SAME PLACE.
OH, THANKS!
YOU'RE AT THE DENDRITIC CELLS
DEN
WE'VE GOT TO HURRY.
REMEMBER THE WAY FOR NEXT TIME.
KTCH
G-GOT IT!
WHITE BLOOD CELL
THIS IS SOME PLACE!
WOW.
YEAH, SURE.
BLOOD VESSELS
WHOA... PLATELETS.
OH, LOOK AT ALL THE LITTLE ONES!
SO CUTE!!
HEAVE HO
HEAVE HO
PLATELET
SCURRY SCURRY

Dendritic Cells
These cells take fragments of bacterial cells and virus-infected cells, and present them as antigens for other cells in the immune system. As their name suggests, they extend branch-like appendages.

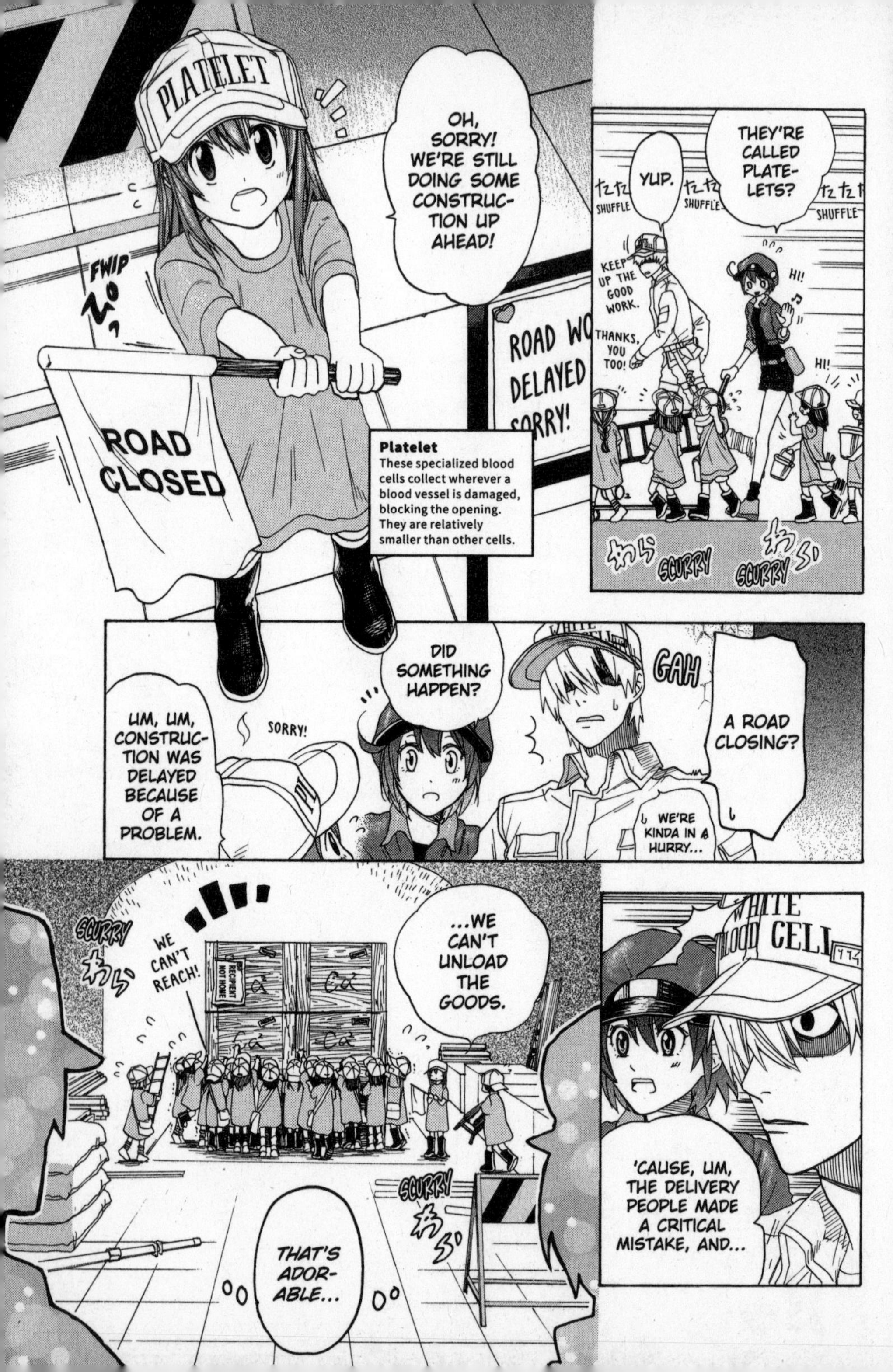

THEY'RE CALLED PLATE-LETS?
YUP.
SHUFFLE
SHUFFLE
SHUFFLE
KEEP UP THE GOOD WORK.
HI!
THANKS, YOU TOO!
HI!
SCURRY
SCURRY
PLATELET
OH, SORRY! WE'RE STILL DOING SOME CONSTRUC-TION UP AHEAD!
FWIP
ROAD CLOSED
ROAD WO
DELAYED
SORRY!
Platelet
These specialized blood cells collect wherever a blood vessel is damaged, blocking the opening. They are relatively smaller than other cells.
GAH
A ROAD CLOSING?
WE'RE KINDA IN A HURRY...
DID SOMETHING HAPPEN?
SORRY!
UM, UM, CONSTRUC-TION WAS DELAYED BECAUSE OF A PROBLEM.
WHITE BLOOD CELL
'CAUSE, UM, THE DELIVERY PEOPLE MADE A CRITICAL MISTAKE, AND...
...WE CAN'T UNLOAD THE GOODS.
WE CAN'T REACH!
SCURRY
RECIPIENT NOT HOME
SCURRY
THAT'S ADOR-ABLE...

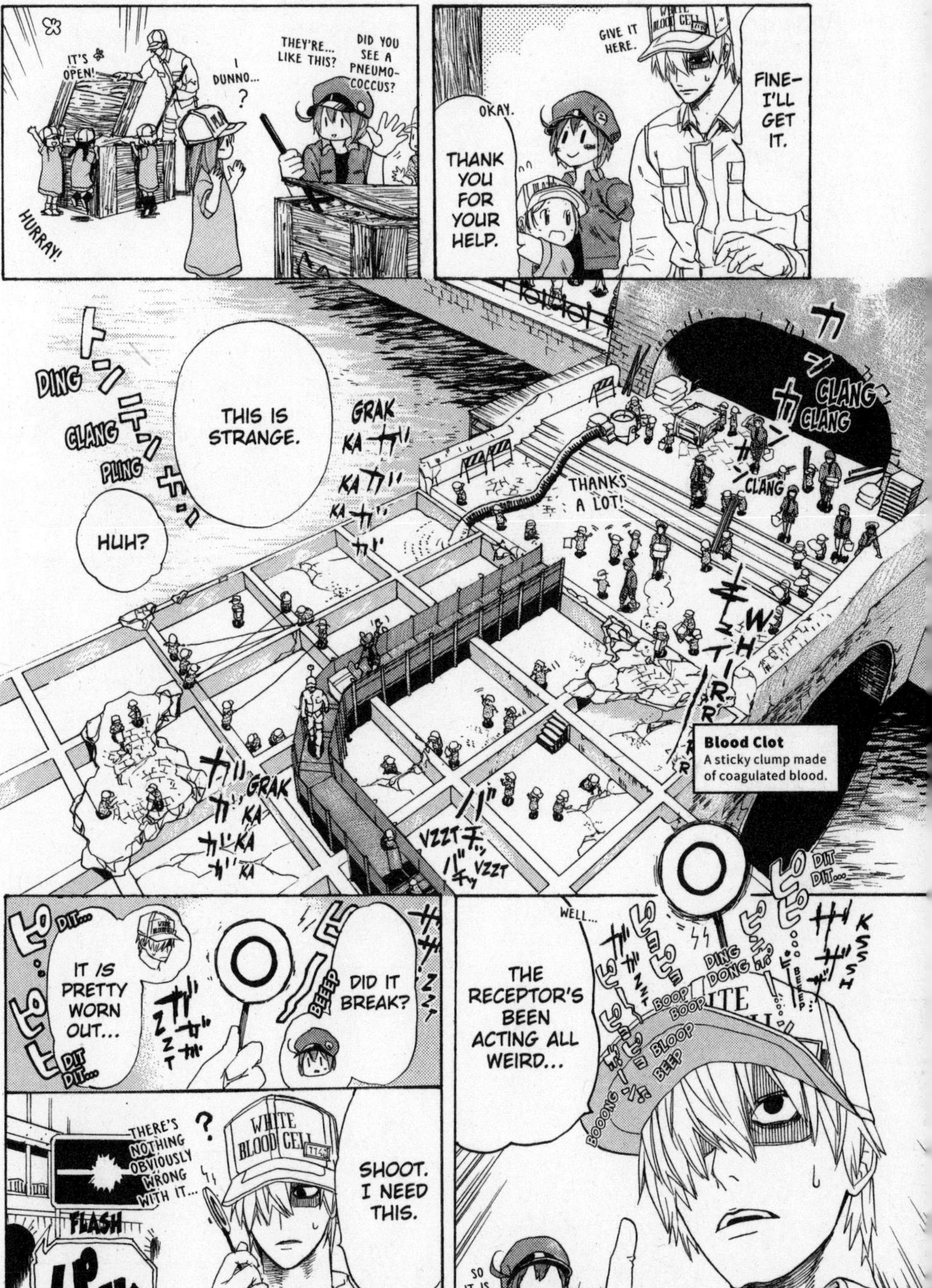
GIVE IT HERE.
OKAY.
FINE— I'LL GET IT.
THANK YOU FOR YOUR HELP.
DID YOU SEE A PNEUMO-COCCUS?
THEY'RE... LIKE THIS?
I DUNNO... ?
IT'S OPEN!
HURRAY!
THIS IS STRANGE.
HUH?
DING
CLANG
PLING
GRAK KA KA KA
THANKS A LOT!
CLANG CLANG
CLANG
WHIRRR
GRAK KA KA KA
VZZT VZZT
DIT DIT...
Blood Clot
A sticky clump made of coagulated blood.
WELL...
THE RECEPTOR'S BEEN ACTING ALL WEIRD...
DING DONG
BOOP BOOP
BLOOP BEEP
BOOONG
BEEEP
KSSSH
SO IT IS.
DID IT BREAK?
BEEEP
IT IS PRETTY WORN OUT...
DIT...
DIT DIT...
SHOOT. I NEED THIS.
THERE'S NOTHING OBVIOUSLY WRONG WITH IT...
FLASH

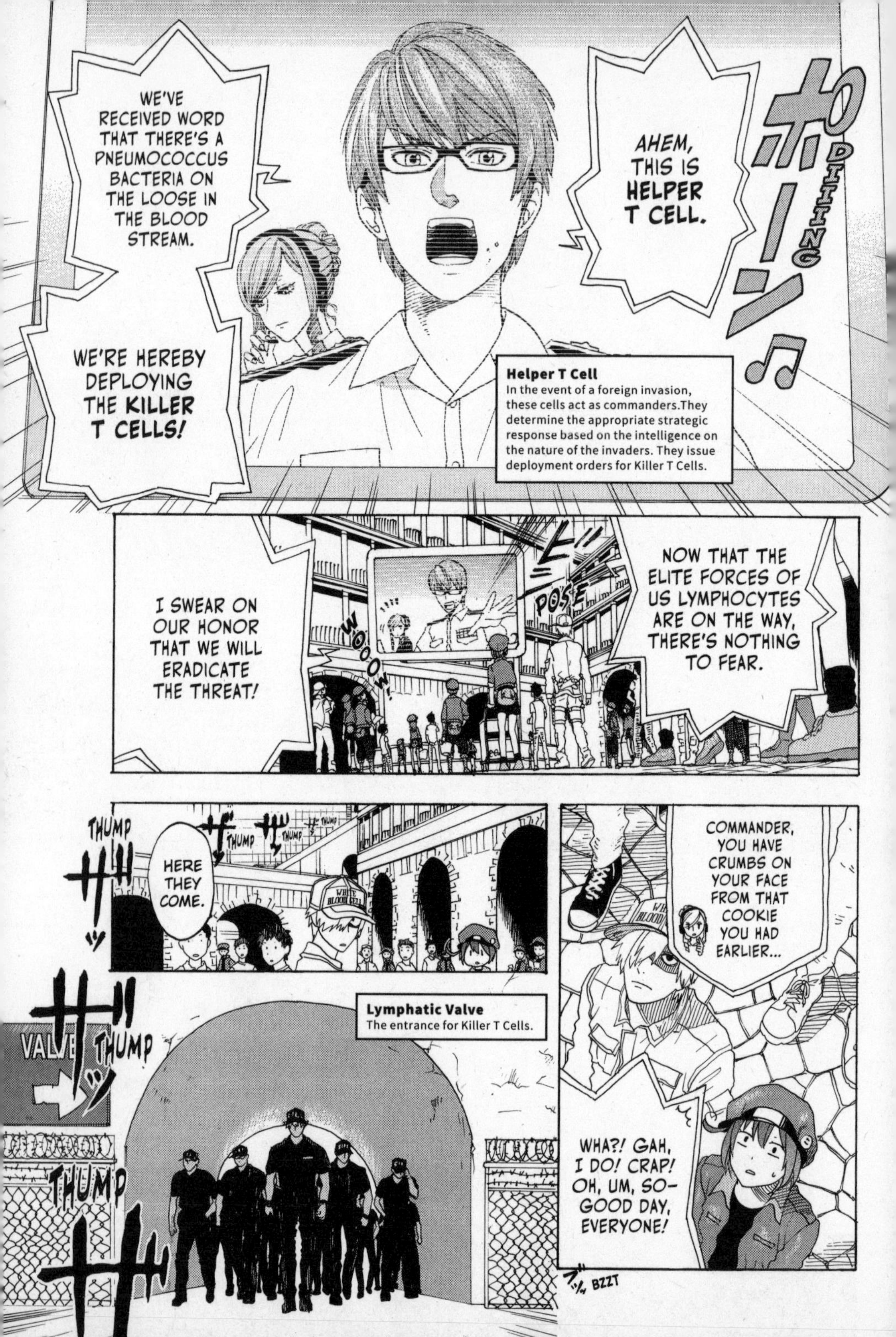
DIIIING
AHEM, THIS IS HELPER T CELL.
WE'VE RECEIVED WORD THAT THERE'S A PNEUMOCOCCUS BACTERIA ON THE LOOSE IN THE BLOOD STREAM.
WE'RE HEREBY DEPLOYING THE KILLER T CELLS!
Helper T Cell
In the event of a foreign invasion, these cells act as commanders.They determine the appropriate strategic response based on the intelligence on the nature of the invaders. They issue deployment orders for Killer T Cells.
NOW THAT THE ELITE FORCES OF US LYMPHOCYTES ARE ON THE WAY, THERE'S NOTHING TO FEAR.
POSE
WOOOW!
I SWEAR ON OUR HONOR THAT WE WILL ERADICATE THE THREAT!
COMMANDER, YOU HAVE CRUMBS ON YOUR FACE FROM THAT COOKIE YOU HAD EARLIER...
WHA?! GAH, I DO! CRAP! OH, UM, SO- GOOD DAY, EVERYONE!
BZZT
THUMP
THUMP
THUMP
THUMP
HERE THEY COME.
WHITE BLOOD CELL
Lymphatic Valve
The entrance for Killer T Cells.
VALVE
THUMP
THUMP

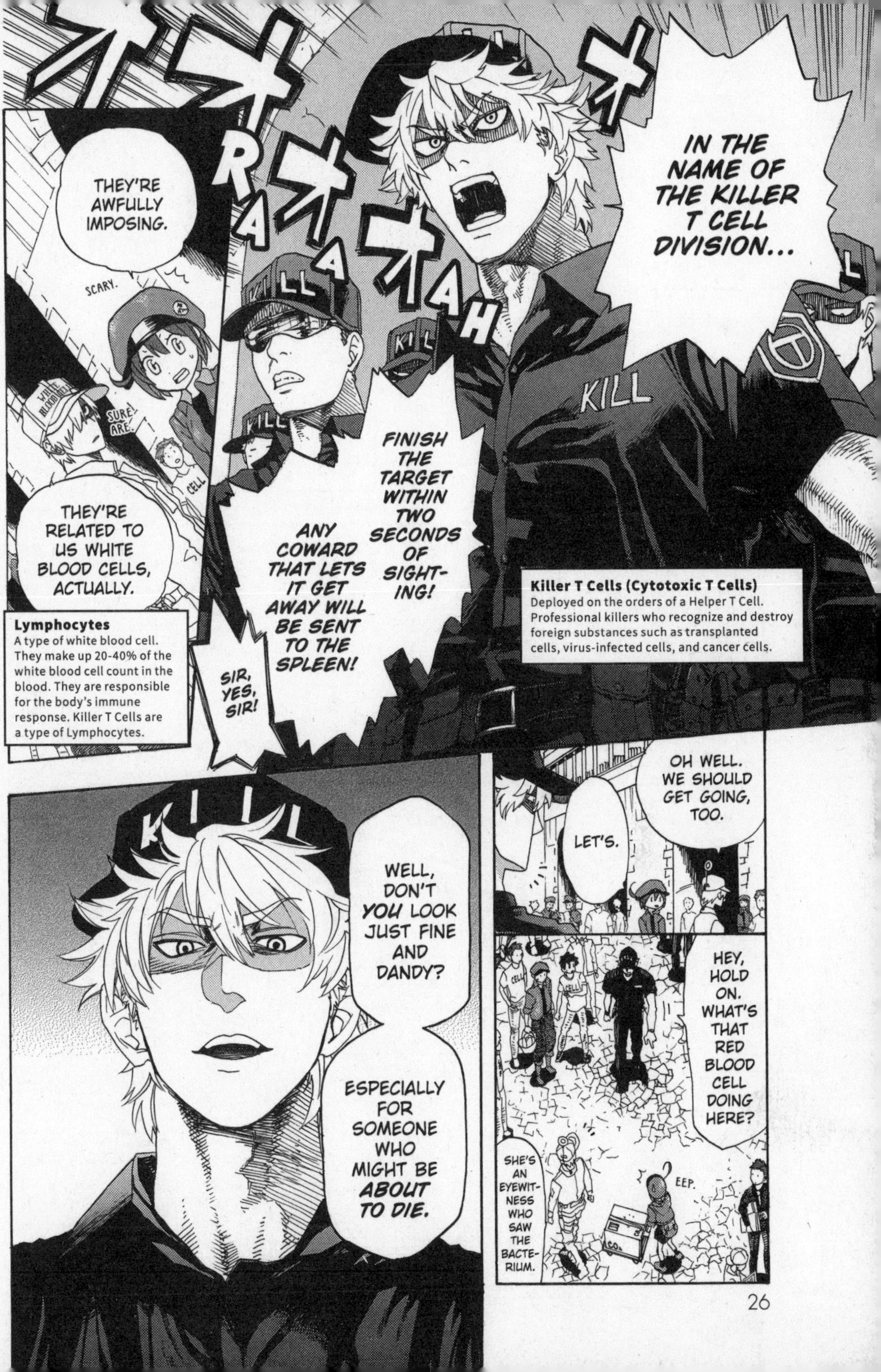
RAAAH
IN THE NAME OF THE KILLER T CELL DIVISION...
FINISH THE TARGET WITHIN TWO SECONDS OF SIGHTING!
ANY COWARD THAT LETS IT GET AWAY WILL BE SENT TO THE SPLEEN!
Killer T Cells (Cytotoxic T Cells)
Deployed on the orders of a Helper T Cell. Professional killers who recognize and destroy foreign substances such as transplanted cells, virus-infected cells, and cancer cells.
SIR, YES, SIR!
KILL
THEY'RE AWFULLY IMPOSING.
SCARY.
SURE ARE.
THEY'RE RELATED TO US WHITE BLOOD CELLS, ACTUALLY.
Lymphocytes
A type of white blood cell. They make up 20-40% of the white blood cell count in the blood. They are responsible for the body's immune response. Killer T Cells are a type of Lymphocytes.
OH WELL. WE SHOULD GET GOING, TOO.
LET'S.
HEY, HOLD ON. WHAT'S THAT RED BLOOD CELL DOING HERE?
SHE'S AN EYEWITNESS WHO SAW THE BACTERIUM.
EEP.
WELL, DON'T YOU LOOK JUST FINE AND DANDY?
ESPECIALLY FOR SOMEONE WHO MIGHT BE ABOUT TO DIE.

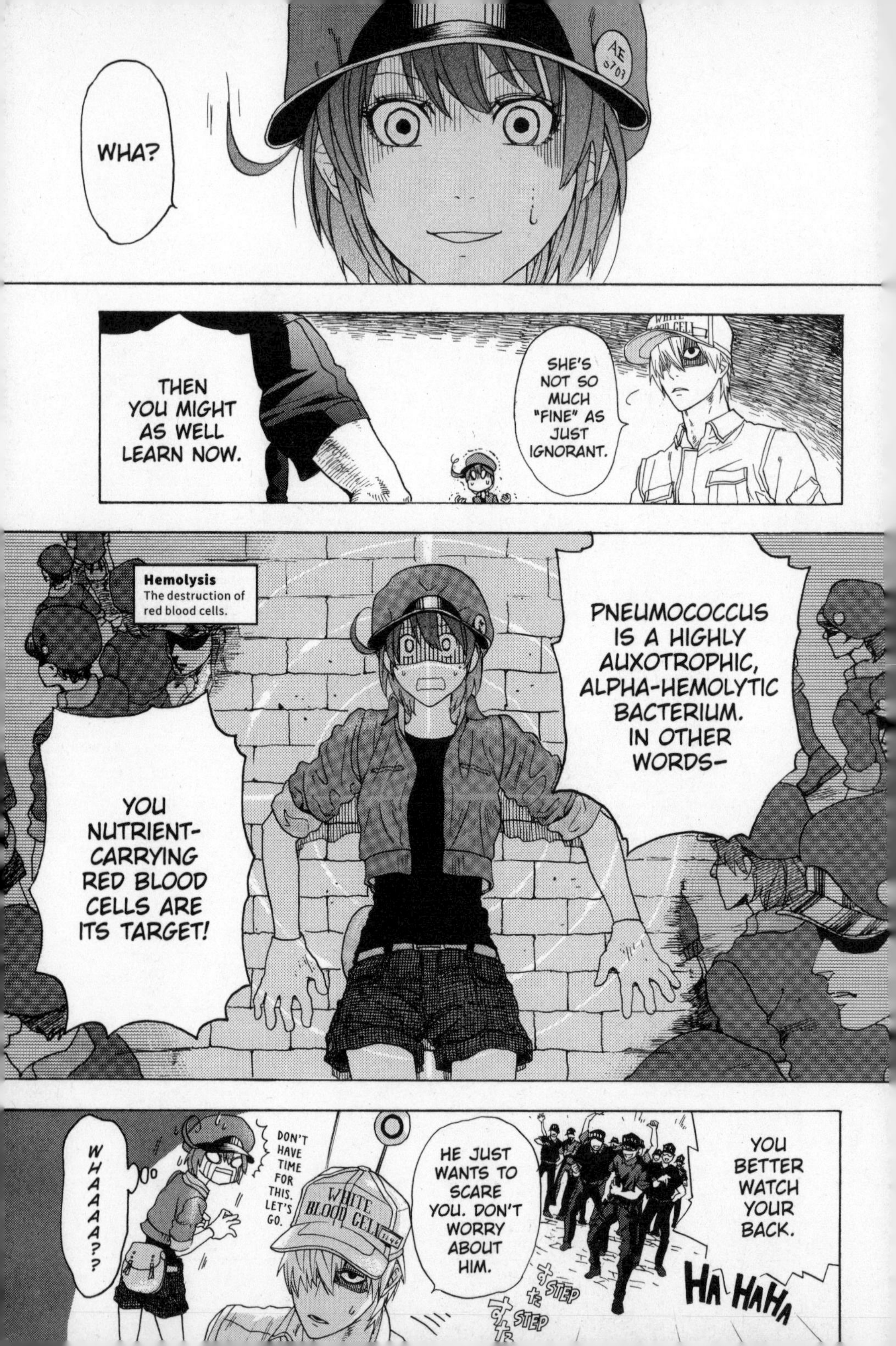
WHA?
SHE'S NOT SO MUCH "FINE" AS JUST IGNORANT.
THEN YOU MIGHT AS WELL LEARN NOW.
PNEUMOCOCCUS IS A HIGHLY AUXOTROPHIC, ALPHA-HEMOLYTIC BACTERIUM. IN OTHER WORDS–
Hemolysis
The destruction of red blood cells.
YOU NUTRIENT-CARRYING RED BLOOD CELLS ARE ITS TARGET!
YOU BETTER WATCH YOUR BACK.
HA HA HA
HE JUST WANTS TO SCARE YOU. DON'T WORRY ABOUT HIM.
STEP
STEP
DON'T HAVE TIME FOR THIS. LET'S GO.
WHAAAAA?!?

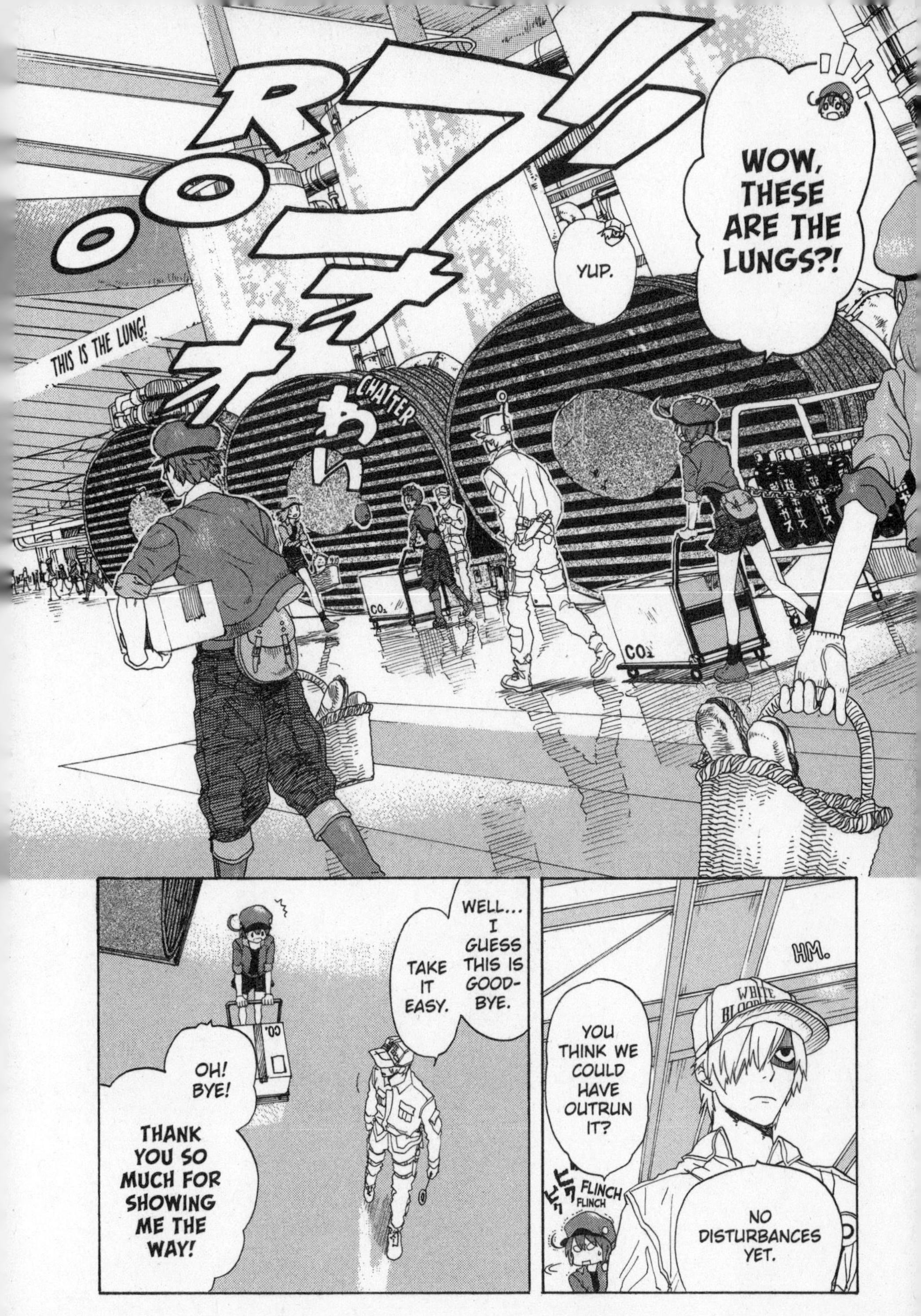
WOW, THESE ARE THE LUNGS?!
YUP.
CHATTER
THIS IS THE LUNG!
CO2
CO2
HM.
YOU THINK WE COULD HAVE OUTRUN IT?
NO DISTURBANCES YET.
FLINCH FLINCH
WELL... I GUESS THIS IS GOOD-BYE.
TAKE IT EASY.
OH! BYE!
THANK YOU SO MUCH FOR SHOWING ME THE WAY!

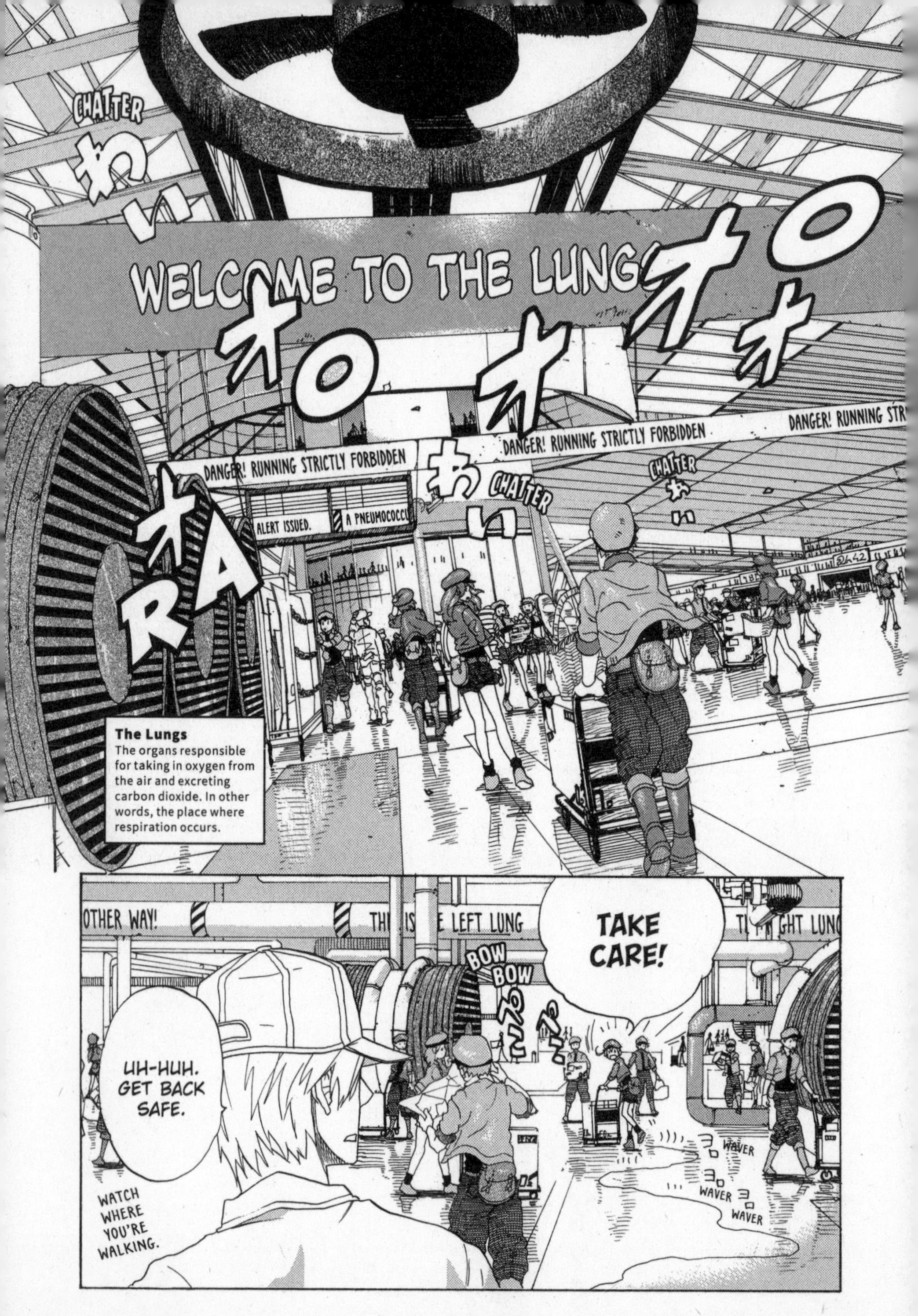
CHATTER
WELCOME TO THE LUNGS
DANGER! RUNNING STRICTLY FORBIDDEN
DANGER! RUNNING STRI
CHATTER
CHATTER
DANGER! RUNNING STRICTLY FORBIDDEN
ALERT ISSUED.
A PNEUMOCOCCU
RA
The Lungs
The organs responsible for taking in oxygen from the air and excreting carbon dioxide. In other words, the place where respiration occurs.
LEFT LUNG
OTHER WAY!
TAKE CARE!
BOW BOW
WAVER
WAVER
WAVER
UH-HUH. GET BACK SAFE.
WATCH WHERE YOU'RE WALKING.

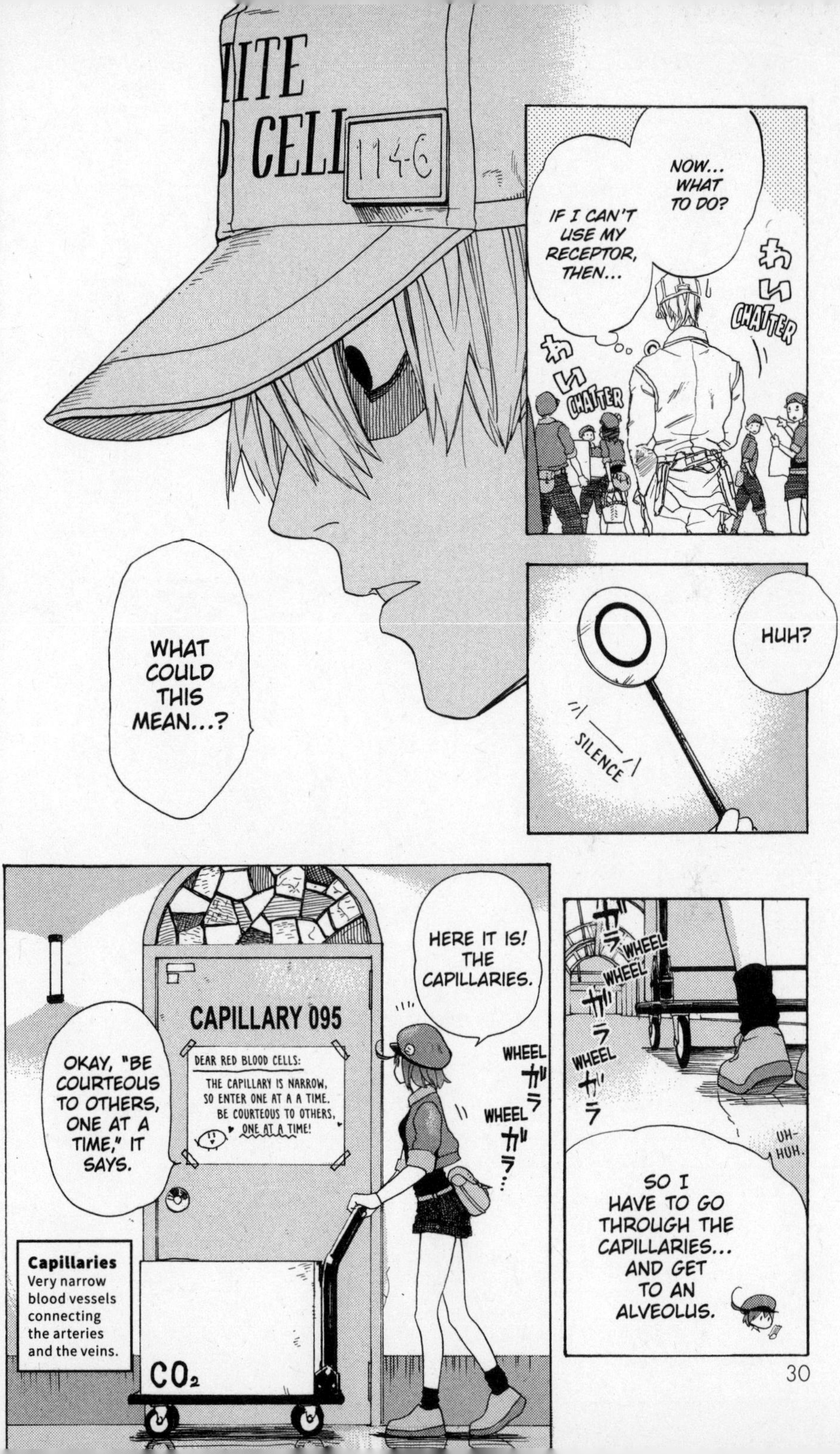
NOW... WHAT TO DO?
IF I CAN'T USE MY RECEPTOR, THEN...
わい CHATTER
わい CHATTER
HUH?
SILENCE
1146
WHAT COULD THIS MEAN...?
ガラ WHEEL
ガラ WHEEL
ガラ WHEEL
UH-HUH.
SO I HAVE TO GO THROUGH THE CAPILLARIES... AND GET TO AN ALVEOLUS.
HERE IT IS! THE CAPILLARIES.
CAPILLARY 095
DEAR RED BLOOD CELLS:
THE CAPILLARY IS NARROW, SO ENTER ONE AT A A TIME. BE COURTEOUS TO OTHERS, ONE AT A TIME!
OKAY, "BE COURTEOUS TO OTHERS, ONE AT A TIME," IT SAYS.
WHEEL ガラ
WHEEL ガラ...
CO_2

Capillaries
Very narrow blood vessels connecting the arteries and the veins.

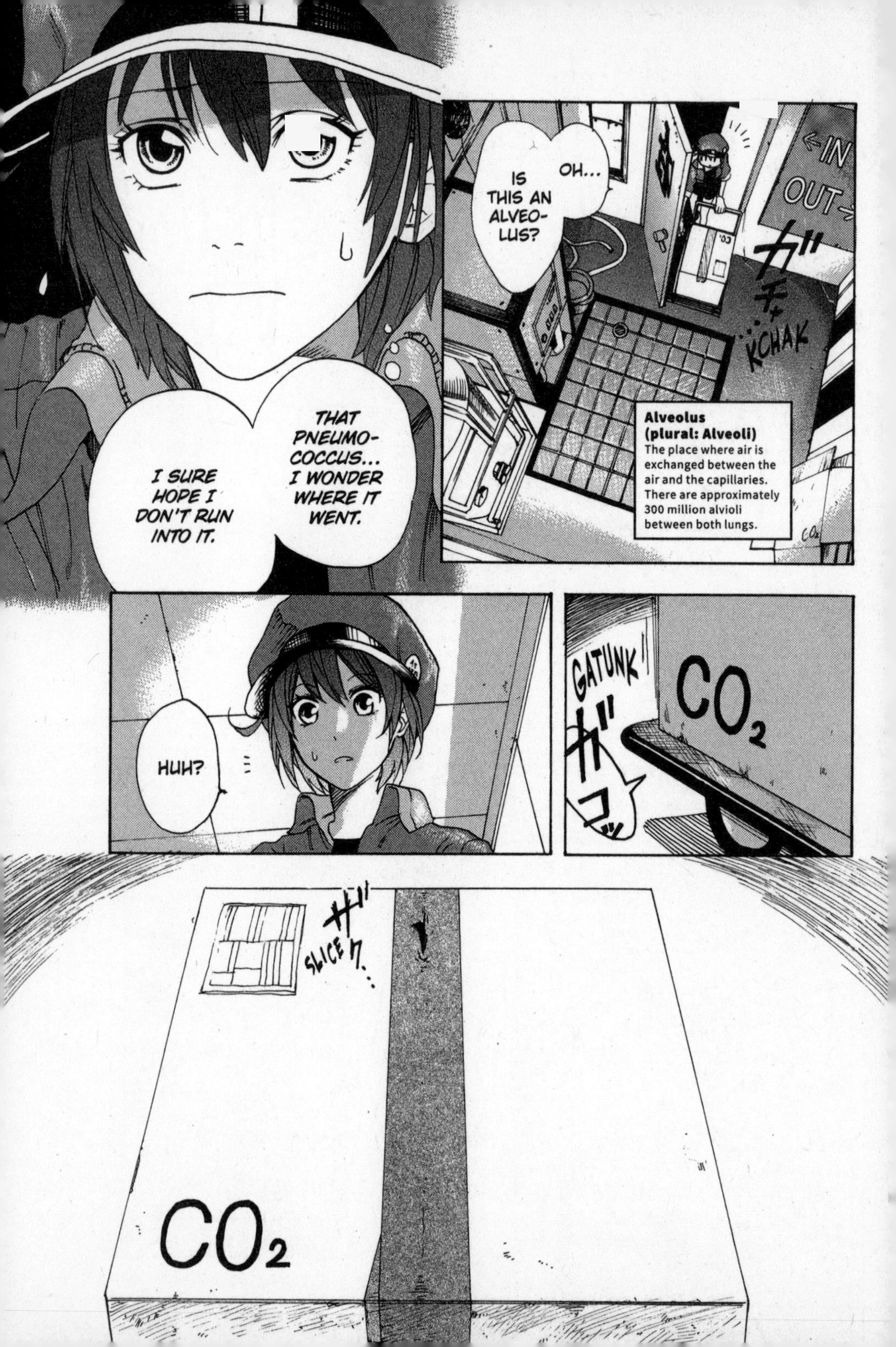

←IN
OUT→
OH...
IS THIS AN ALVEOLUS?
KCHAK
Alveolus (plural: Alveoli)
The place where air is exchanged between the air and the capillaries. There are approximately 300 million alvioli between both lungs.
CO2
THAT PNEUMOCOCCUS... I WONDER WHERE IT WENT.
I SURE HOPE I DON'T RUN INTO IT.
GATUNK
CO2
HUH?
SLICE
CO2

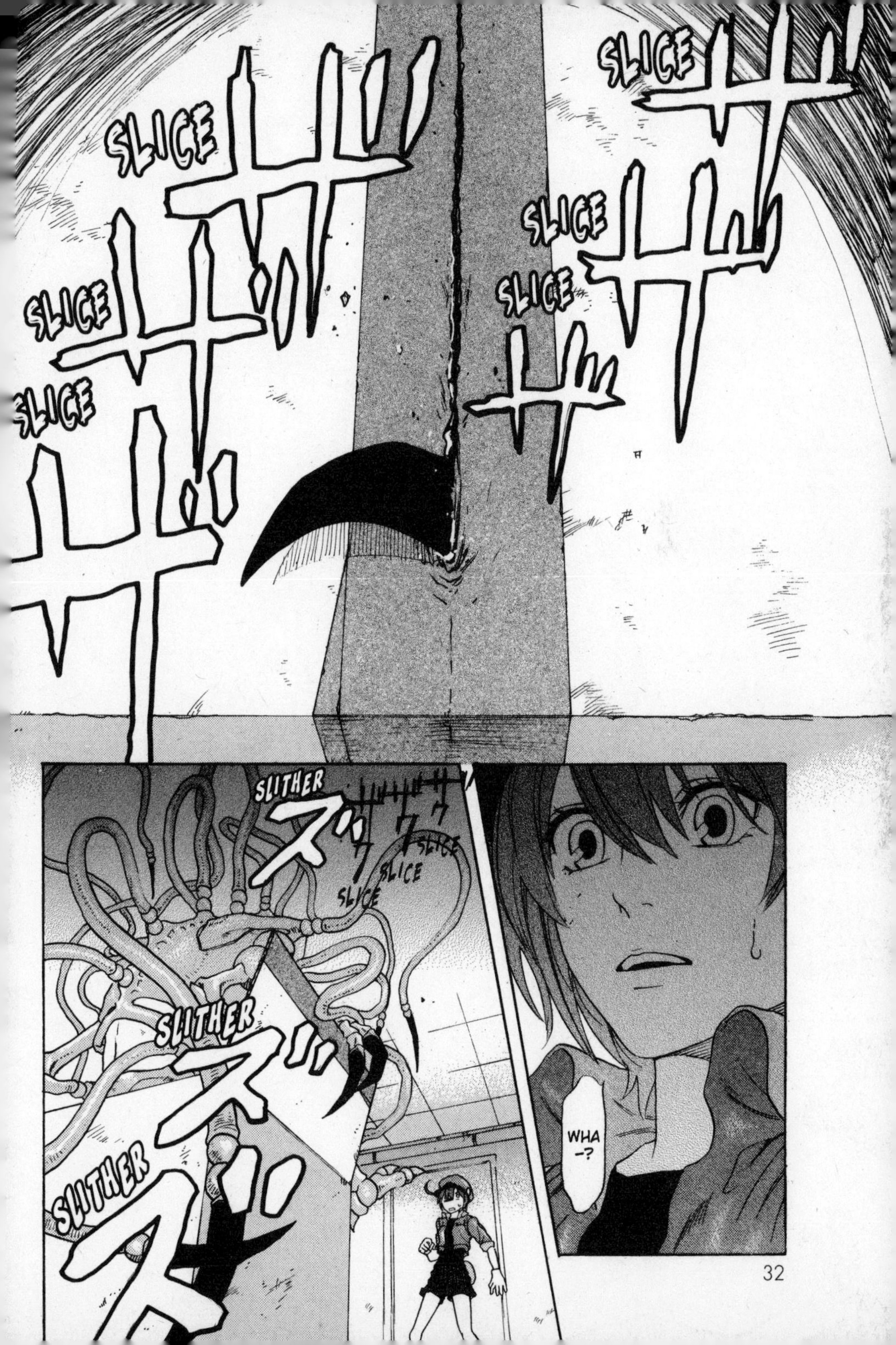
SLICE
SLICE
SLICE
SLICE
SLICE
SLICE
WHA –?
SLITHER
SLICE
SLICE
SLICE
SLITHER
SLITHER

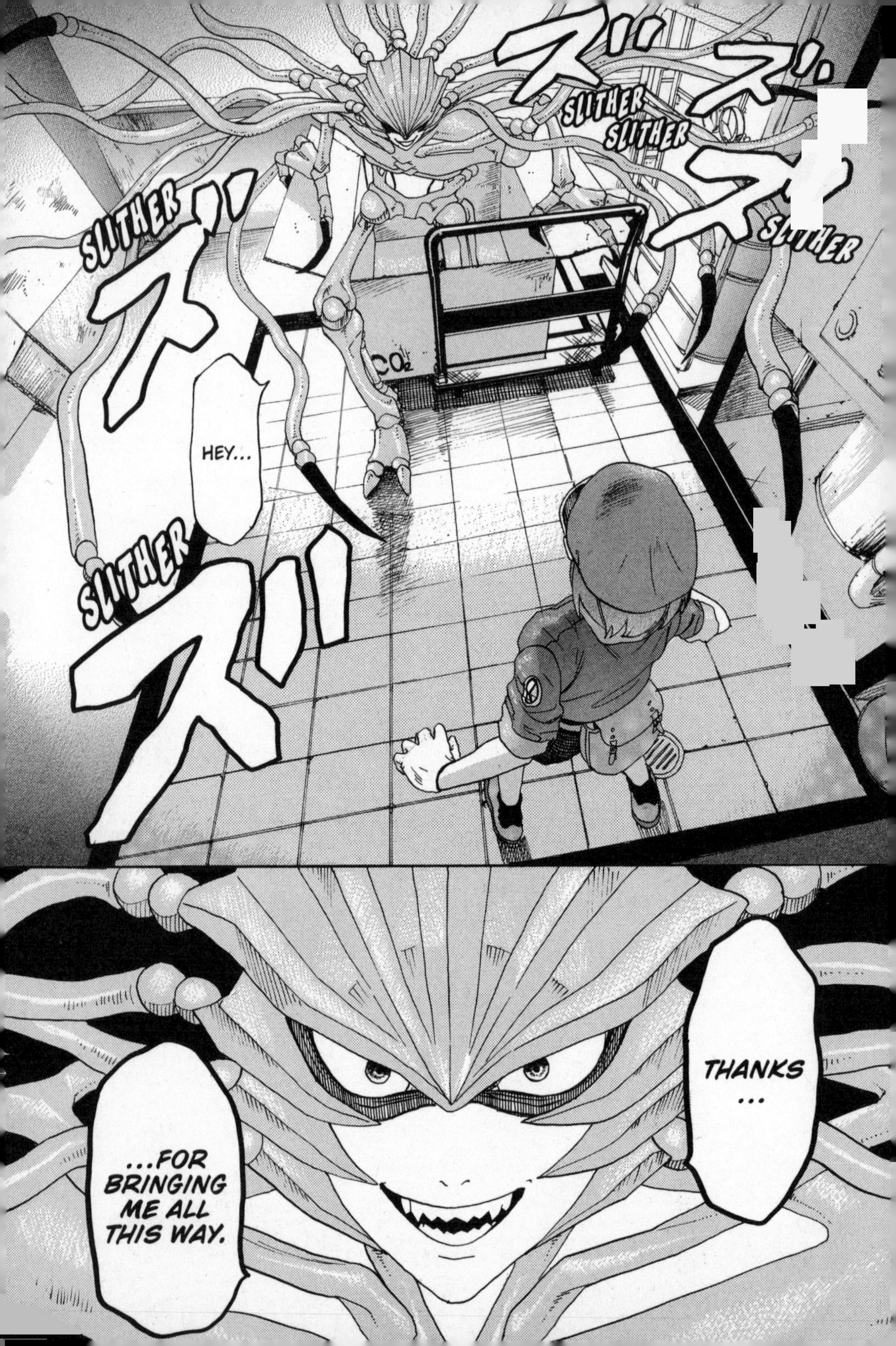
SLITHER
SLITHER
SLITHER
SLITHER
CO2
HEY...
SLITHER
THANKS...
...FOR BRINGING ME ALL THIS WAY.

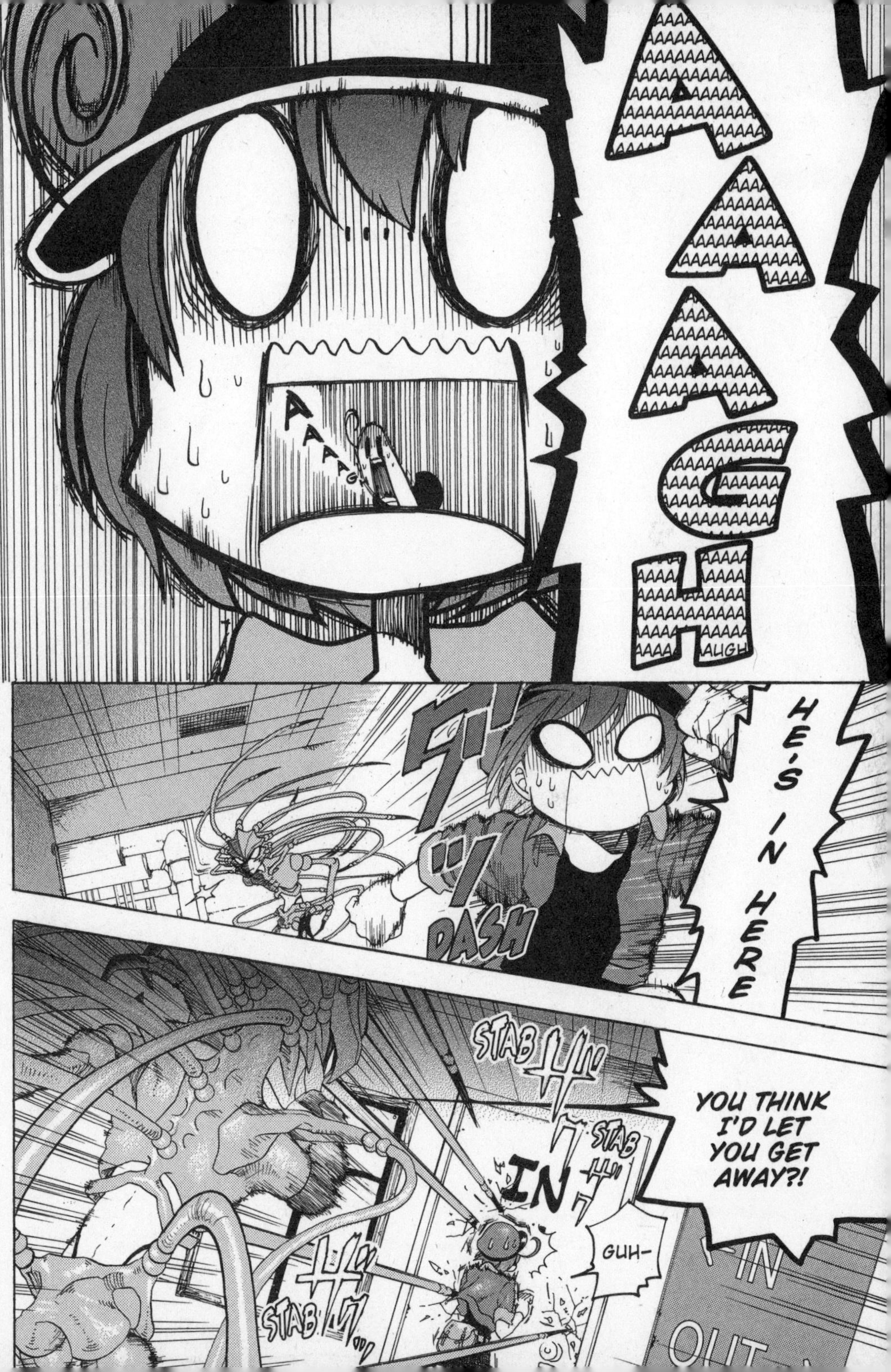
AAAAGH
AAAAG
HE'S IN HERE
DASH
YOU THINK I'D LET YOU GET AWAY?!
STAB
STAB
GUH-
IN
OUT
STAB

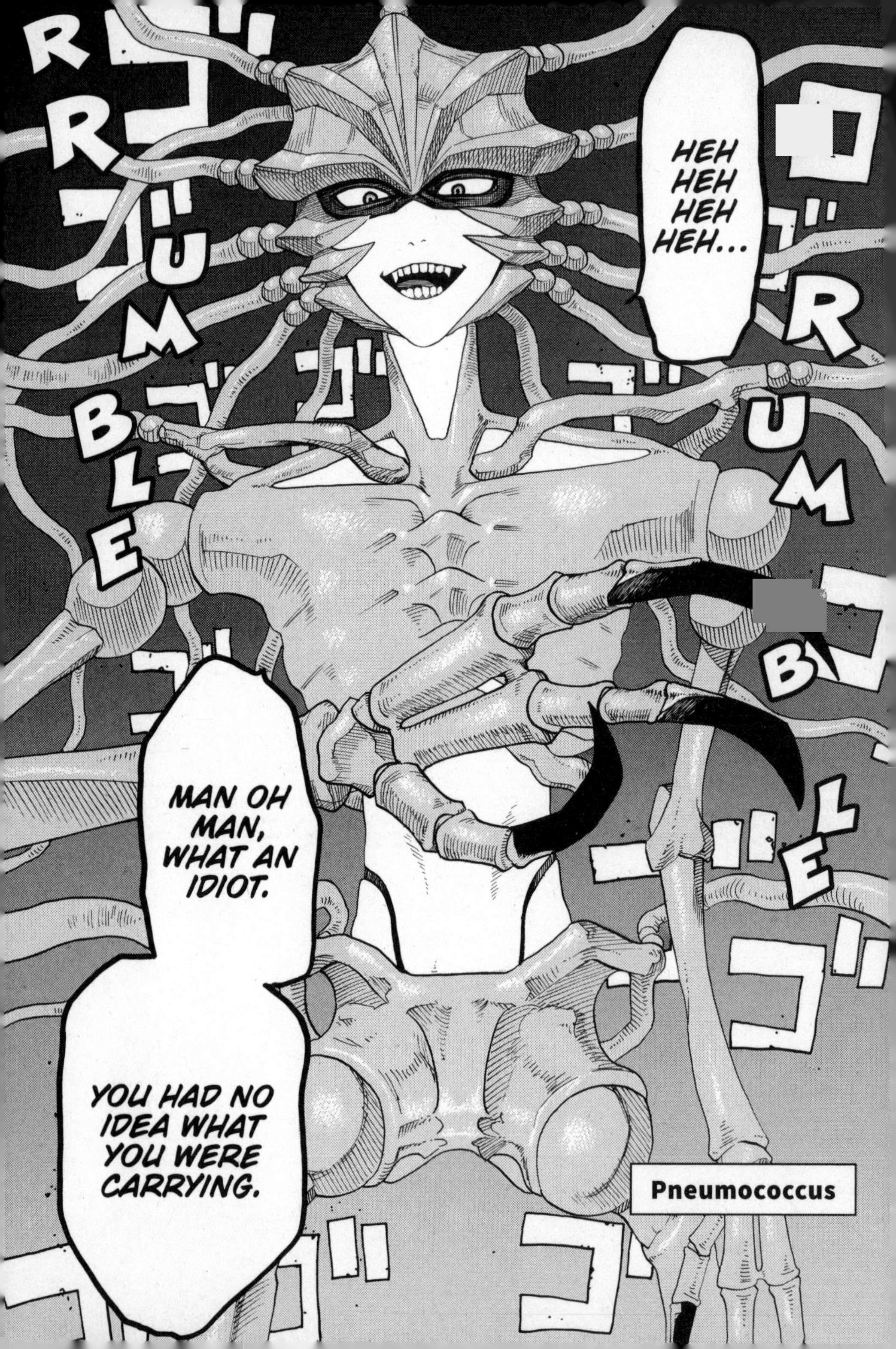

HEH HEH HEH HEH...
RRUMBLE
RRUMBLE
MAN OH MAN, WHAT AN IDIOT.
YOU HAD NO IDEA WHAT YOU WERE CARRYING.
Pneumococcus

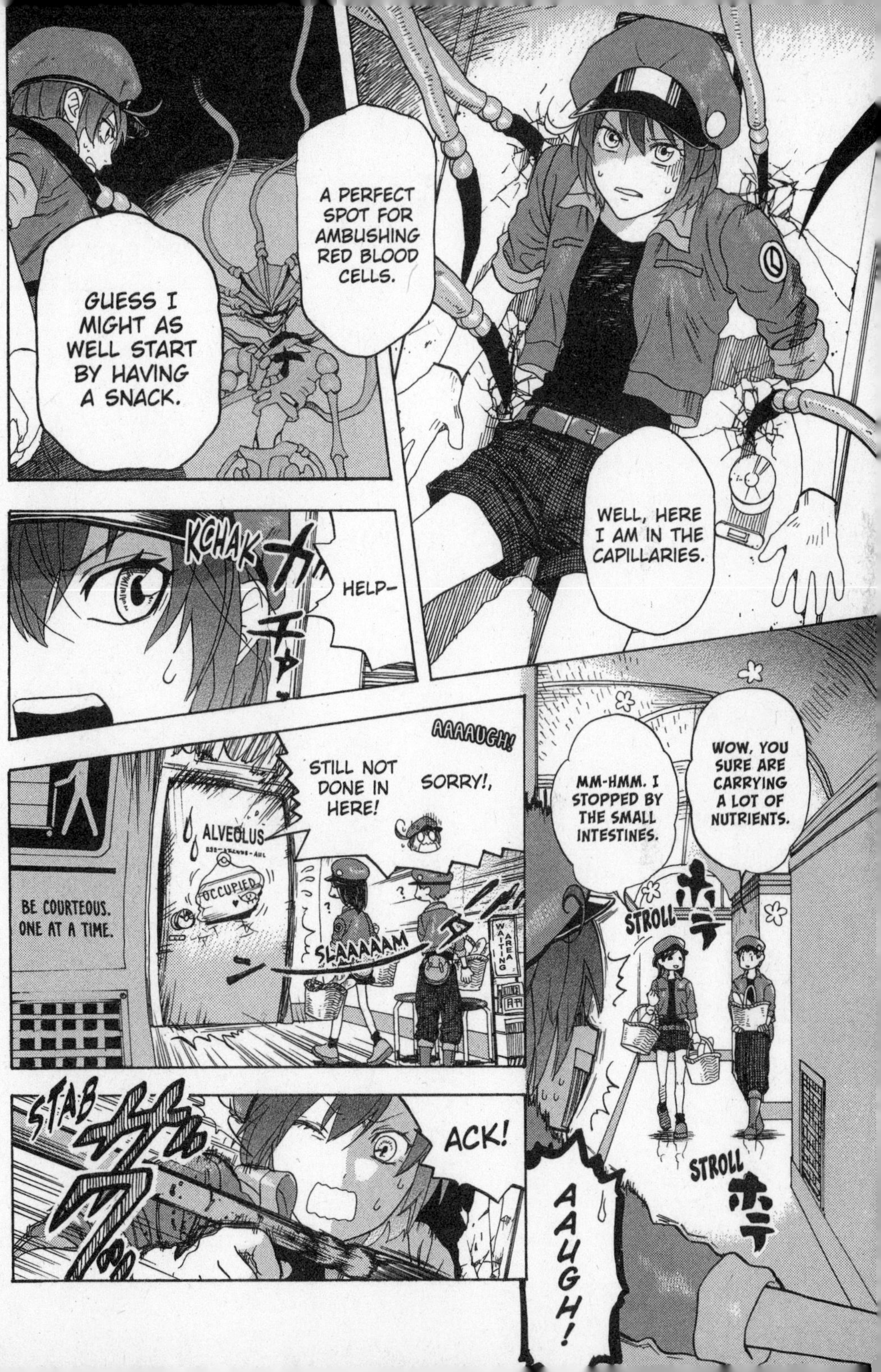
WELL, HERE I AM IN THE CAPILLARIES.
A PERFECT SPOT FOR AMBUSHING RED BLOOD CELLS.
GUESS I MIGHT AS WELL START BY HAVING A SNACK.
KCHAK
HELP-
WOW, YOU SURE ARE CARRYING A LOT OF NUTRIENTS.
MM-HMM. I STOPPED BY THE SMALL INTESTINES.
STROLL
STROLL
AAUGH!
AAAAUGH!
STILL NOT DONE IN HERE!
SORRY!,
ALVEOLUS
OCCUPIED
WAITING AREA
BE COURTEOUS. ONE AT A TIME.
SLAAAAAM
STAB
ACK!

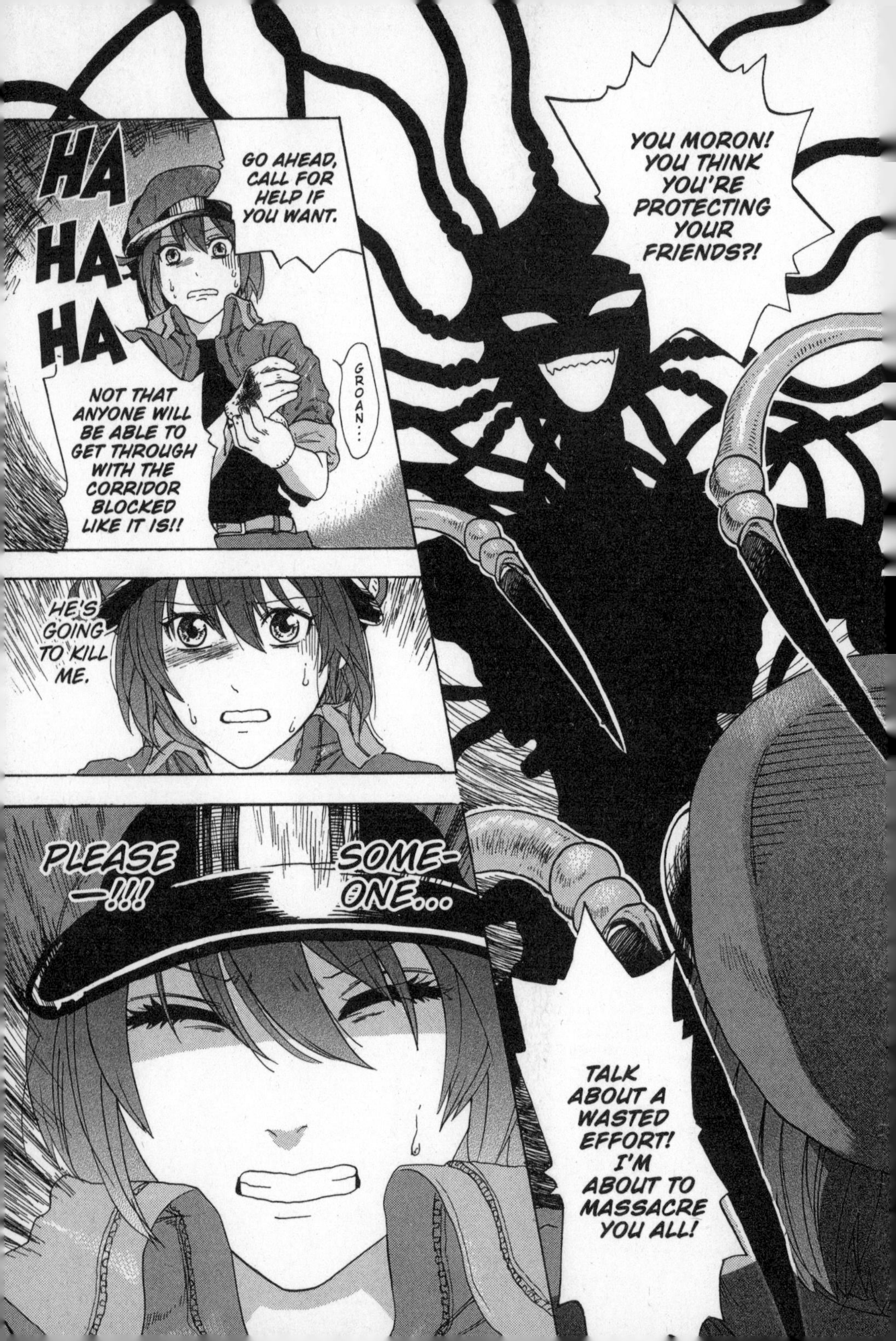
YOU MORON! YOU THINK YOU'RE PROTECTING YOUR FRIENDS?!
TALK ABOUT A WASTED EFFORT! I'M ABOUT TO MASSACRE YOU ALL!
GO AHEAD, CALL FOR HELP IF YOU WANT.
HA HA HA HA
GROAN...
NOT THAT ANYONE WILL BE ABLE TO GET THROUGH WITH THE CORRIDOR BLOCKED LIKE IT IS!!
HE'S GOING TO KILL ME.
SOME-ONE...
PLEASE—!!!

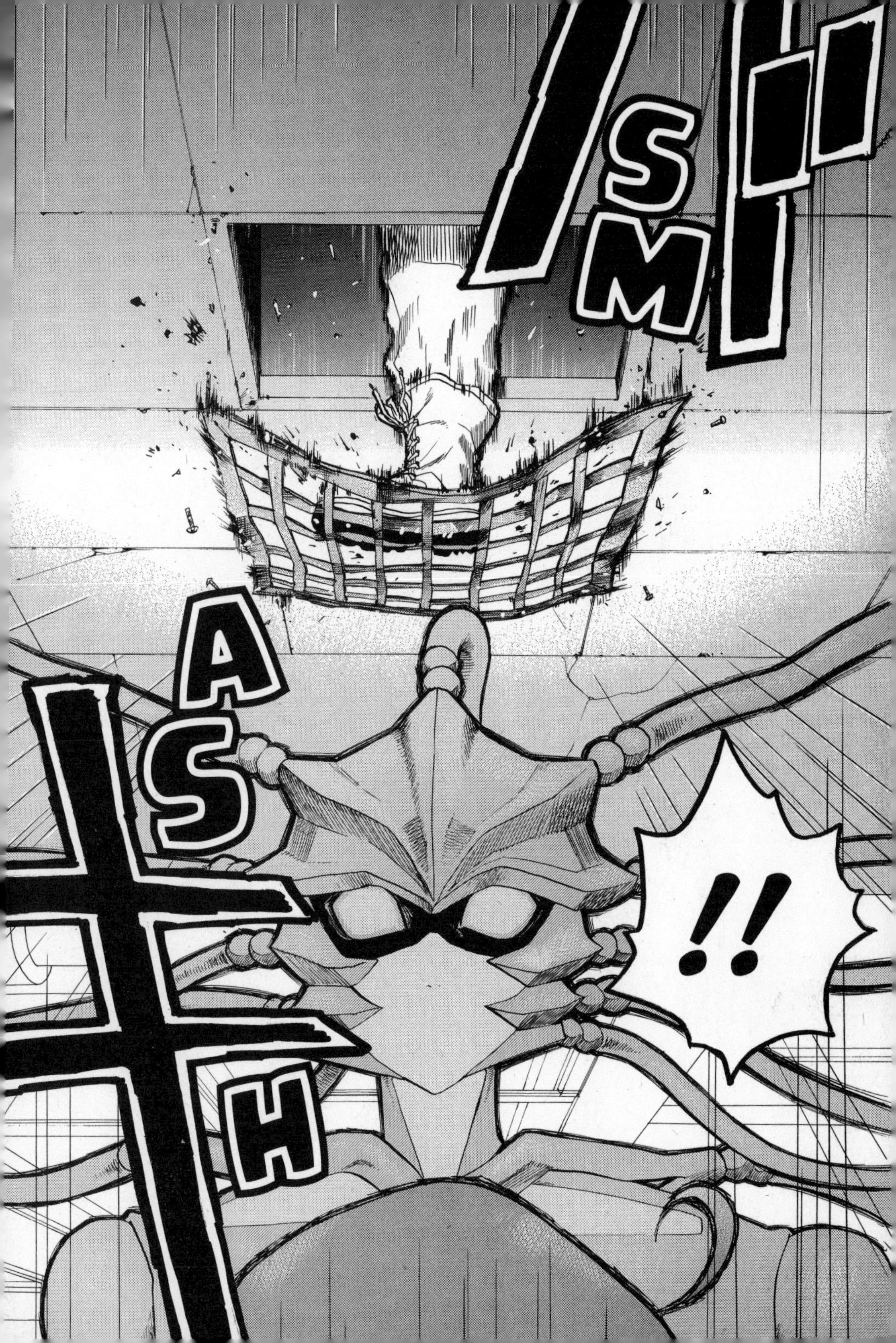
SM
ASH
!!

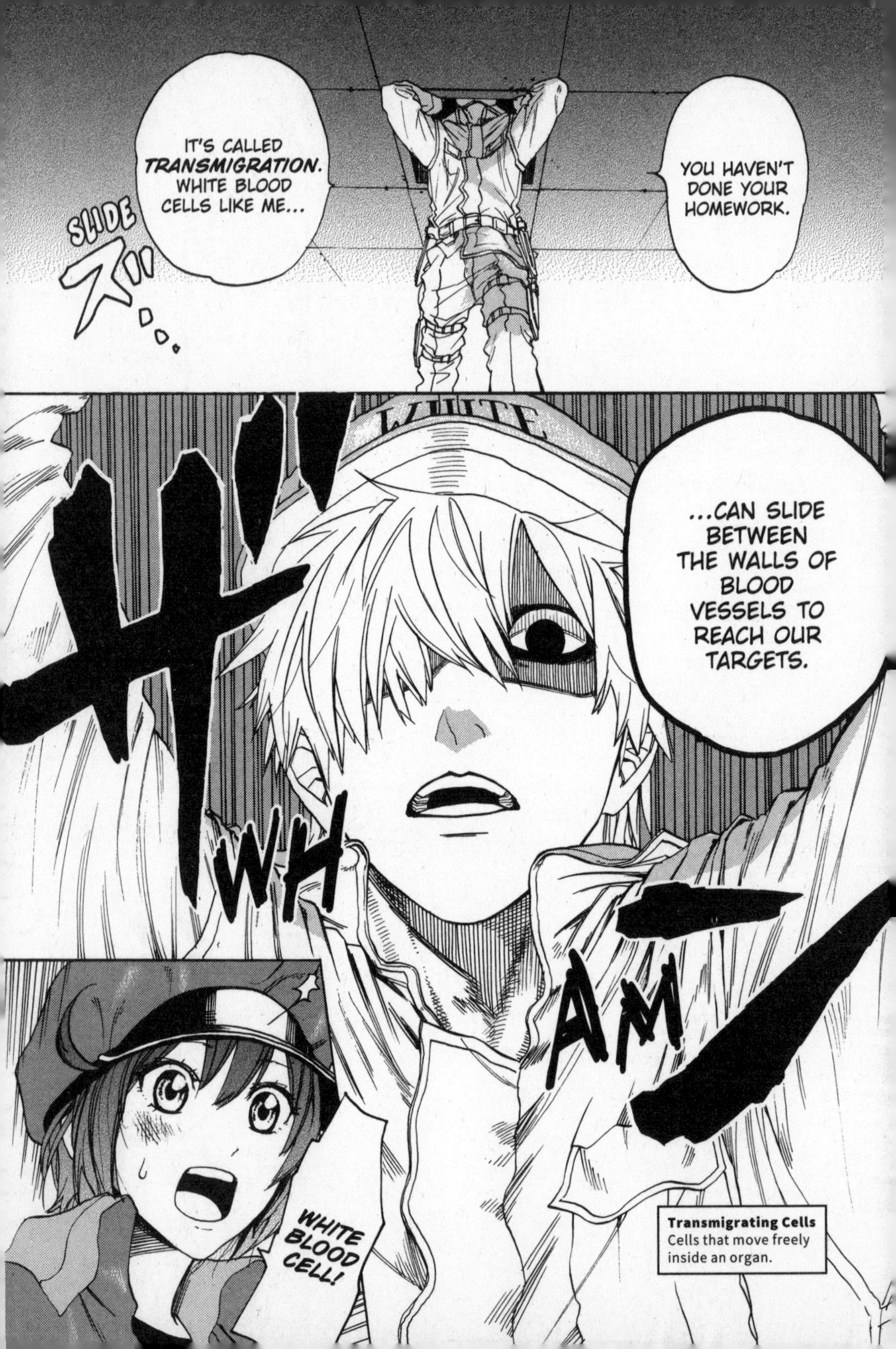

YOU HAVEN'T DONE YOUR HOMEWORK.
IT'S CALLED *TRANSMIGRATION*. WHITE BLOOD CELLS LIKE ME...
SLIDE
...CAN SLIDE BETWEEN THE WALLS OF BLOOD VESSELS TO REACH OUR TARGETS.
WH
AM
WHITE BLOOD CELL!
Transmigrating Cells
Cells that move freely inside an organ.

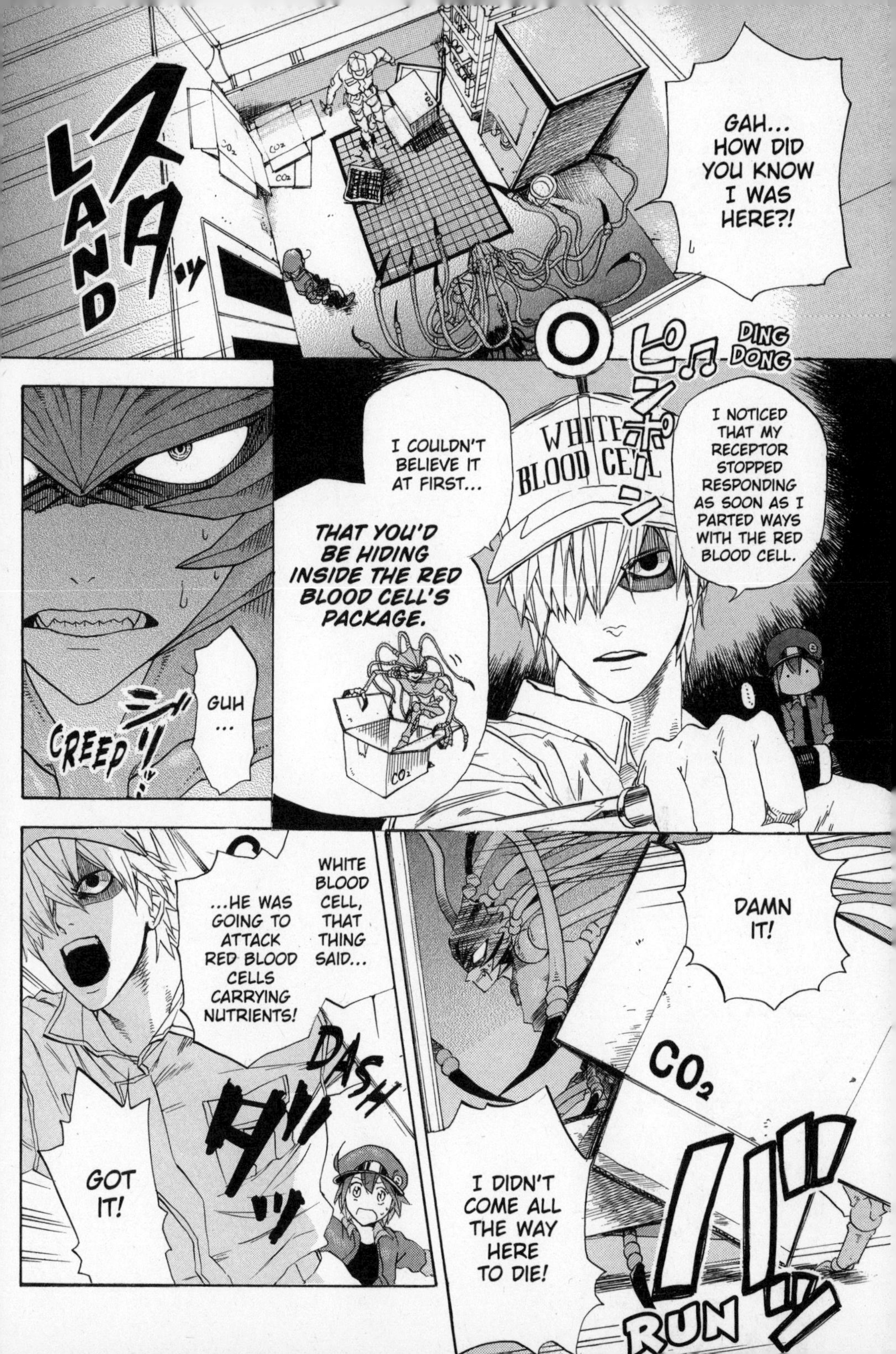
LAND
GAH... HOW DID YOU KNOW I WAS HERE?!
DING DONG
I NOTICED THAT MY RECEPTOR STOPPED RESPONDING AS SOON AS I PARTED WAYS WITH THE RED BLOOD CELL.
WHITE BLOOD CELL
I COULDN'T BELIEVE IT AT FIRST...
THAT YOU'D BE HIDING INSIDE THE RED BLOOD CELL'S PACKAGE.
GUH...
CREEP
DAMN IT!
CO_2
I DIDN'T COME ALL THE WAY HERE TO DIE!
RUN
WHITE BLOOD CELL, THAT THING SAID...
...HE WAS GOING TO ATTACK RED BLOOD CELLS CARRYING NUTRIENTS!
DASH
GOT IT!

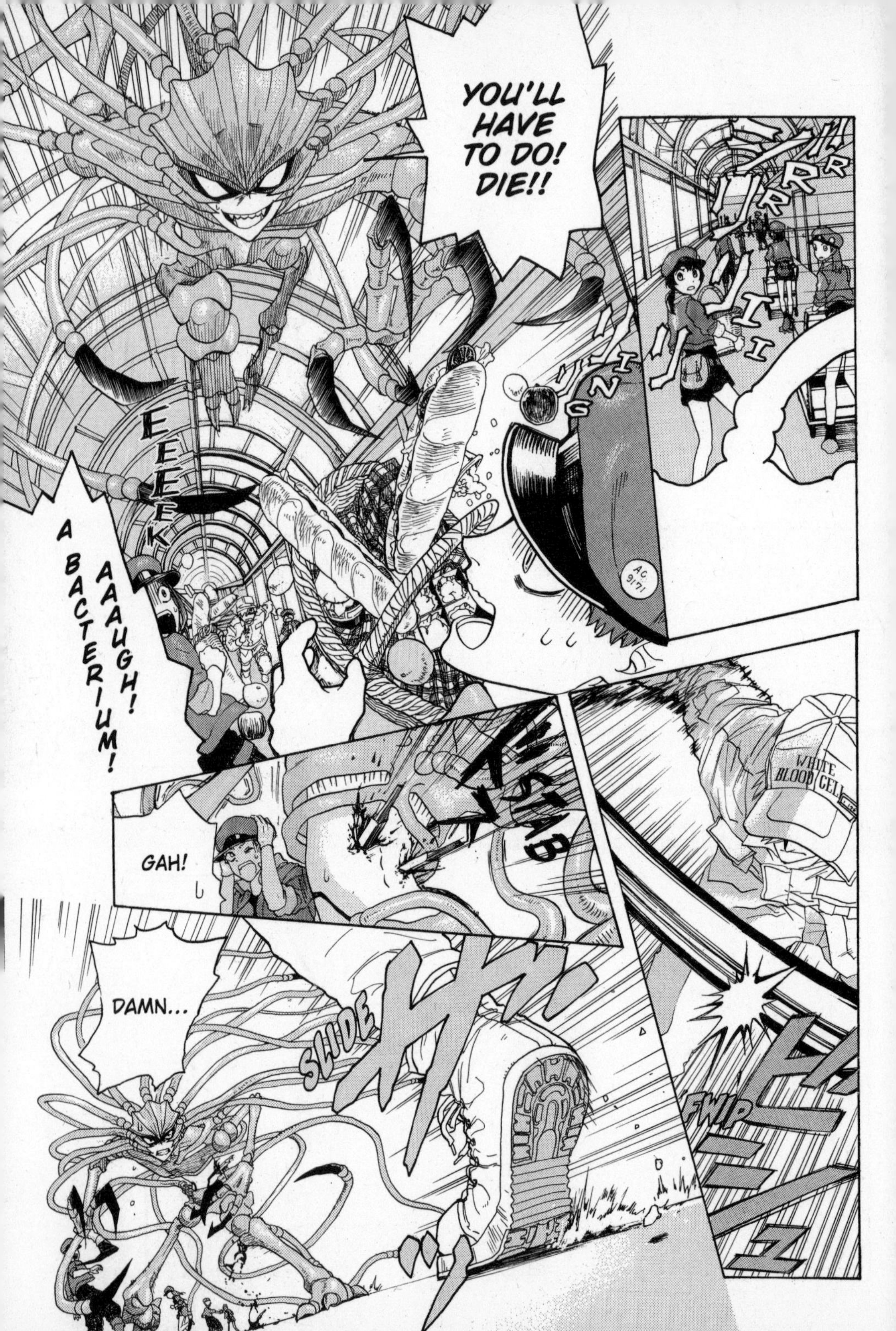
YOU'LL HAVE TO DO! DIE!!
EEEEK
A BACTERIUM!
AAAAUGH!
STAB
GAH!
FWIP
SLIDE
DAMN...

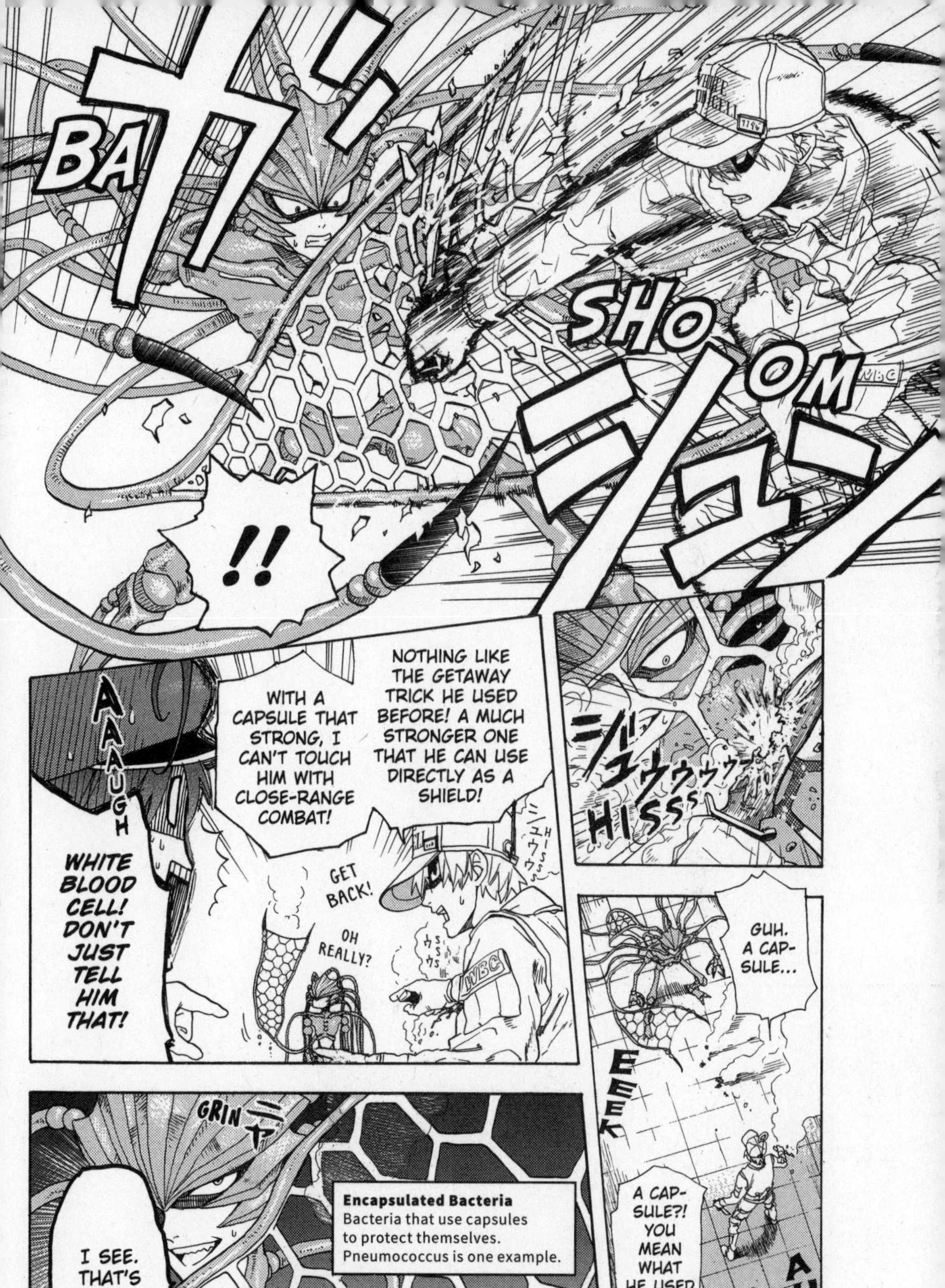

BA
SHOOM
!!
HISSS
NOTHING LIKE THE GETAWAY TRICK HE USED BEFORE! A MUCH STRONGER ONE THAT HE CAN USE DIRECTLY AS A SHIELD!
WITH A CAPSULE THAT STRONG, I CAN'T TOUCH HIM WITH CLOSE-RANGE COMBAT!
HISSS
GET BACK!
OH REALLY?
AAAAUGH
WHITE BLOOD CELL! DON'T JUST TELL HIM THAT!
GUH. A CAP-SULE...
A CAP-SULE?! YOU MEAN WHAT HE USED BEFORE -?!
EEEK
AUGH AUGH
GRIN
Encapsulated Bacteria
Bacteria that use capsules to protect themselves. Pneumococcus is one example.
I SEE. THAT'S GOOD TO KNOW.

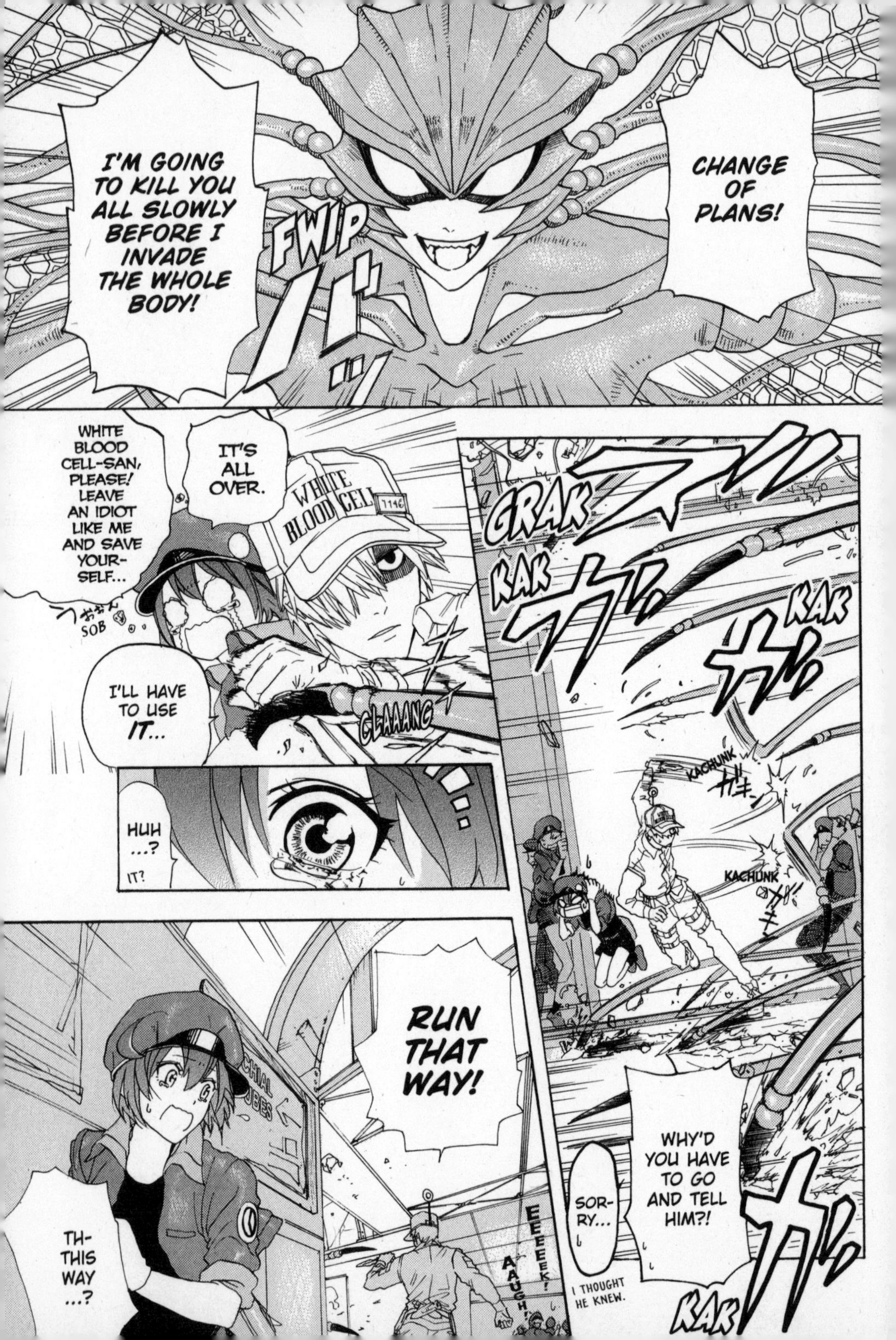
CHANGE OF PLANS!
I'M GOING TO KILL YOU ALL SLOWLY BEFORE I INVADE THE WHOLE BODY!
FWIP
GRAK
KAK
KAK
KACHUNK
KACHUNK
IT'S ALL OVER.
WHITE BLOOD CELL 1146
WHITE BLOOD CELL-SAN, PLEASE! LEAVE AN IDIOT LIKE ME AND SAVE YOURSELF...
SOB
I'LL HAVE TO USE IT...
CLAAANG
HUH ...?
IT?
WHY'D YOU HAVE TO GO AND TELL HIM?!
SORRY...
I THOUGHT HE KNEW.
KAK
EEEEEK!
AAUGH!
RUN THAT WAY!
TH-THIS WAY ...?

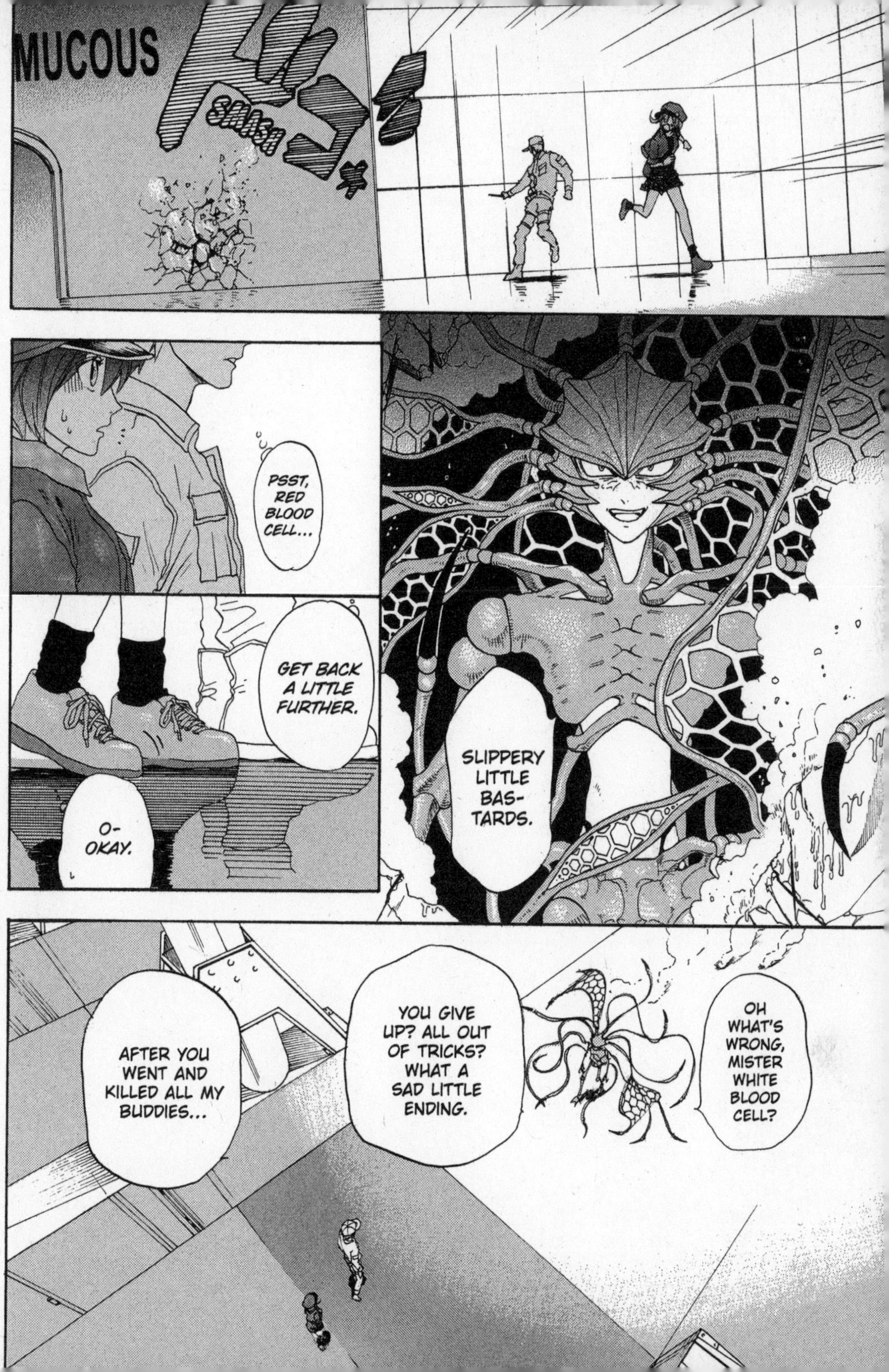
MUCOUS
SMASH!!
SLIPPERY LITTLE BAS-TARDS.
PSST, RED BLOOD CELL...
GET BACK A LITTLE FURTHER.
O-OKAY.
OH WHAT'S WRONG, MISTER WHITE BLOOD CELL?
YOU GIVE UP? ALL OUT OF TRICKS? WHAT A SAD LITTLE ENDING.
AFTER YOU WENT AND KILLED ALL MY BUDDIES...

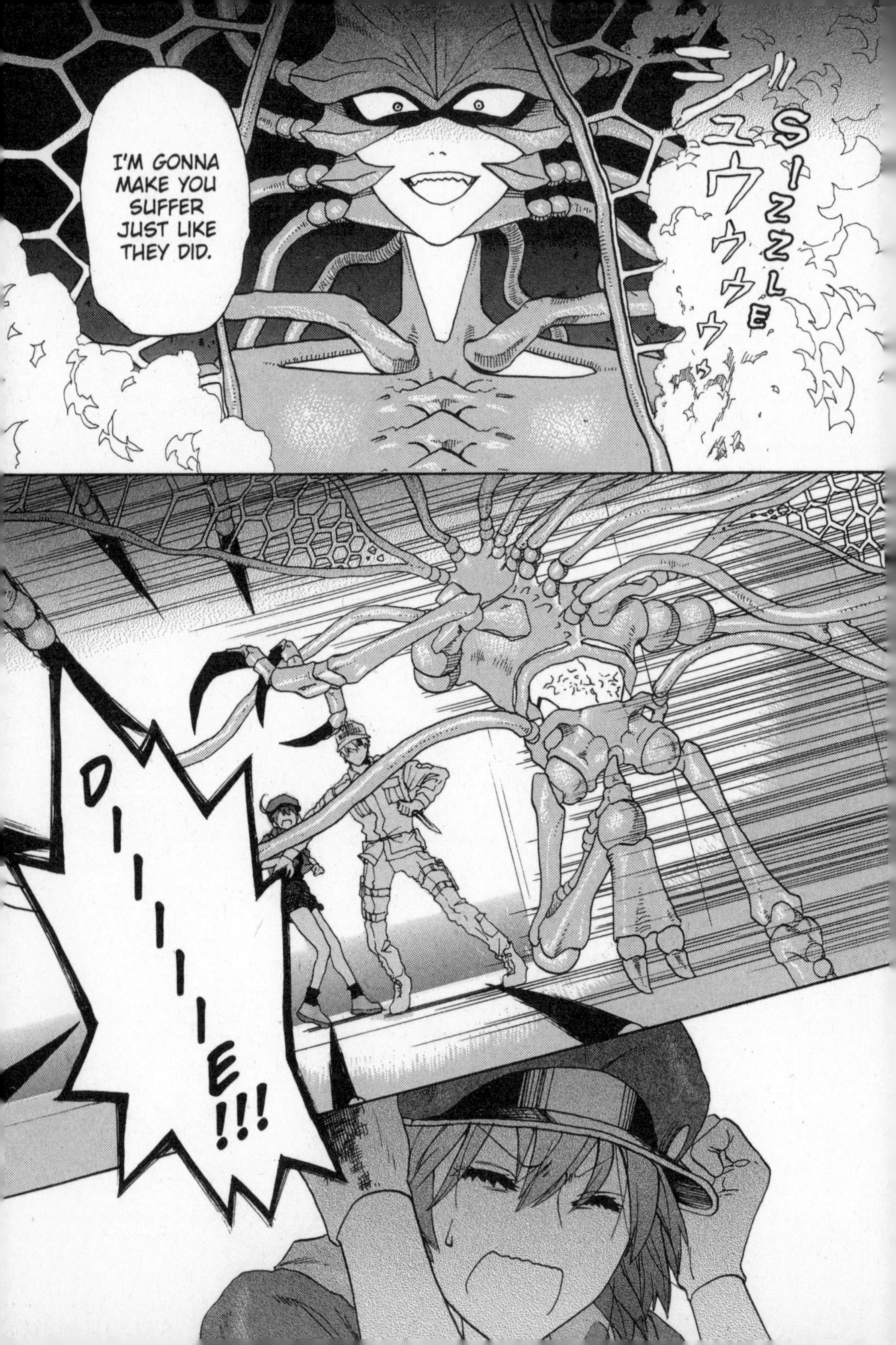

SIZZLE
ジュウウウウウ
I'M GONNA MAKE YOU SUFFER JUST LIKE THEY DID.
DIIIIIE!!!

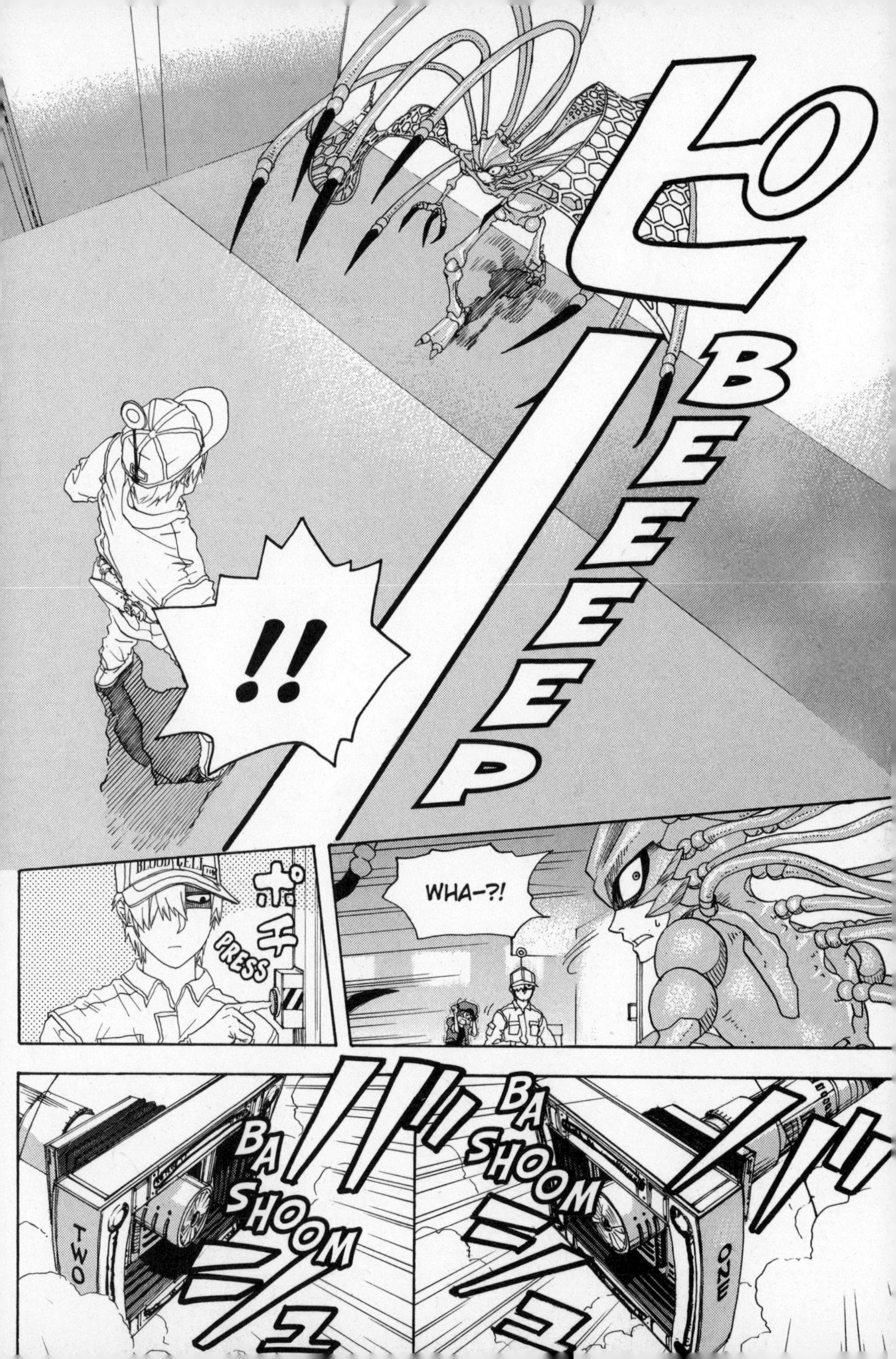

ピ
BEEEEEEP
!!
WHA-?!
ポチ
PRESS
BLOOD CELL
BA SHOOM
BA SHOOM
TWO

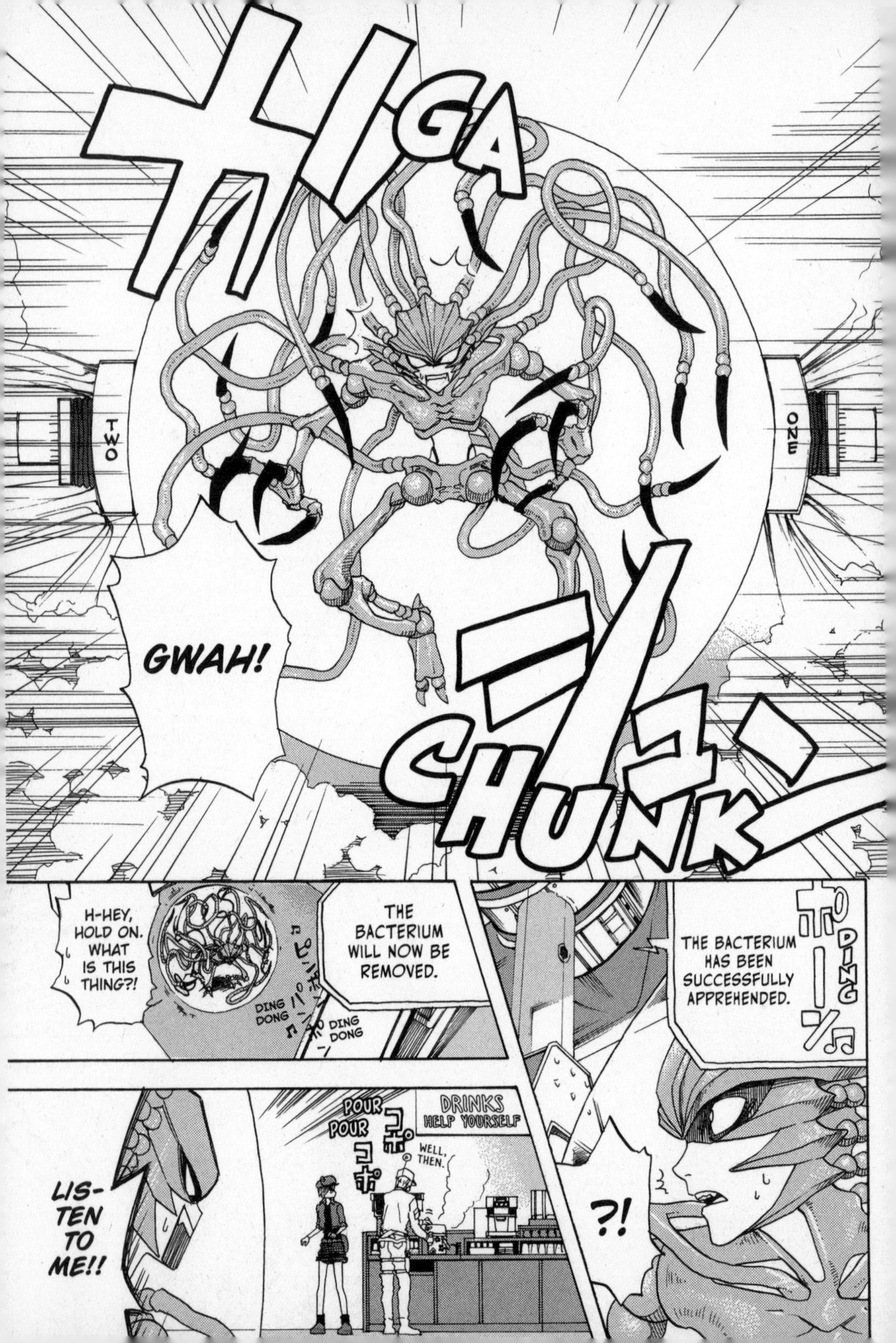
GA
ONE
TWO
GWAH!
CHUNK
THE BACTERIUM HAS BEEN SUCCESSFULLY APPREHENDED.
DING
THE BACTERIUM WILL NOW BE REMOVED.
DING DONG
DING DONG
H-HEY, HOLD ON. WHAT IS THIS THING?!
?!
DRINKS HELP YOURSELF
POUR POUR
WELL, THEN.
LIS-TEN TO ME!!

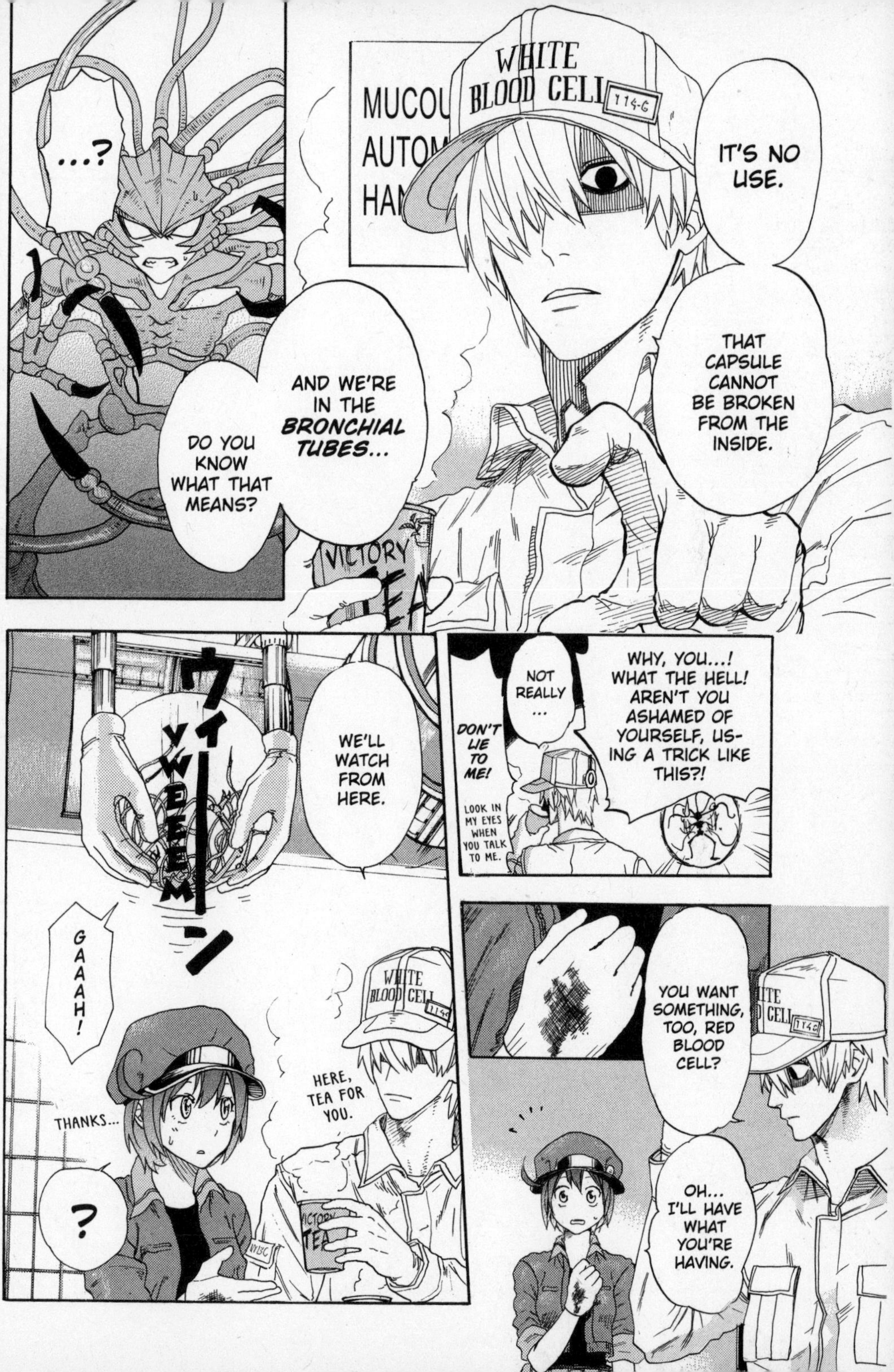

WHITE BLOOD CELL
1146
IT'S NO USE.
THAT CAPSULE CANNOT BE BROKEN FROM THE INSIDE.
AND WE'RE IN THE BRONCHIAL TUBES...
DO YOU KNOW WHAT THAT MEANS?
VICTORY TEA
...?
WHY, YOU...! WHAT THE HELL! AREN'T YOU ASHAMED OF YOURSELF, USING A TRICK LIKE THIS?!
NOT REALLY...
DON'T LIE TO ME!
LOOK IN MY EYES WHEN YOU TALK TO ME.
WE'LL WATCH FROM HERE.
ウィーン
WEEEM
GAAAH!
YOU WANT SOMETHING, TOO, RED BLOOD CELL?
OH... I'LL HAVE WHAT YOU'RE HAVING.
HERE, TEA FOR YOU.
THANKS...
?

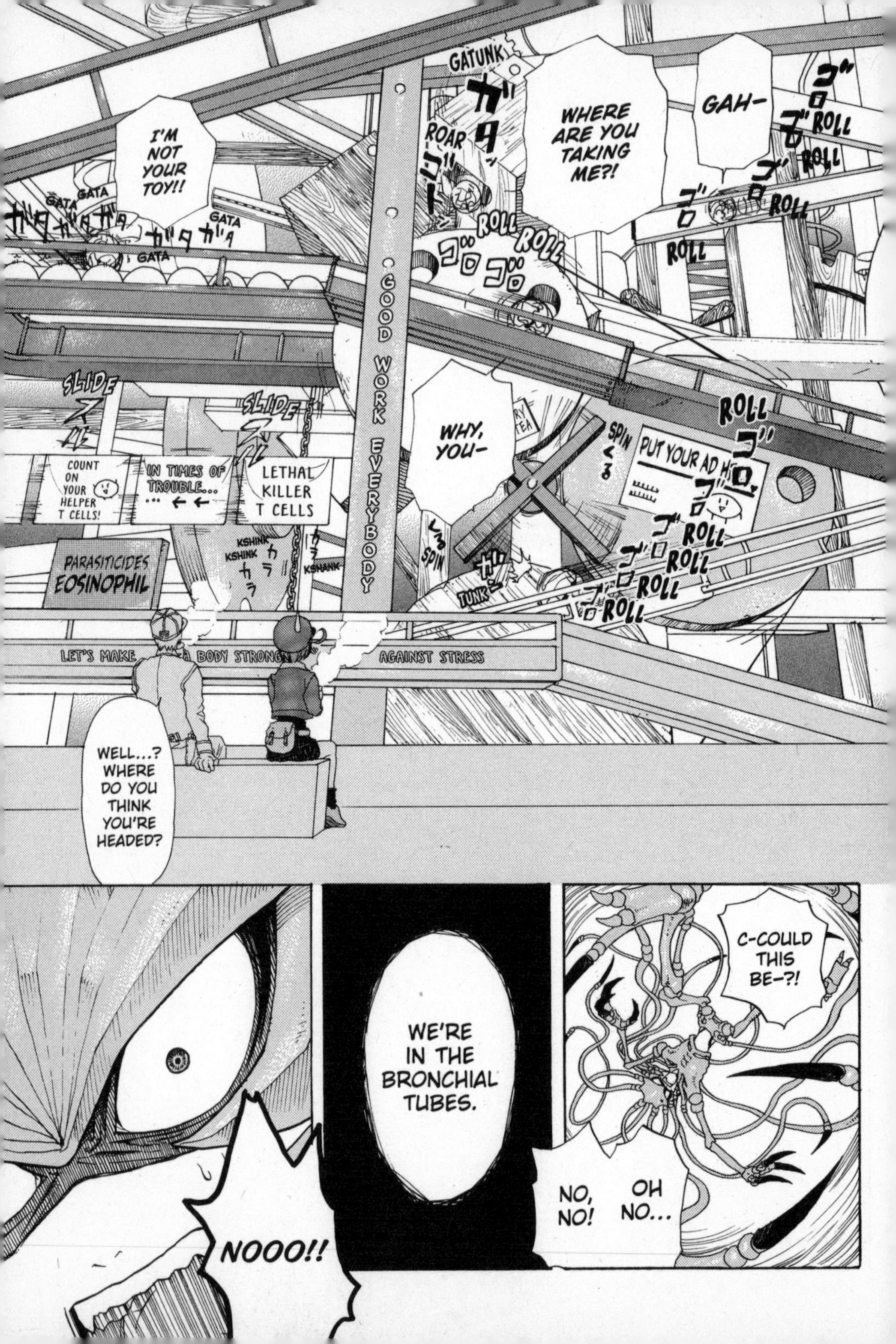
GAH-
ROLL ROLL ROLL ROLL
WHERE ARE YOU TAKING ME?!
GATUNK
ROAR
ROLL ROLL
I'M NOT YOUR TOY!!
GATA GATA GATA GATA
GOOD WORK EVERYBODY
ROLL ROLL ROLL ROLL ROLL
PUT YOUR AD H
SPIN SPIN
TUNK
WHY, YOU-
SLIDE
SLIDE
LETHAL KILLER T CELLS
IN TIMES OF TROUBLE... ... ← ←
COUNT ON YOUR HELPER T CELLS!
KSHINK KSHINK KSHANK
PARASITICIDES EOSINOPHIL
LET'S MAKE A BODY STRONG AGAINST STRESS
WELL...? WHERE DO YOU THINK YOU'RE HEADED?
C-COULD THIS BE-?!
OH NO...
NO, NO!
WE'RE IN THE BRONCHIAL TUBES.
NOOO!!

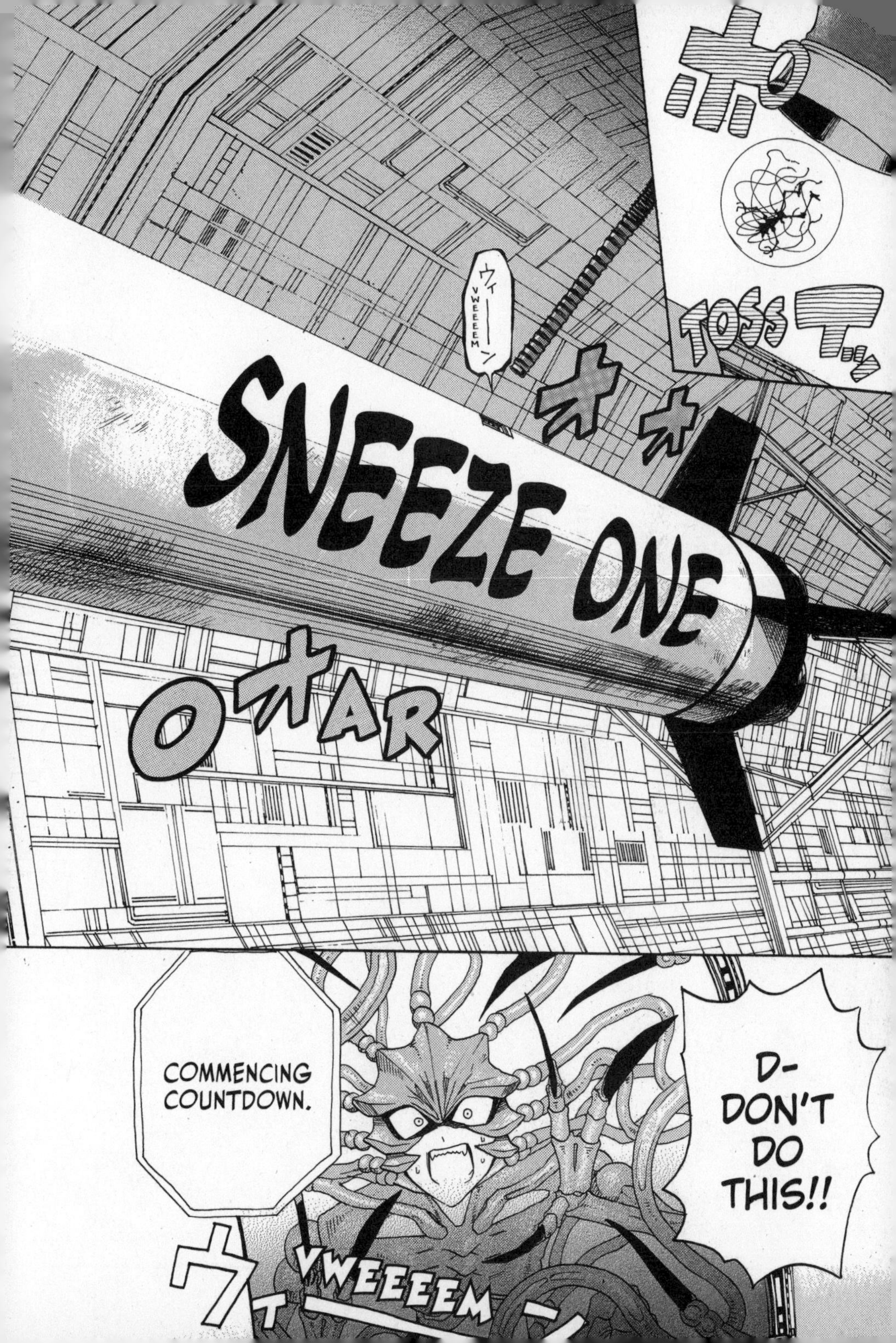
TOSS
VWEEEEM
SNEEZE ONE
D-DON'T DO THIS!!
COMMENCING COUNTDOWN.
VWEEEEM

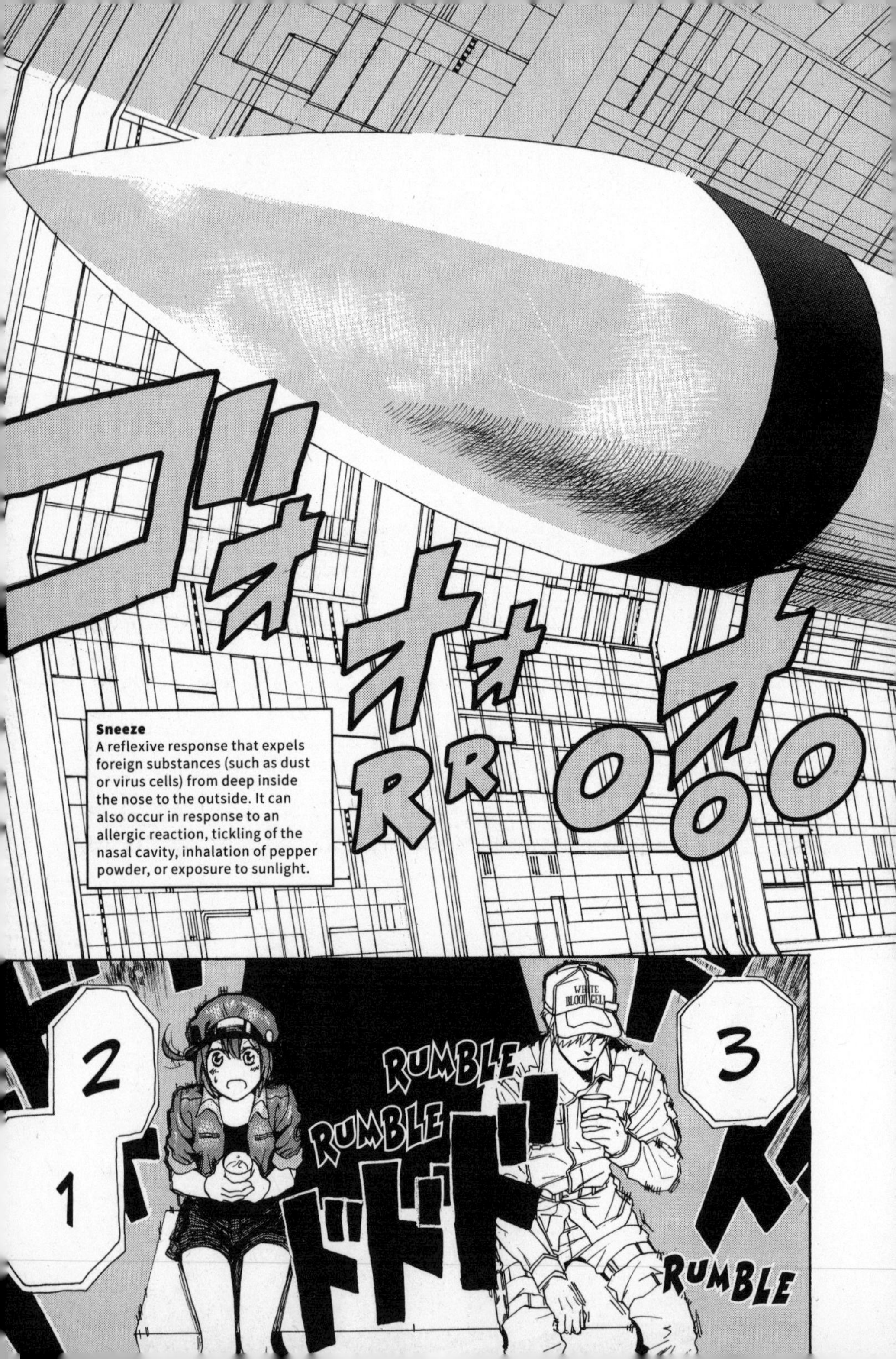
ゴオオォオ
RROOO
Sneeze
A reflexive response that expels foreign substances (such as dust or virus cells) from deep inside the nose to the outside. It can also occur in response to an allergic reaction, tickling of the nasal cavity, inhalation of pepper powder, or exposure to sunlight.
3
WHITE BLOOD CELL
RUMBLE
RUMBLE
RUMBLE
ドドド
2
1

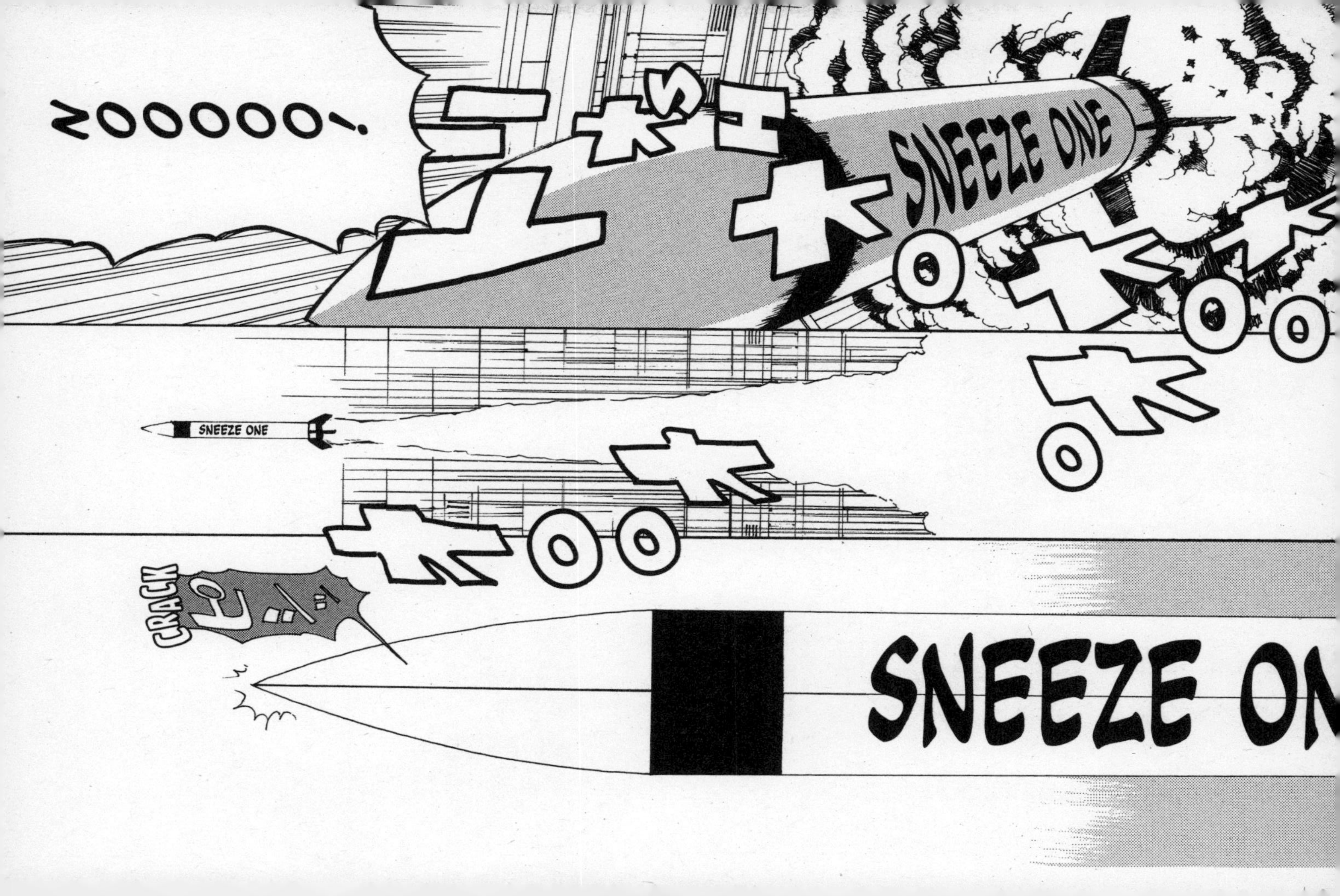
NOOOOO!
SH
SNEEZE ONE
SNEEZE ONE
CRACK
SNEEZE ON

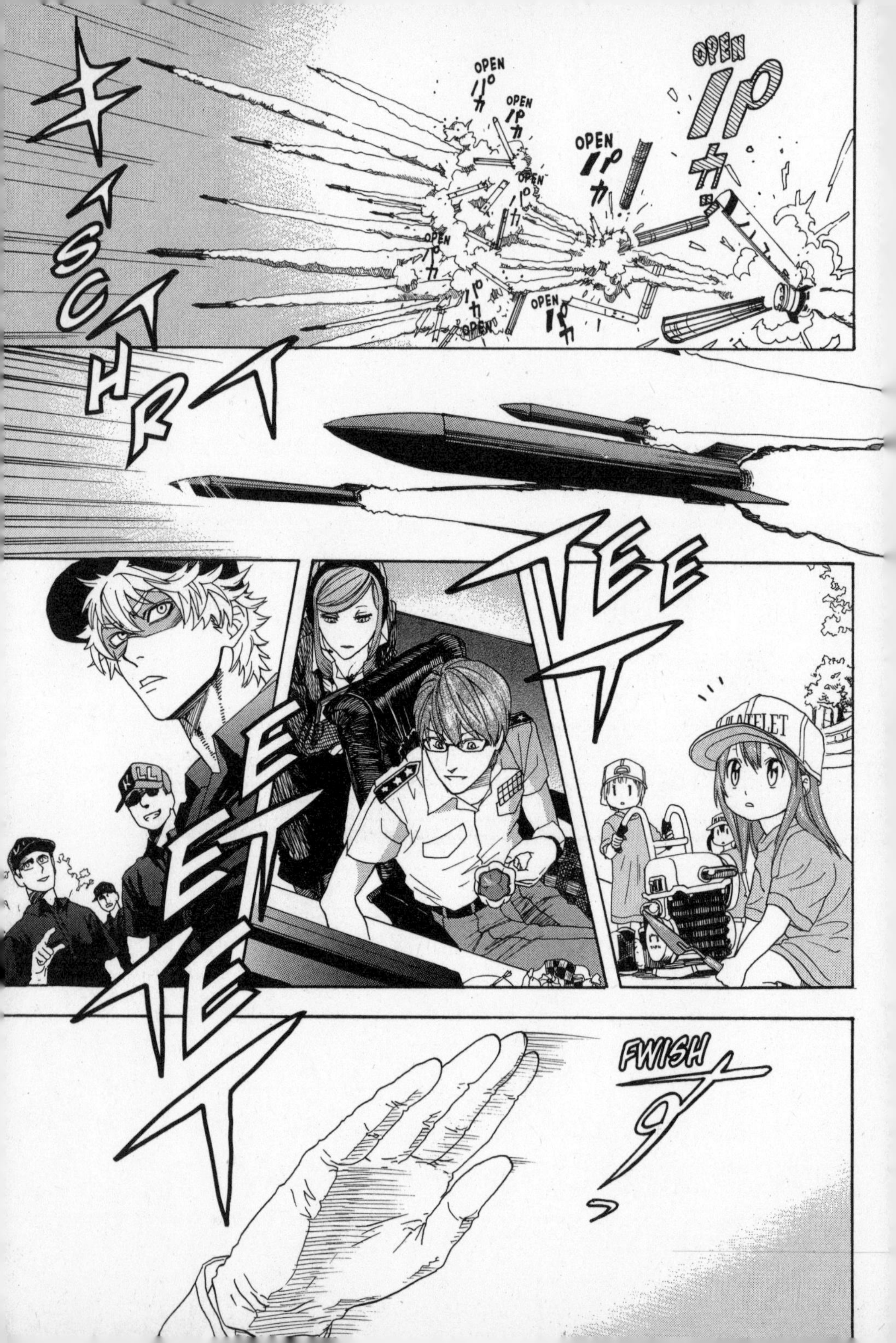
OPEN
OPEN
OPEN
OPEN
OPEN
OPEN
OPEN
SCHR
TEE
FWISH

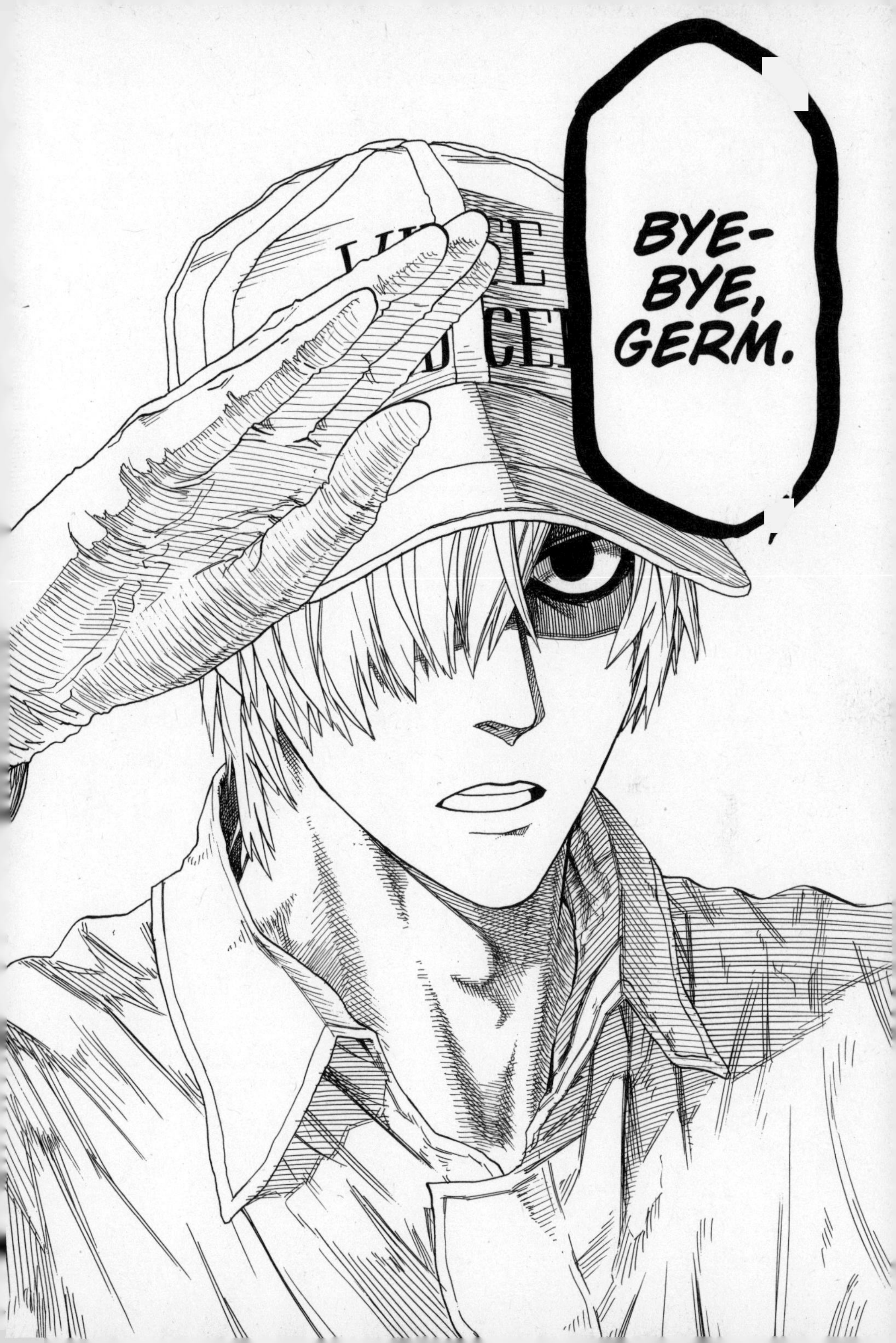
BYE-BYE, GERM.

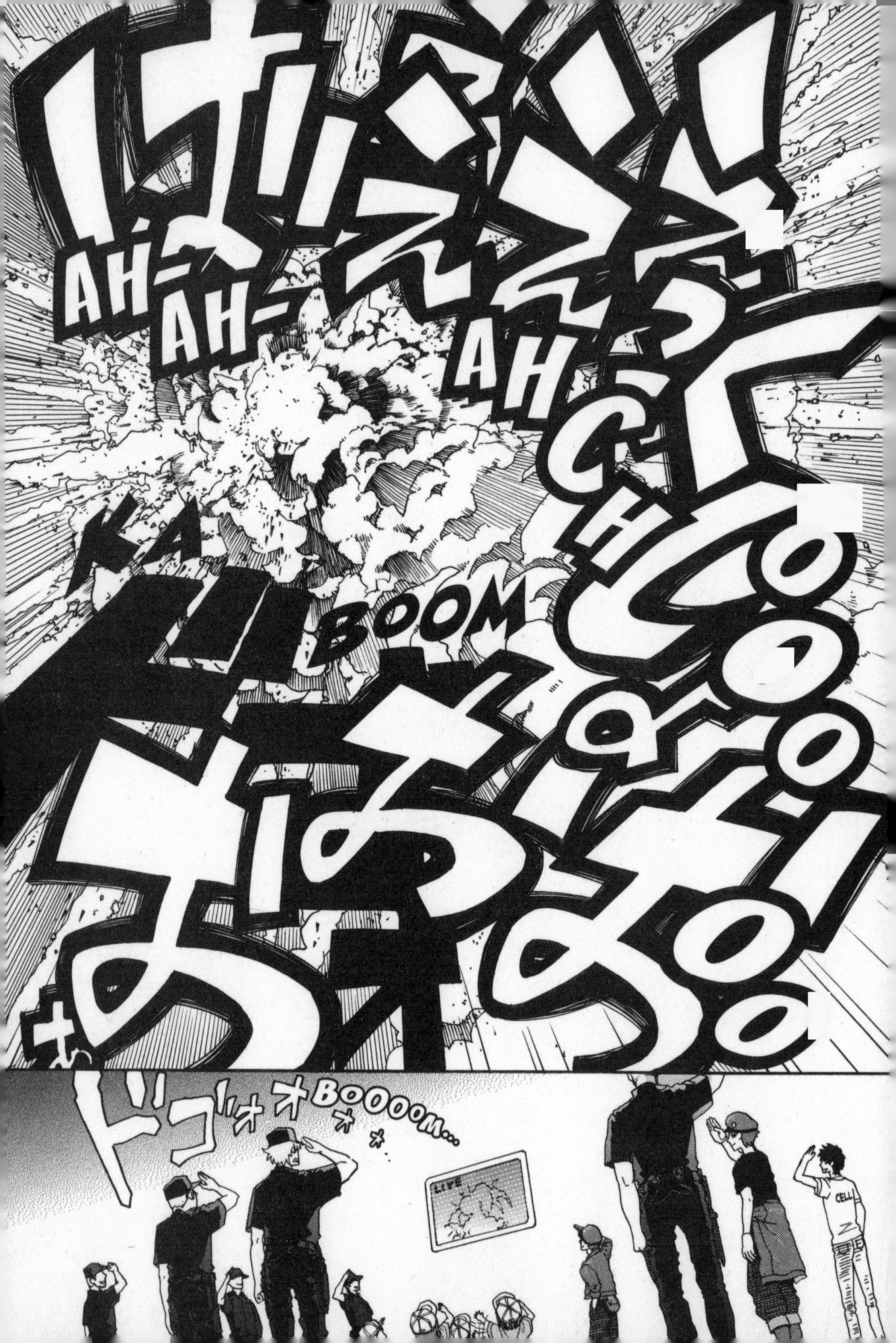
AH– AH– AH–
G– H–
KA BOOM
BOOOOOM...
LIVE
CELL

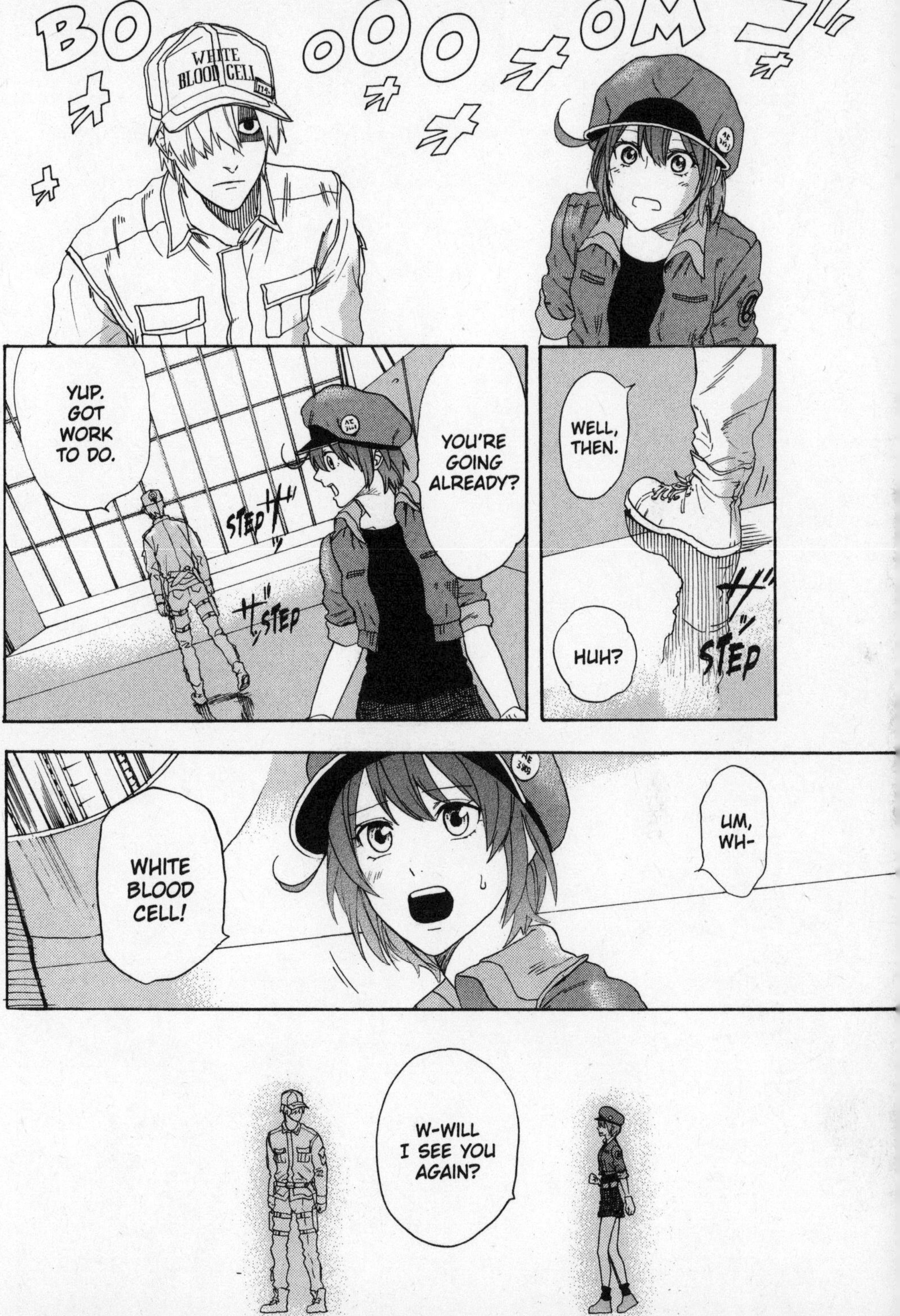
BOoOOOoOM
WHITE BLOOD CELL
WELL, THEN.
STEP
HUH?
YOU'RE GOING ALREADY?
STEP
YUP. GOT WORK TO DO.
STEP
UM, WH-
WHITE BLOOD CELL!
W-WILL I SEE YOU AGAIN?

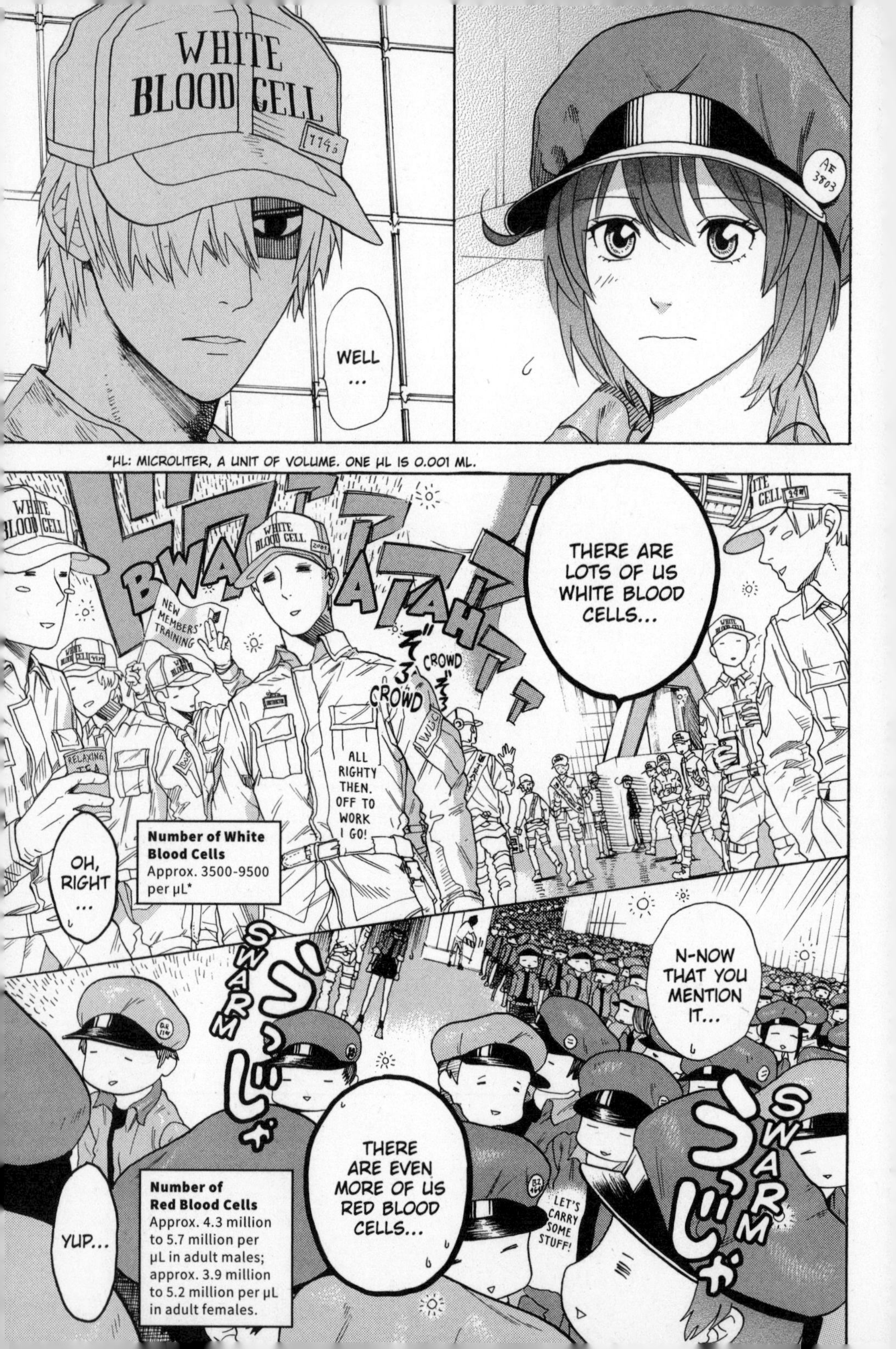
WHITE BLOOD CELL
WELL...
THERE ARE LOTS OF US WHITE BLOOD CELLS...
CROWD
CROWD
BWAAAAH
ALL RIGHTY THEN. OFF TO WORK I GO!
NEW MEMBERS' TRAINING
RELAXING TEA
Number of White Blood Cells
Approx. 3500-9500 per μL*
OH, RIGHT...
N-NOW THAT YOU MENTION IT...
SWARM
THERE ARE EVEN MORE OF US RED BLOOD CELLS...
LET'S CARRY SOME STUFF!
Number of Red Blood Cells
Approx. 4.3 million to 5.7 million per μL in adult males; approx. 3.9 million to 5.2 million per μL in adult females.
YUP...
SWARM

*μL: MICROLITER, A UNIT OF VOLUME. ONE μL IS 0.001 ML.

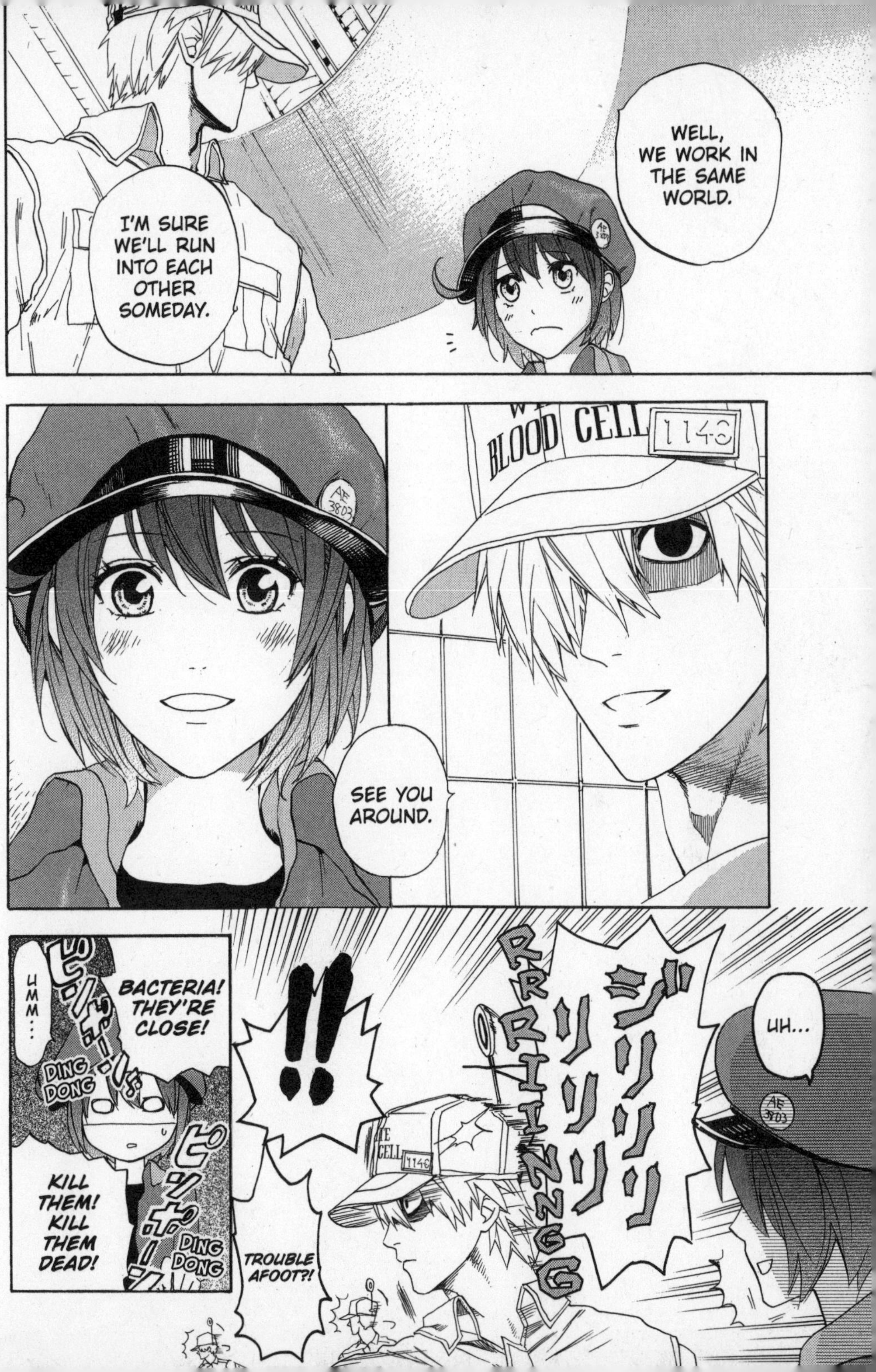
WELL, WE WORK IN THE SAME WORLD.
I'M SURE WE'LL RUN INTO EACH OTHER SOMEDAY.
BLOOD CELL
1146
SEE YOU AROUND.
UH...
ジリリリ
リリリ
RRRIINNGG
!!
TE CELL
1146
TROUBLE AFOOT?!
BACTERIA! THEY'RE CLOSE!
UMM...
DING DONG
KILL THEM! KILL THEM DEAD!
DING DONG

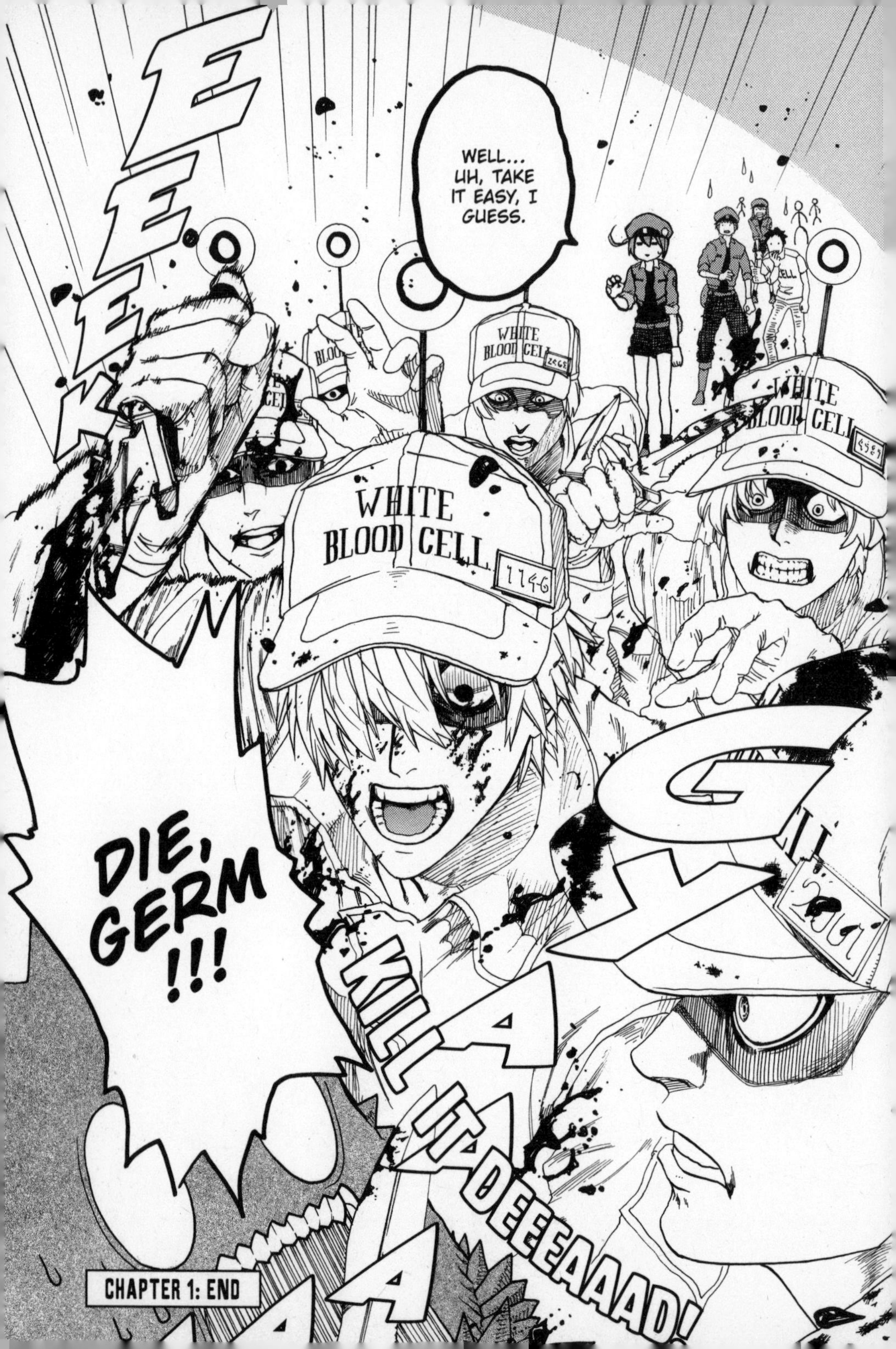
WELL... UH, TAKE IT EASY, I GUESS.
EEEK
WHITE BLOOD CELL
WHITE BLOOD CELL 1146
WHITE BLOOD CELL
KILL IT DEEEAAAD!
DIE, GERM!!!
CHAPTER 1: END

Cells at Work!
はたらく細胞

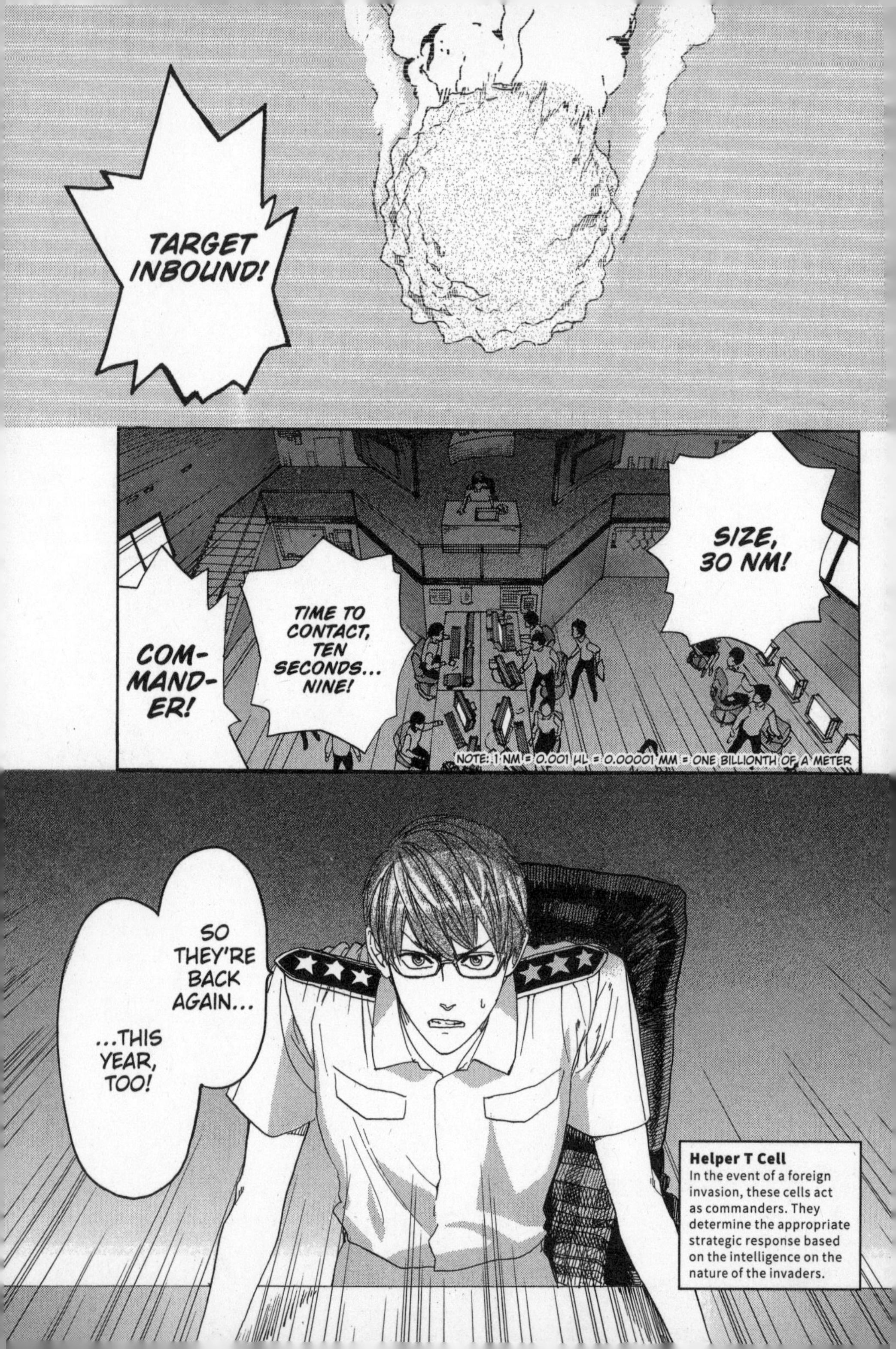
TARGET INBOUND!
SIZE, 30 NM!
TIME TO CONTACT, TEN SECONDS... NINE!
COM-MAND-ER!
NOTE: 1 NM = 0.001 µL = 0.00001 MM = ONE BILLIONTH OF A METER
SO THEY'RE BACK AGAIN...
...THIS YEAR, TOO!
Helper T Cell
In the event of a foreign invasion, these cells act as commanders. They determine the appropriate strategic response based on the intelligence on the nature of the invaders.

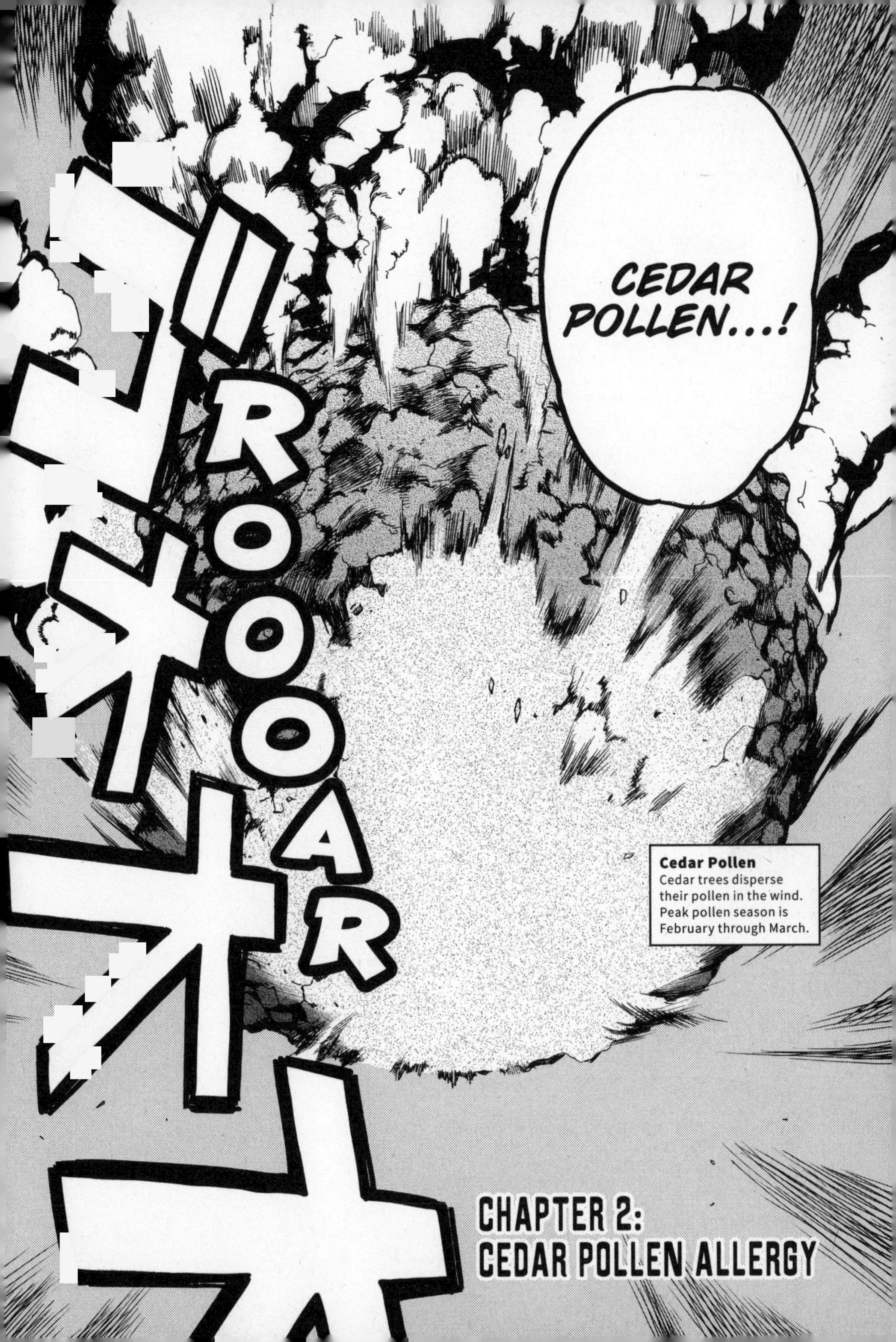

CHAPTER 2: CEDAR POLLEN ALLERGY

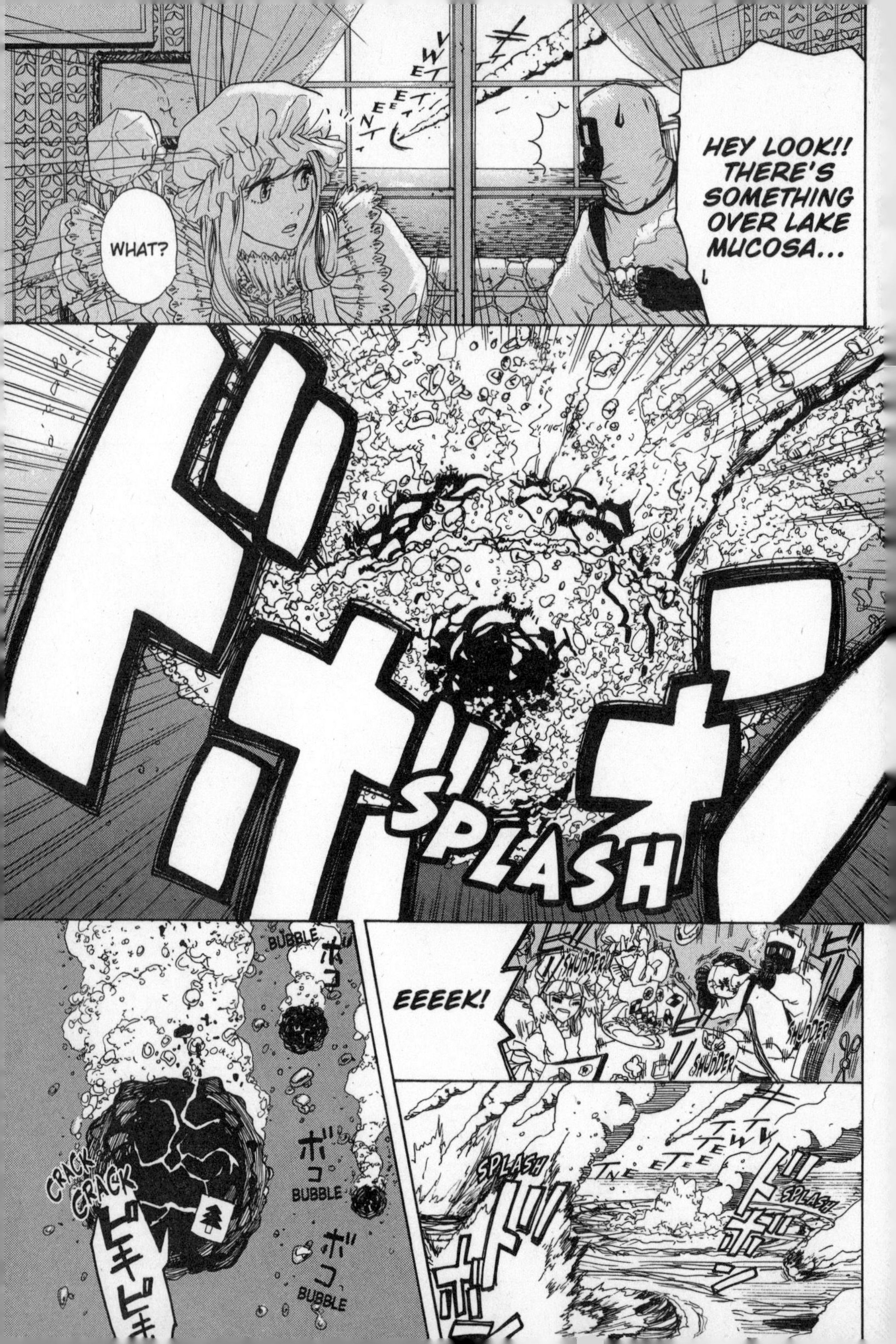
HEY LOOK!! THERE'S SOMETHING OVER LAKE MUCOSA...
WHAT?
SPLASH
EEEEK!
SHUDDER!!
SHUDDER
SHUDDER
SPLASH!!
SPLASH
BUBBLE
ボコ
BUBBLE
ボコ
BUBBLE
CRACK CRACK
ピキピキ

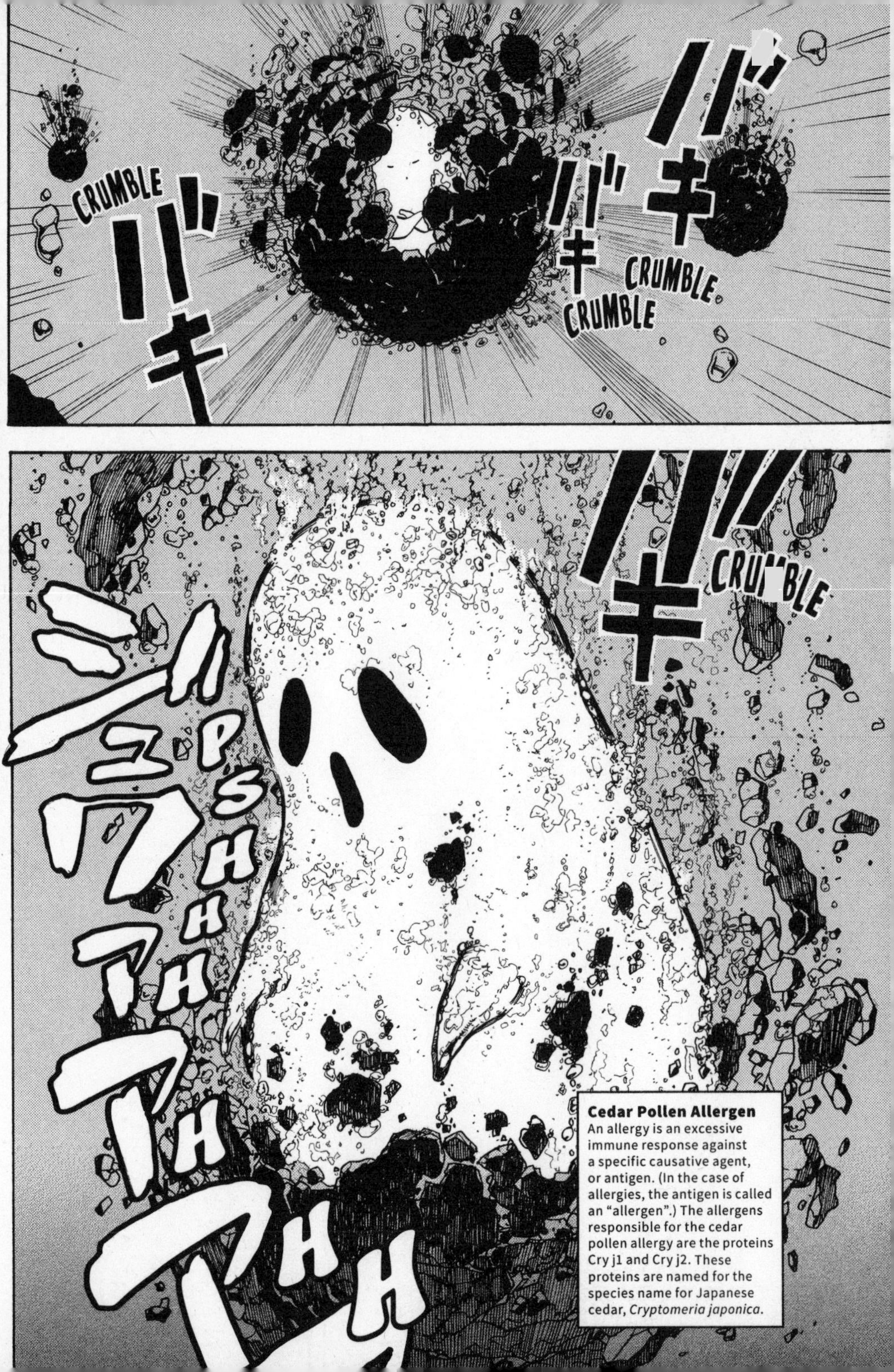
バキ
バキ
CRUMBLE
CRUMBLE
CRUMBLE
バキ
バキ
CRUMBLE
シュワァァァ
PSHHHHHH
Cedar Pollen Allergen
An allergy is an excessive immune response against a specific causative agent, or antigen. (In the case of allergies, the antigen is called an "allergen".) The allergens responsible for the cedar pollen allergy are the proteins Cry j1 and Cry j2. These proteins are named for the species name for Japanese cedar, *Cryptomeria japonica*.

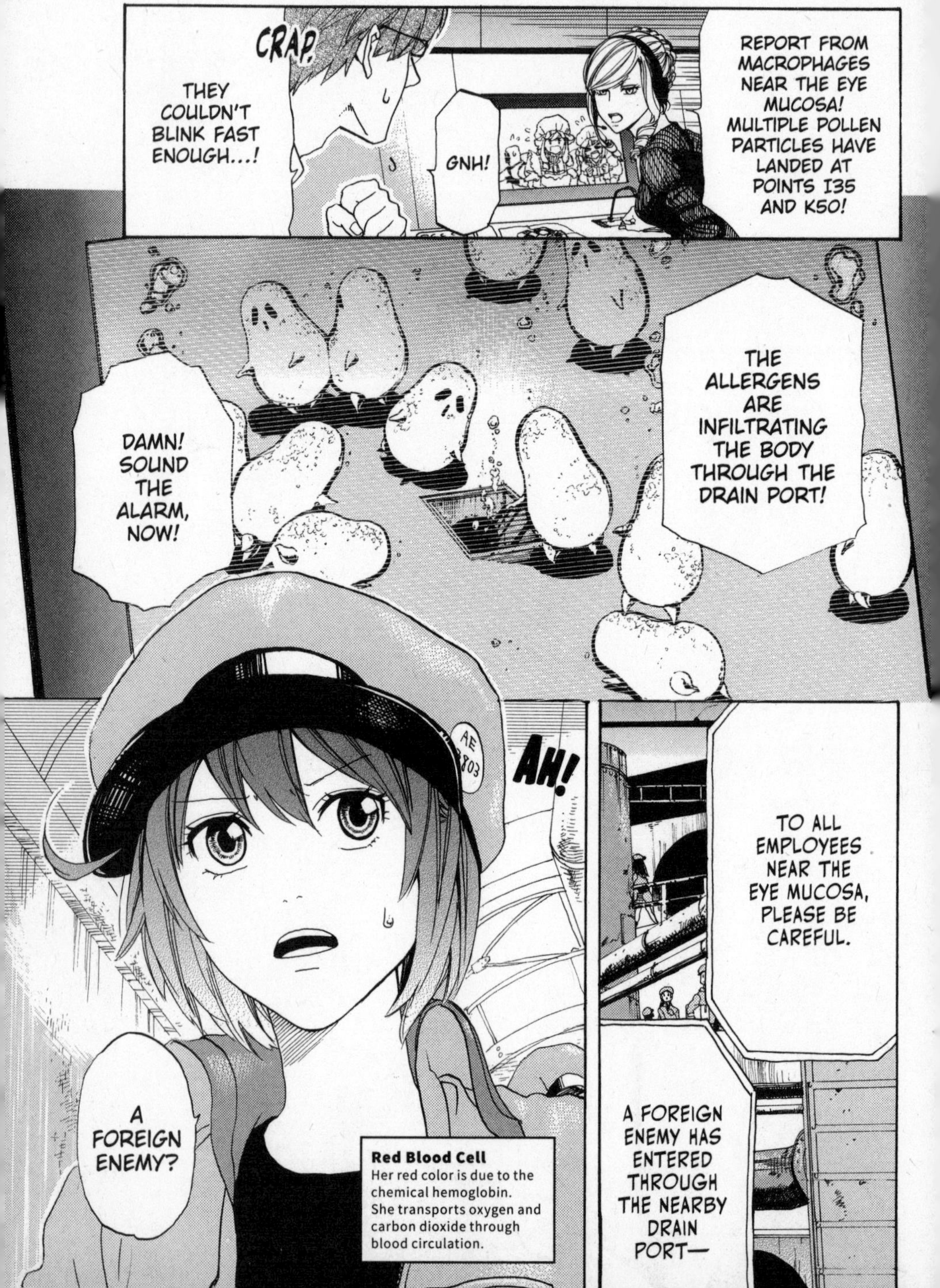
REPORT FROM MACROPHAGES NEAR THE EYE MUCOSA! MULTIPLE POLLEN PARTICLES HAVE LANDED AT POINTS I35 AND K50!
GNH!
CRAP.
THEY COULDN'T BLINK FAST ENOUGH...!
THE ALLERGENS ARE INFILTRATING THE BODY THROUGH THE DRAIN PORT!
DAMN! SOUND THE ALARM, NOW!
TO ALL EMPLOYEES NEAR THE EYE MUCOSA, PLEASE BE CAREFUL.
A FOREIGN ENEMY HAS ENTERED THROUGH THE NEARBY DRAIN PORT—
AH!
A FOREIGN ENEMY?
Red Blood Cell
Her red color is due to the chemical hemoglobin. She transports oxygen and carbon dioxide through blood circulation.

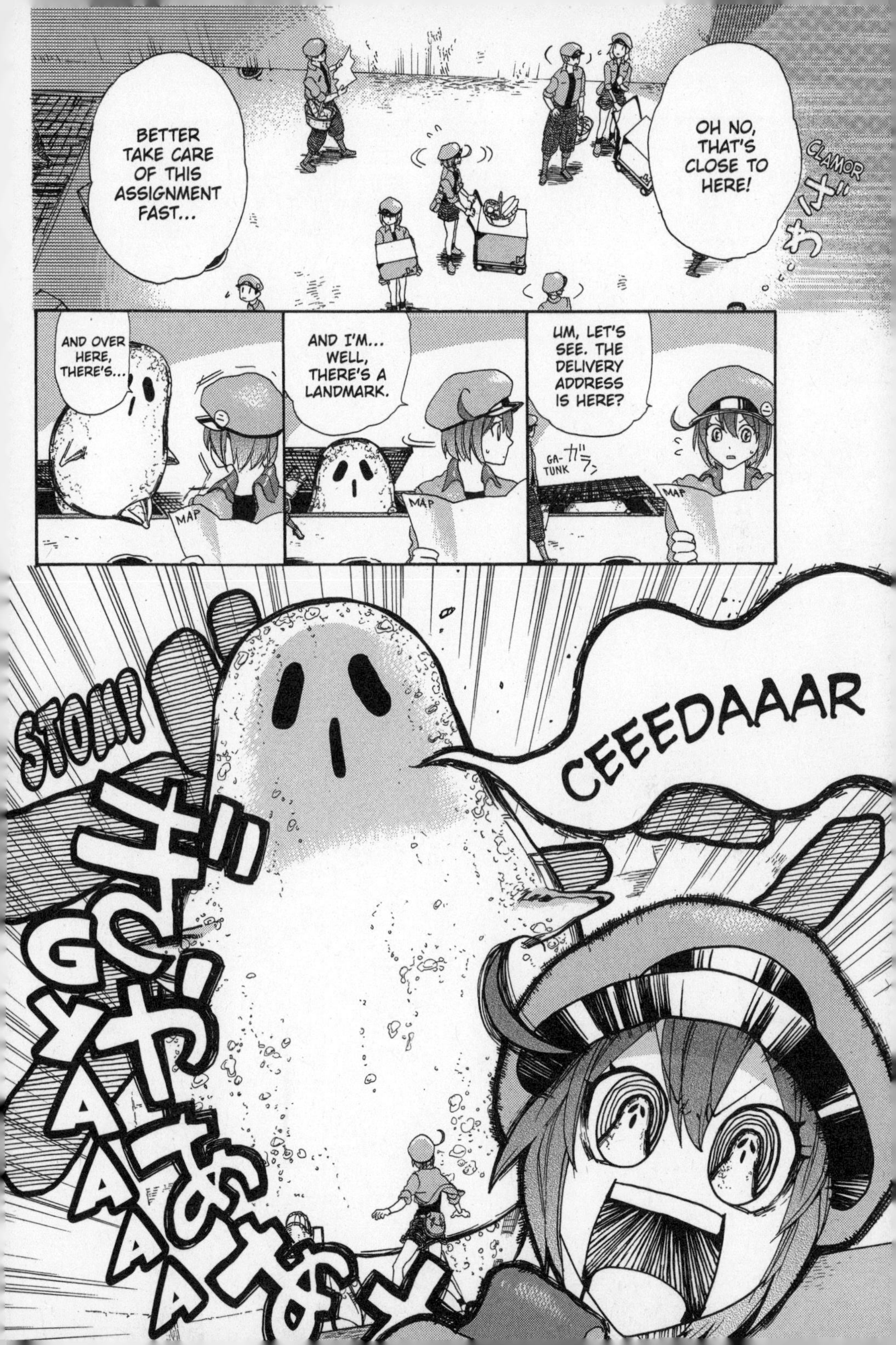
OH NO, THAT'S CLOSE TO HERE!
CLAMOR
BETTER TAKE CARE OF THIS ASSIGNMENT FAST...
UM, LET'S SEE. THE DELIVERY ADDRESS IS HERE?
GA-TUNK
AND I'M... WELL, THERE'S A LANDMARK.
MAP
AND OVER HERE, THERE'S...
MAP
CEEEDAAAR
STOMP
GYAAAA

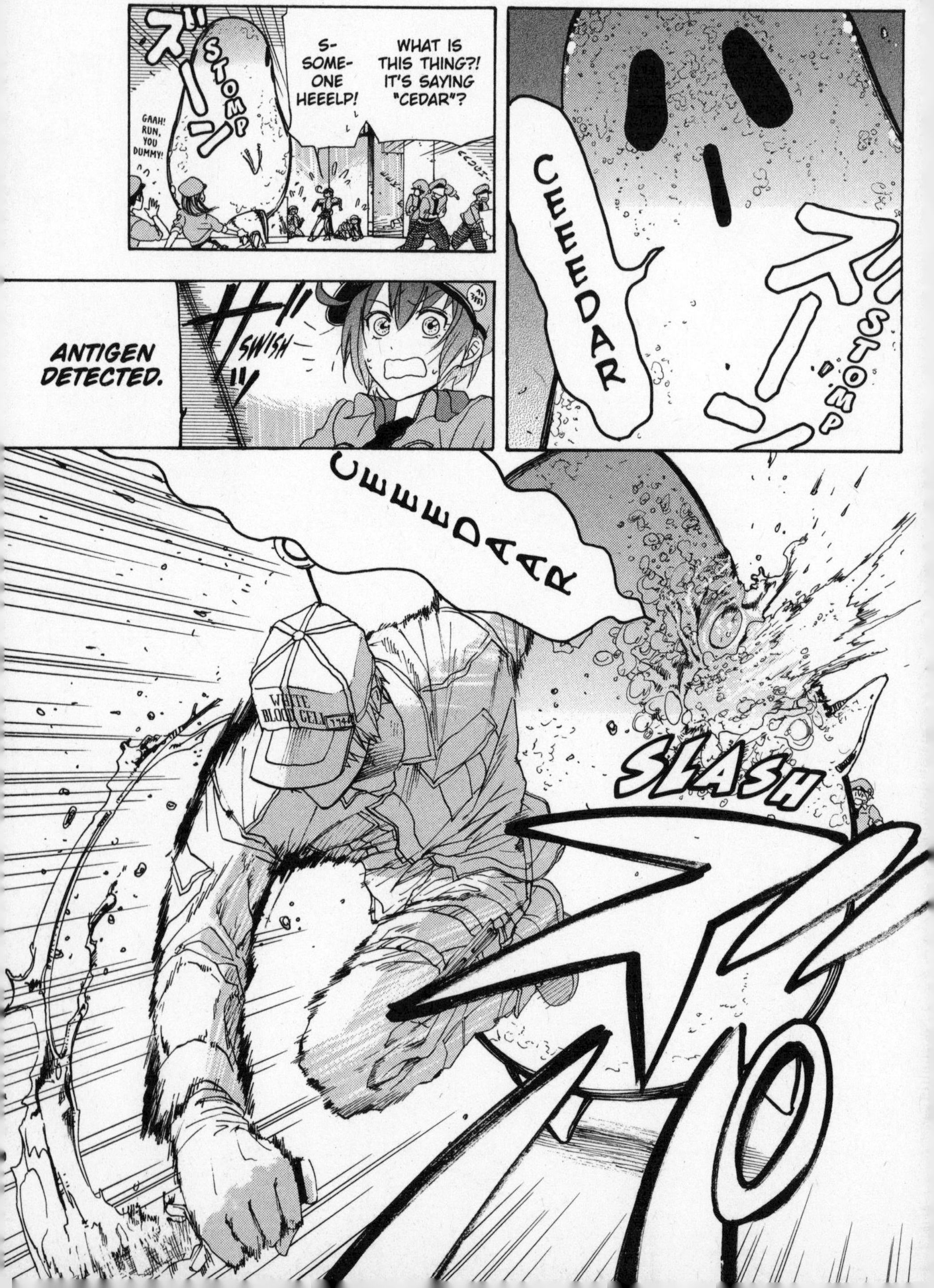
CEEEDAR
STOMP
WHAT IS THIS THING?! IT'S SAYING "CEDAR"?
S-SOME-ONE HEEELP!
STOMP
GAAH! RUN, YOU DUMMY!
ANTIGEN DETECTED.
SWISH
CEEEDAR
WHITE BLOOD CELL
SLASH

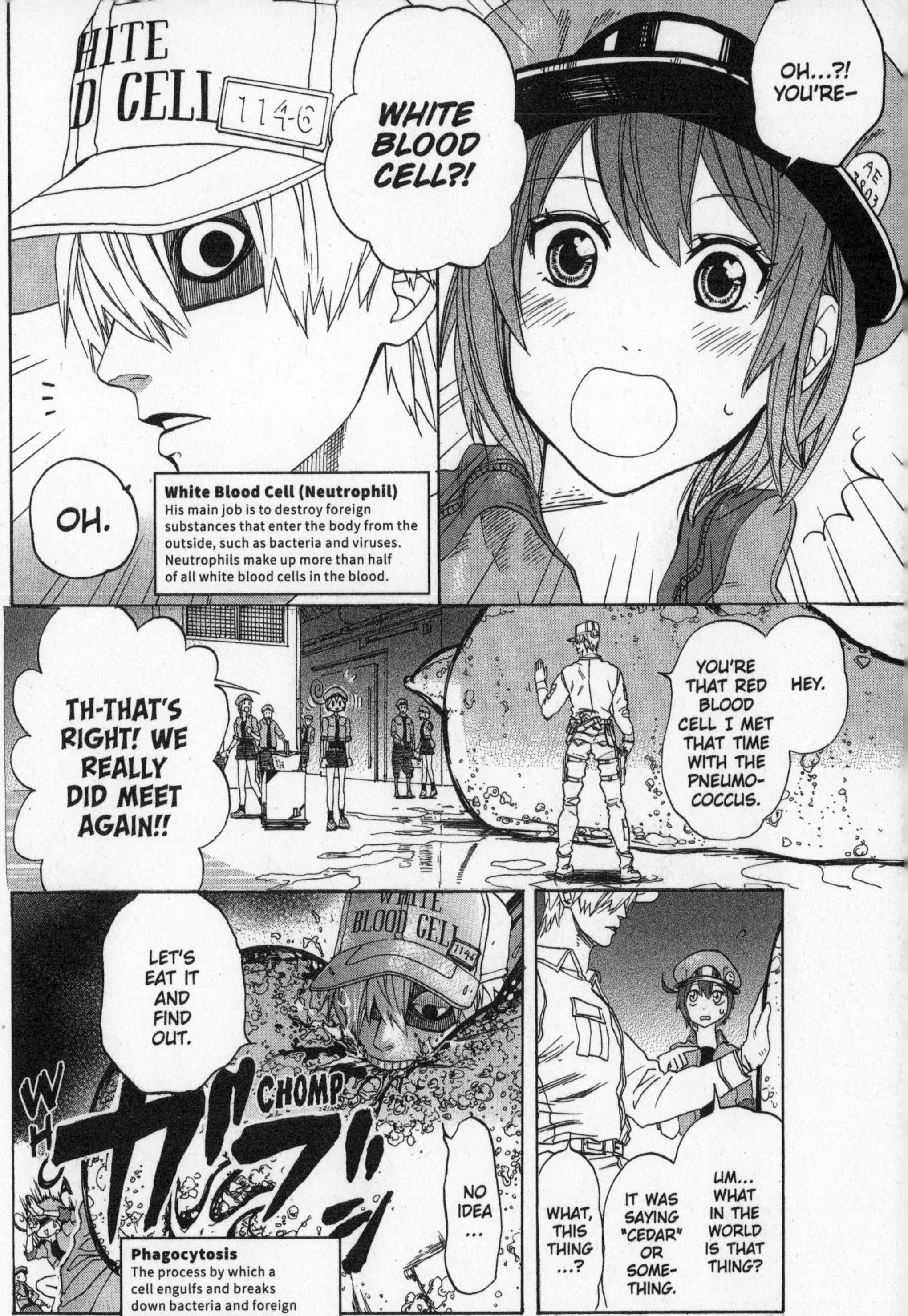

OH...?! YOU'RE-
WHITE BLOOD CELL?!
OH.
White Blood Cell (Neutrophil)
His main job is to destroy foreign substances that enter the body from the outside, such as bacteria and viruses. Neutrophils make up more than half of all white blood cells in the blood.
HEY.
YOU'RE THAT RED BLOOD CELL I MET THAT TIME WITH THE PNEUMO-COCCUS.
TH-THAT'S RIGHT! WE REALLY DID MEET AGAIN!!
UM... WHAT IN THE WORLD IS THAT THING?
IT WAS SAYING "CEDAR" OR SOME-THING.
WHAT, THIS THING ...?
NO IDEA ...
LET'S EAT IT AND FIND OUT.
CHOMP
WHA
Phagocytosis
The process by which a cell engulfs and breaks down bacteria and foreign substances. Cells that can do this (such as monocytes, macrophages, and neutrophils) are called phagocytes.

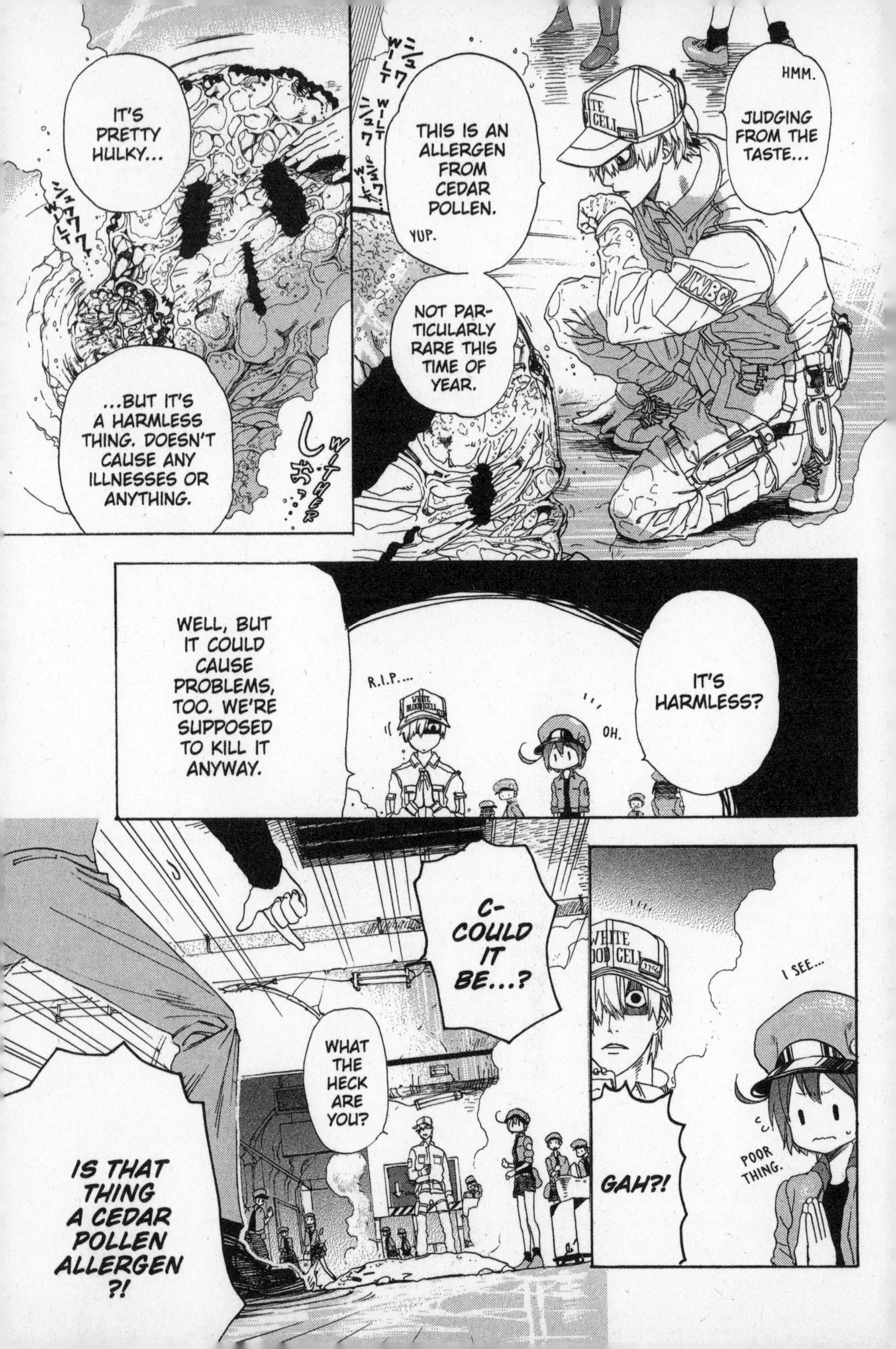
HMM.
JUDGING FROM THE TASTE...
WILT WILT WILT
THIS IS AN ALLERGEN FROM CEDAR POLLEN.
YUP.
NOT PARTICULARLY RARE THIS TIME OF YEAR.
IT'S PRETTY HULKY...
WILT
...BUT IT'S A HARMLESS THING. DOESN'T CAUSE ANY ILLNESSES OR ANYTHING.
WITHER
IT'S HARMLESS?
OH.
R.I.P....
WELL, BUT IT COULD CAUSE PROBLEMS, TOO. WE'RE SUPPOSED TO KILL IT ANYWAY.
I SEE...
POOR THING.
GAH?!
C-COULD IT BE...?
WHAT THE HECK ARE YOU?
IS THAT THING A CEDAR POLLEN ALLERGEN?!

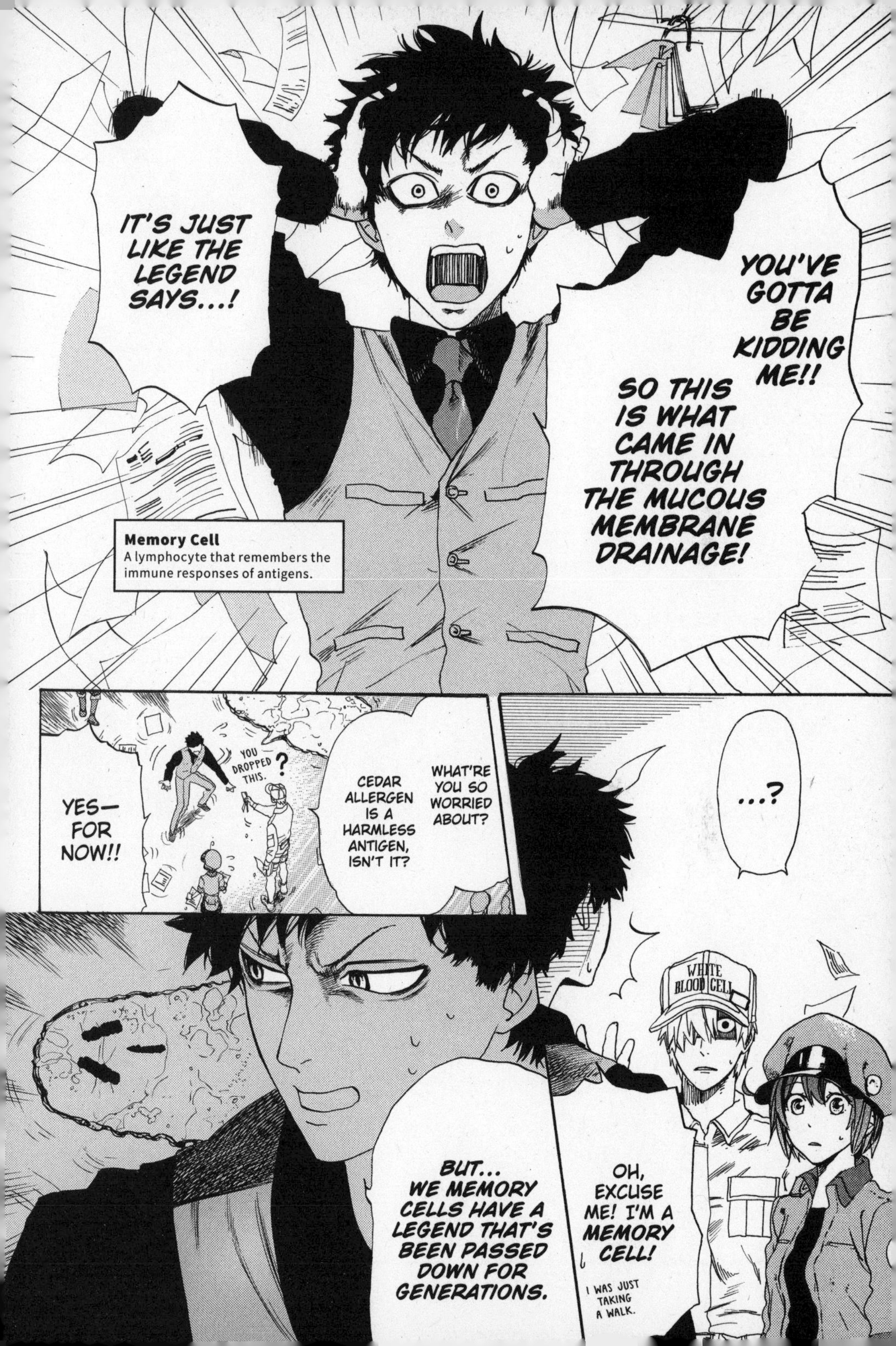
YOU'VE GOTTA BE KIDDING ME!!
SO THIS IS WHAT CAME IN THROUGH THE MUCOUS MEMBRANE DRAINAGE!
IT'S JUST LIKE THE LEGEND SAYS...!
Memory Cell
A lymphocyte that remembers the immune responses of antigens.
...?
WHAT'RE YOU SO WORRIED ABOUT?
CEDAR ALLERGEN IS A HARMLESS ANTIGEN, ISN'T IT?
YOU DROPPED THIS.
?
YES— FOR NOW!!
OH, EXCUSE ME! I'M A MEMORY CELL!
I WAS JUST TAKING A WALK.
BUT... WE MEMORY CELLS HAVE A LEGEND THAT'S BEEN PASSED DOWN FOR GENERATIONS.

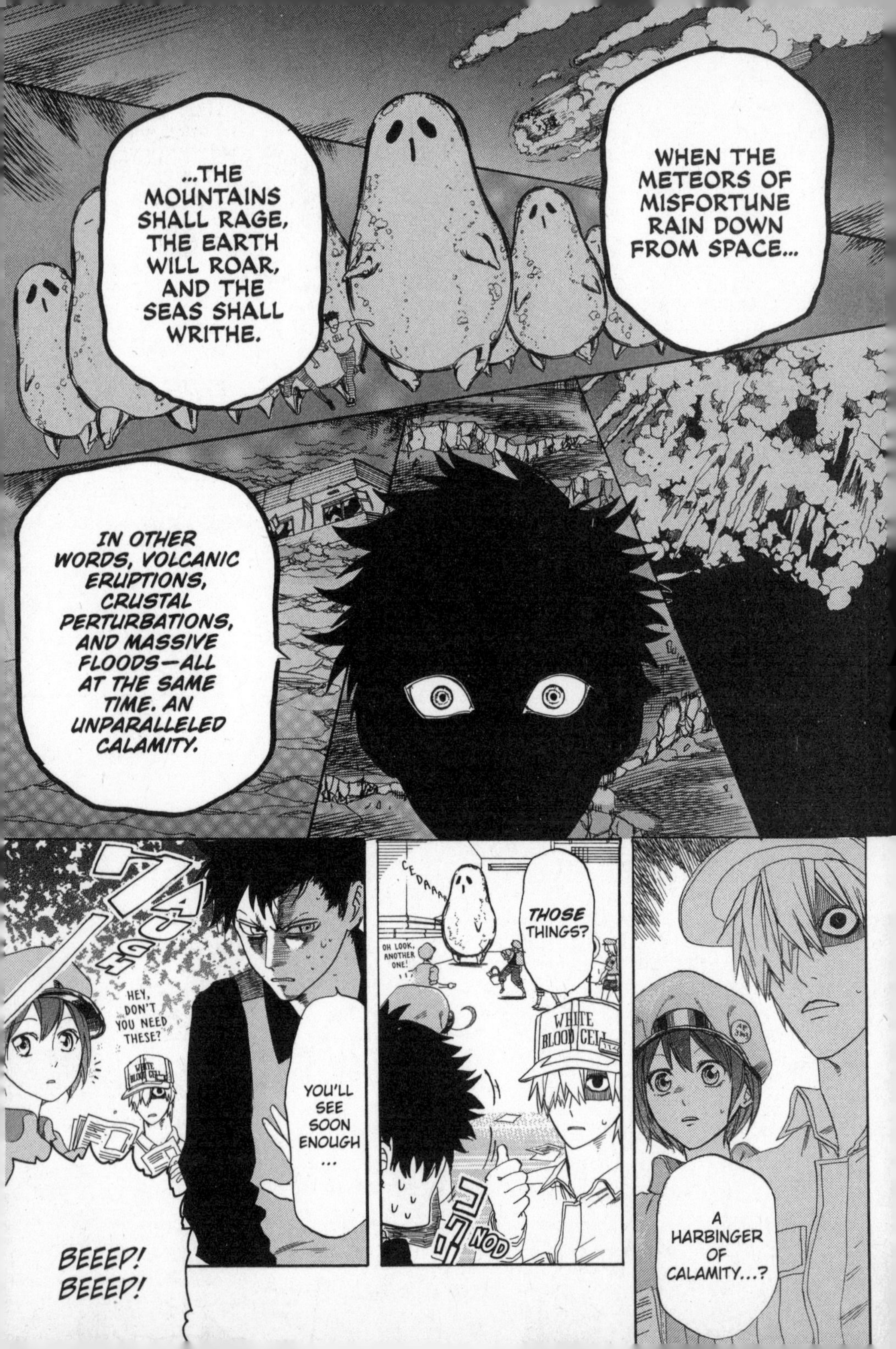
WHEN THE METEORS OF MISFORTUNE RAIN DOWN FROM SPACE...
...THE MOUNTAINS SHALL RAGE, THE EARTH WILL ROAR, AND THE SEAS SHALL WRITHE.
IN OTHER WORDS, VOLCANIC ERUPTIONS, CRUSTAL PERTURBATIONS, AND MASSIVE FLOODS—ALL AT THE SAME TIME. AN UNPARALLELED CALAMITY.
A HARBINGER OF CALAMITY...?
THOSE THINGS?
OH LOOK, ANOTHER ONE!
WHITE BLOOD CELL
NOD
YOU'LL SEE SOON ENOUGH...
HEY, DON'T YOU NEED THESE?
BEEEP! BEEEP!

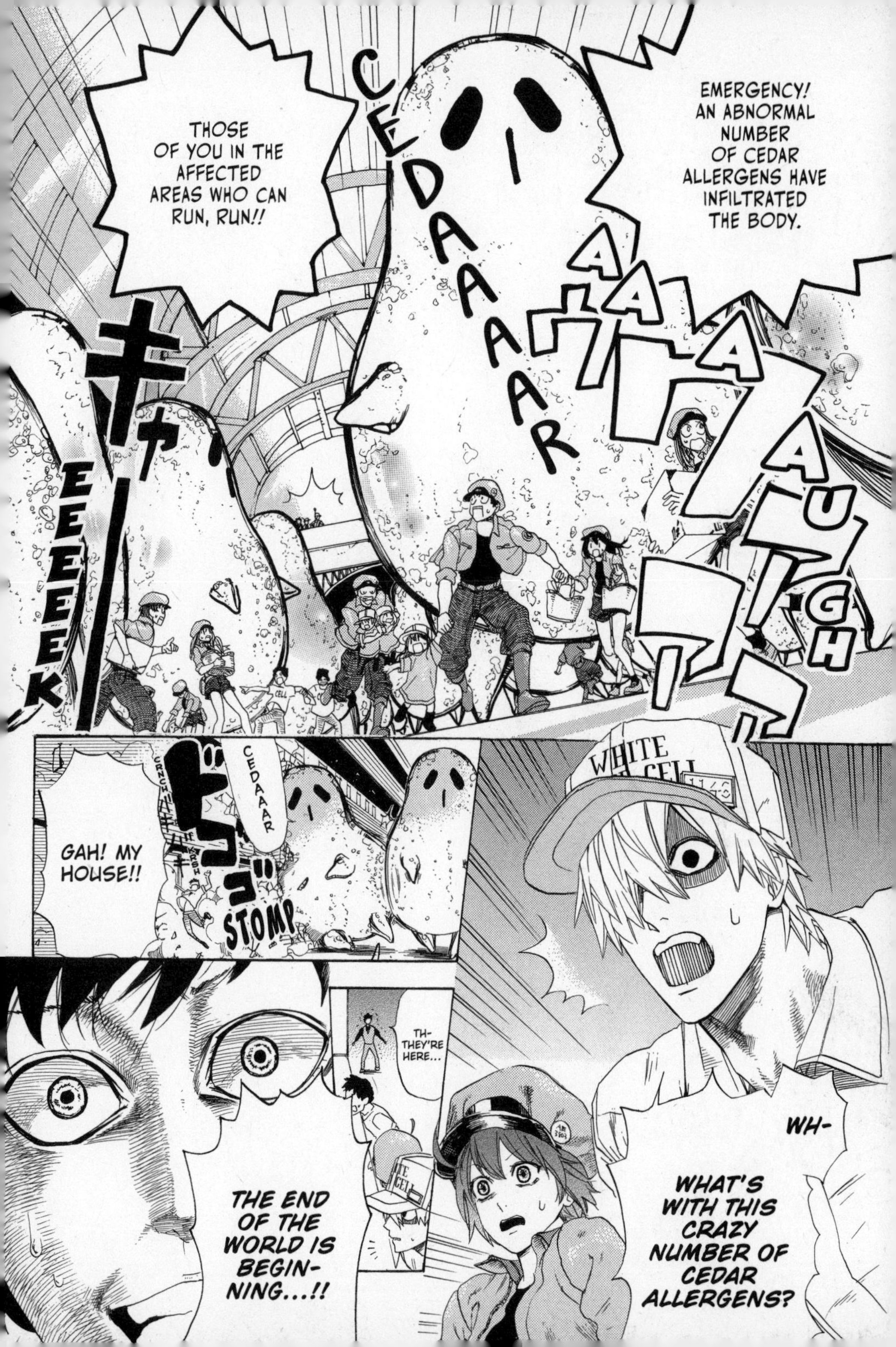

EMERGENCY! AN ABNORMAL NUMBER OF CEDAR ALLERGENS HAVE INFILTRATED THE BODY.
CEDAAAR
AAAAAUGH!!
THOSE OF YOU IN THE AFFECTED AREAS WHO CAN RUN, RUN!!
キャー
EEEEEK
CEDAAAR
CRNCH
KRSH
STOMP
GAH! MY HOUSE!!
WH-
WHAT'S WITH THIS CRAZY NUMBER OF CEDAR ALLERGENS?
TH-THEY'RE HERE...
THE END OF THE WORLD IS BEGIN-NING...!!

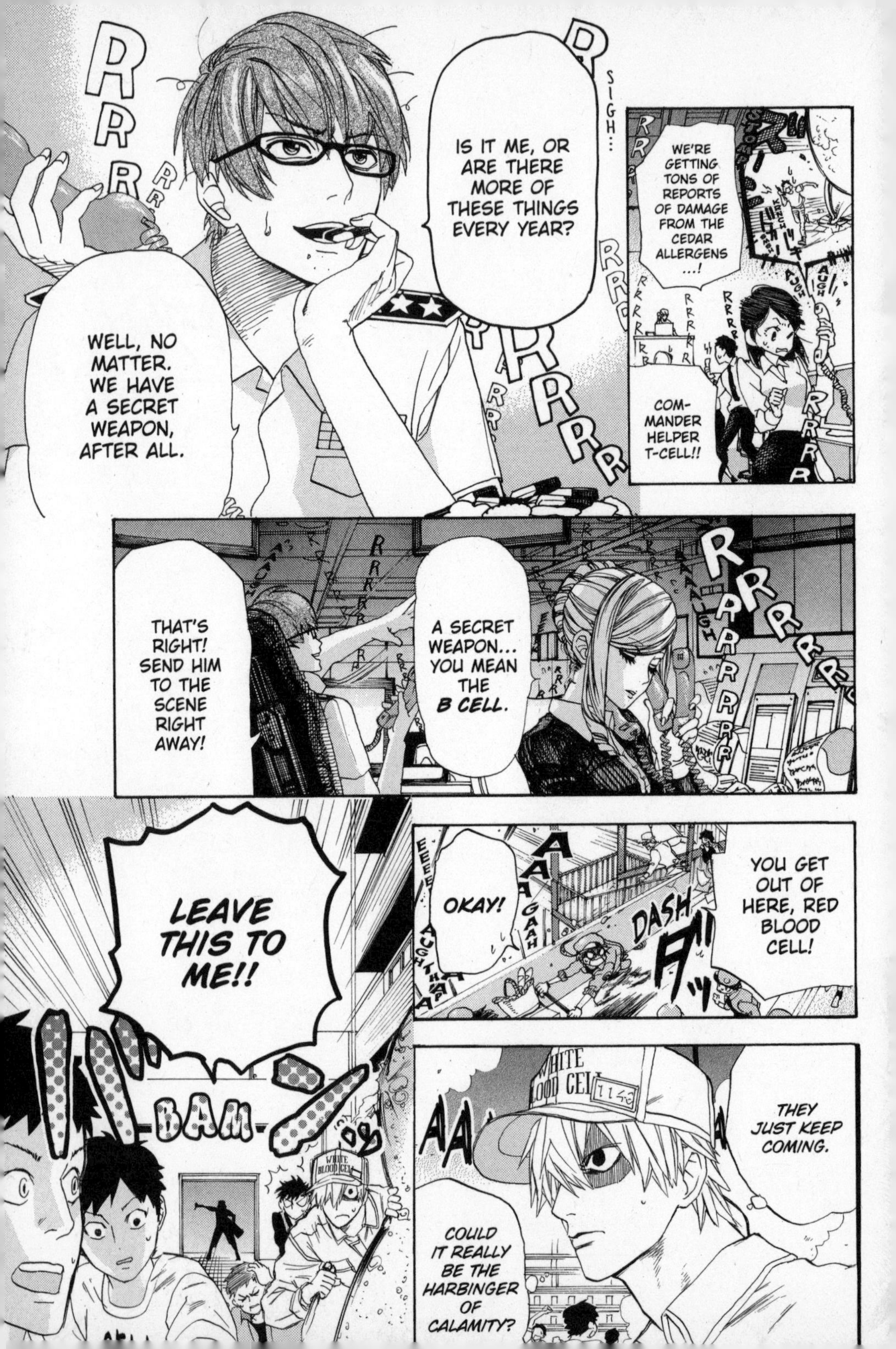
WE'RE GETTING TONS OF REPORTS OF DAMAGE FROM THE CEDAR ALLERGENS ...!
COMMANDER HELPER T-CELL!!
SIGH...
IS IT ME, OR ARE THERE MORE OF THESE THINGS EVERY YEAR?
WELL, NO MATTER. WE HAVE A SECRET WEAPON, AFTER ALL.
A SECRET WEAPON... YOU MEAN THE *B CELL*.
THAT'S RIGHT! SEND HIM TO THE SCENE RIGHT AWAY!
YOU GET OUT OF HERE, RED BLOOD CELL!
DASH
OKAY!
THEY JUST KEEP COMING.
COULD IT REALLY BE THE HARBINGER OF CALAMITY?
LEAVE THIS TO ME!!
BAM

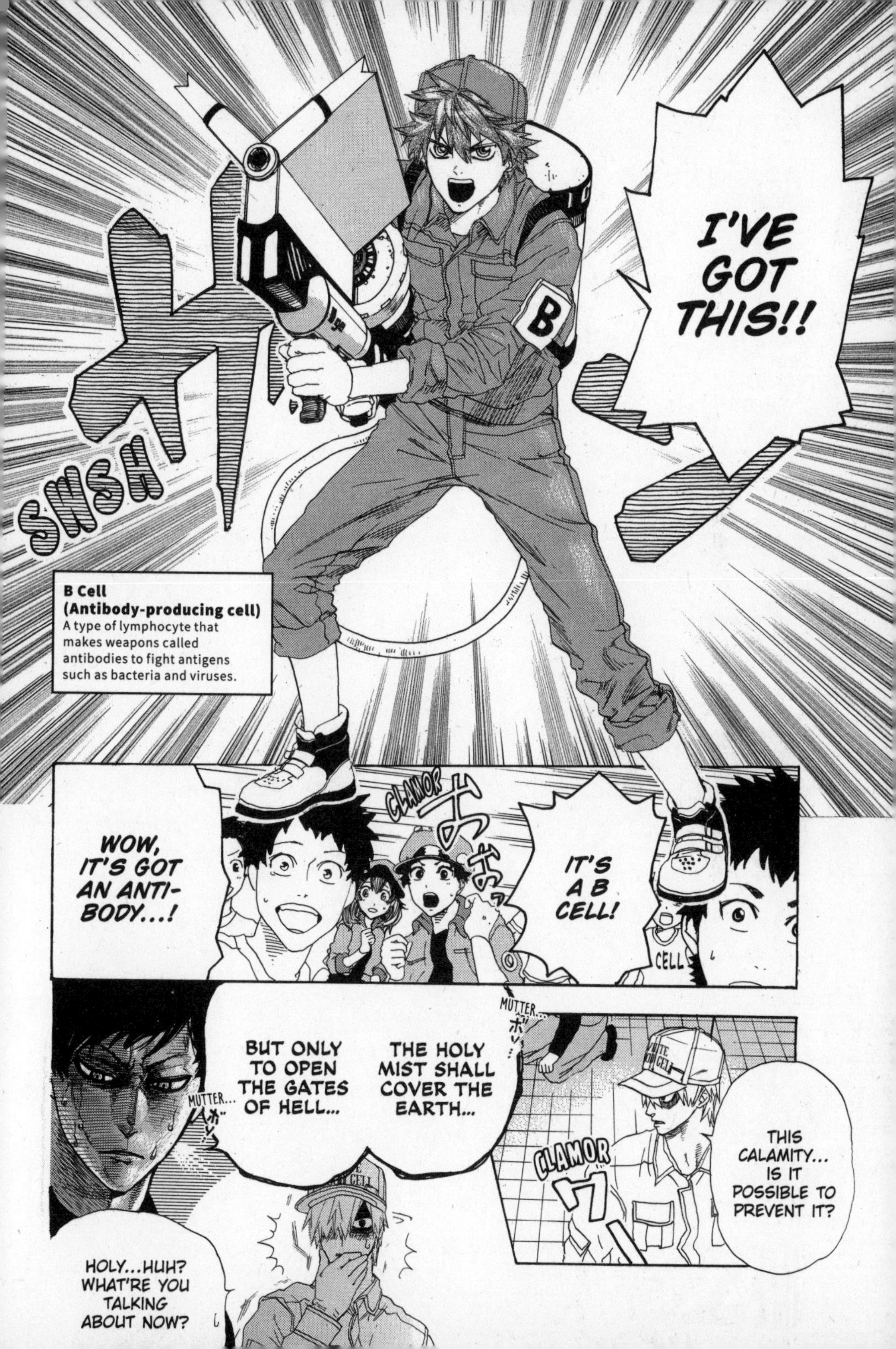
I'VE GOT THIS!!
SWSH
B Cell
(Antibody-producing cell)
A type of lymphocyte that makes weapons called antibodies to fight antigens such as bacteria and viruses.
IT'S A B CELL!
CLAMOR
WOW, IT'S GOT AN ANTI-BODY...!
THIS CALAMITY... IS IT POSSIBLE TO PREVENT IT?
CLAMOR
MUTTER...
THE HOLY MIST SHALL COVER THE EARTH...
BUT ONLY TO OPEN THE GATES OF HELL...
MUTTER...
HOLY...HUH? WHAT'RE YOU TALKING ABOUT NOW?

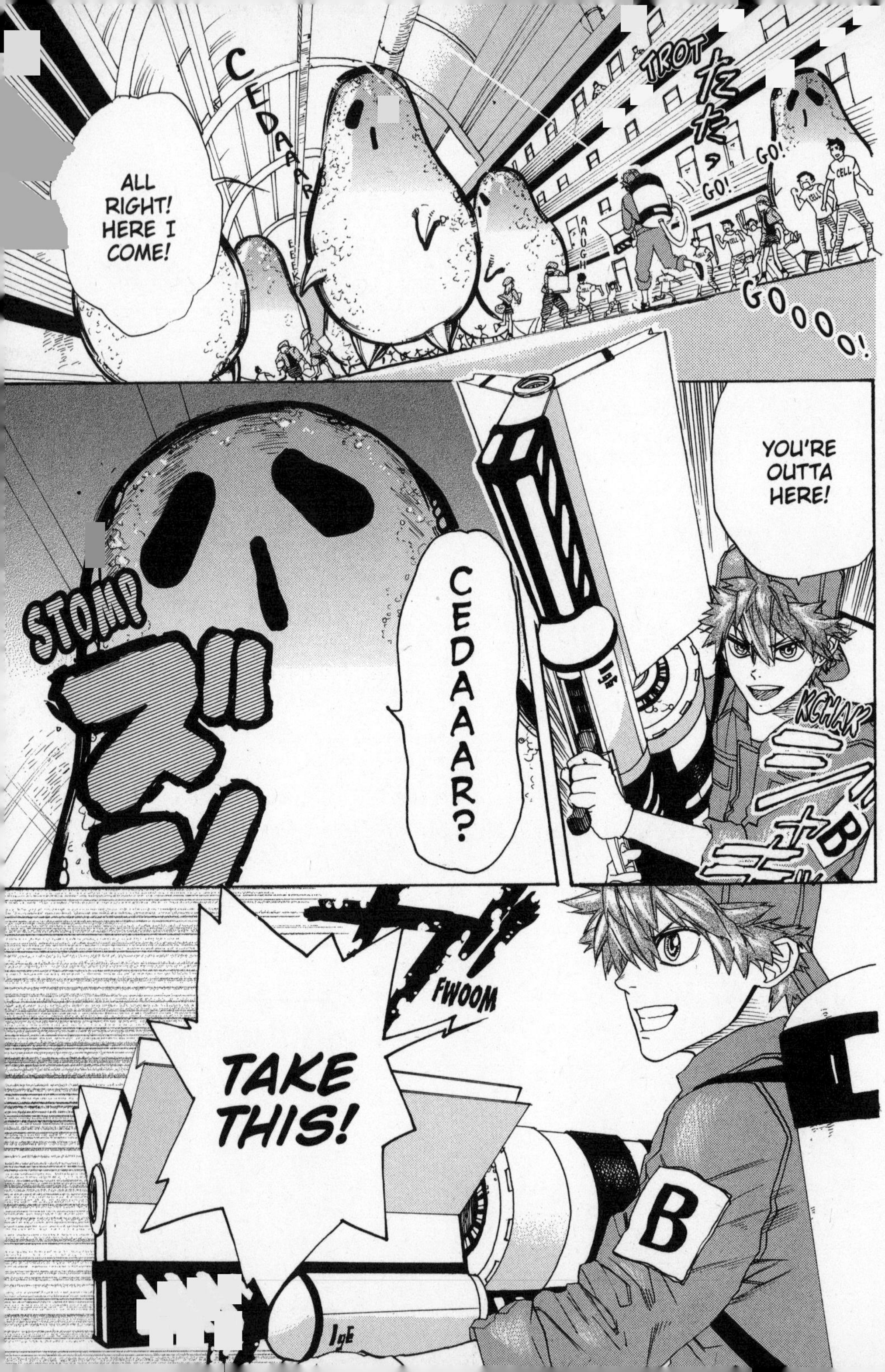
TROT
たた
GO!
GO!
AAUGH
GOOOOO!
CEDAAAR
ALL RIGHT! HERE I COME!
YOU'RE OUTTA HERE!
KCHAK
CEDAAAR?
STOMP
FWOOM
TAKE THIS!

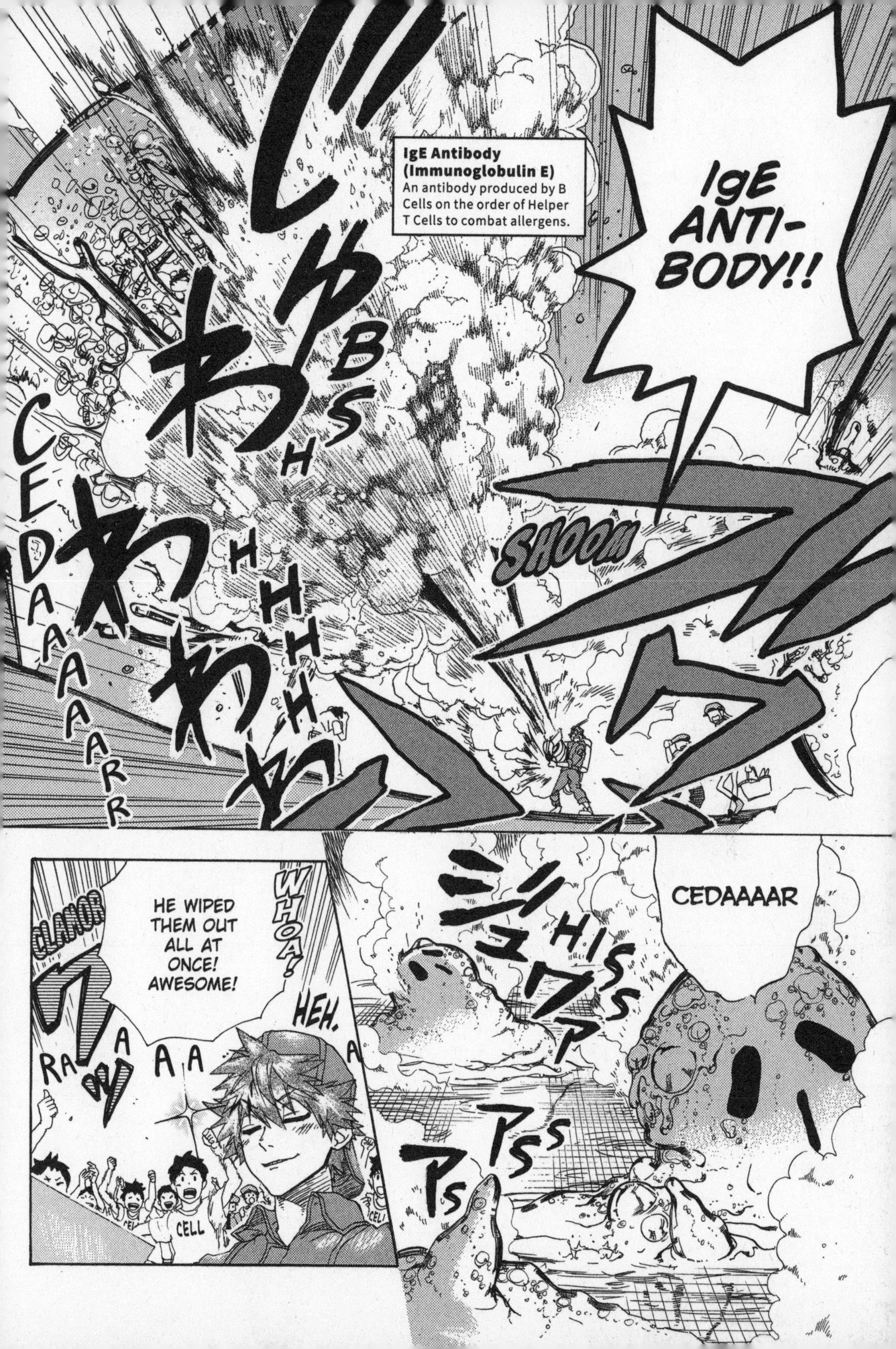
IgE ANTI-BODY!!
IgE Antibody (Immunoglobulin E)
An antibody produced by B Cells on the order of Helper T Cells to combat allergens.
SHOOM
じゅわわわわ
BSHHHHHHH
CEDAAAAARR
CEDAAAAR
シュワア
HISSS
アア
PSSS
HE WIPED THEM OUT ALL AT ONCE! AWESOME!
WHOA!
HEH.
CLAMOR
RAAAAAA
CELL

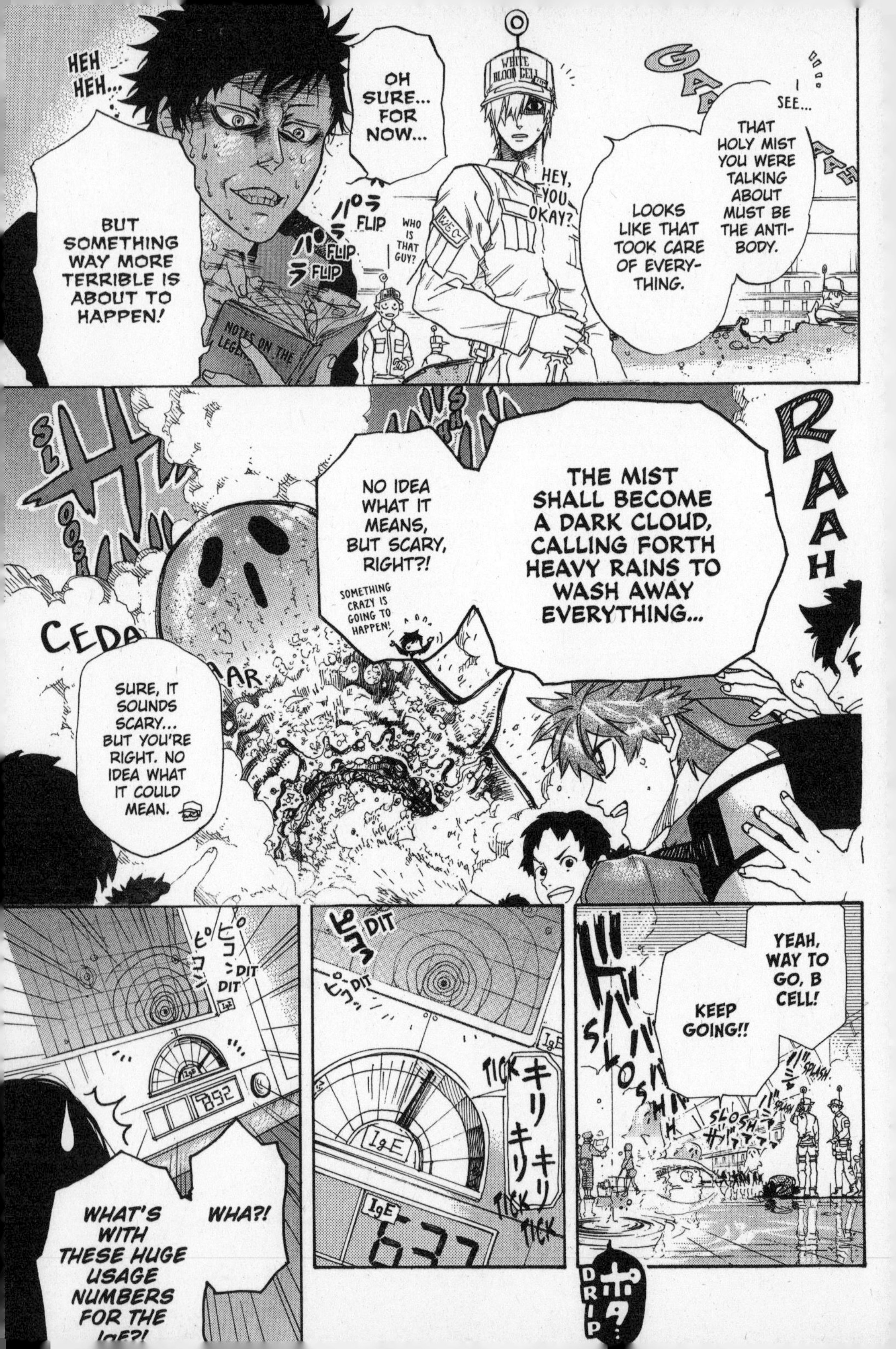

GAAAAAH
I SEE...
THAT HOLY MIST YOU WERE TALKING ABOUT MUST BE THE ANTI-BODY.
LOOKS LIKE THAT TOOK CARE OF EVERY-THING.
HEY, YOU OKAY?
WHO IS THAT GUY?
WHITE BLOOD CELL
パラ FLIP
パラ FLIP
パラ FLIP
OH SURE... FOR NOW...
HEH HEH...
BUT SOMETHING WAY MORE TERRIBLE IS ABOUT TO HAPPEN!
NOTES ON THE LEGE...
RAAH
THE MIST SHALL BECOME A DARK CLOUD, CALLING FORTH HEAVY RAINS TO WASH AWAY EVERYTHING...
NO IDEA WHAT IT MEANS, BUT SCARY, RIGHT?!
SOMETHING CRAZY IS GOING TO HAPPEN!
CEDA
AAR
SURE, IT SOUNDS SCARY... BUT YOU'RE RIGHT. NO IDEA WHAT IT COULD MEAN.
YEAH, WAY TO GO, B CELL!
KEEP GOING!!
SLOSH
SPLASH
SLOSH
DRIP
ピコ DIT
ピコ DIT
TICK
キリ TICK
キリ TICK
IgE
637
ピコ DIT
ピコ DIT
IgE
892
WHA?!
WHAT'S WITH THESE HUGE USAGE NUMBERS FOR THE IgE?!

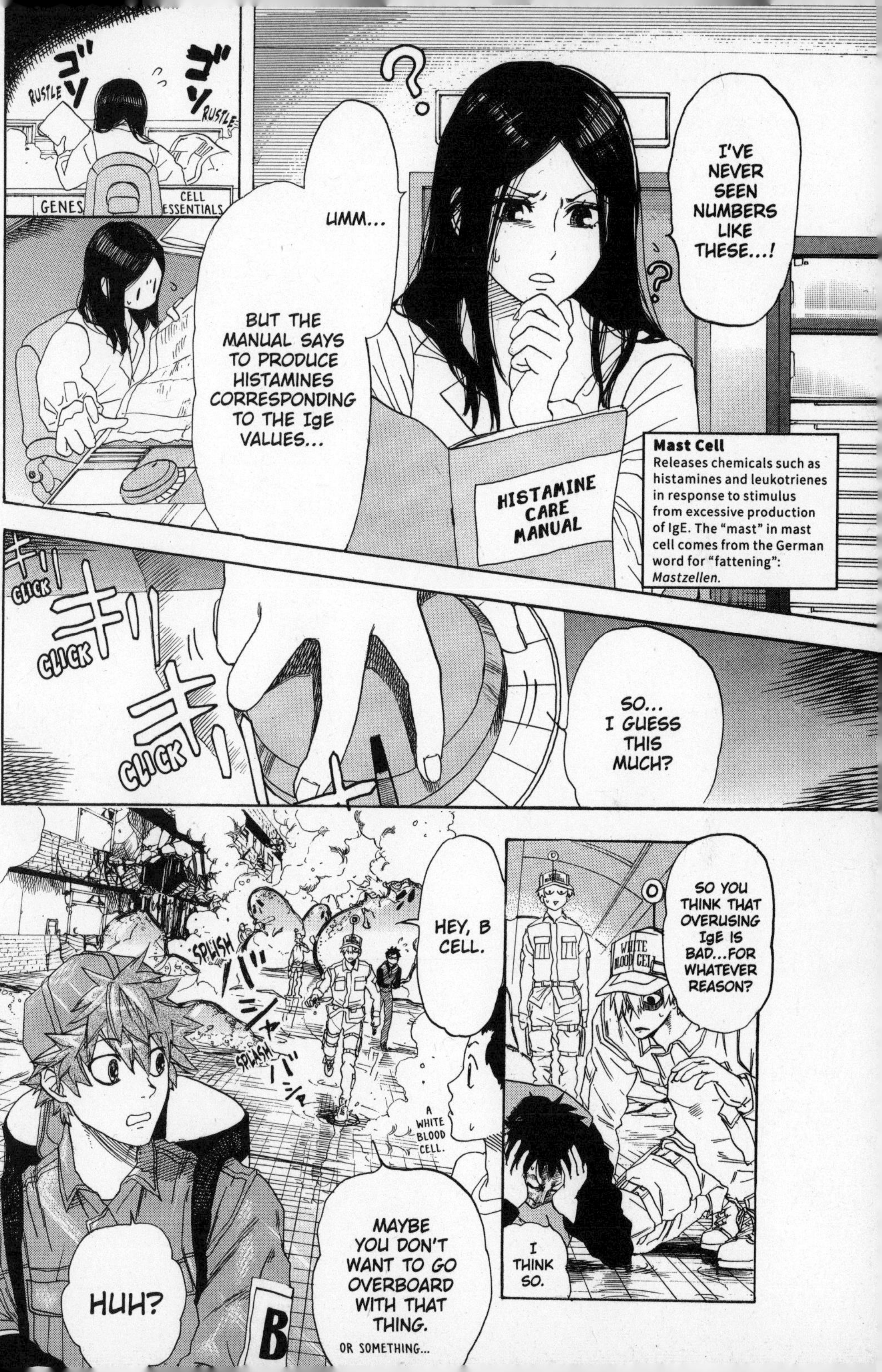
I'VE NEVER SEEN NUMBERS LIKE THESE...!
UMM...
BUT THE MANUAL SAYS TO PRODUCE HISTAMINES CORRESPONDING TO THE IgE VALUES...
HISTAMINE CARE MANUAL
Mast Cell
Releases chemicals such as histamines and leukotrienes in response to stimulus from excessive production of IgE. The "mast" in mast cell comes from the German word for "fattening": *Mastzellen.*
RUSTLE
RUSTLE
GENES
CELL ESSENTIALS
SO... I GUESS THIS MUCH?
CLICK
CLICK
CLICK
SO YOU THINK THAT OVERUSING IgE IS BAD...FOR WHATEVER REASON?
WHITE BLOOD CELL
I THINK SO.
HEY, B CELL.
SPLASH
SPLASH
A WHITE BLOOD CELL.
MAYBE YOU DON'T WANT TO GO OVERBOARD WITH THAT THING.
OR SOMETHING...
HUH?
B

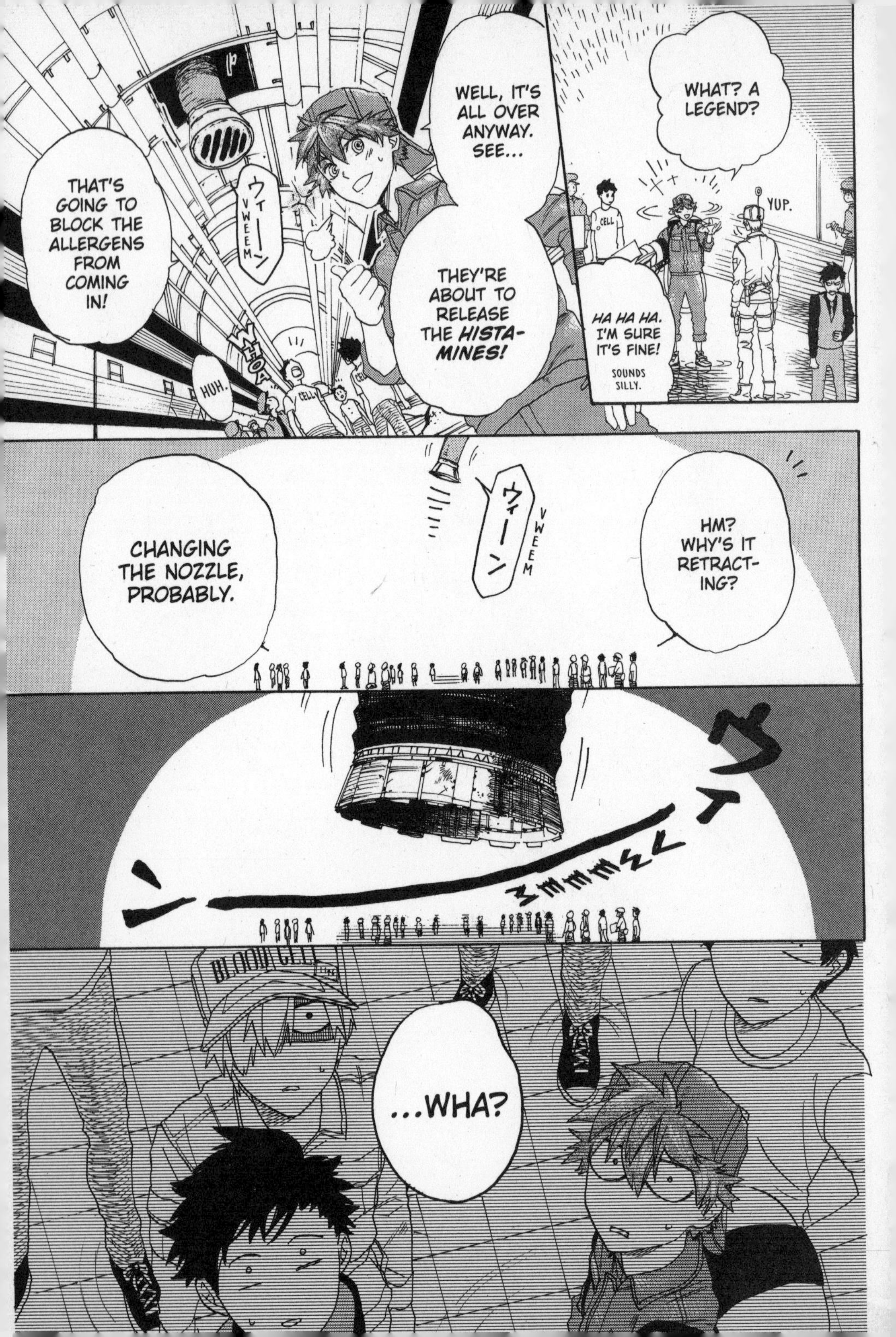
WHAT? A LEGEND?
YUP.
HA HA HA. I'M SURE IT'S FINE!
SOUNDS SILLY.
WELL, IT'S ALL OVER ANYWAY. SEE...
THEY'RE ABOUT TO RELEASE THE *HISTAMINES!*
ウィーン
VWEEM
THAT'S GOING TO BLOCK THE ALLERGENS FROM COMING IN!
WHOA
HUH.
HM? WHY'S IT RETRACTING?
ウィーン
VWEEM
CHANGING THE NOZZLE, PROBABLY.
ウィーン
VWEEEEEM
BLOOD CELL
...WHA?

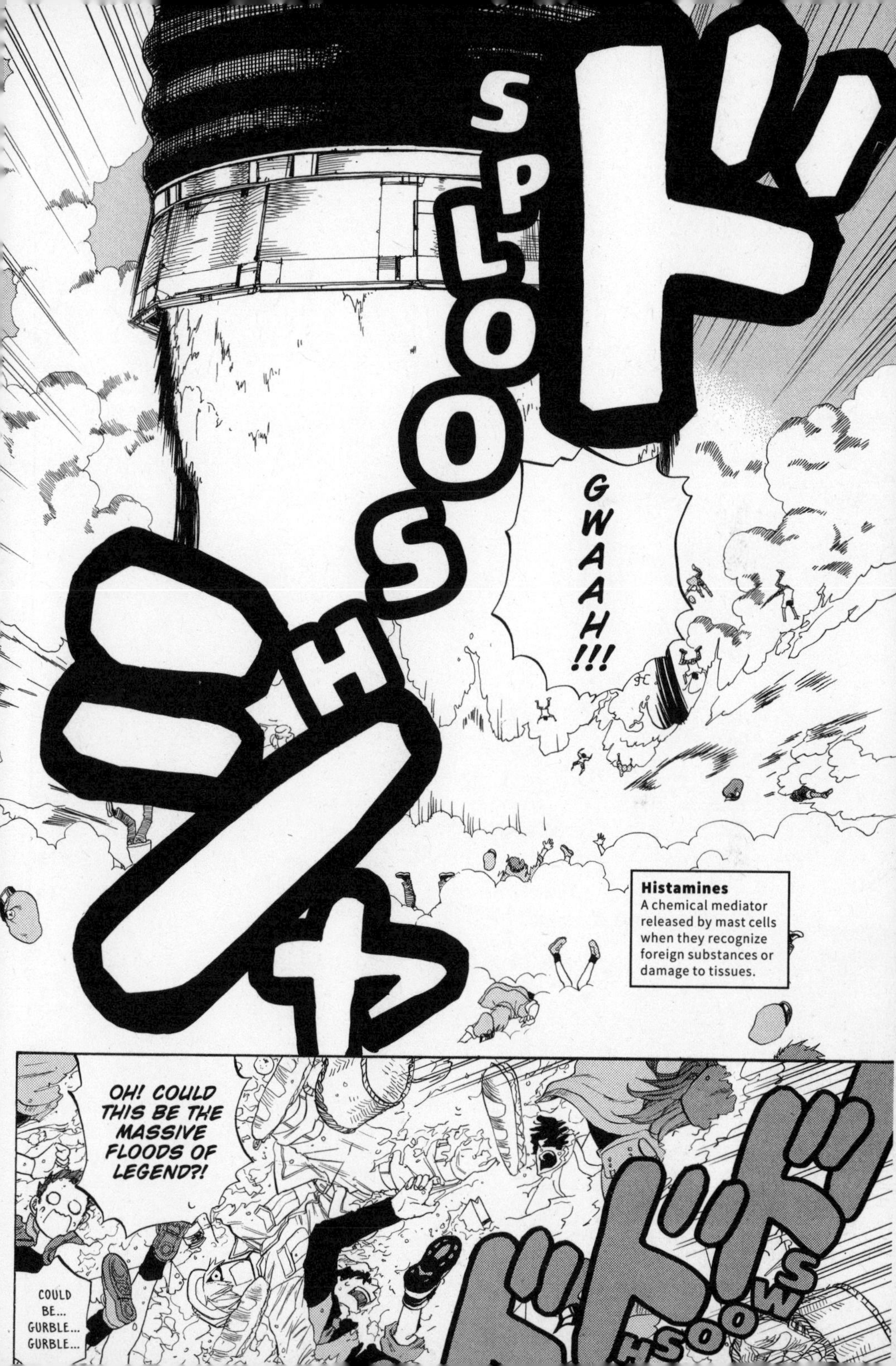
SPLOOSH
GWAAAH!!!
Histamines
A chemical mediator released by mast cells when they recognize foreign substances or damage to tissues.
SWOOSH
OH! COULD THIS BE THE MASSIVE FLOODS OF LEGEND?!
COULD BE... GURBLE... GURBLE...

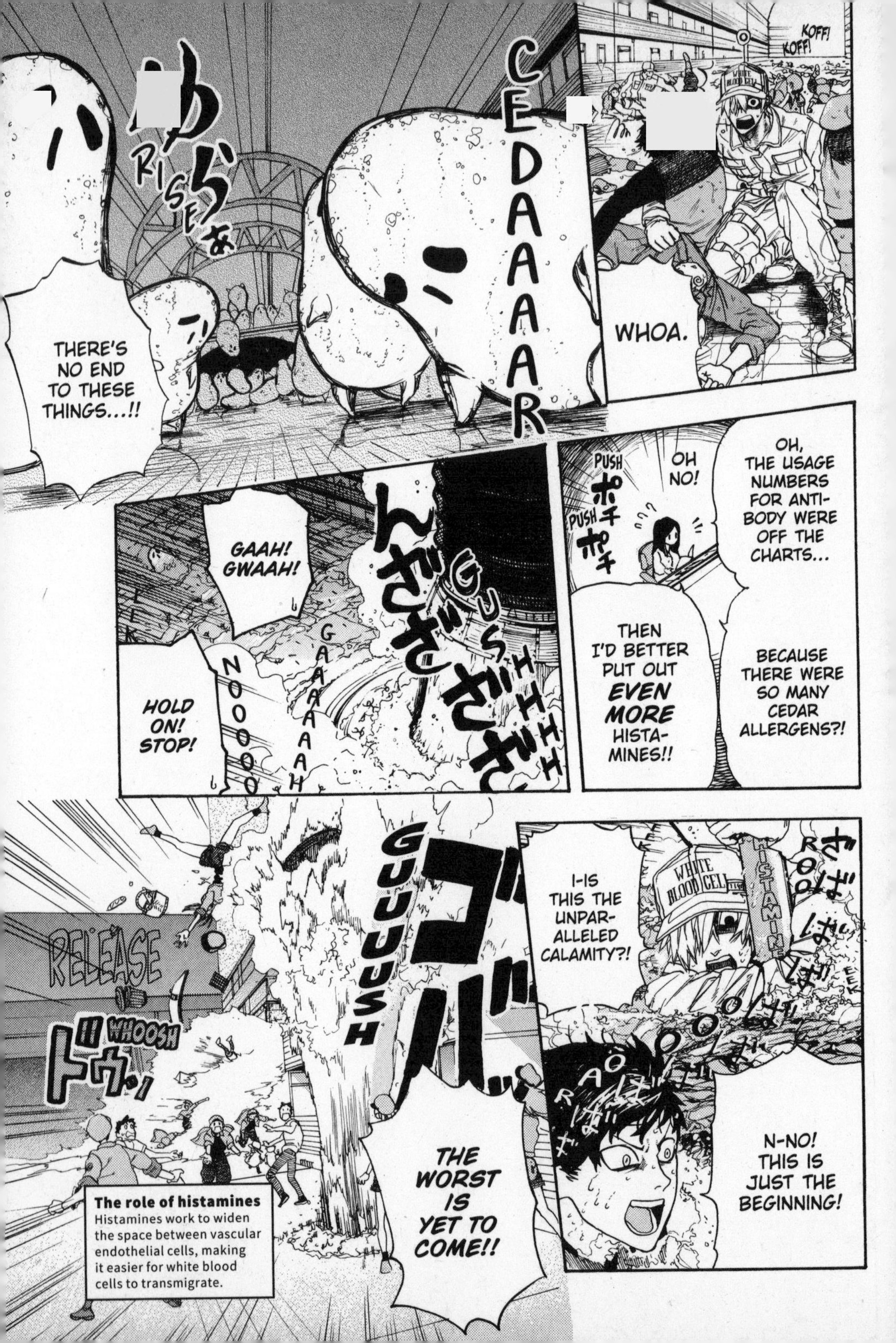
KOFF! KOFF!
WHITE BLOOD CELL
WHOA.
CEDAAAAAR
RISE
THERE'S NO END TO THESE THINGS...!!
PUSH ポチ PUSH ポチ
OH NO!
OH, THE USAGE NUMBERS FOR ANTI-BODY WERE OFF THE CHARTS...
BECAUSE THERE WERE SO MANY CEDAR ALLERGENS?!
THEN I'D BETTER PUT OUT EVEN MORE HISTA-MINES!!
GUSHHHHHH
GAAH! GWAAH!
GAAAAAAAH
NOOOOO
HOLD ON! STOP!
WHITE BLOOD CELL
HISTAMINE
I-IS THIS THE UNPAR-ALLELED CALAMITY?!
EEEK
N-NO! THIS IS JUST THE BEGINNING!
GUUUUUSH
THE WORST IS YET TO COME!!
RELEASE
WHOOSH
The role of histamines
Histamines work to widen the space between vascular endothelial cells, making it easier for white blood cells to transmigrate.

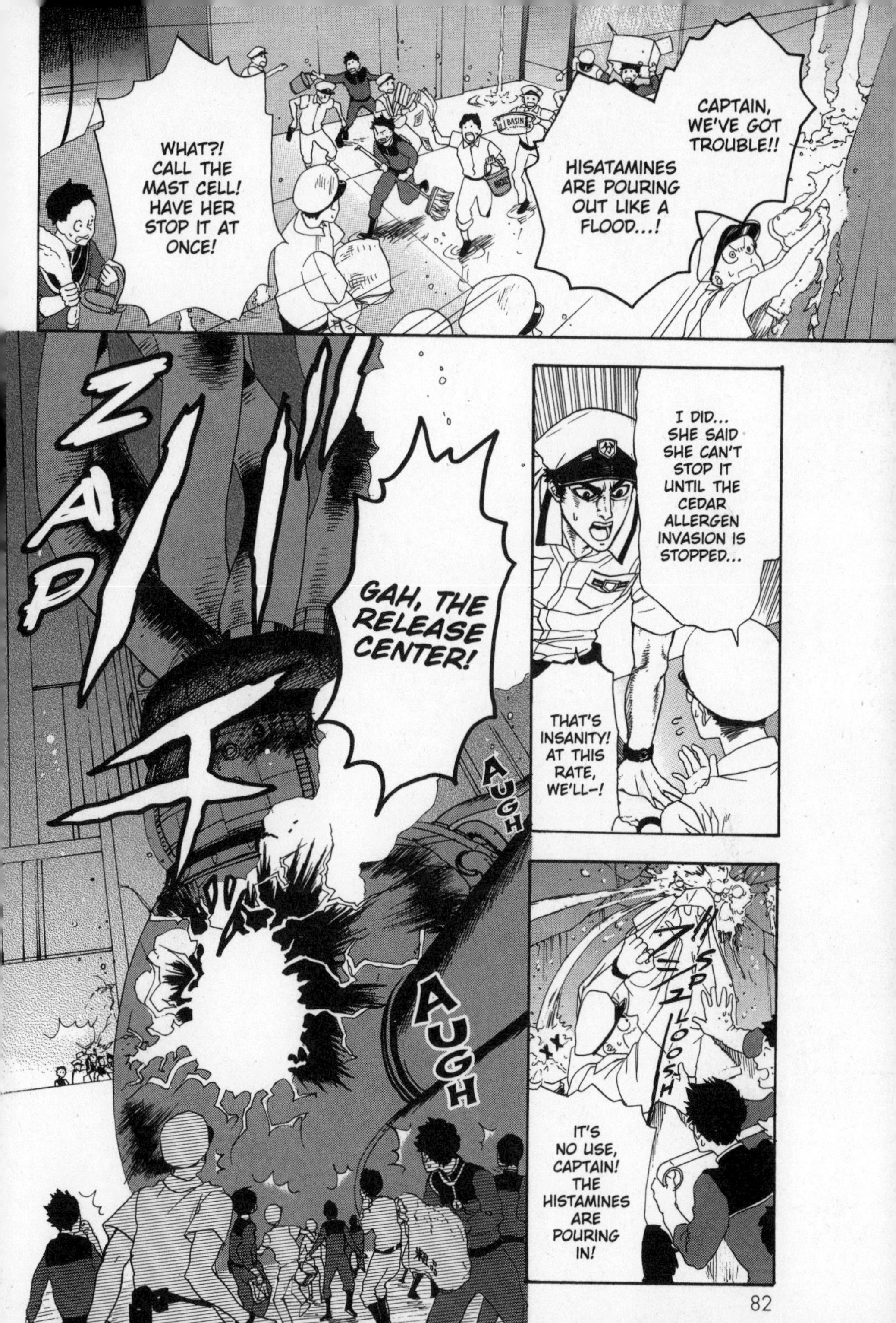
CAPTAIN, WE'VE GOT TROUBLE!!
HISATAMINES ARE POURING OUT LIKE A FLOOD...!
WHAT?! CALL THE MAST CELL! HAVE HER STOP IT AT ONCE!
BASIN
I DID... SHE SAID SHE CAN'T STOP IT UNTIL THE CEDAR ALLERGEN INVASION IS STOPPED...
THAT'S INSANITY! AT THIS RATE, WE'LL–!
SPLOOSH
IT'S NO USE, CAPTAIN! THE HISTAMINES ARE POURING IN!
ZAP
GAH, THE RELEASE CENTER!
AUGH
AUGH

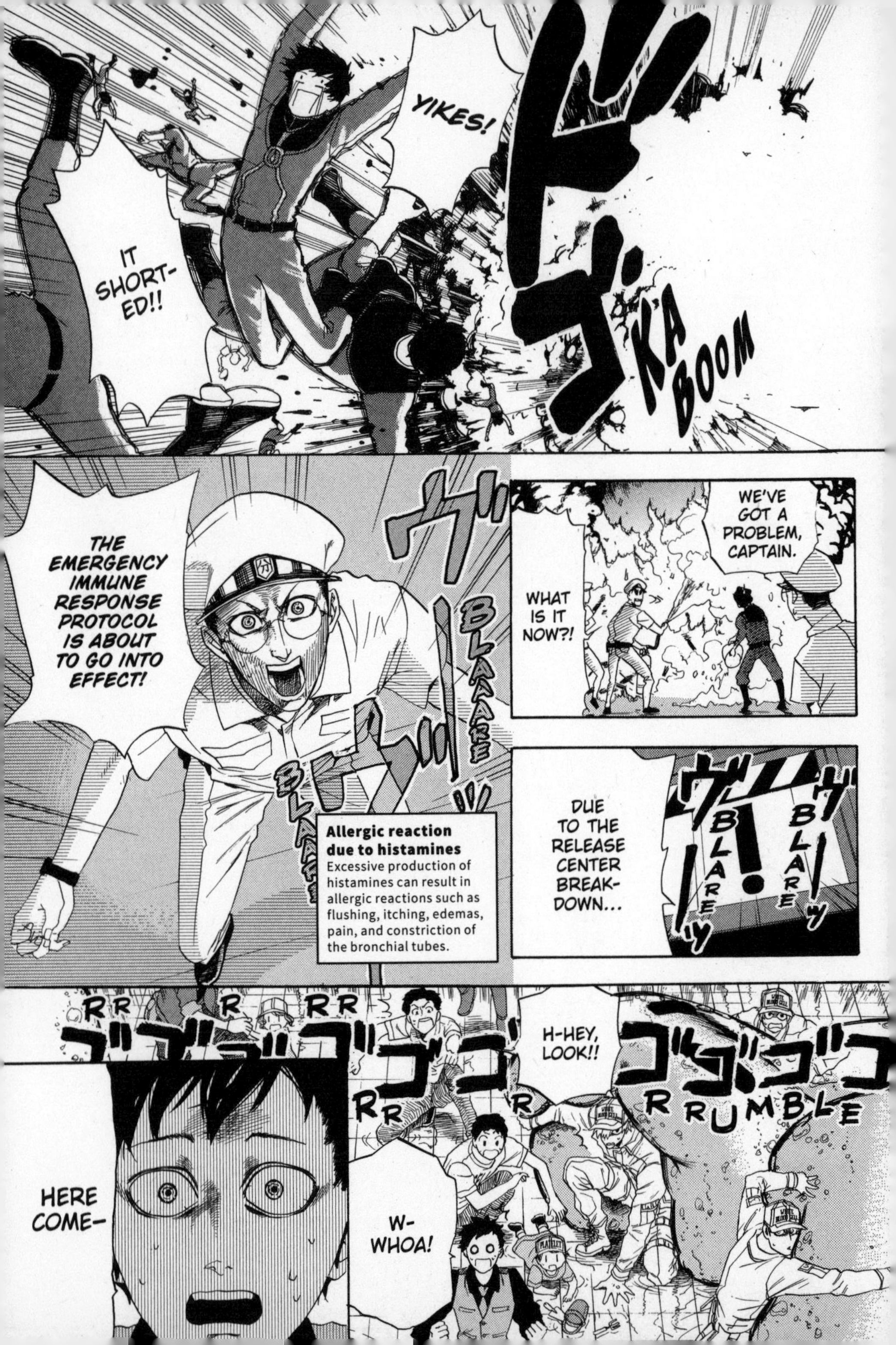
KA BOOM
YIKES!
IT SHORTED!!
WE'VE GOT A PROBLEM, CAPTAIN.
WHAT IS IT NOW?!
BLARE BLARE
DUE TO THE RELEASE CENTER BREAKDOWN...
BLAAARE
THE EMERGENCY IMMUNE RESPONSE PROTOCOL IS ABOUT TO GO INTO EFFECT!
BLAAARE
Allergic reaction due to histamines
Excessive production of histamines can result in allergic reactions such as flushing, itching, edemas, pain, and constriction of the bronchial tubes.
RRRUMBLE
H-HEY, LOOK!!
RR R RR RR R
W-WHOA!
HERE COME-

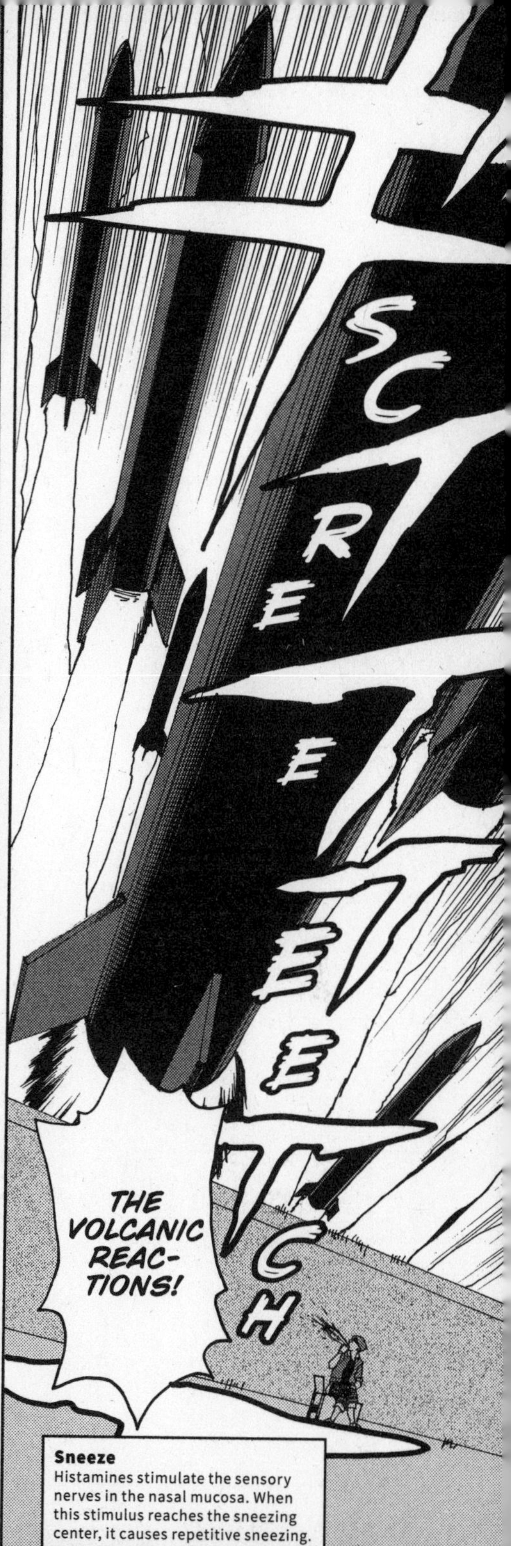
SCREEEETCH
THE VOLCANIC REAC-TIONS!
Sneeze
Histamines stimulate the sensory nerves in the nasal mucosa. When this stimulus reaches the sneezing center, it causes repetitive sneezing.
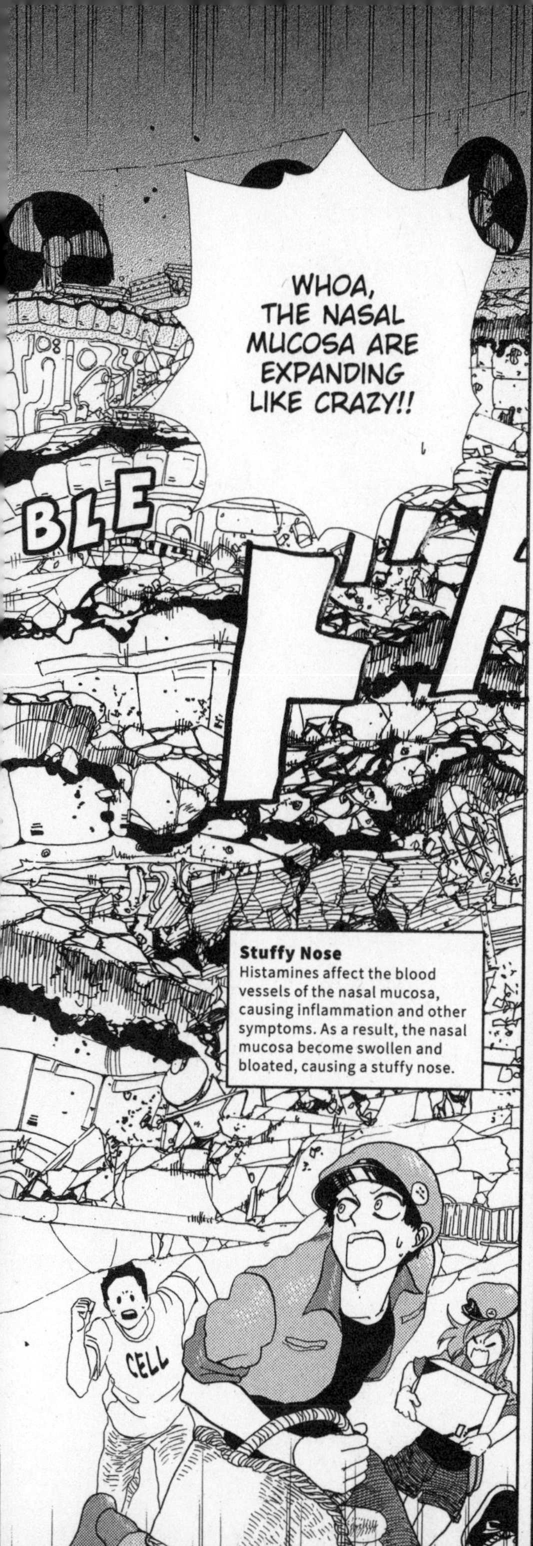
WHOA, THE NASAL MUCOSA ARE EXPANDING LIKE CRAZY!!
BLE
Stuffy Nose
Histamines affect the blood vessels of the nasal mucosa, causing inflammation and other symptoms. As a result, the nasal mucosa become swollen and bloated, causing a stuffy nose.
CELL

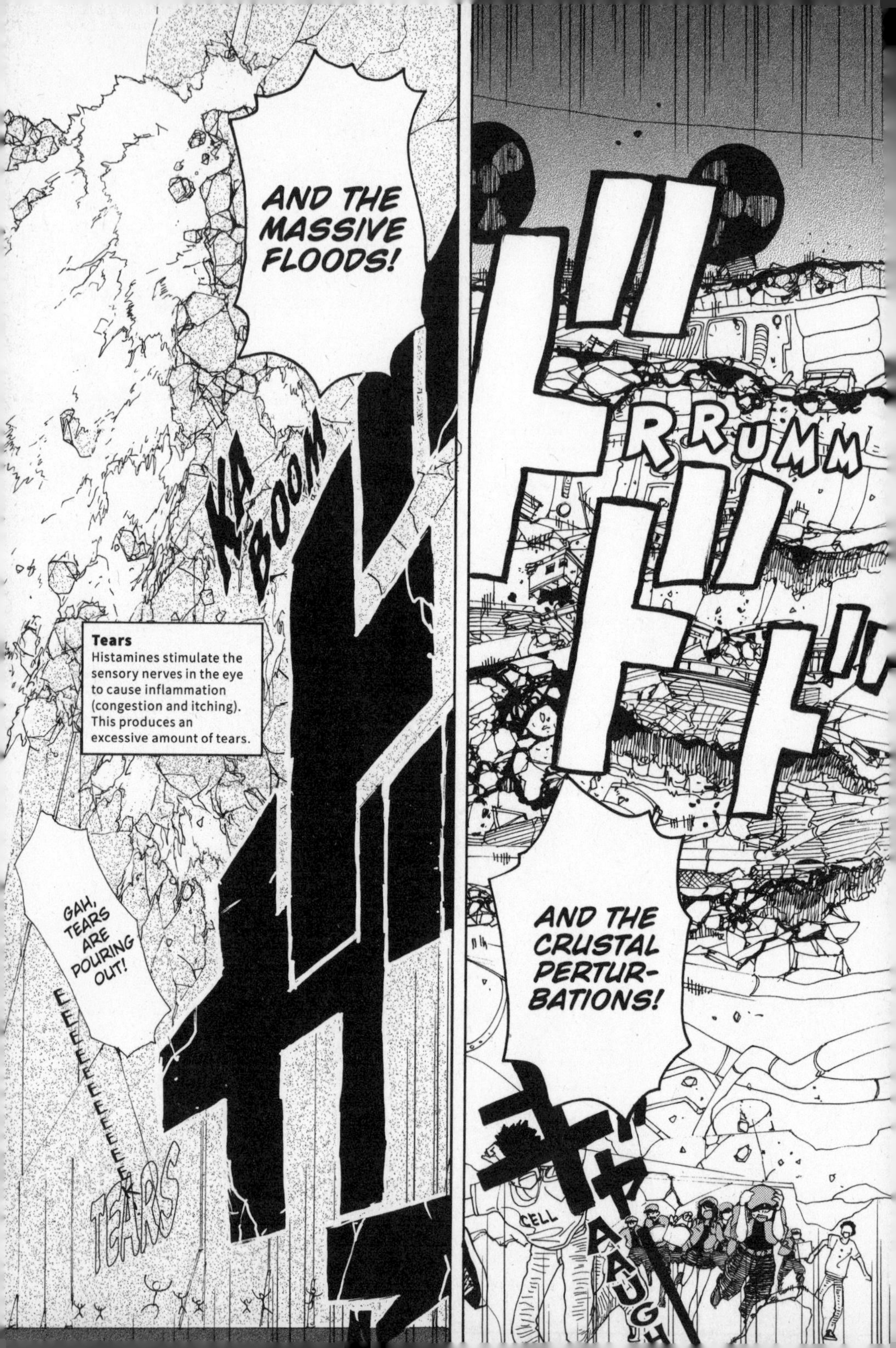
RRUMM
AND THE CRUSTAL PERTUR-BATIONS!
CELL
AAUGH
AND THE MASSIVE FLOODS!
KA-BOOM
Tears
Histamines stimulate the sensory nerves in the eye to cause inflammation (congestion and itching). This produces an excessive amount of tears.
GAH, TEARS ARE POURING OUT!
EEEEEEEEEEE
TEARS

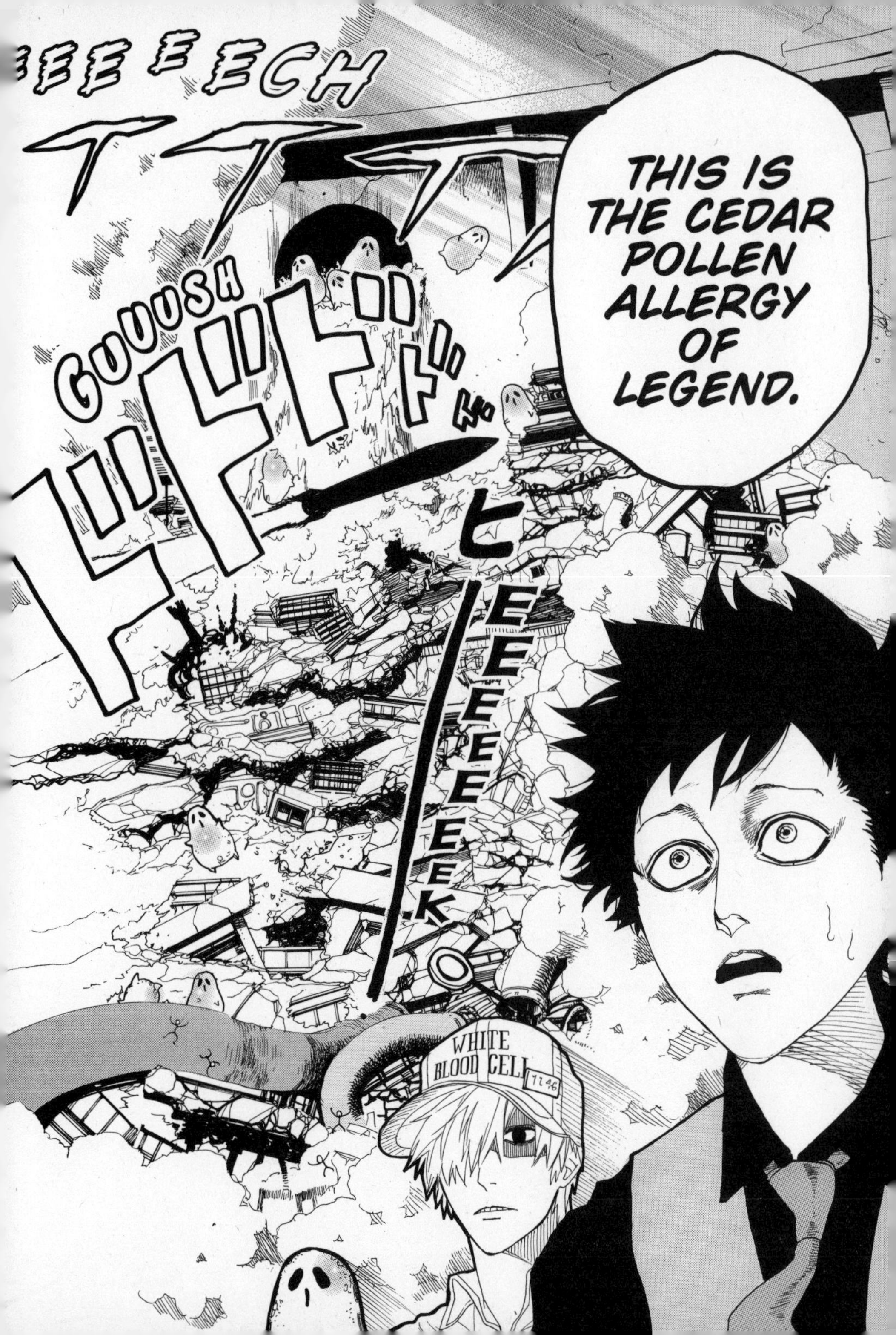

THIS IS THE CEDAR POLLEN ALLERGY OF LEGEND.
EE E ECH
GUUUSH
EEEEEEEEK
WHITE BLOOD CELL
1146

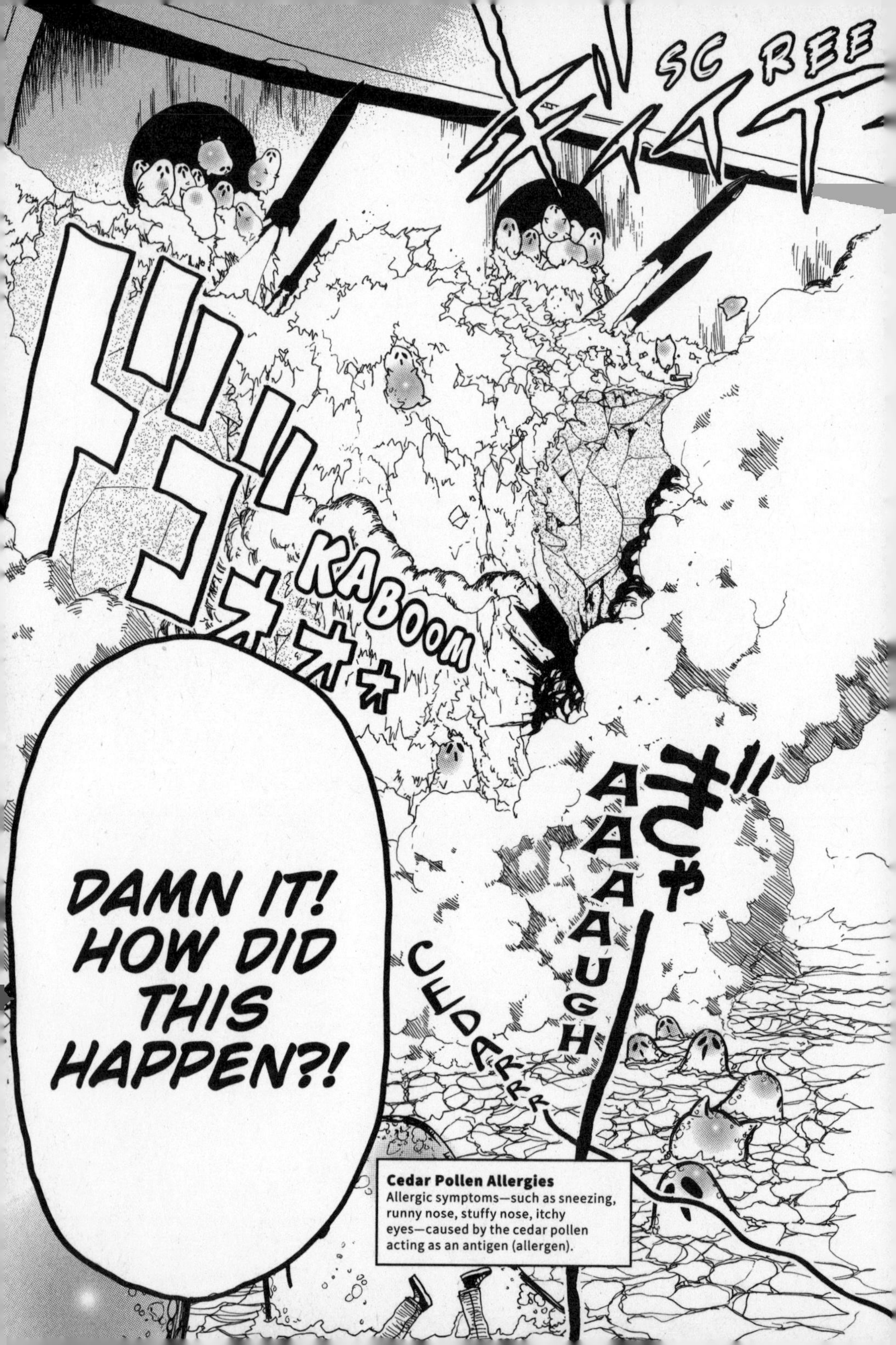
SCREE
KABOOM
AAAAAUGH
CEDARRR
DAMN IT! HOW DID THIS HAPPEN?!
Cedar Pollen Allergies
Allergic symptoms—such as sneezing, runny nose, stuffy nose, itchy eyes—caused by the cedar pollen acting as an antigen (allergen).

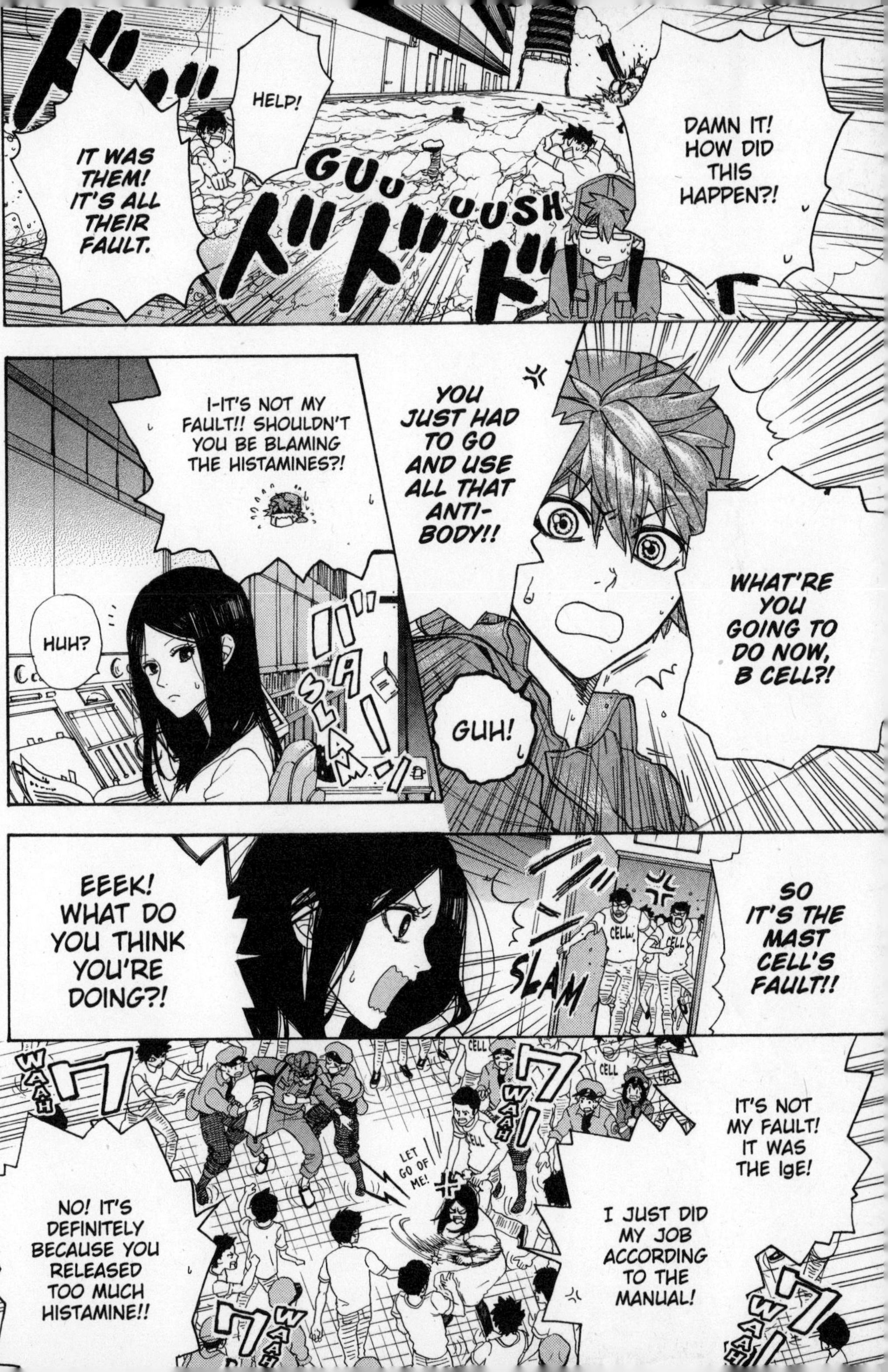
DAMN IT! HOW DID THIS HAPPEN?!
HELP!
GUUUUUSH
IT WAS THEM! IT'S ALL THEIR FAULT.
WHAT'RE YOU GOING TO DO NOW, B CELL?!
YOU JUST HAD TO GO AND USE ALL THAT ANTI-BODY!!
GUH!
I-IT'S NOT MY FAULT!! SHOULDN'T YOU BE BLAMING THE HISTAMINES?!
HUH?
SLAM
SO IT'S THE MAST CELL'S FAULT!!
SLAM
EEEK! WHAT DO YOU THINK YOU'RE DOING?!
WAAH
IT'S NOT MY FAULT! IT WAS THE IgE!
I JUST DID MY JOB ACCORDING TO THE MANUAL!
WAAH
LET GO OF ME!
WAAH
NO! IT'S DEFINITELY BECAUSE YOU RELEASED TOO MUCH HISTAMINE!!
WAAH

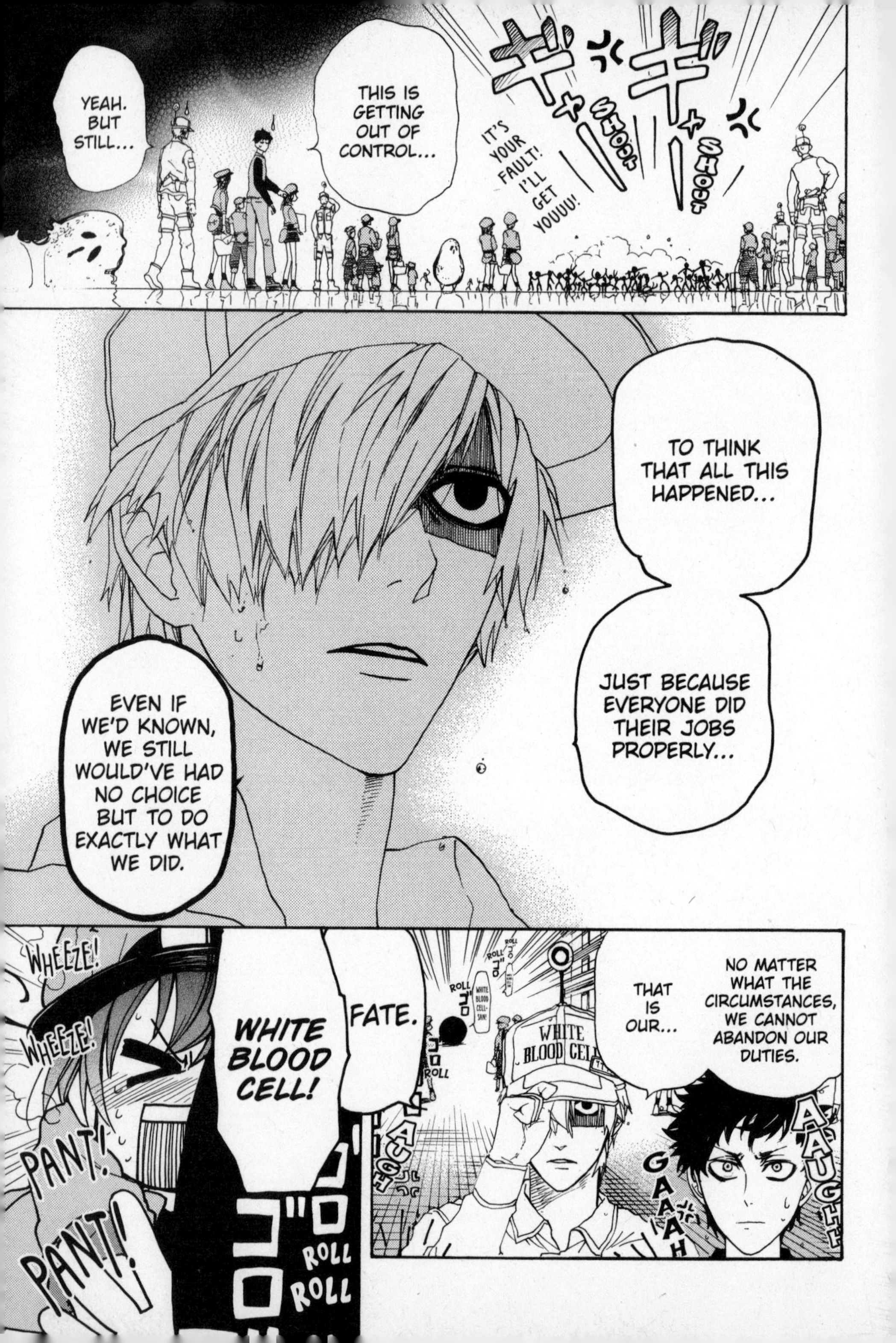
SHOOT
SHOOT
IT'S YOUR FAULT! I'LL GET YOUUU!
THIS IS GETTING OUT OF CONTROL...
YEAH. BUT STILL...
TO THINK THAT ALL THIS HAPPENED...
JUST BECAUSE EVERYONE DID THEIR JOBS PROPERLY...
EVEN IF WE'D KNOWN, WE STILL WOULD'VE HAD NO CHOICE BUT TO DO EXACTLY WHAT WE DID.
NO MATTER WHAT THE CIRCUMSTANCES, WE CANNOT ABANDON OUR DUTIES.
THAT IS OUR...
AAUGH
GAAAH
WHITE BLOOD CELL
AAUGH
ROLL
ROLL
ROLL
WHITE BLOOD CELL-SAN!
ROLL
FATE.
WHITE BLOOD CELL!
ROLL
ROLL
WHEEZE!
WHEEZE!
PANT!
PANT!

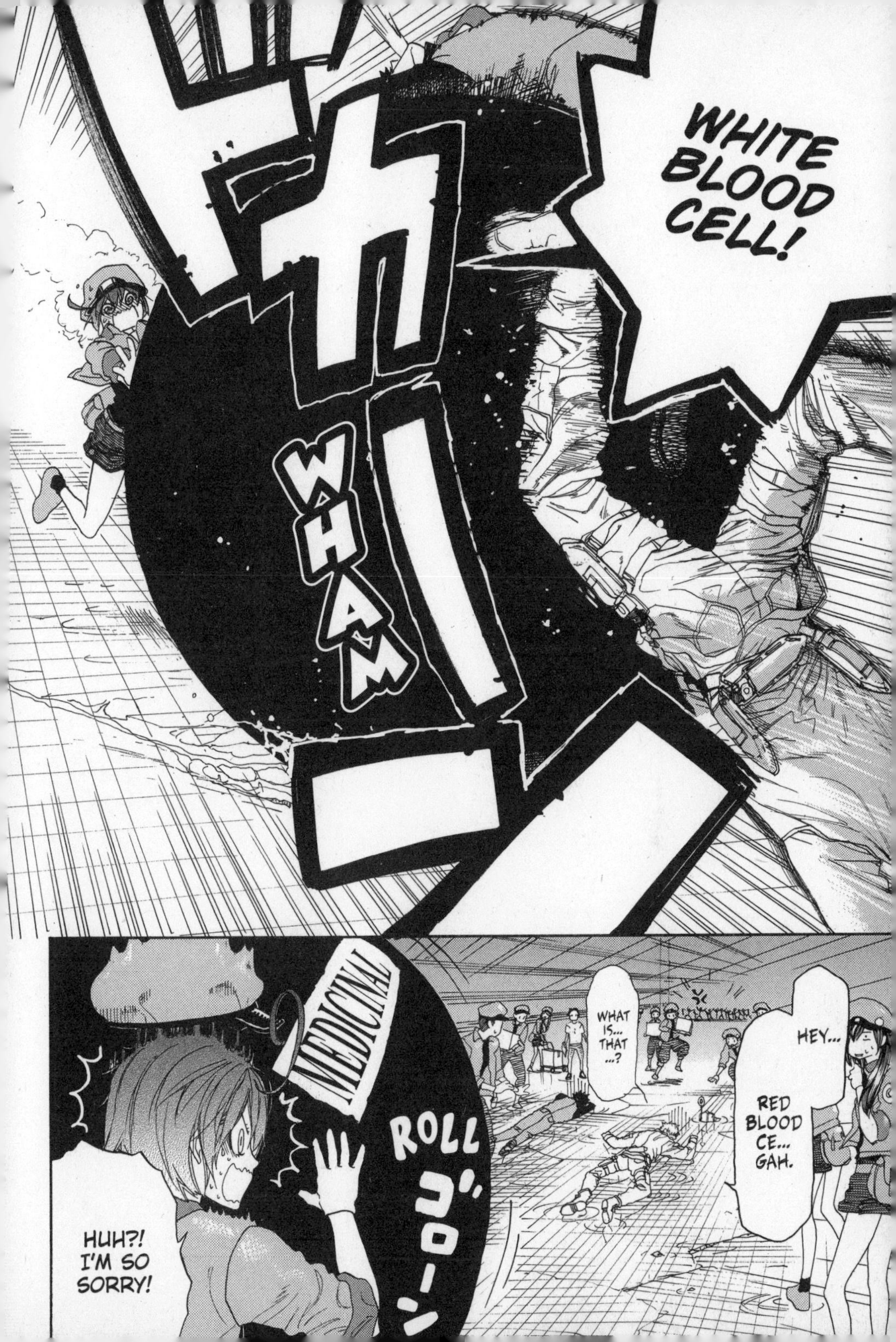
WHITE BLOOD CELL!
WHAM
HEY...
RED BLOOD CE... GAH.
WHAT IS... THAT ...?
MEDICINAL
ROLL
ゴローン
HUH?! I'M SO SORRY!

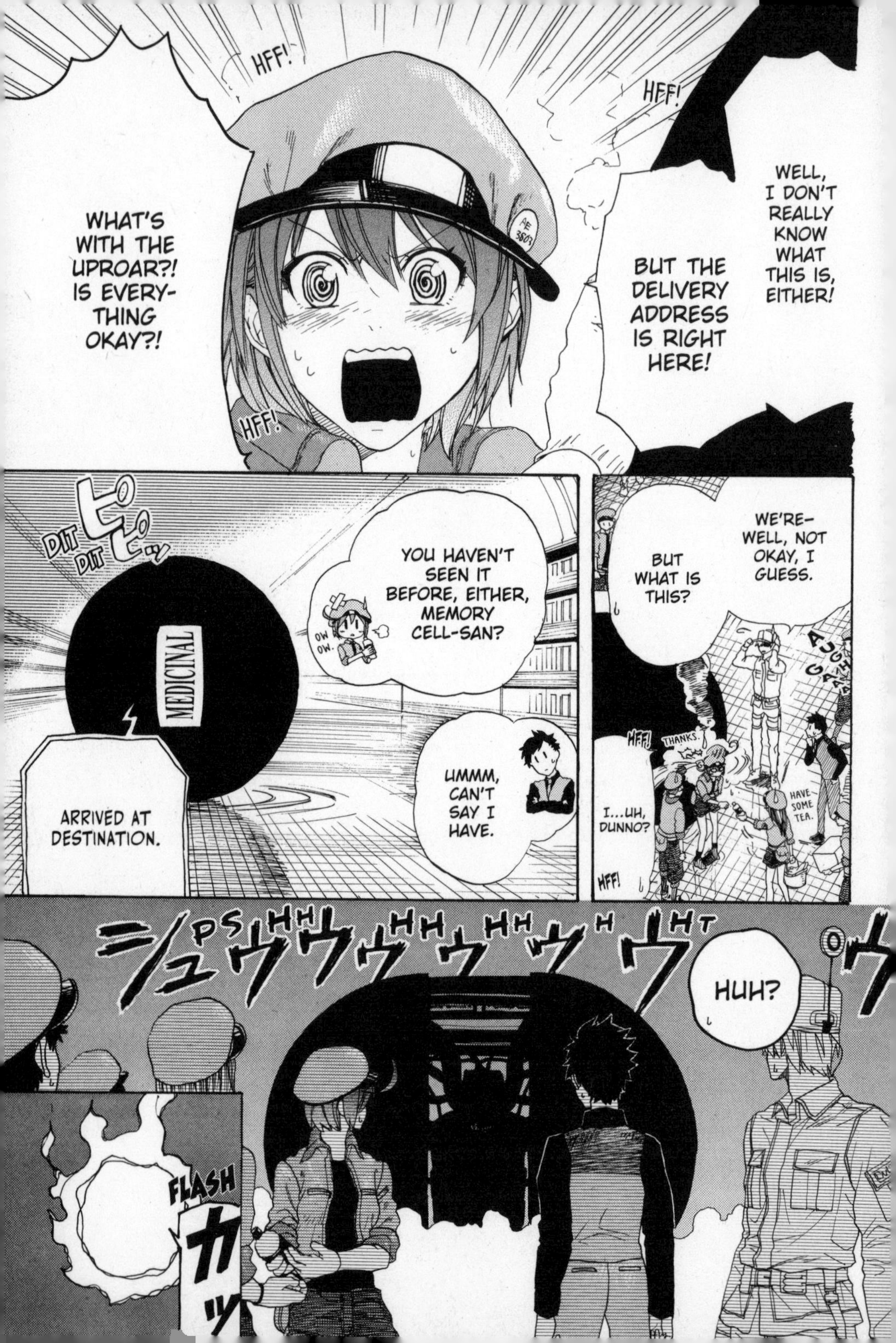
HFF!
HFF!
WELL, I DON'T REALLY KNOW WHAT THIS IS, EITHER!
BUT THE DELIVERY ADDRESS IS RIGHT HERE!
WHAT'S WITH THE UPROAR?! IS EVERY-THING OKAY?!
HFF!
WE'RE—WELL, NOT OKAY, I GUESS.
BUT WHAT IS THIS?
AUGGAHH
HFF!
THANKS.
HAVE SOME TEA.
I...UH, DUNNO?
HFF!
YOU HAVEN'T SEEN IT BEFORE, EITHER, MEMORY CELL-SAN?
OW OW.
UMMM, CAN'T SAY I HAVE.
DIT DIT
MEDICINAL
ARRIVED AT DESTINATION.
PSHHHHHHHHHHT
HUH?
FLASH

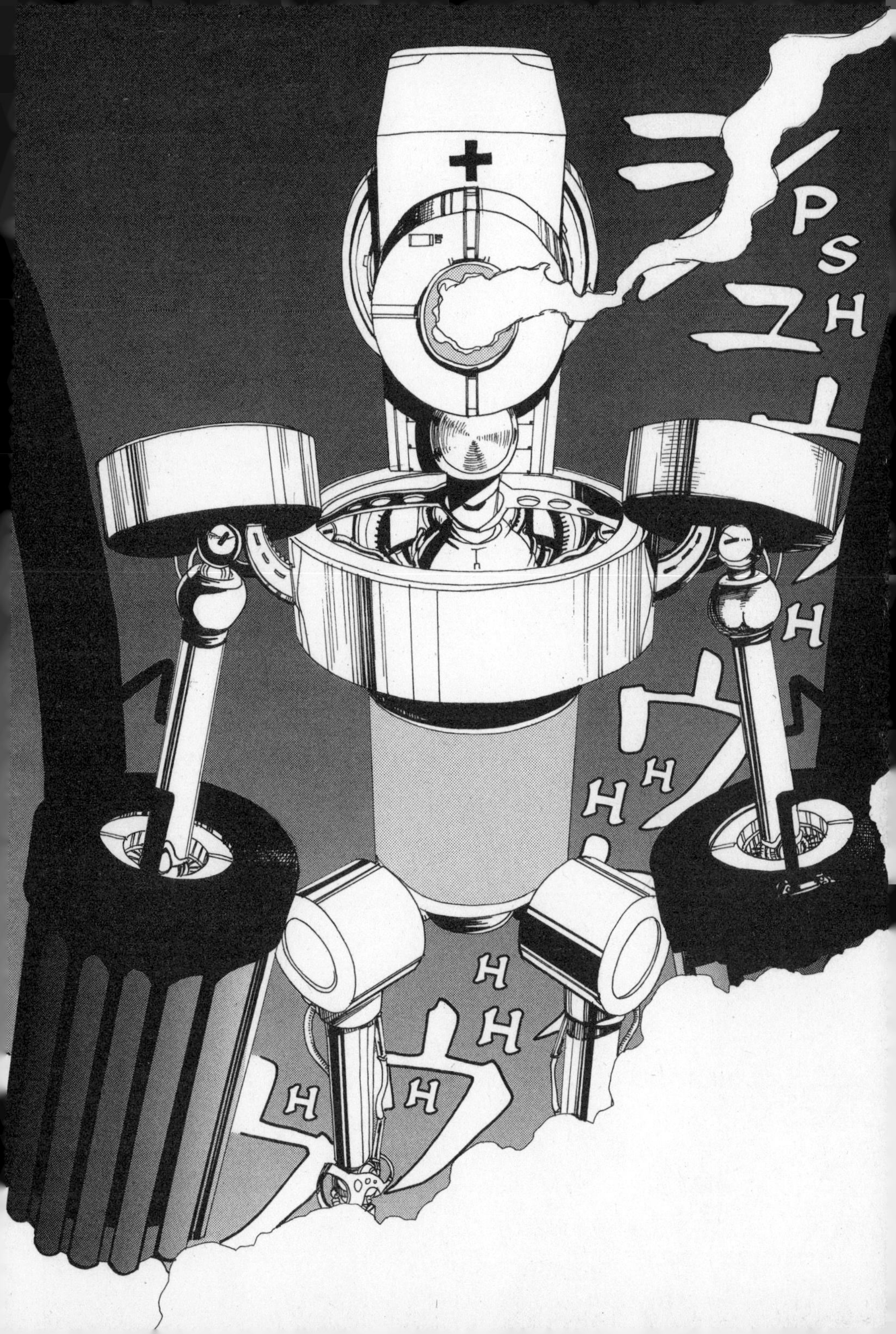
PSH
H
HH
HH
HH

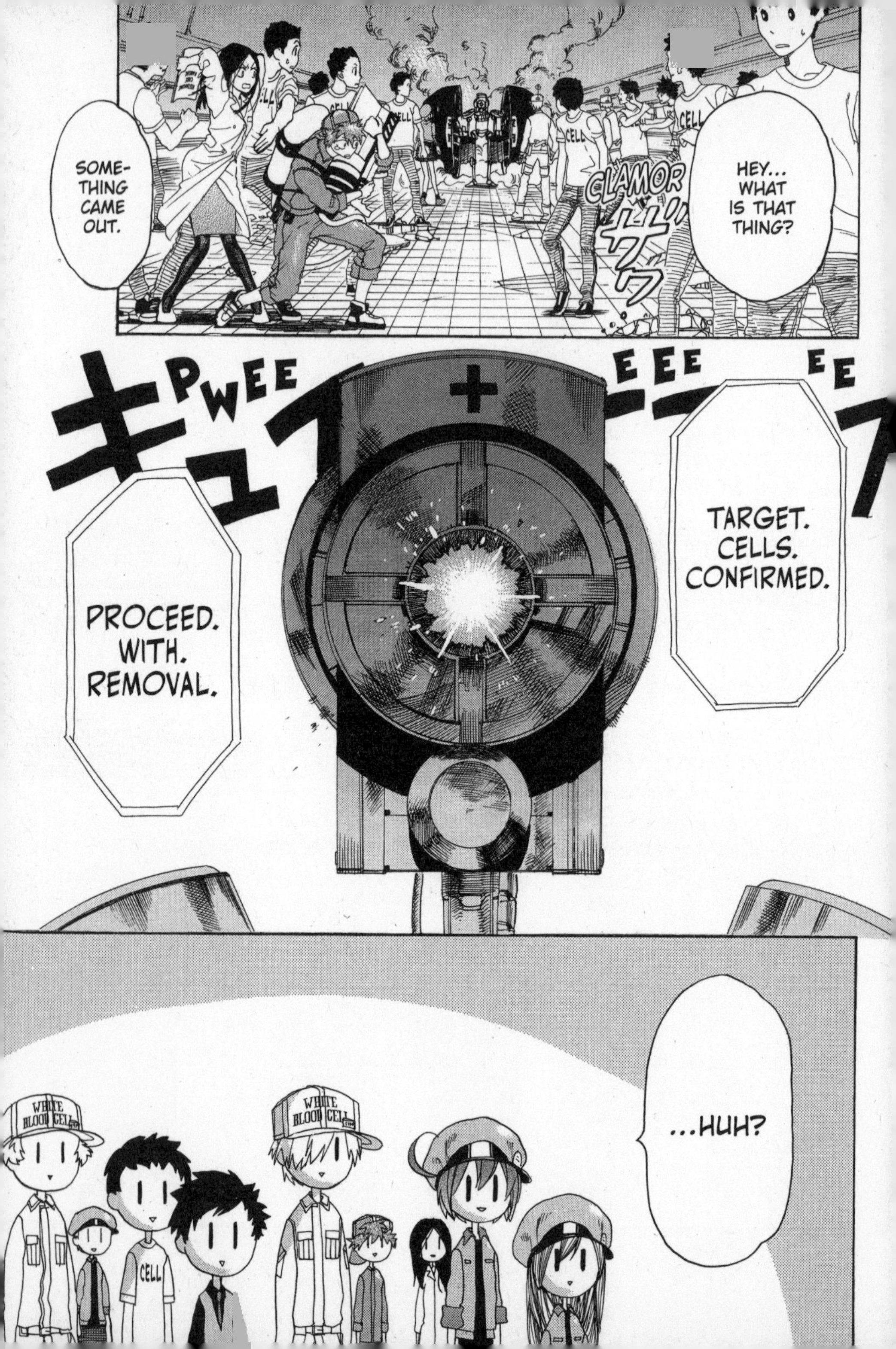
HEY... WHAT IS THAT THING?
CLAMOR
SOME-THING CAME OUT.
PWEE EEE EE
TARGET. CELLS. CONFIRMED.
PROCEED. WITH. REMOVAL.
...HUH?

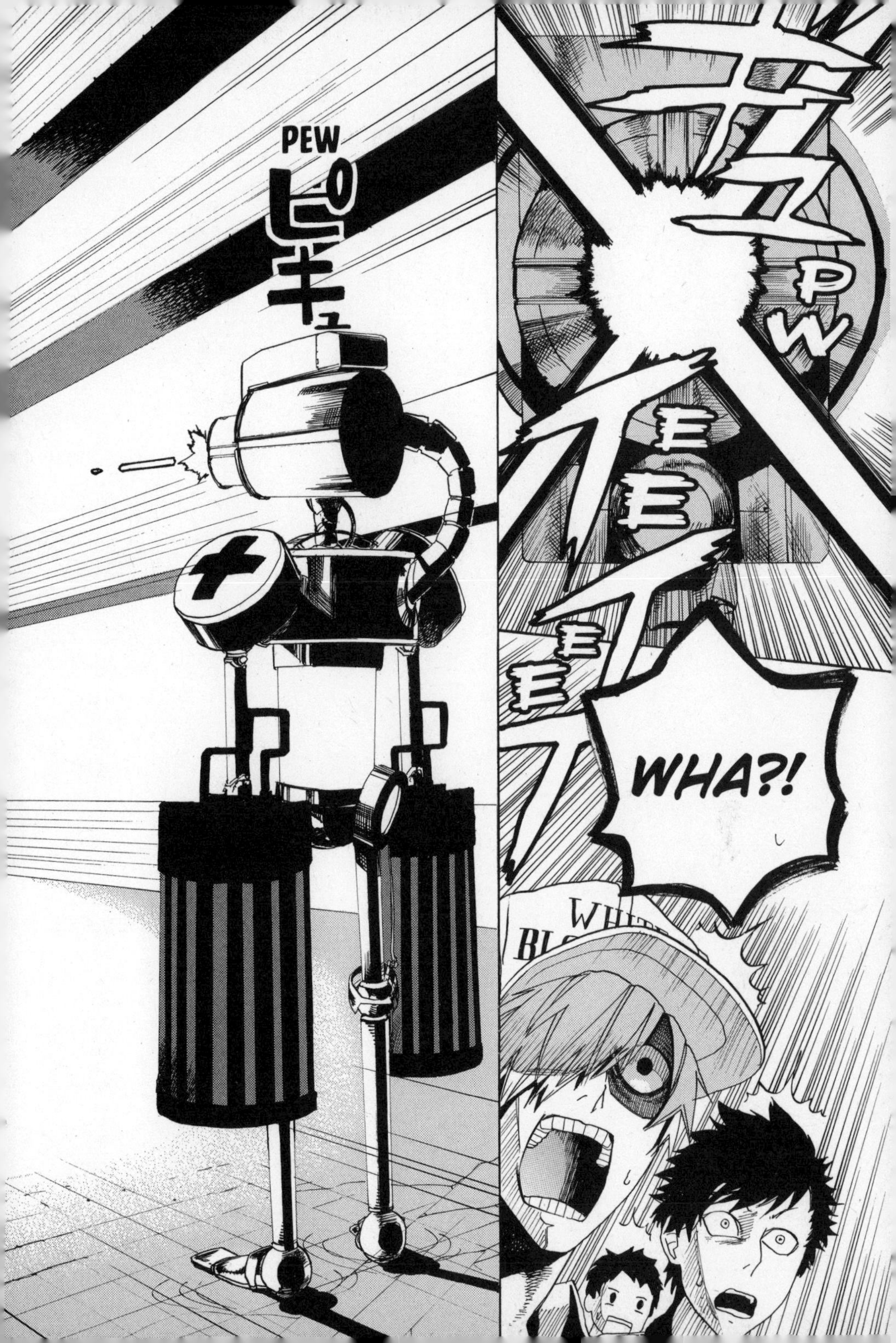
PW
EE
EE
WHA?!
PEW
ピキュ

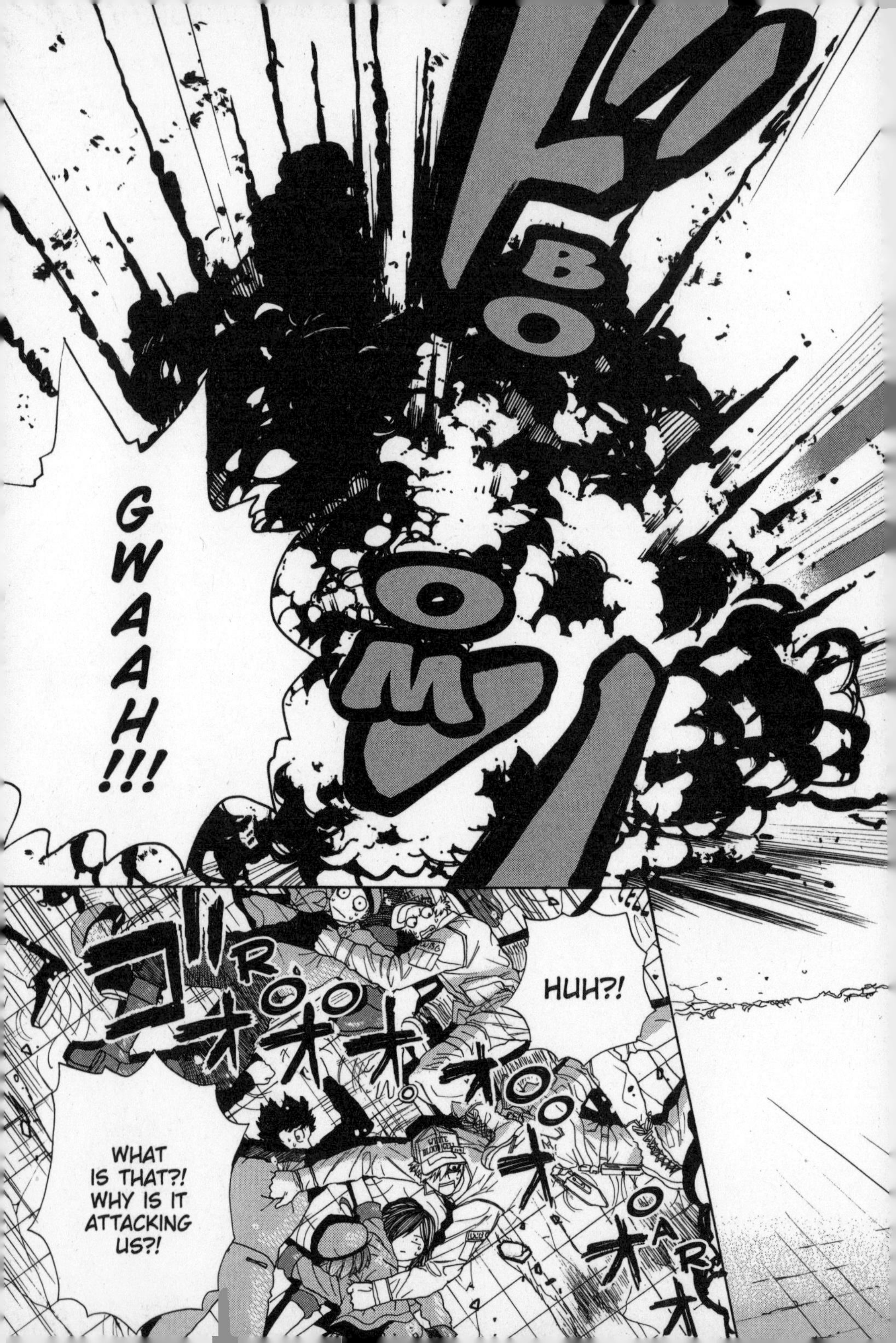
BOOM
GWAAAH!!!
HUH?!
ROOOOOOOAR
WHAT IS THAT?! WHY IS IT ATTACKING US?!

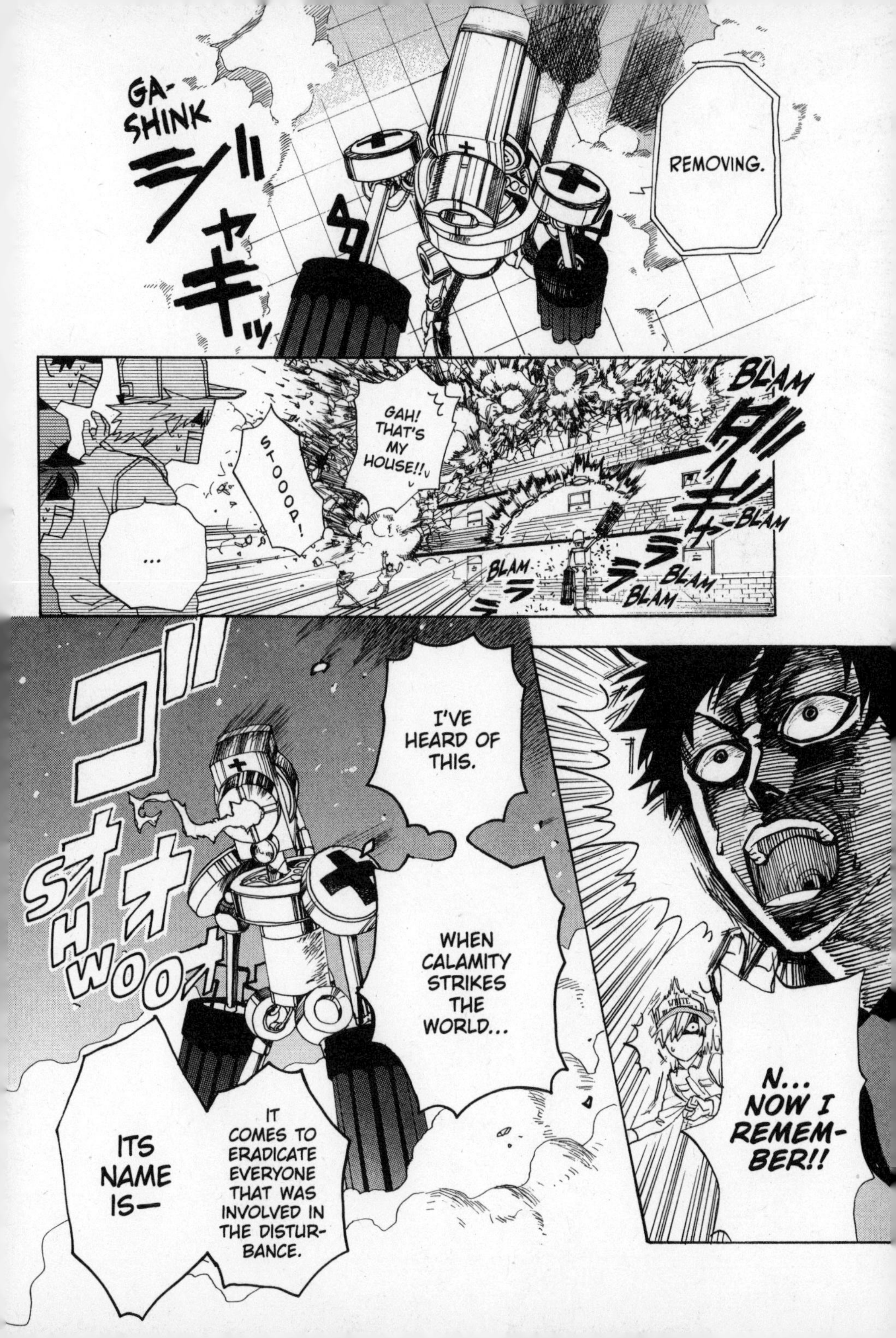
REMOVING.
GA-SHINK
BLAM
BLAM
BLAM
BLAM
BLAM
GAH! THAT'S MY HOUSE!!
STOOOP!
...
N... NOW I REMEMBER!!
I'VE HEARD OF THIS.
WHEN CALAMITY STRIKES THE WORLD...
IT COMES TO ERADICATE EVERYONE THAT WAS INVOLVED IN THE DISTURBANCE.
ITS NAME IS—
SHWOO

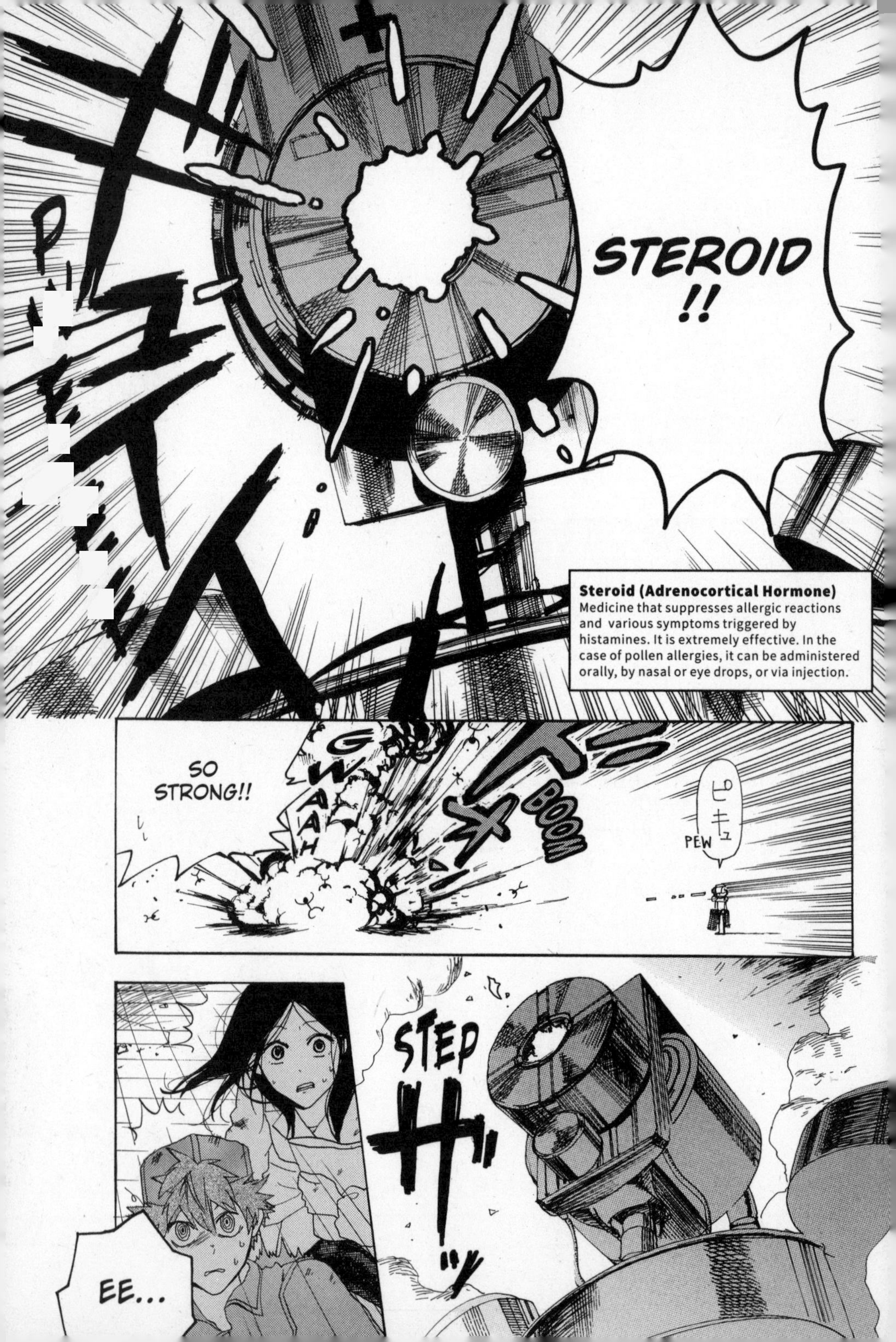
STEROID !!
Steroid (Adrenocortical Hormone)
Medicine that suppresses allergic reactions and various symptoms triggered by histamines. It is extremely effective. In the case of pollen allergies, it can be administered orally, by nasal or eye drops, or via injection.
ピキュ
PEW
BOOM
GWAAAH
SO STRONG!!
STEP
EE...

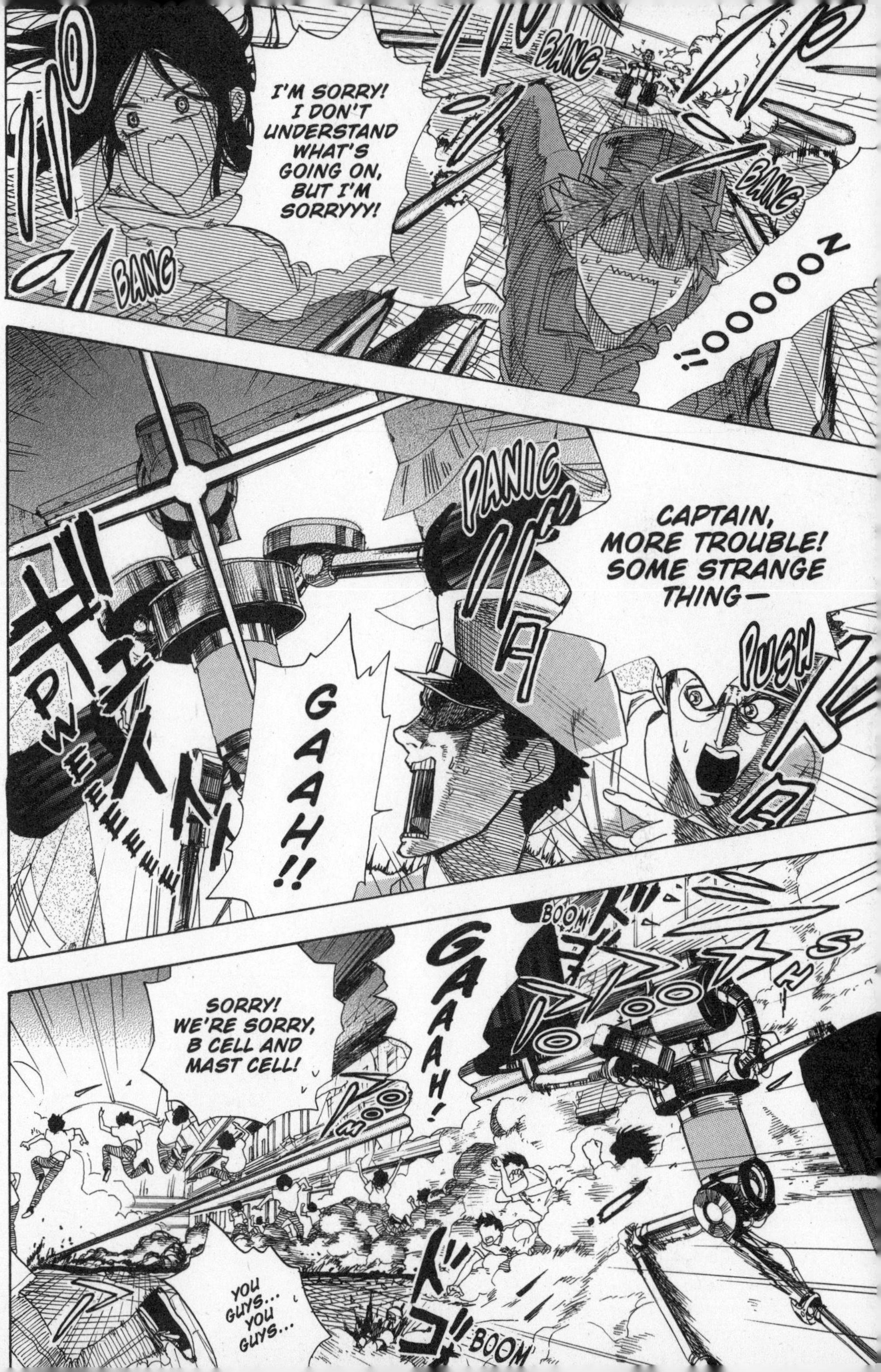
BANG
BANG
NOOOOOO!!
I'M SORRY! I DON'T UNDERSTAND WHAT'S GOING ON, BUT I'M SORRYYY!
BANG
PUSH
CAPTAIN, MORE TROUBLE! SOME STRANGE THING—
PANIC
GAAAH!!
PWEEEEEEE
SHH
BOOM
GAAAAH!
SORRY! WE'RE SORRY, B CELL AND MAST CELL!
BOOM
YOU GUYS... YOU GUYS...

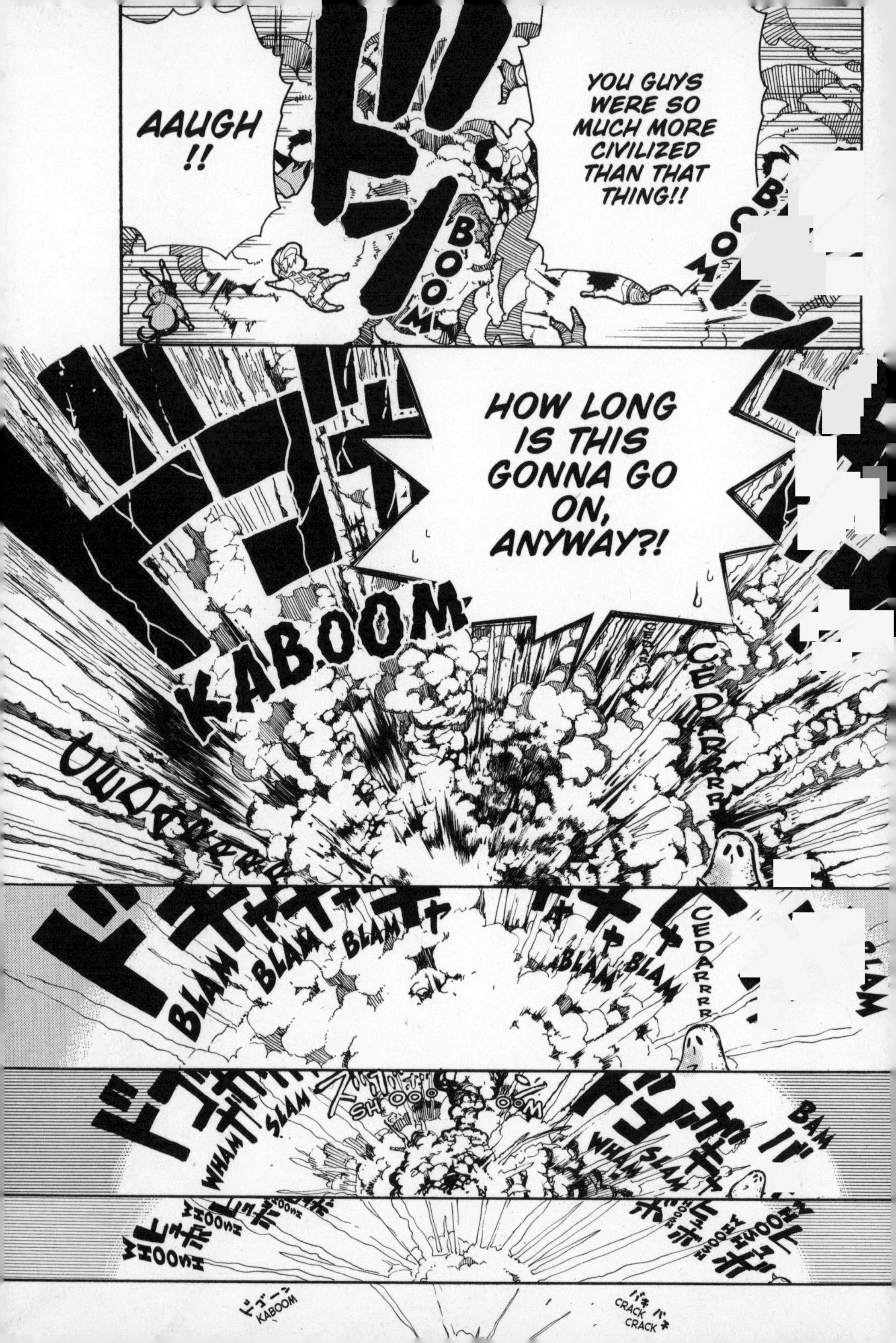
BOOM
YOU GUYS WERE SO MUCH MORE CIVILIZED THAN THAT THING!!
BOOOM
AAUGH !!
HOW LONG IS THIS GONNA GO ON, ANYWAY?!
CEDARRR
CEDARRR
KABOOM
CEDARRR
BLAM BLAM
BLAM
BLAM
BLAM
BLAM
SLAM
BAM
WHAM SLAM
SHOOOOOM
WHAM
SLAM
WHOOSH
WHOOSH
WHOOSH
WHOOSH
CRACK CRACK
KABOOM

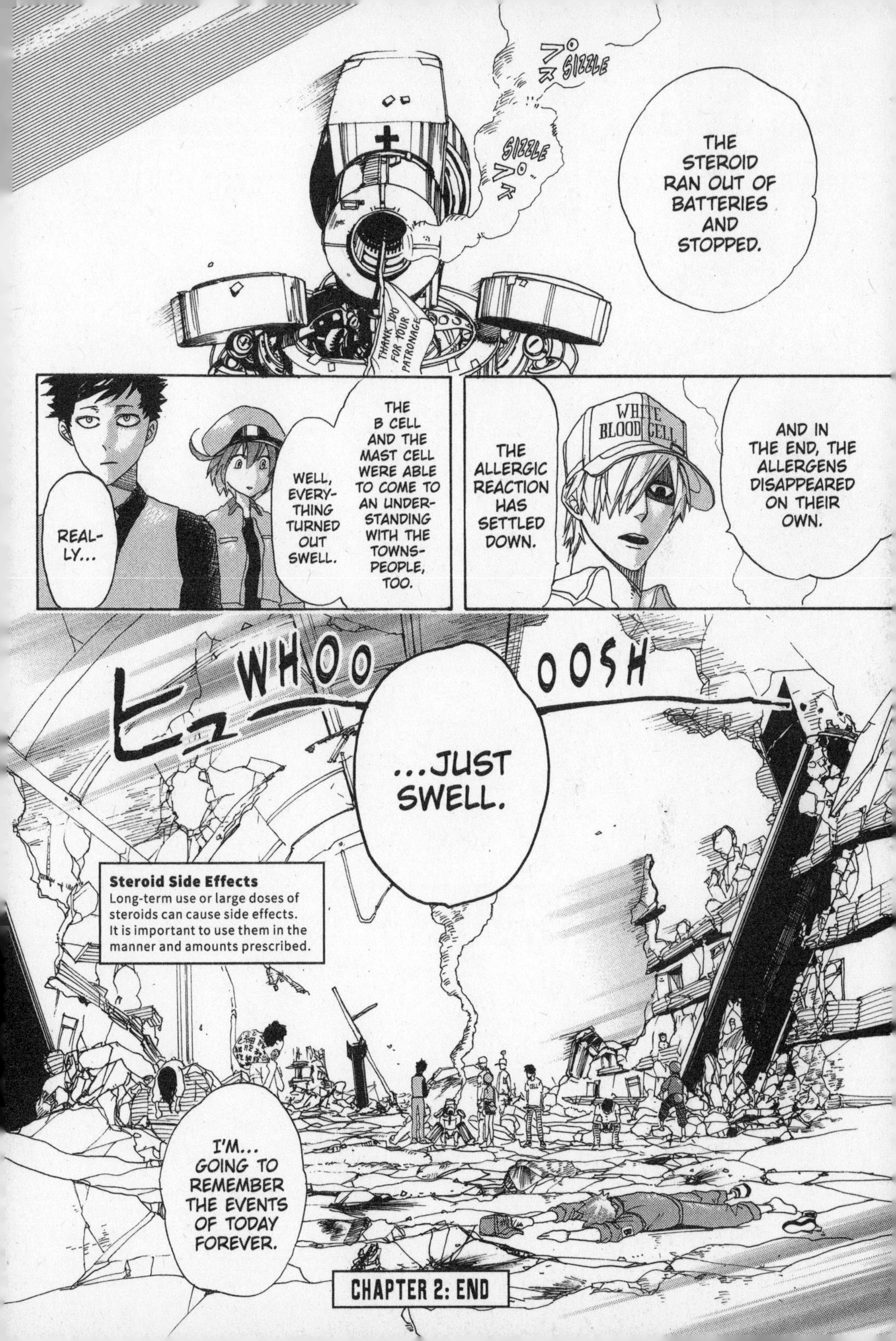
SIZZLE
SIZZLE
THE STEROID RAN OUT OF BATTERIES AND STOPPED.
THANK YOU FOR YOUR PATRONAGE
AND IN THE END, THE ALLERGENS DISAPPEARED ON THEIR OWN.
WHITE BLOOD CELL
THE ALLERGIC REACTION HAS SETTLED DOWN.
THE B CELL AND THE MAST CELL WERE ABLE TO COME TO AN UNDERSTANDING WITH THE TOWNSPEOPLE, TOO.
WELL, EVERYTHING TURNED OUT SWELL.
REAL-LY...
ヒュー
WHOOOOSH
...JUST SWELL.
Steroid Side Effects
Long-term use or large doses of steroids can cause side effects. It is important to use them in the manner and amounts prescribed.
I'M... GOING TO REMEMBER THE EVENTS OF TODAY FOREVER.
CHAPTER 2: END

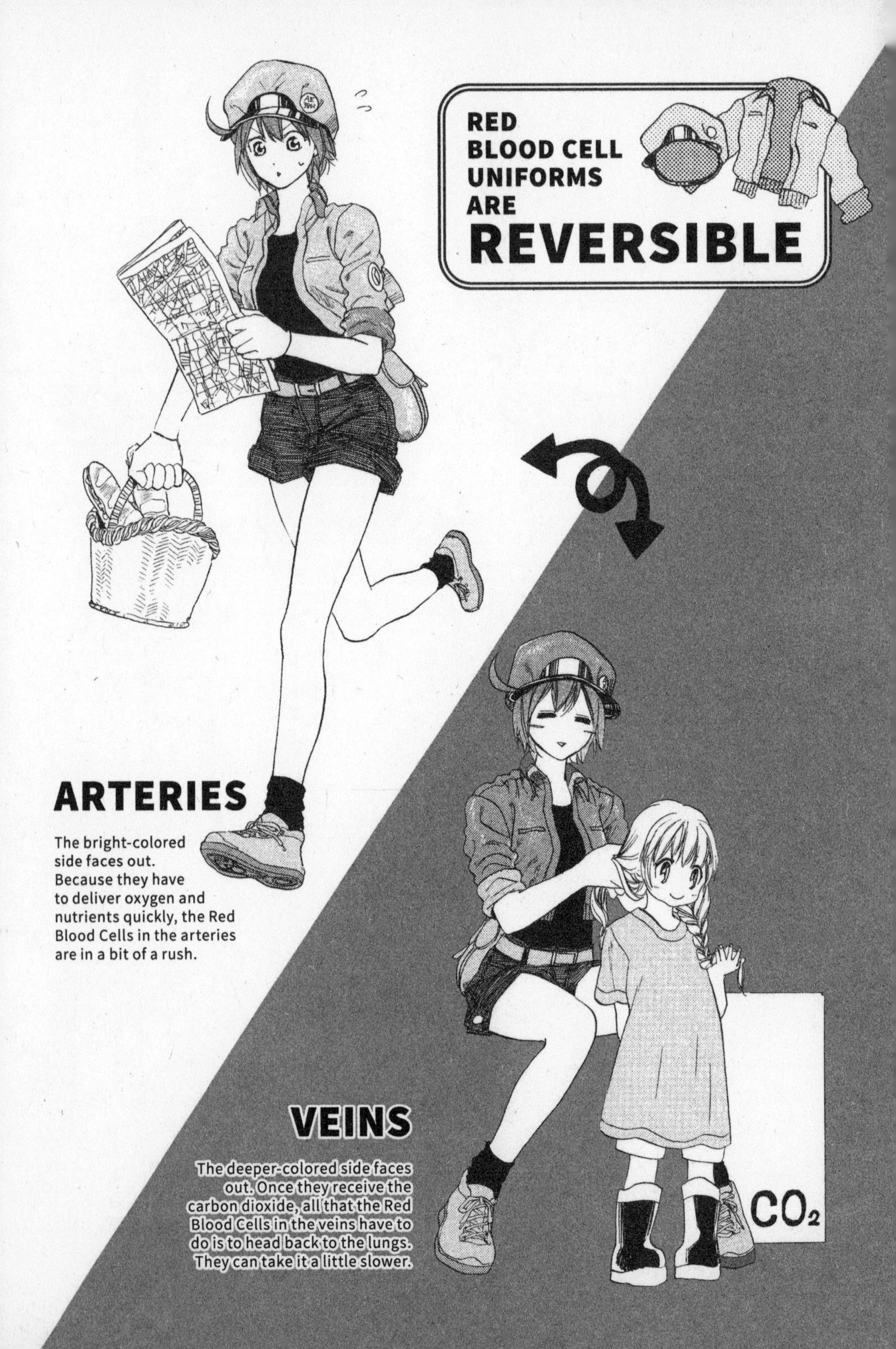
RED BLOOD CELL UNIFORMS ARE REVERSIBLE
ARTERIES
The bright-colored side faces out. Because they have to deliver oxygen and nutrients quickly, the Red Blood Cells in the arteries are in a bit of a rush.
VEINS
The deeper-colored side faces out. Once they receive the carbon dioxide, all that the Red Blood Cells in the veins have to do is to head back to the lungs. They can take it a little slower.
CO_2

Cells at Work!
はたらく細胞

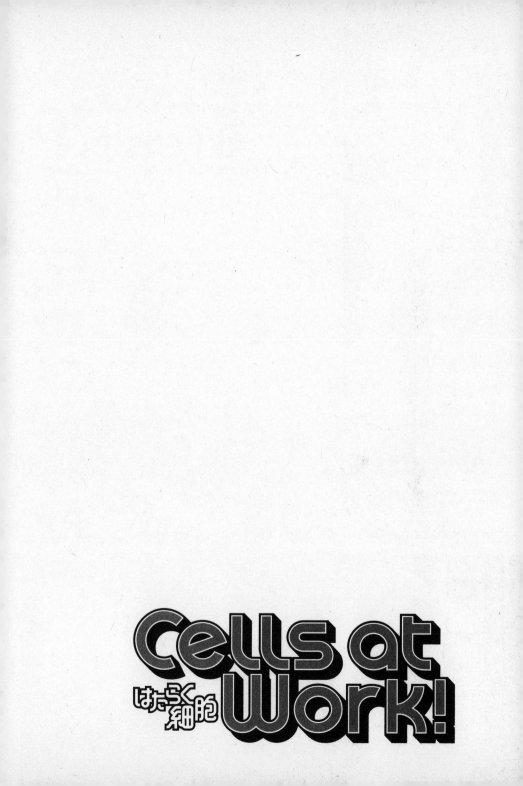

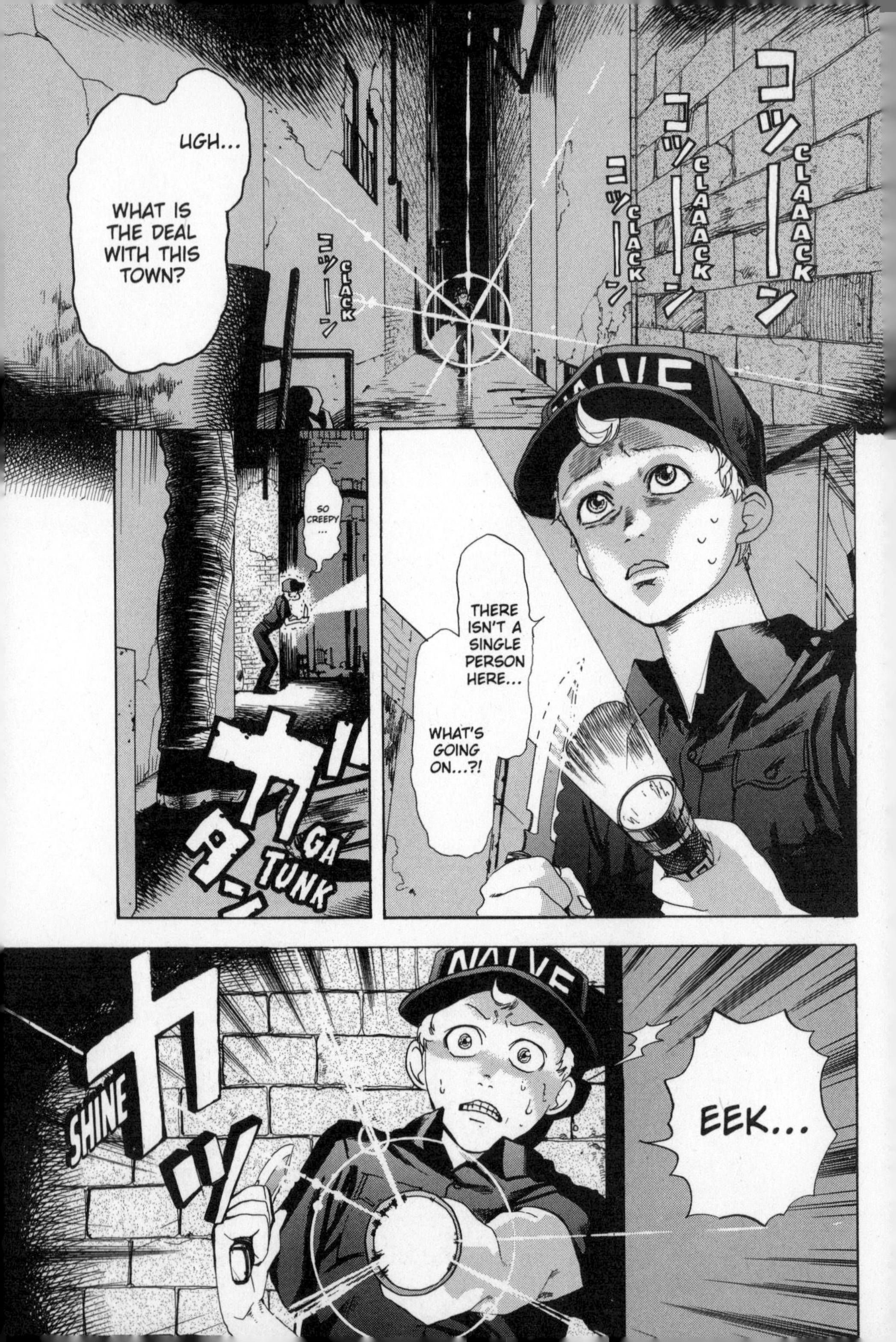
CLAAACK
CLAAACK
CLACK
CLACK
UGH...
WHAT IS THE DEAL WITH THIS TOWN?
THERE ISN'T A SINGLE PERSON HERE...
WHAT'S GOING ON...?!
SO CREEPY...
GA TUNK
EEK...
SHINE

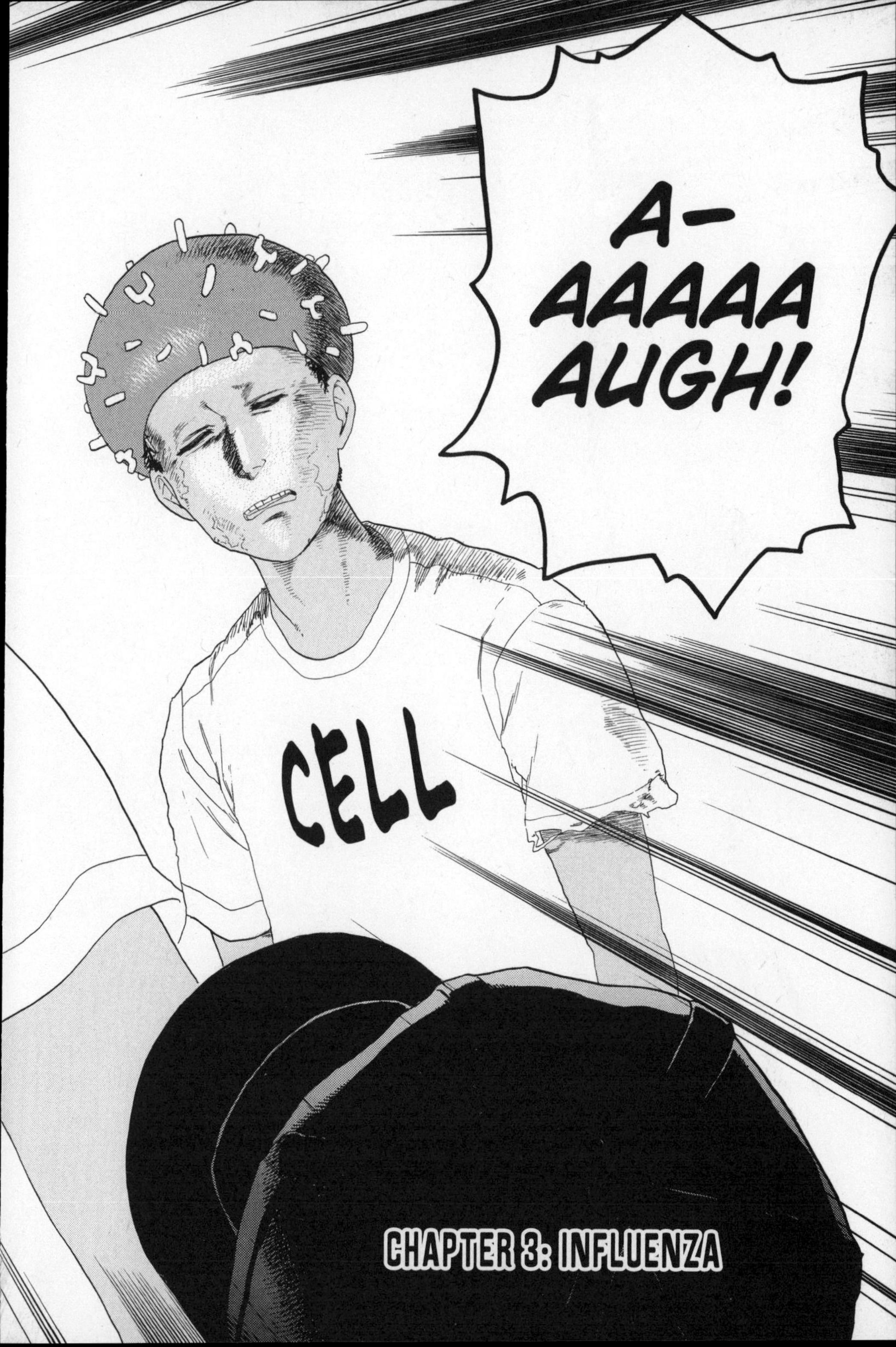
A-AAAAA AUGH!
CELL
CHAPTER 3: INFLUENZA

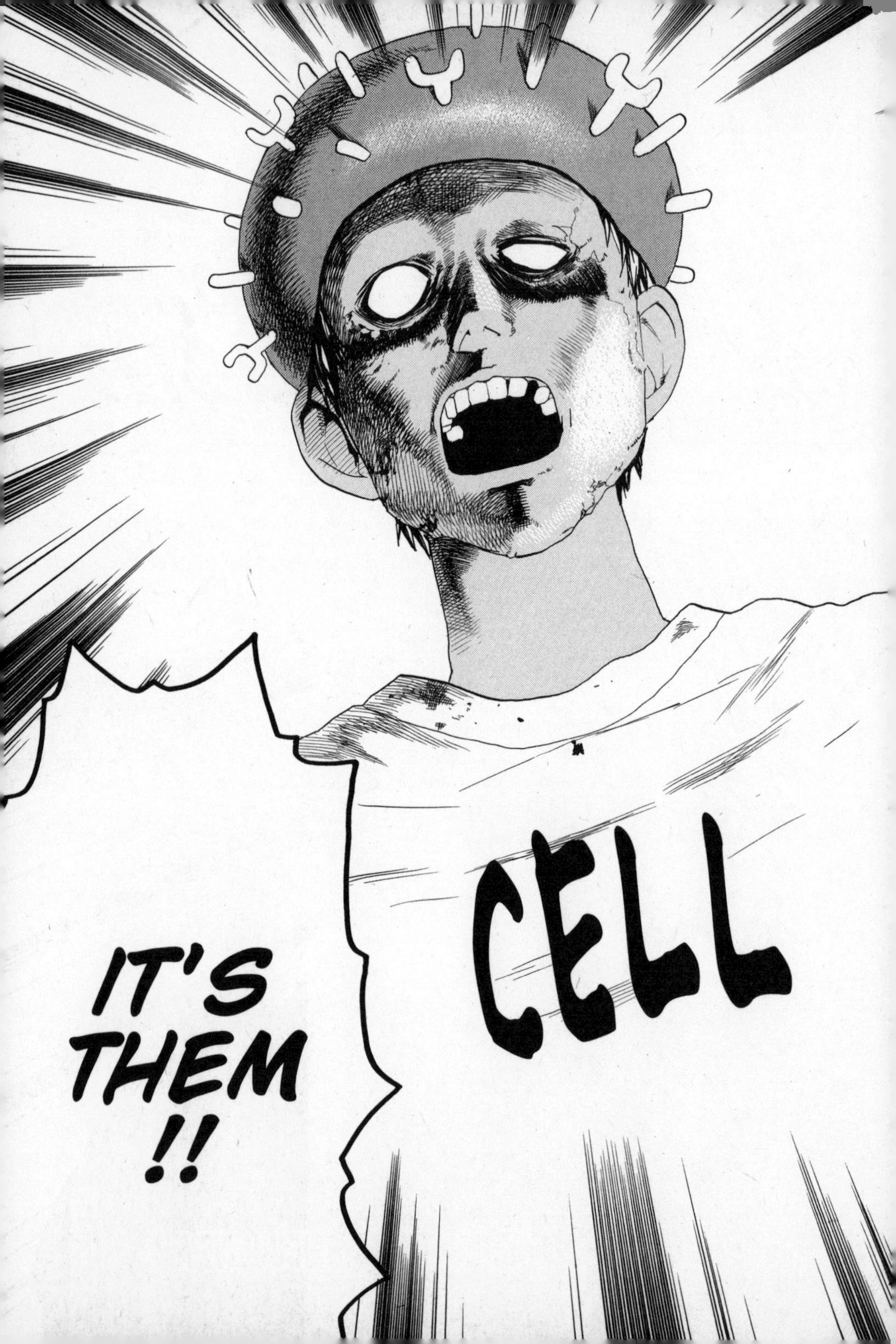
CELL
IT'S THEM !!

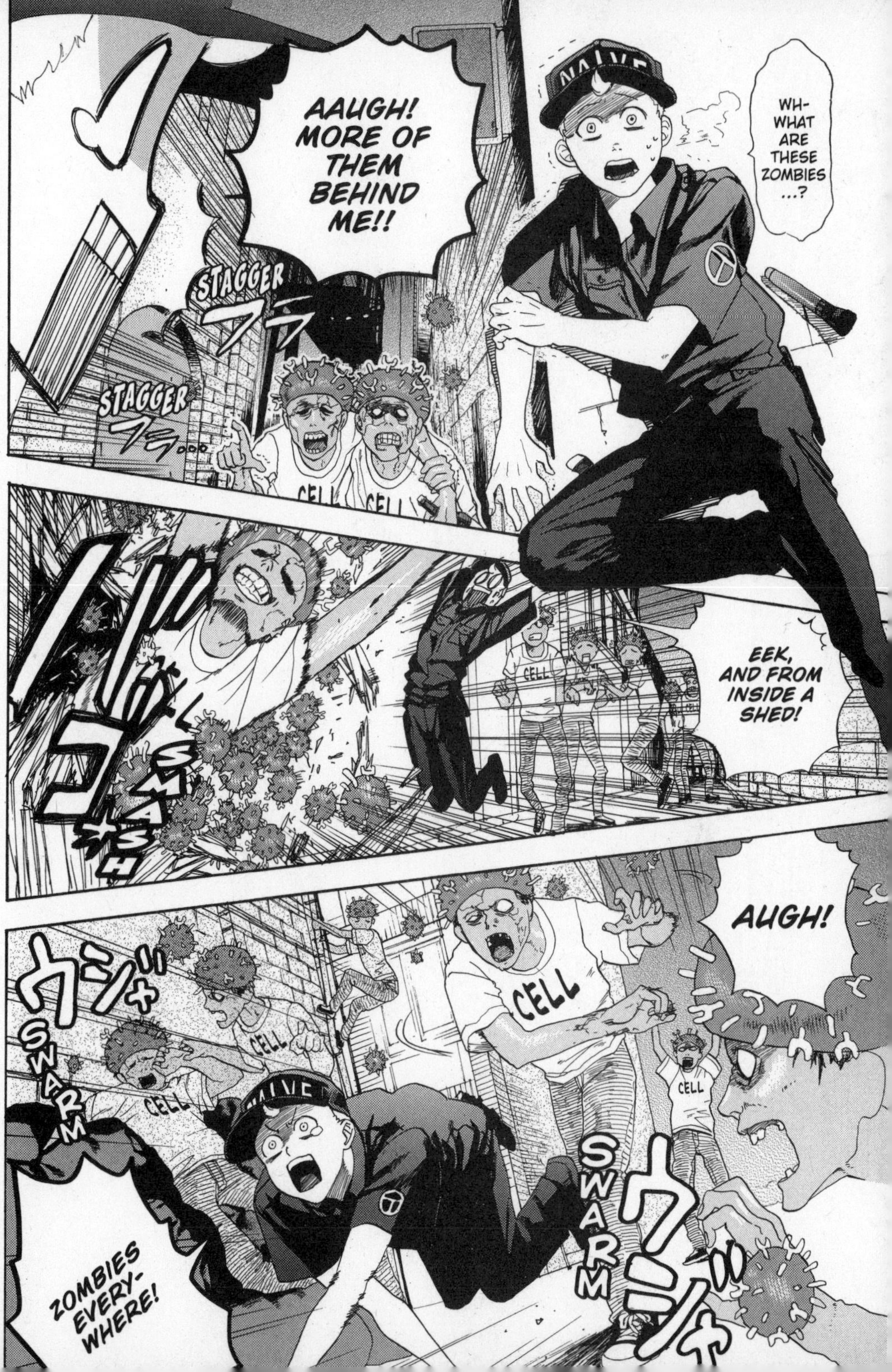
WH- WHAT ARE THESE ZOMBIES ...?
AAUGH! MORE OF THEM BEHIND ME!!
STAGGER
フラ
STAGGER
フラ...
EEK, AND FROM INSIDE A SHED!
SMASH
AUGH!
SWARM
SWARM
ZOMBIES EVERY-WHERE!

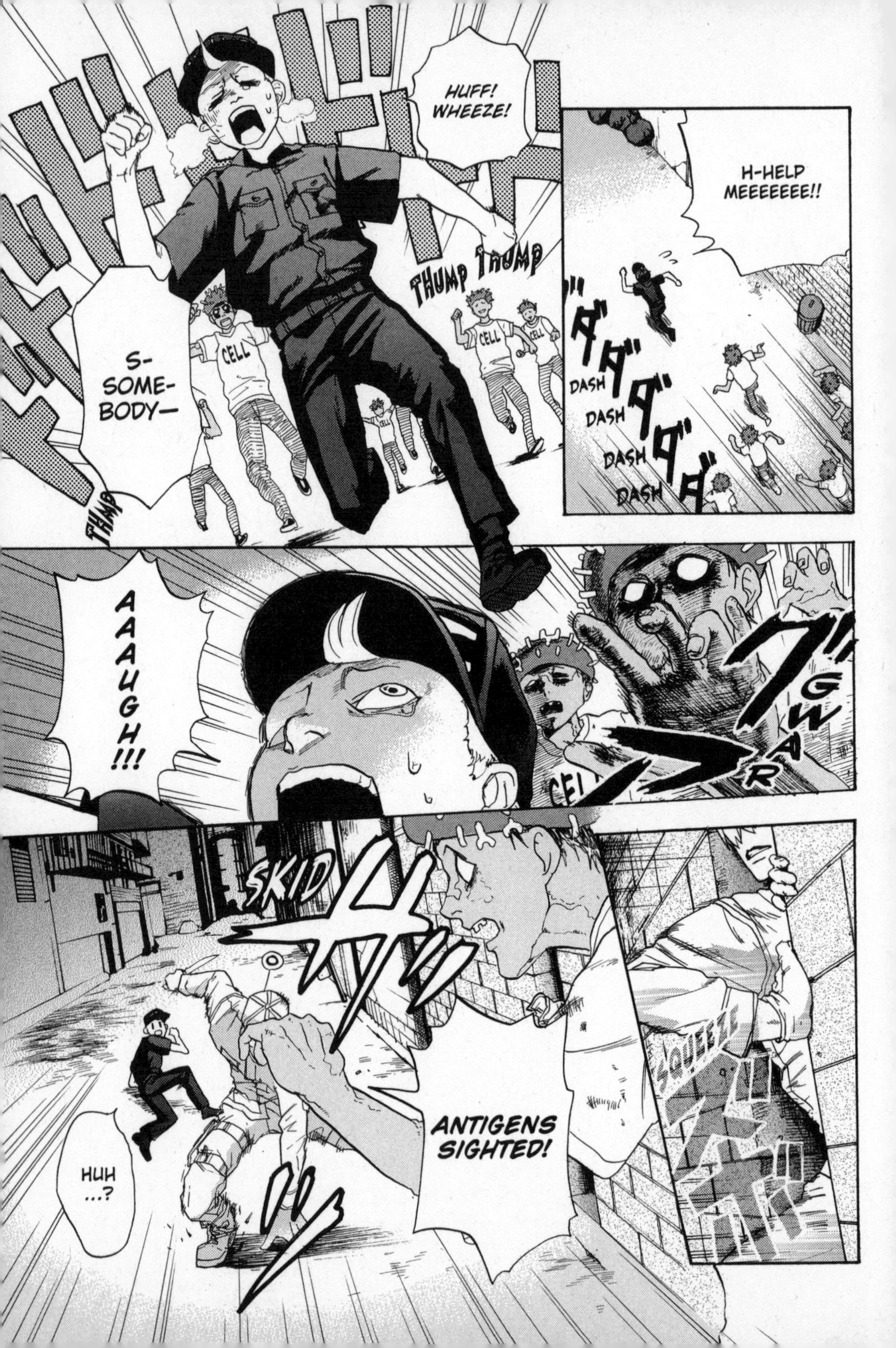
H-HELP MEEEEEEE!!
DASH
DASH
DASH
DASH
HUFF! WHEEZE!
THUMP THUMP
S- SOME- BODY—
THMP
GWAR
AAAAUGH!!!
SKID
SQUEEZE
ANTIGENS SIGHTED!
HUH ...?

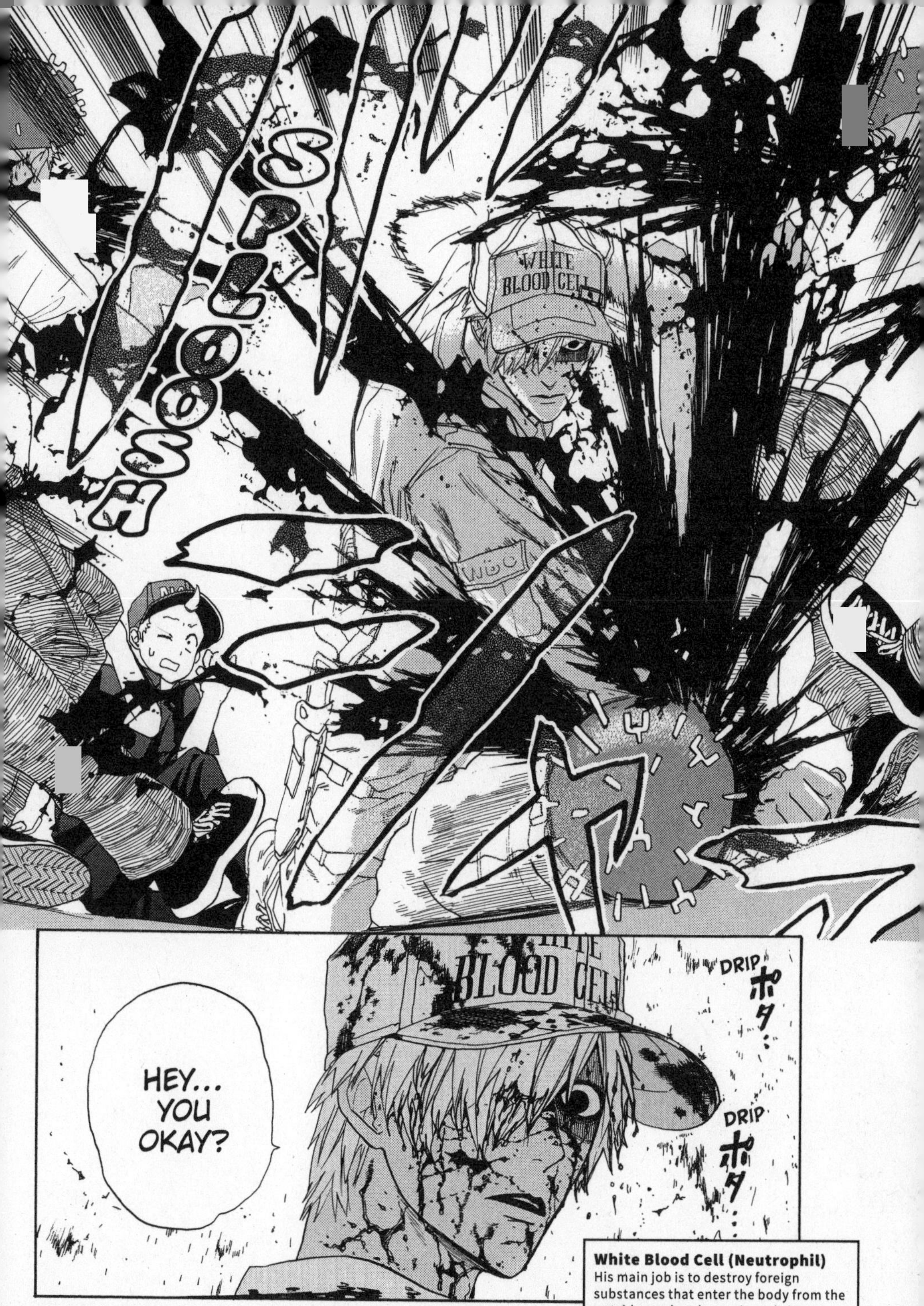
SPLOOSH
DRIP ポタ
DRIP ポタ
HEY... YOU OKAY?

White Blood Cell (Neutrophil)
His main job is to destroy foreign substances that enter the body from the outside, such as bacteria and viruses. Neutrophils make up more than half of all white blood cells in the blood.

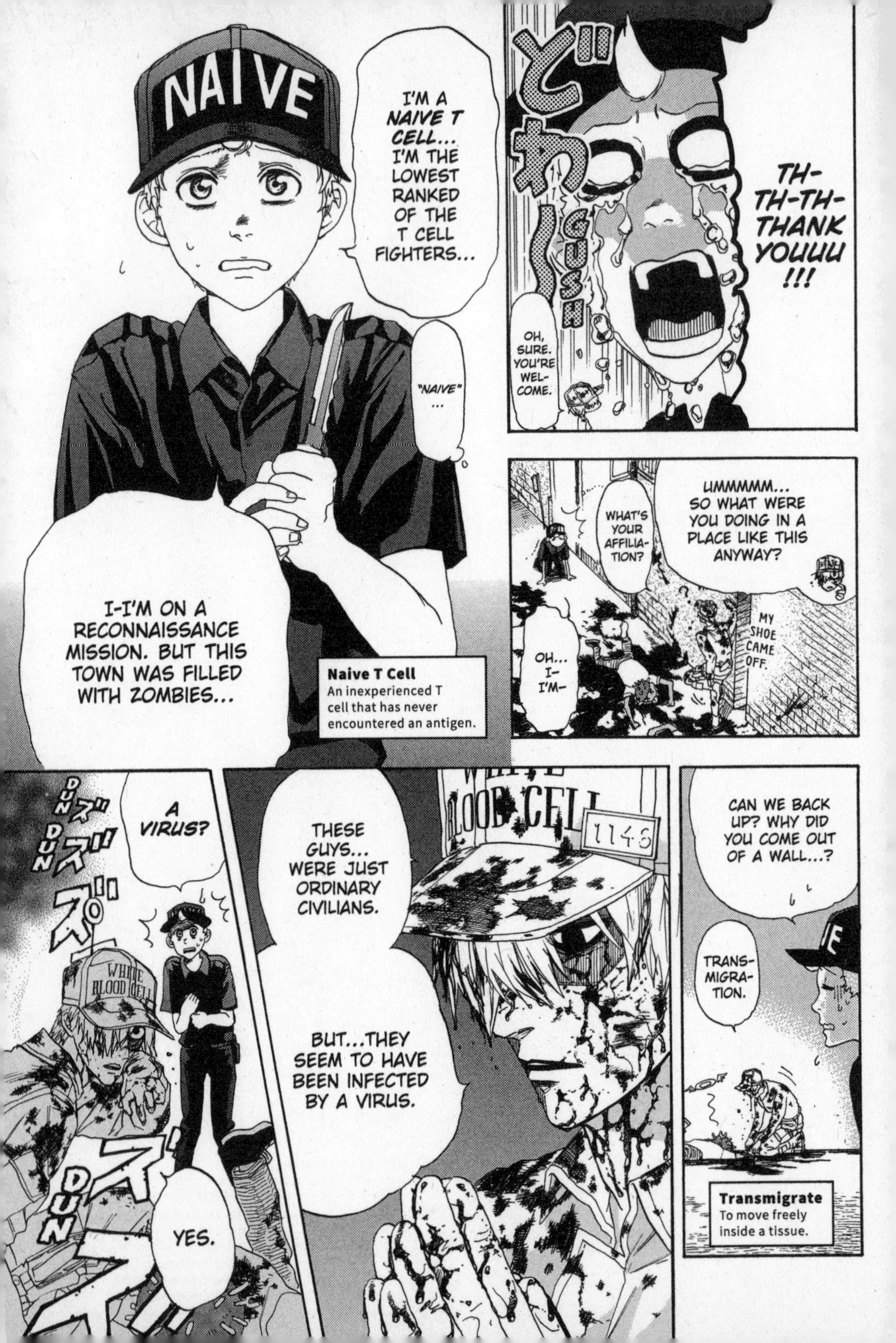
どわ
GUSH
TH-TH-TH-THANK YOUUU!!!
OH, SURE. YOU'RE WEL-COME.
UMMMMM... SO WHAT WERE YOU DOING IN A PLACE LIKE THIS ANYWAY?
MY SHOE CAME OFF.
WHAT'S YOUR AFFILIA-TION?
OH... I— I'M—
I'M A NAIVE T CELL... I'M THE LOWEST RANKED OF THE T CELL FIGHTERS...
"NAIVE"...
I-I'M ON A RECONNAISSANCE MISSION. BUT THIS TOWN WAS FILLED WITH ZOMBIES...
Naive T Cell
An inexperienced T cell that has never encountered an antigen.
CAN WE BACK UP? WHY DID YOU COME OUT OF A WALL...?
TRANS-MIGRA-TION.
Transmigrate
To move freely inside a tissue.
WHITE BLOOD CELL
1146
THESE GUYS... WERE JUST ORDINARY CIVILIANS.
BUT...THEY SEEM TO HAVE BEEN INFECTED BY A VIRUS.
A VIRUS?
DUN DUN
WHITE BLOOD CELL
DUN
YES.

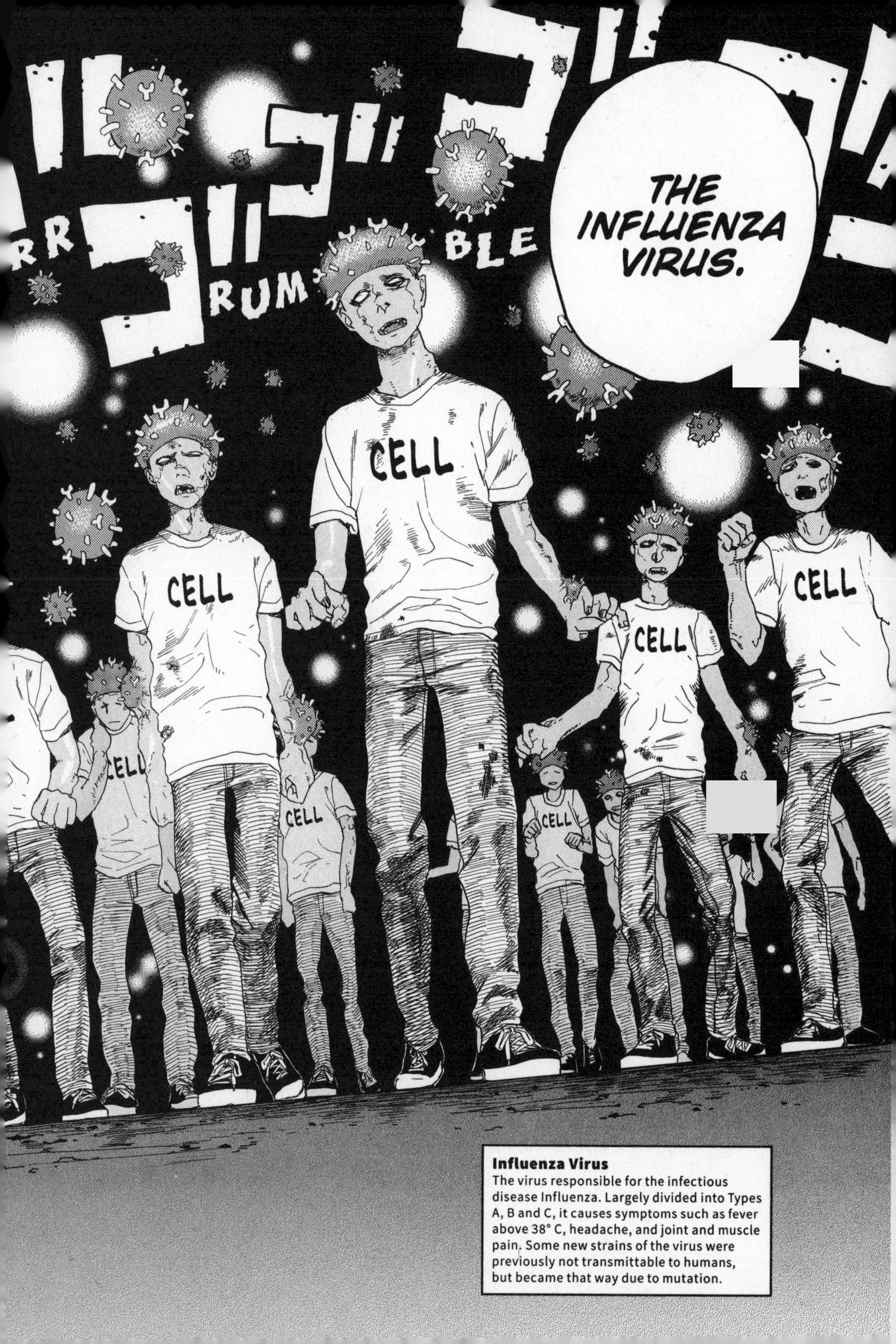
THE INFLUENZA VIRUS.
RR
RUM
BLE
CELL
CELL
CELL
CELL
CELL
CELL
CELL

Influenza Virus
The virus responsible for the infectious disease Influenza. Largely divided into Types A, B and C, it causes symptoms such as fever above 38° C, headache, and joint and muscle pain. Some new strains of the virus were previously not transmittable to humans, but became that way due to mutation.

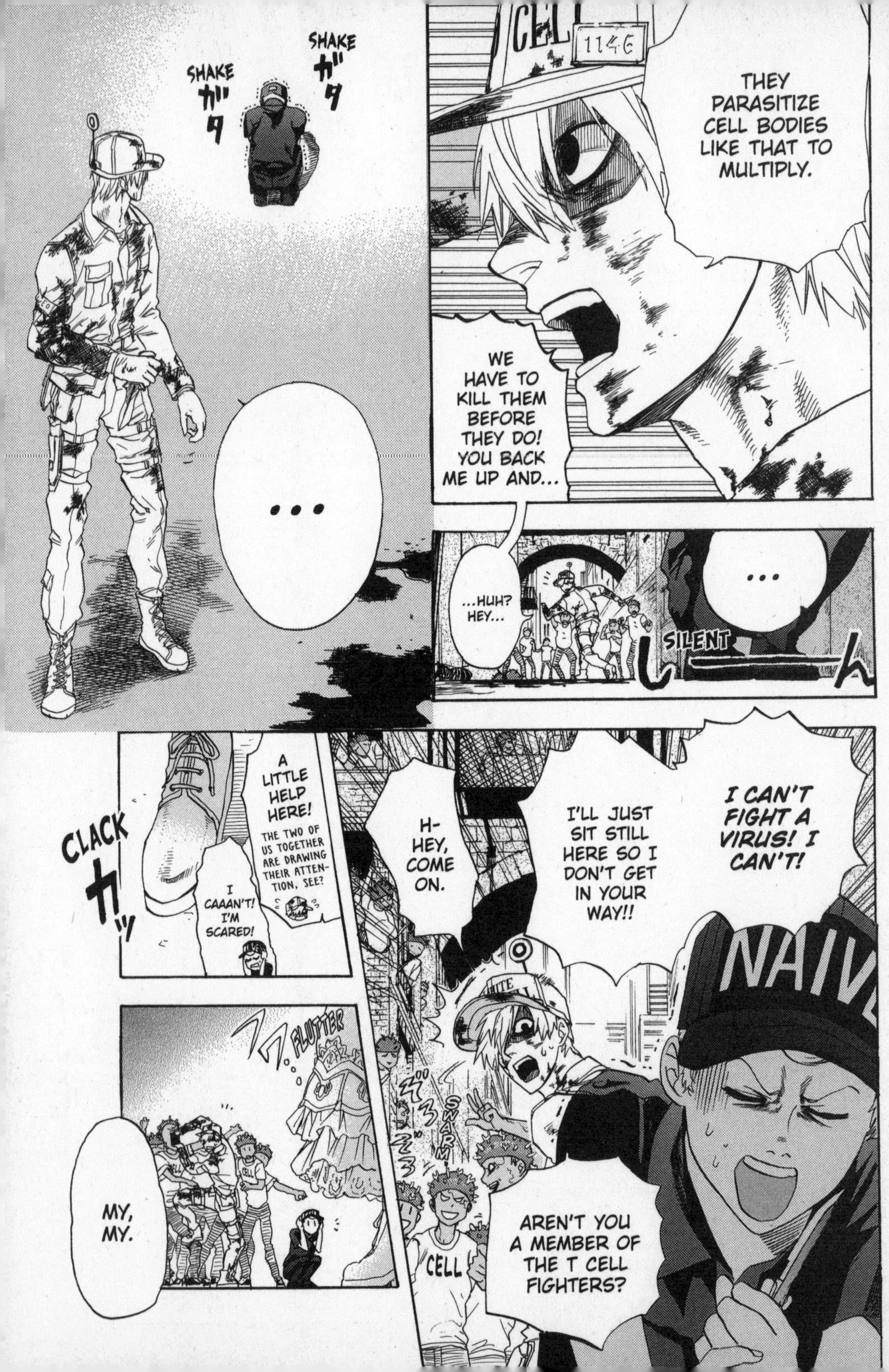
CELL
1146
THEY PARASITIZE CELL BODIES LIKE THAT TO MULTIPLY.
WE HAVE TO KILL THEM BEFORE THEY DO! YOU BACK ME UP AND...
...HUH? HEY...
...
SILENT
SHAKE
SHAKE
...
I CAN'T FIGHT A VIRUS! I CAN'T!
I'LL JUST SIT STILL HERE SO I DON'T GET IN YOUR WAY!!
H-HEY, COME ON.
NAIVE
SWARM
CELL
AREN'T YOU A MEMBER OF THE T CELL FIGHTERS?
A LITTLE HELP HERE!
THE TWO OF US TOGETHER ARE DRAWING THEIR ATTENTION, SEE?
I CAAAN'T! I'M SCARED!
CLACK
FLUTTER
CELL
MY, MY.

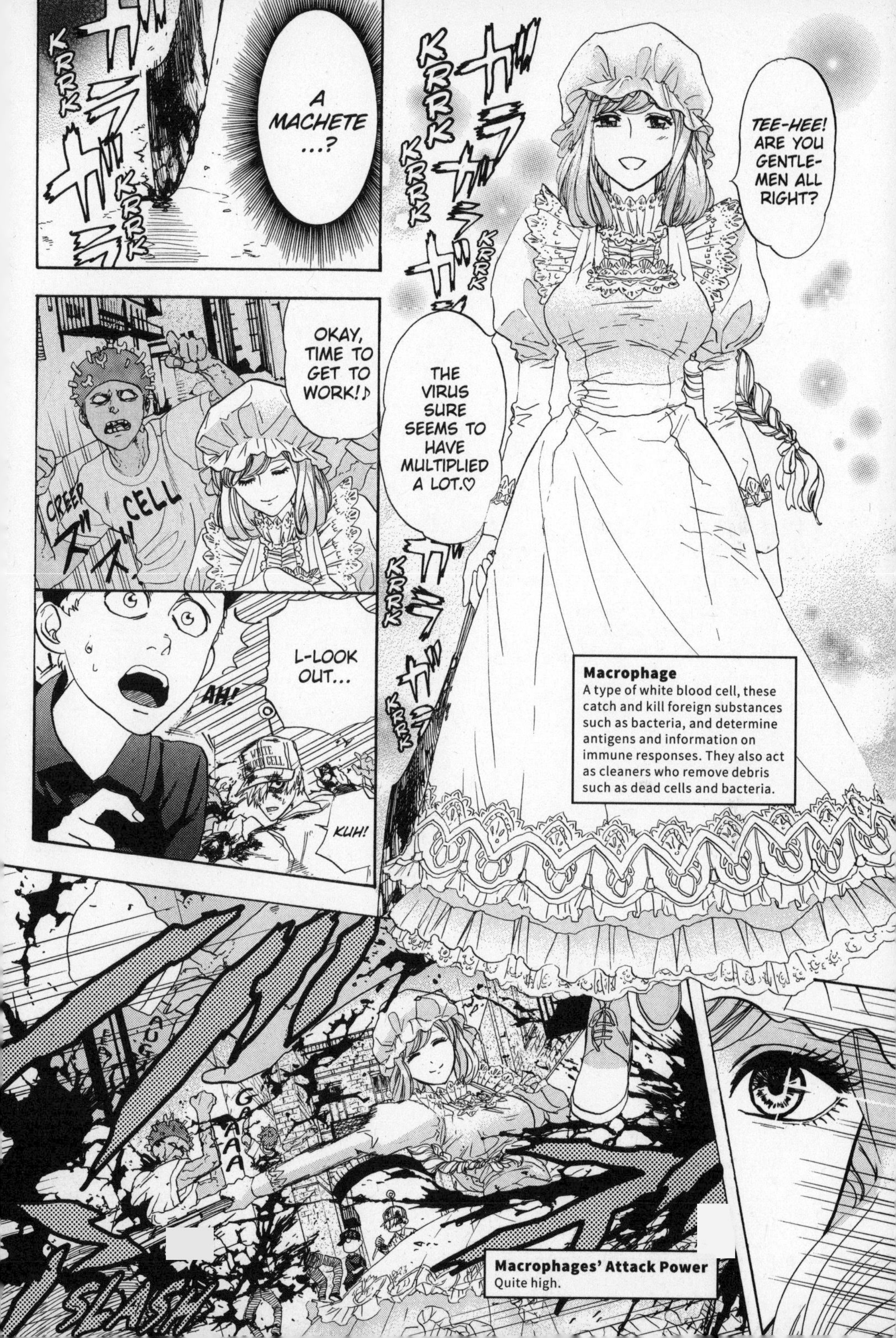

TEE-HEE! ARE YOU GENTLEMEN ALL RIGHT?
KRRK KRRK KRRK
THE VIRUS SURE SEEMS TO HAVE MULTIPLIED A LOT.♡
KRRK KRRK
Macrophage
A type of white blood cell, these catch and kill foreign substances such as bacteria, and determine antigens and information on immune responses. They also act as cleaners who remove debris such as dead cells and bacteria.
A MACHETE ...?
KRRK KRRK
OKAY, TIME TO GET TO WORK!♪
CREEP
CELL
L-LOOK OUT...
AH!
WHITE BLOOD CELL
KUH!
Macrophages' Attack Power
Quite high.
SLASH

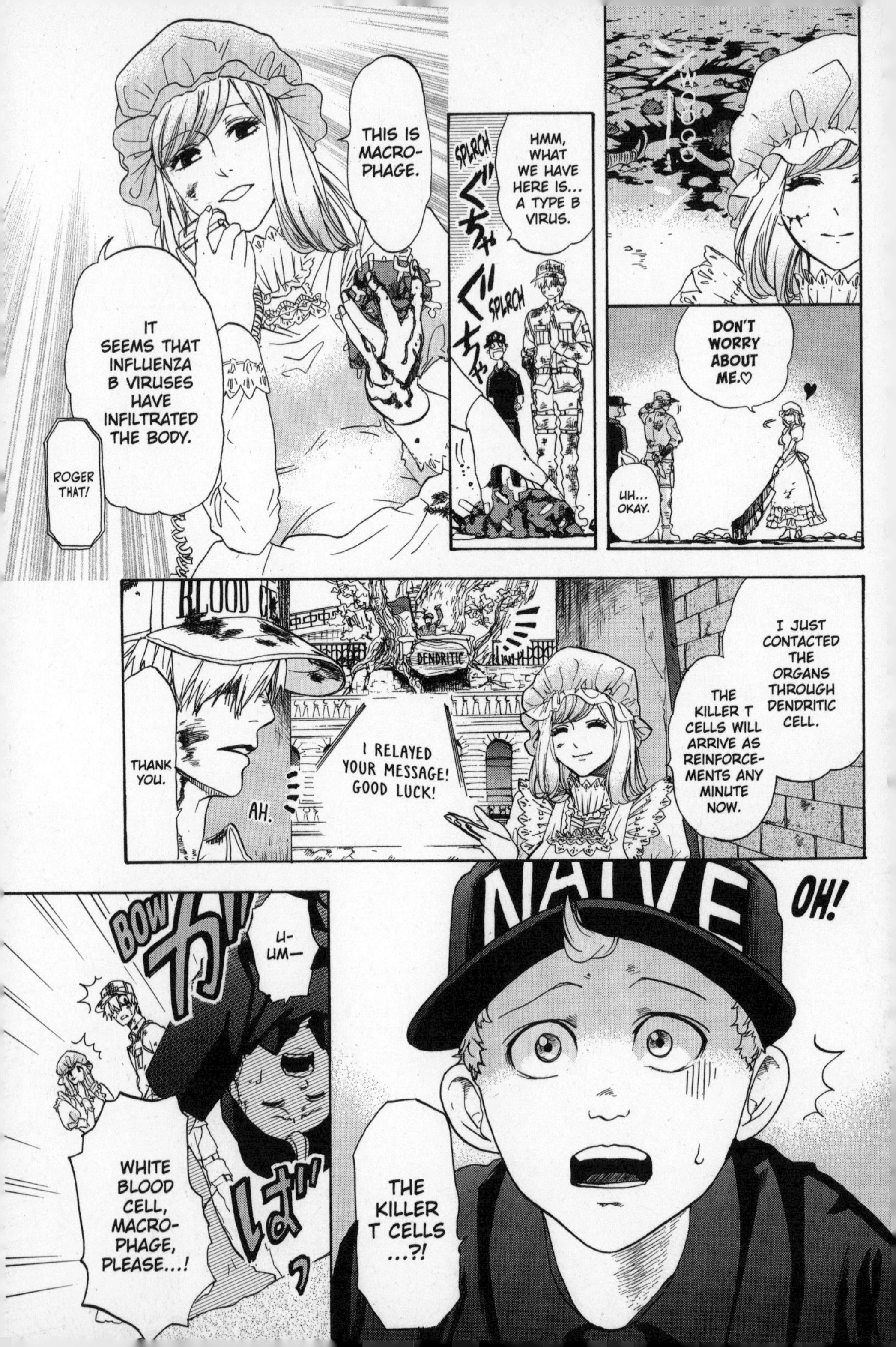

DON'T WORRY ABOUT ME.♡
UH... OKAY.
SPLRCH
SPLRCH
HMM, WHAT WE HAVE HERE IS... A TYPE B VIRUS.
THIS IS MACRO-PHAGE.
IT SEEMS THAT INFLUENZA B VIRUSES HAVE INFILTRATED THE BODY.
ROGER THAT!
I JUST CONTACTED THE ORGANS THROUGH DENDRITIC CELL.
THE KILLER T CELLS WILL ARRIVE AS REINFORCE-MENTS ANY MINUTE NOW.
DENDRITIC
I RELAYED YOUR MESSAGE! GOOD LUCK!
AH.
THANK YOU.
BLOOD CE
NAIVE
OH!
THE KILLER T CELLS ...?!
U-UM—
BOW
WHITE BLOOD CELL, MACRO-PHAGE, PLEASE...!

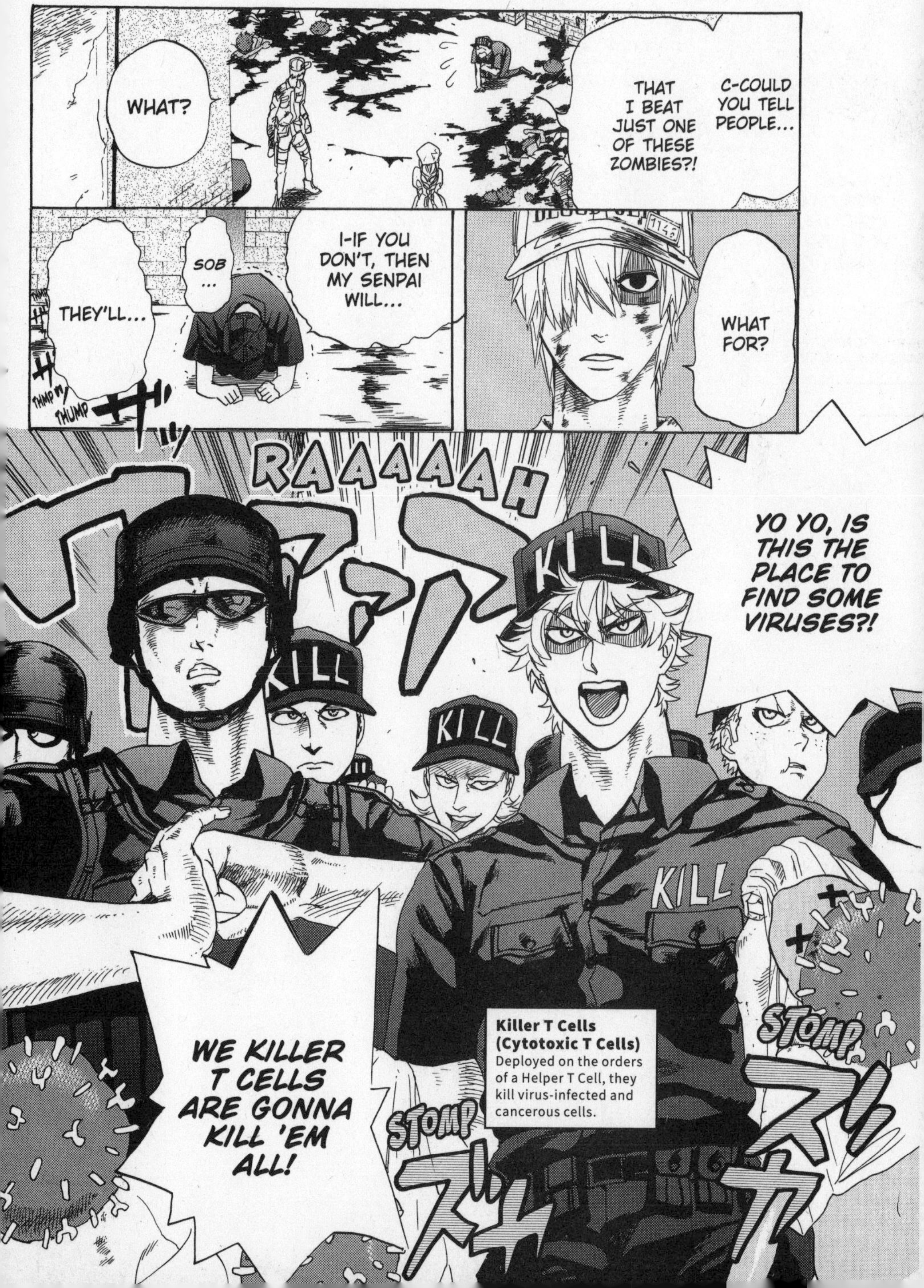

C-COULD YOU TELL PEOPLE...
THAT I BEAT JUST ONE OF THESE ZOMBIES?!
WHAT?
WHAT FOR?
I-IF YOU DON'T, THEN MY SENPAI WILL...
SOB...
THEY'LL...
THUMP THUMP THUMP
RAAAAAAH
YO YO, IS THIS THE PLACE TO FIND SOME VIRUSES?!
WE KILLER T CELLS ARE GONNA KILL 'EM ALL!
Killer T Cells (Cytotoxic T Cells)
Deployed on the orders of a Helper T Cell, they kill virus-infected and cancerous cells.
STOMP
STOMP

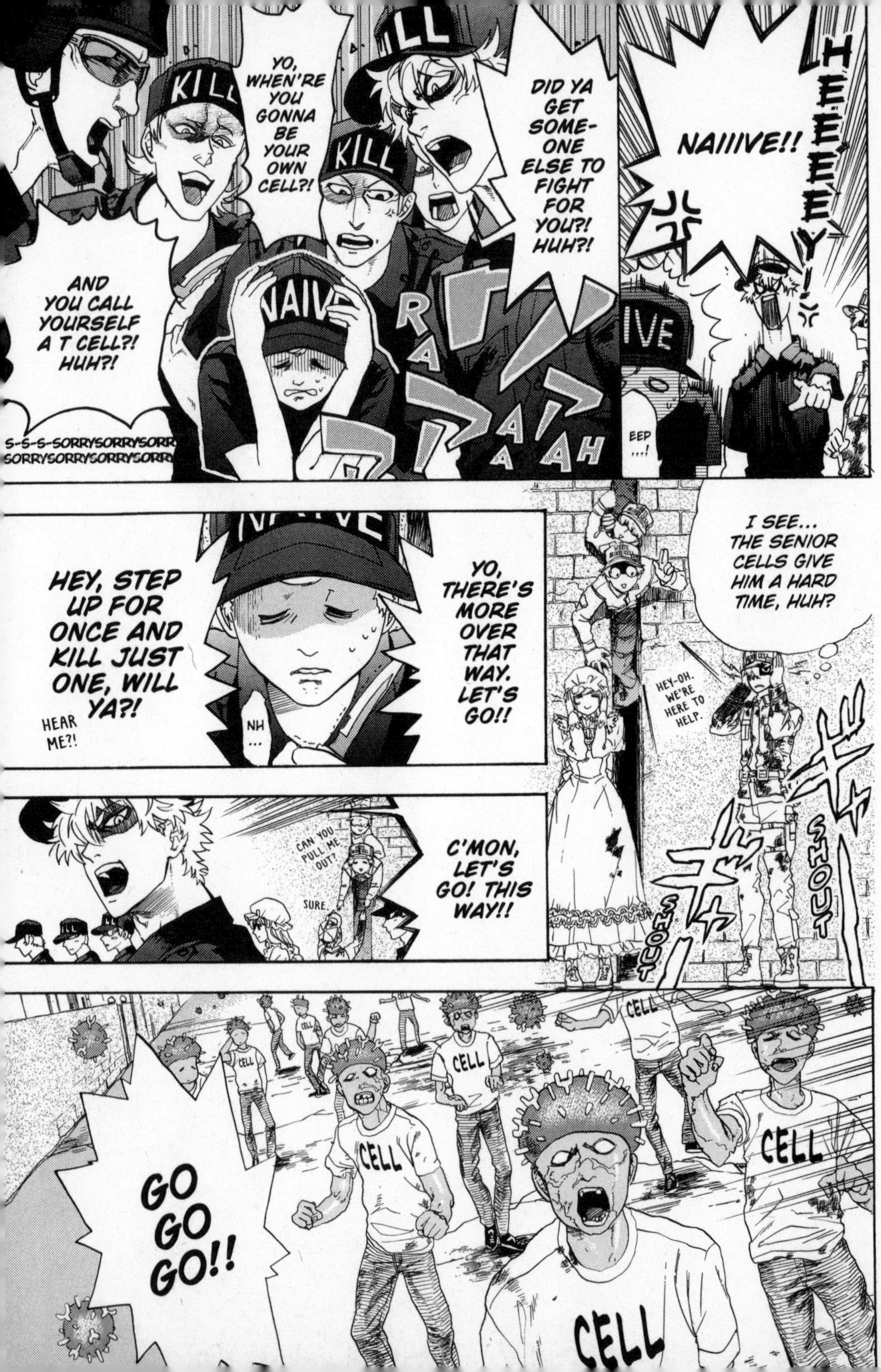
HEEEEEY!!
NAIIIVE!!
EEP...!
DID YA GET SOMEONE ELSE TO FIGHT FOR YOU?! HUH?!
RAAAAAAH
YO, WHEN'RE YOU GONNA BE YOUR OWN CELL?!
AND YOU CALL YOURSELF A T CELL?! HUH?!
S-S-S-SORRYSORRYSORR
SORRYSORRYSORRYSORR
I SEE... THE SENIOR CELLS GIVE HIM A HARD TIME, HUH?
HEY-OH. WE'RE HERE TO HELP.
SHOUT
SHOUT
YO, THERE'S MORE OVER THAT WAY. LET'S GO!!
NH...
HEY, STEP UP FOR ONCE AND KILL JUST ONE, WILL YA?!
HEAR ME?!
C'MON, LET'S GO! THIS WAY!!
CAN YOU PULL ME OUT?
SURE.
GO GO GO!!

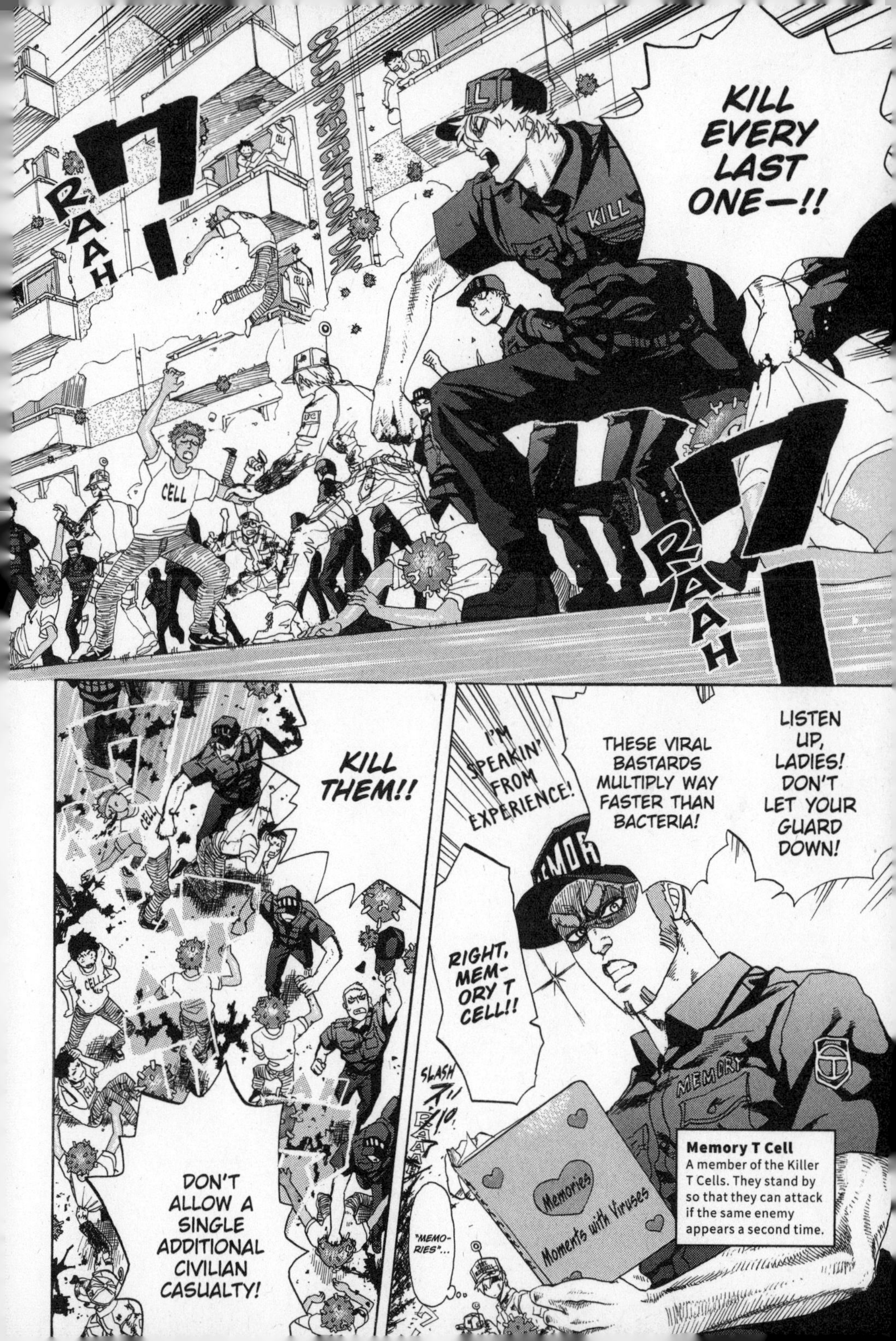
KILL EVERY LAST ONE—!!
RAAH
RAAH
LISTEN UP, LADIES! DON'T LET YOUR GUARD DOWN!
THESE VIRAL BASTARDS MULTIPLY WAY FASTER THAN BACTERIA!
I'M SPEAKIN' FROM EXPERIENCE!
RIGHT, MEMORY T CELL!!
SLASH
"MEMORIES"...
Memories
Moments with Viruses
Memory T Cell
A member of the Killer T Cells. They stand by so that they can attack if the same enemy appears a second time.
KILL THEM!!
DON'T ALLOW A SINGLE ADDITIONAL CIVILIAN CASUALTY!

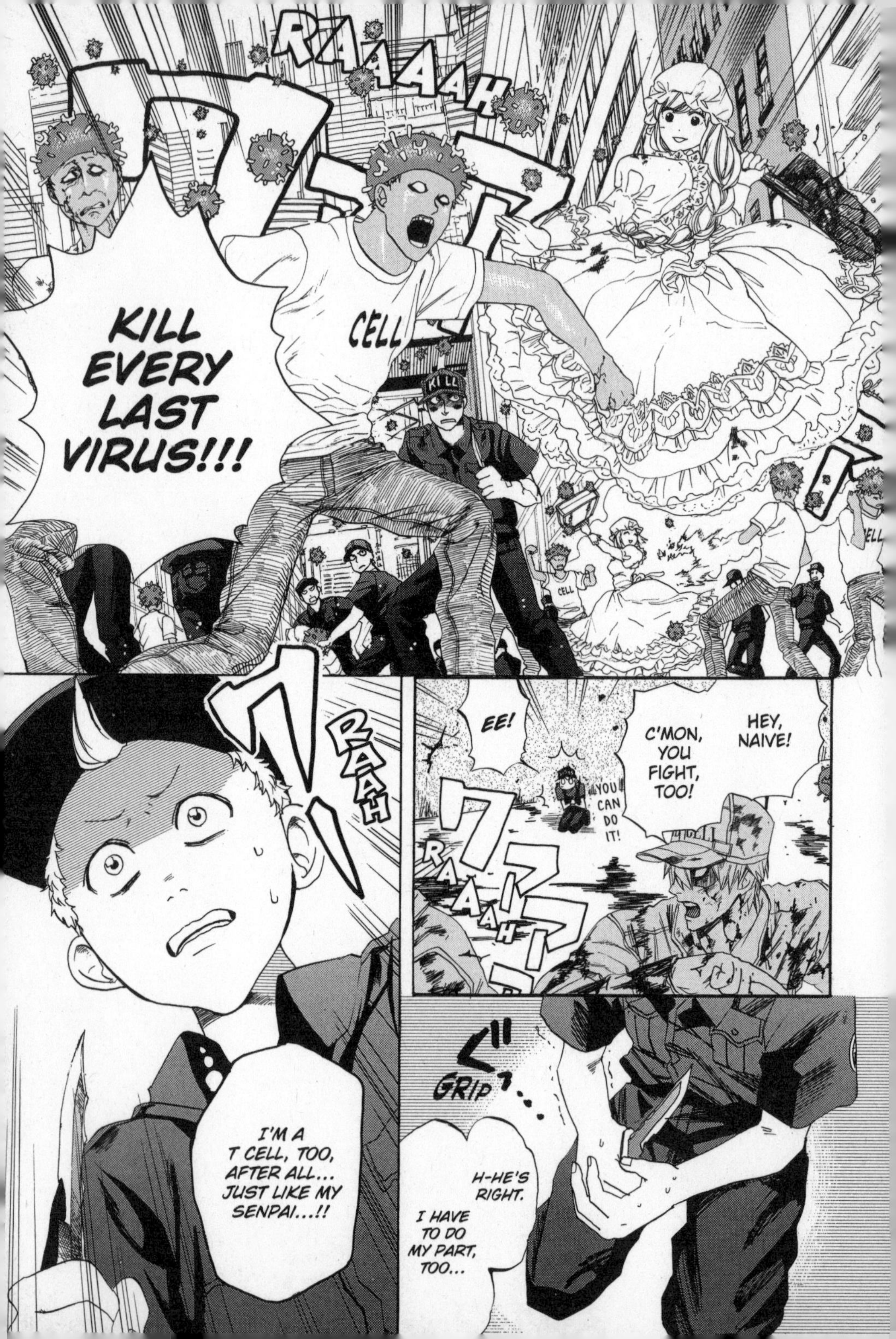
RAAAAH
KILL EVERY LAST VIRUS!!!
HEY, NAIVE!
C'MON, YOU FIGHT, TOO!
EE!
YOU CAN DO IT!
RAAAAH
RAAAH
GRIP
H-HE'S RIGHT.
I HAVE TO DO MY PART, TOO...
I'M A T CELL, TOO, AFTER ALL... JUST LIKE MY SENPAI...!!

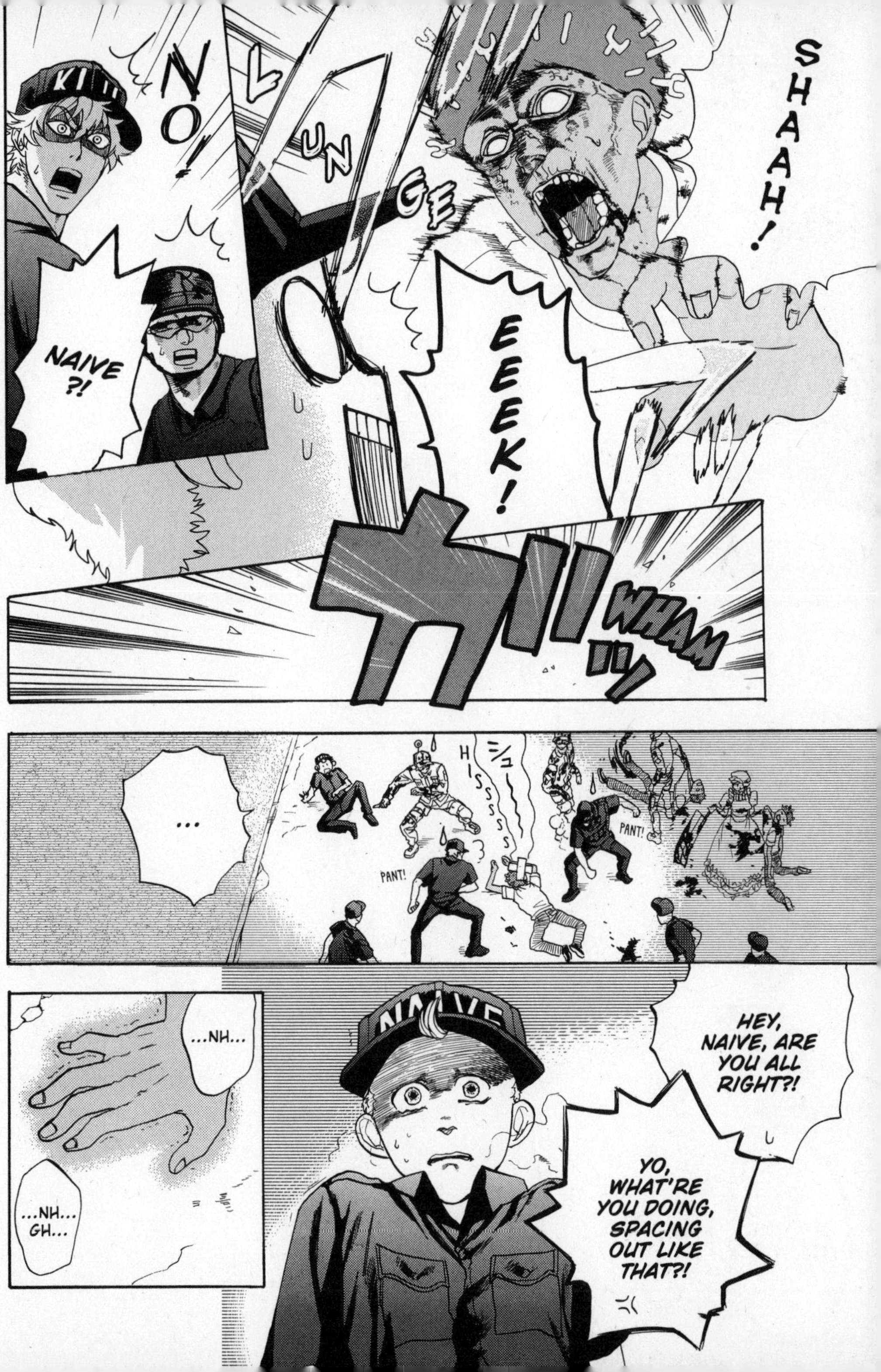
SHAAH!
LUNGE
EEEEK!
NO!
NAIVE ?!
カッ
WHAM
...
HISSSSS
シュー
PANT!
PANT!
HEY, NAIVE, ARE YOU ALL RIGHT?!
YO, WHAT'RE YOU DOING, SPACING OUT LIKE THAT?!
...NH...
...NH... GH...

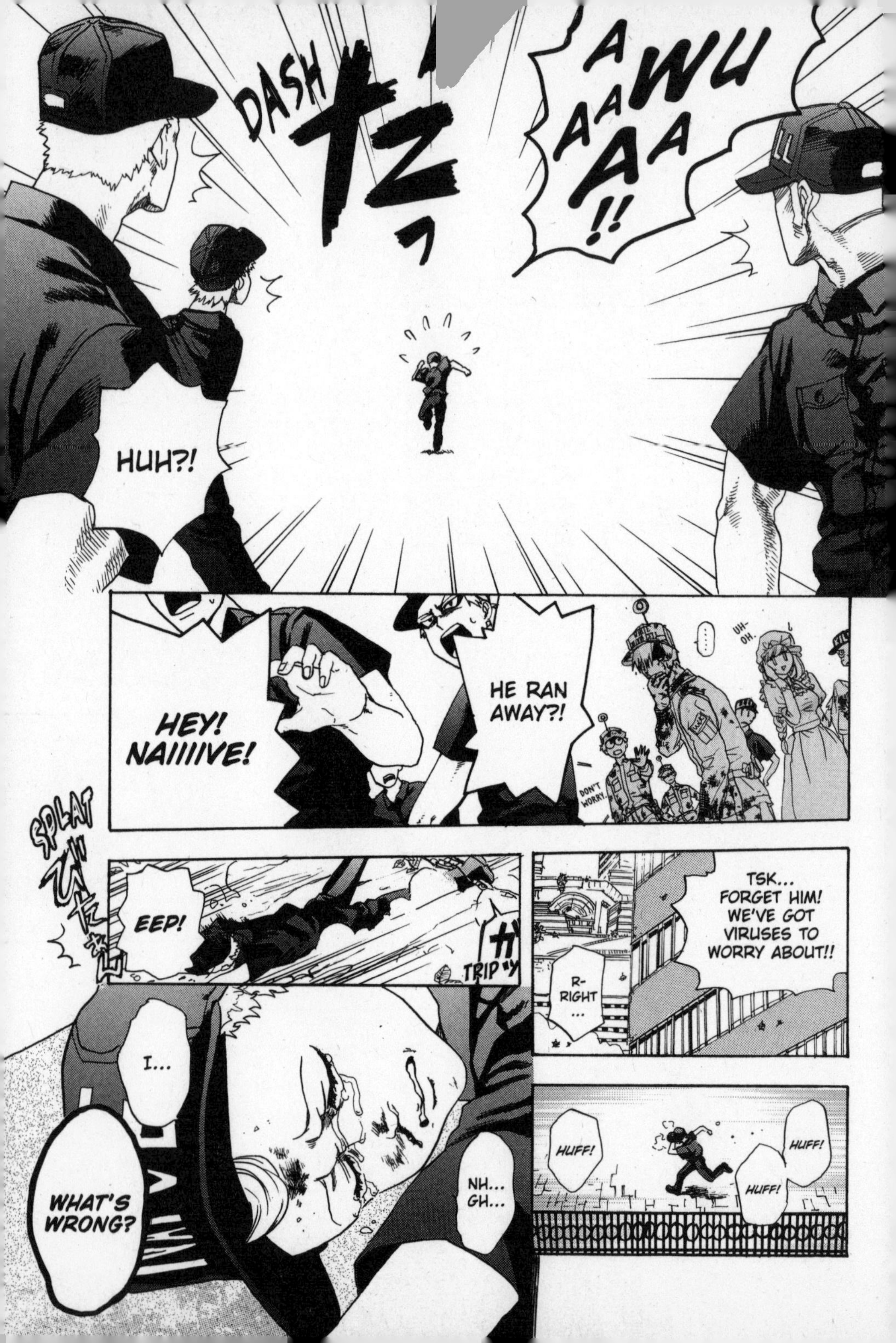
AAAWUAAAA!!
DASH
HUH?!
UH-OH.
...
DON'T WORRY.
HE RAN AWAY?!
HEY! NAIIIIVE!
TSK... FORGET HIM! WE'VE GOT VIRUSES TO WORRY ABOUT!!
R-RIGHT...
TRIP
EEP!
SPLAT
HUFF!
HUFF!
HUFF!
NH... GH...
I...
WHAT'S WRONG?

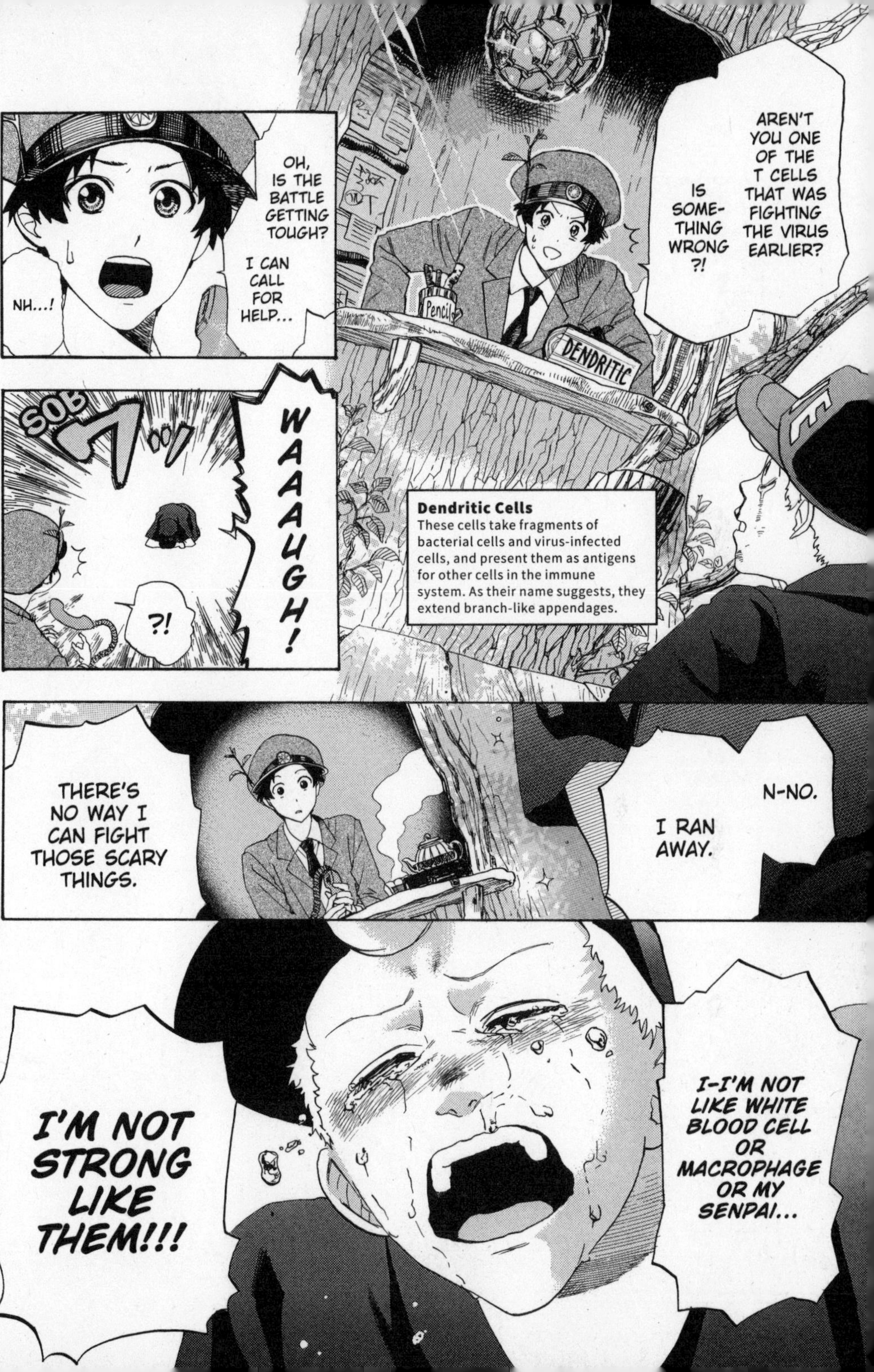
AREN'T YOU ONE OF THE T CELLS THAT WAS FIGHTING THE VIRUS EARLIER?
IS SOMETHING WRONG?!
DENDRITIC
Pencil
OH, IS THE BATTLE GETTING TOUGH?
I CAN CALL FOR HELP...
NH...!
Dendritic Cells
These cells take fragments of bacterial cells and virus-infected cells, and present them as antigens for other cells in the immune system. As their name suggests, they extend branch-like appendages.
WAAAAUGH!
SOB
?!
N-NO.
I RAN AWAY.
THERE'S NO WAY I CAN FIGHT THOSE SCARY THINGS.
I-I'M NOT LIKE WHITE BLOOD CELL OR MACROPHAGE OR MY SENPAI...
I'M NOT STRONG LIKE THEM!!!

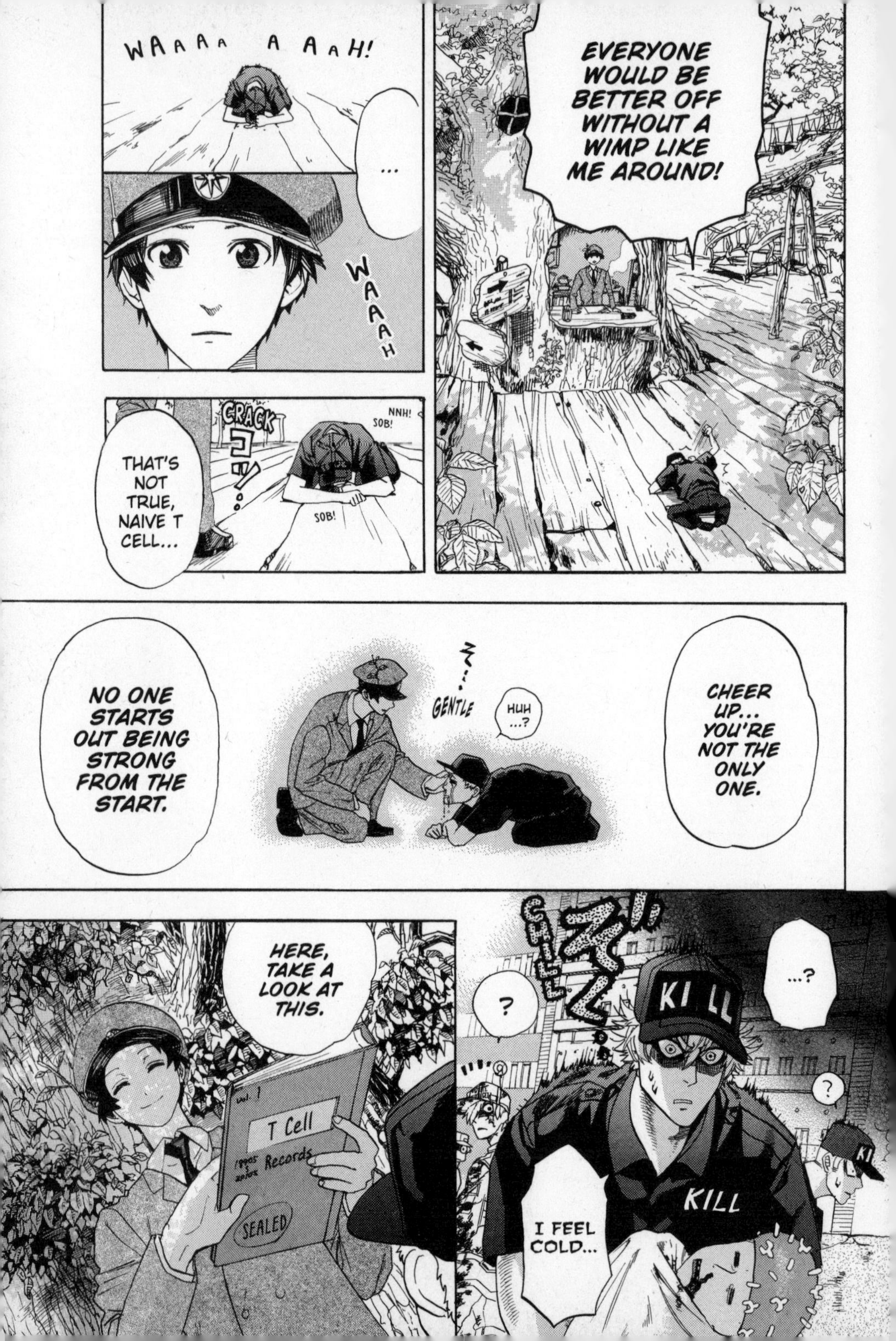
EVERYONE WOULD BE BETTER OFF WITHOUT A WIMP LIKE ME AROUND!
WAAAA AAAH!
...
WAAAAH
CRACK
NNH! SOB!
THAT'S NOT TRUE, NAIVE T CELL...
SOB!
CHEER UP... YOU'RE NOT THE ONLY ONE.
HUH ...?
GENTLE
NO ONE STARTS OUT BEING STRONG FROM THE START.
...?
CHILL
KILL
?
?
KILL
I FEEL COLD...
HERE, TAKE A LOOK AT THIS.
vol. 1
T Cell
Records
SEALED

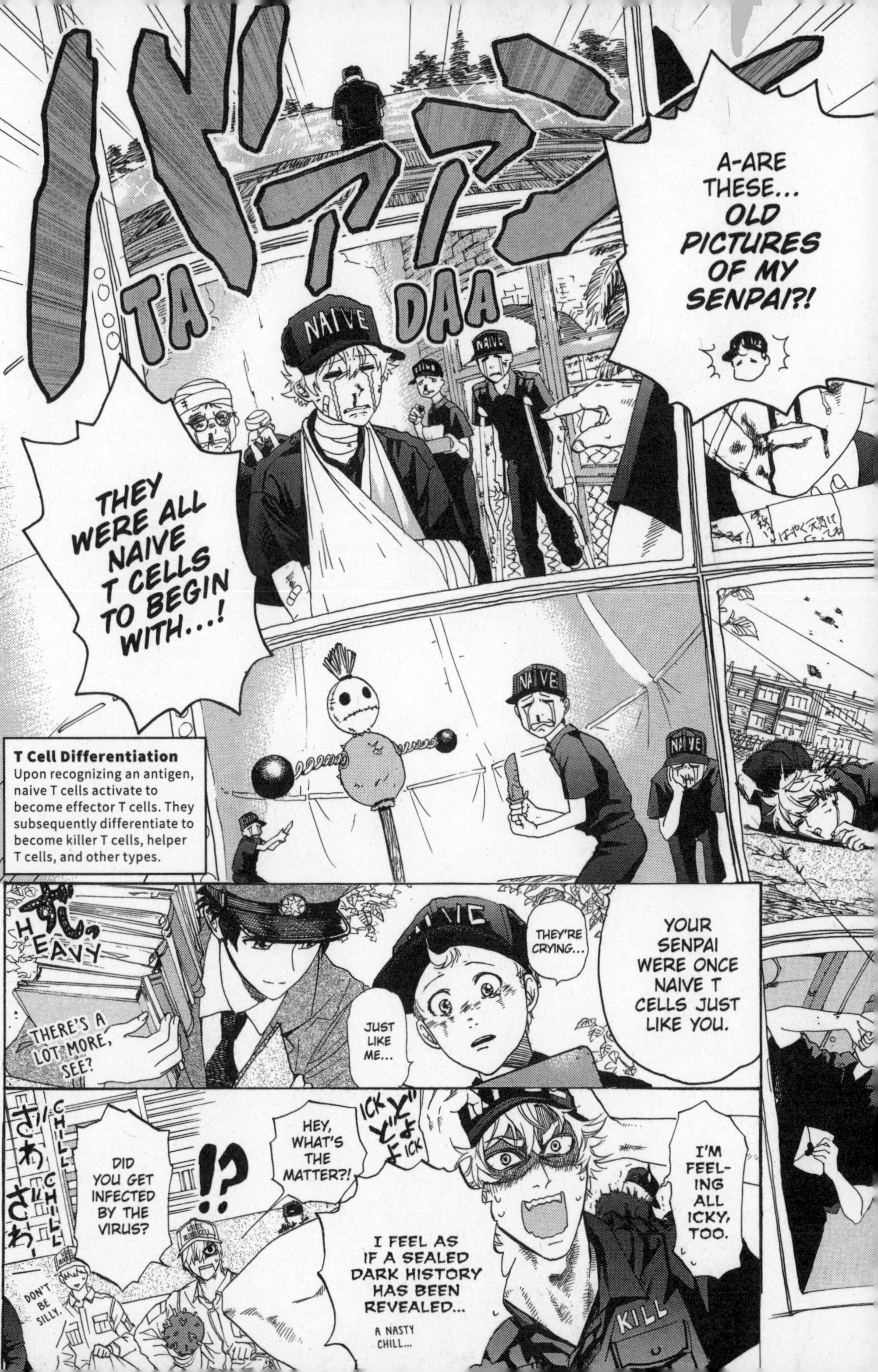

A-ARE THESE... OLD PICTURES OF MY SENPAI?!
TA DAA
THEY WERE ALL NAIVE T CELLS TO BEGIN WITH...!
NAIVE
T Cell Differentiation
Upon recognizing an antigen, naive T cells activate to become effector T cells. They subsequently differentiate to become killer T cells, helper T cells, and other types.
YOUR SENPAI WERE ONCE NAIVE T CELLS JUST LIKE YOU.
THEY'RE CRYING...
JUST LIKE ME...
HEAVY
THERE'S A LOT MORE, SEE?
I'M FEELING ALL ICKY, TOO.
I FEEL AS IF A SEALED DARK HISTORY HAS BEEN REVEALED...
A NASTY CHILL...
KILL
ICK ICK
HEY, WHAT'S THE MATTER?!
!?
DID YOU GET INFECTED BY THE VIRUS?
CHILL CHILL
DON'T BE SILLY.

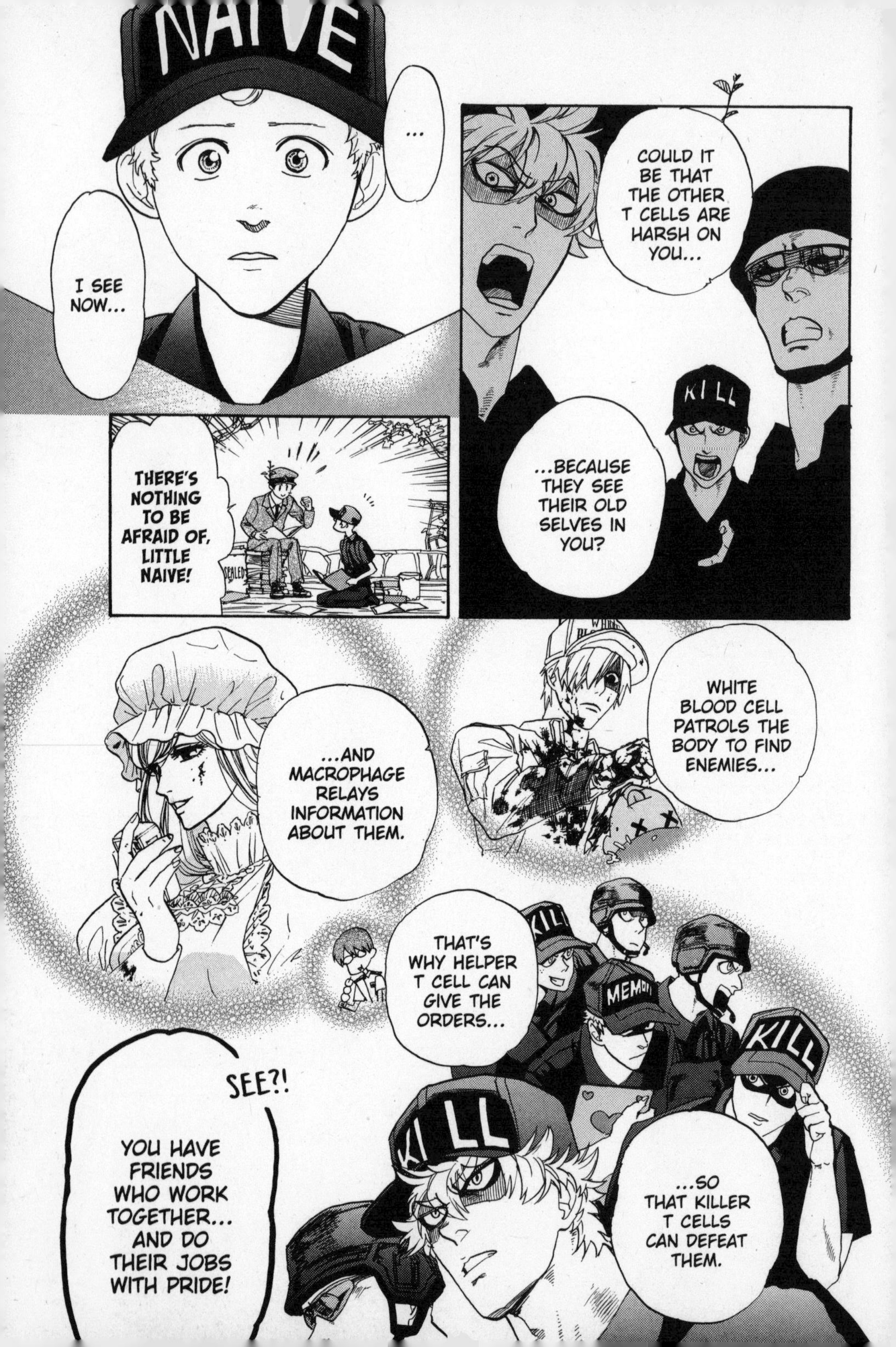
COULD IT BE THAT THE OTHER T CELLS ARE HARSH ON YOU...
...BECAUSE THEY SEE THEIR OLD SELVES IN YOU?
...
I SEE NOW...
THERE'S NOTHING TO BE AFRAID OF, LITTLE NAIVE!
WHITE BLOOD CELL PATROLS THE BODY TO FIND ENEMIES...
...AND MACROPHAGE RELAYS INFORMATION ABOUT THEM.
THAT'S WHY HELPER T CELL CAN GIVE THE ORDERS...
...SO THAT KILLER T CELLS CAN DEFEAT THEM.
SEE?!
YOU HAVE FRIENDS WHO WORK TOGETHER... AND DO THEIR JOBS WITH PRIDE!

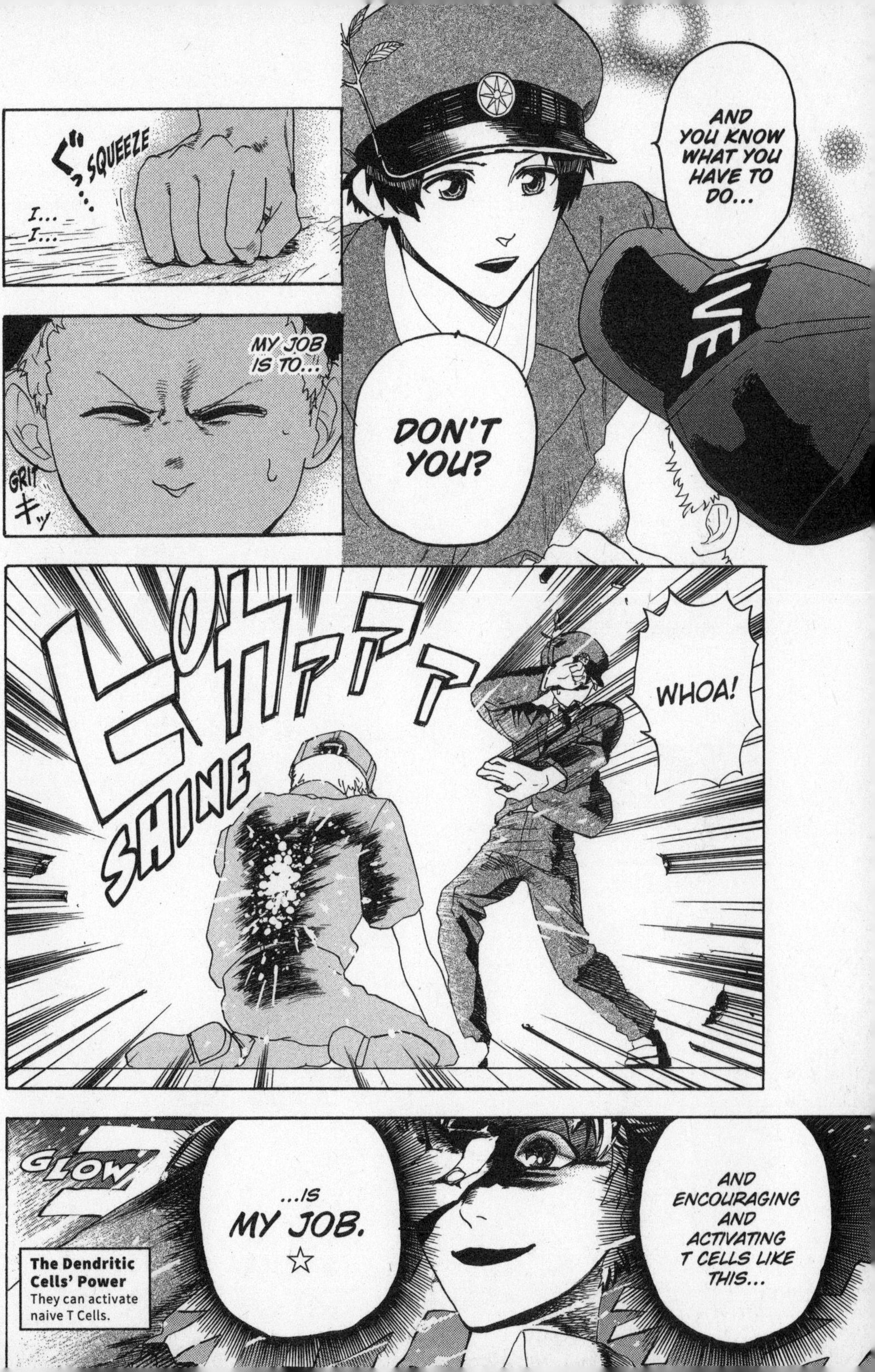
AND YOU KNOW WHAT YOU HAVE TO DO...
DON'T YOU?
SQUEEZE
I... I...
MY JOB IS TO...
GRIT
WHOA!
SHINE
AND ENCOURAGING AND ACTIVATING T CELLS LIKE THIS...
...IS MY JOB. ☆
GLOW
The Dendritic Cells' Power
They can activate naive T Cells.

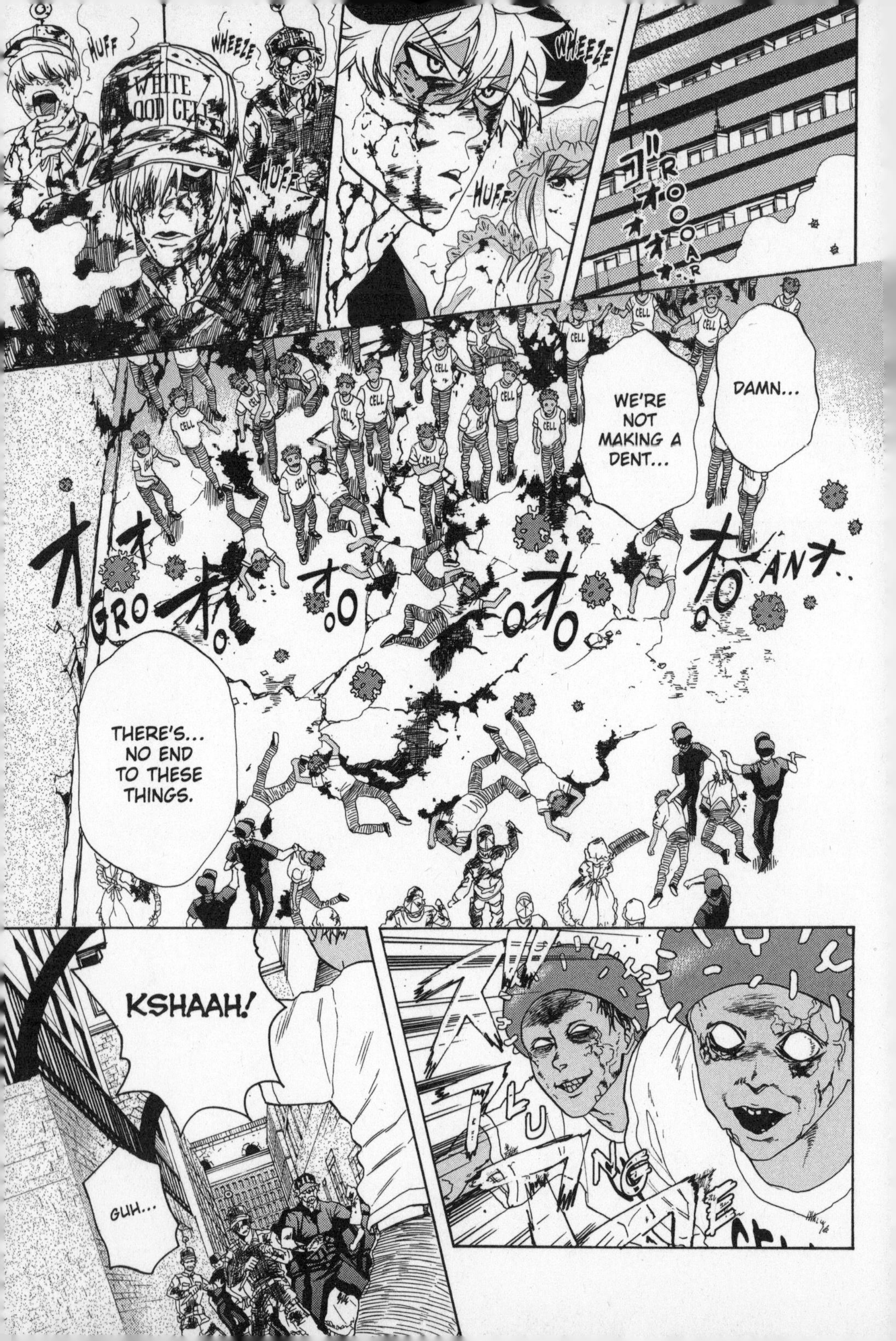
ROOOAR
WHEEZE
HUFF
HUFF
WHEEZE
HUFF
WHITE BLOOD CELL
DAMN...
WE'RE NOT MAKING A DENT...
GROOOOOAN
THERE'S... NO END TO THESE THINGS.
KSHAAH!
GUH...

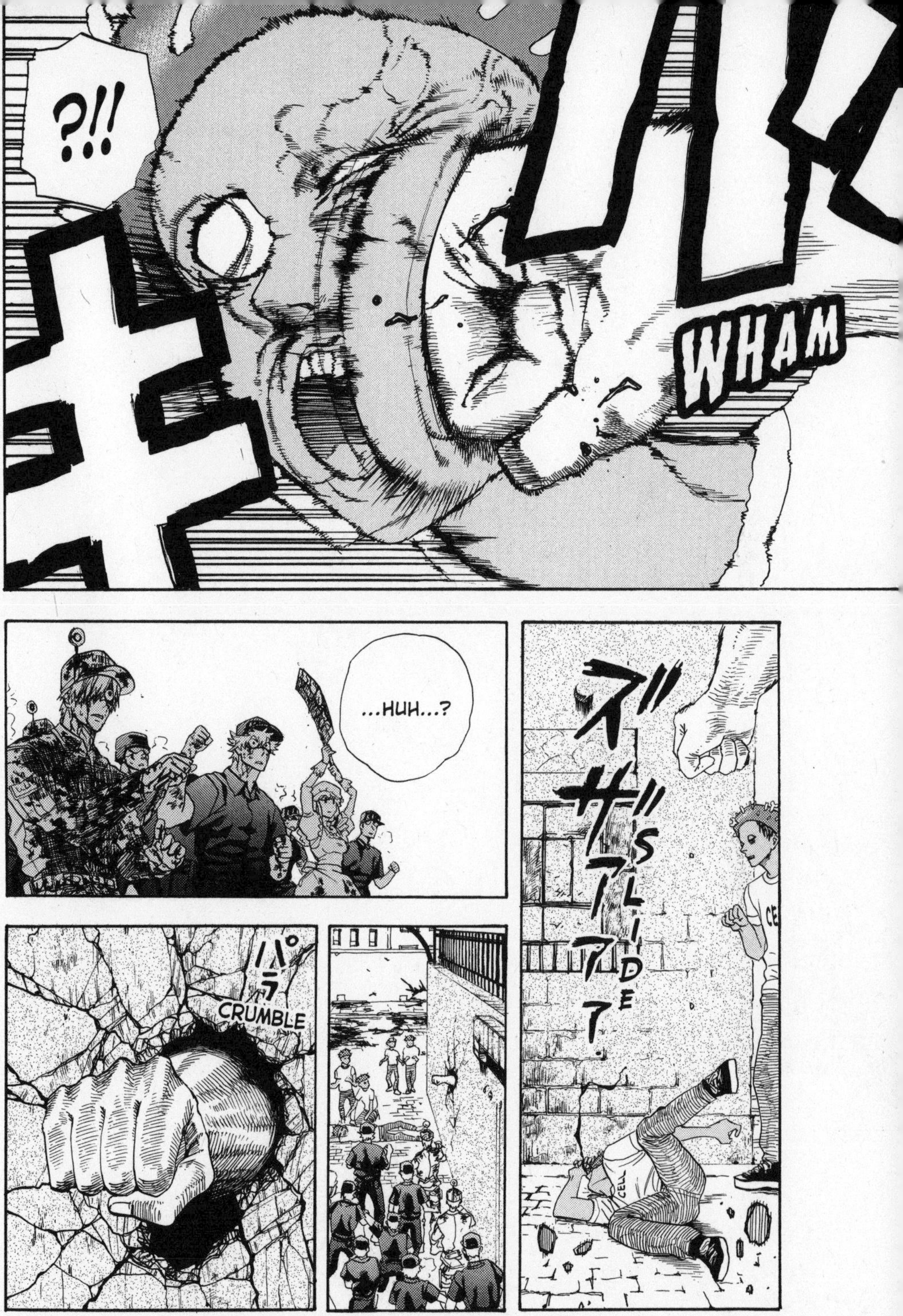
?!!
WHAM
SLIDE
...HUH...?
パラ
CRUMBLE

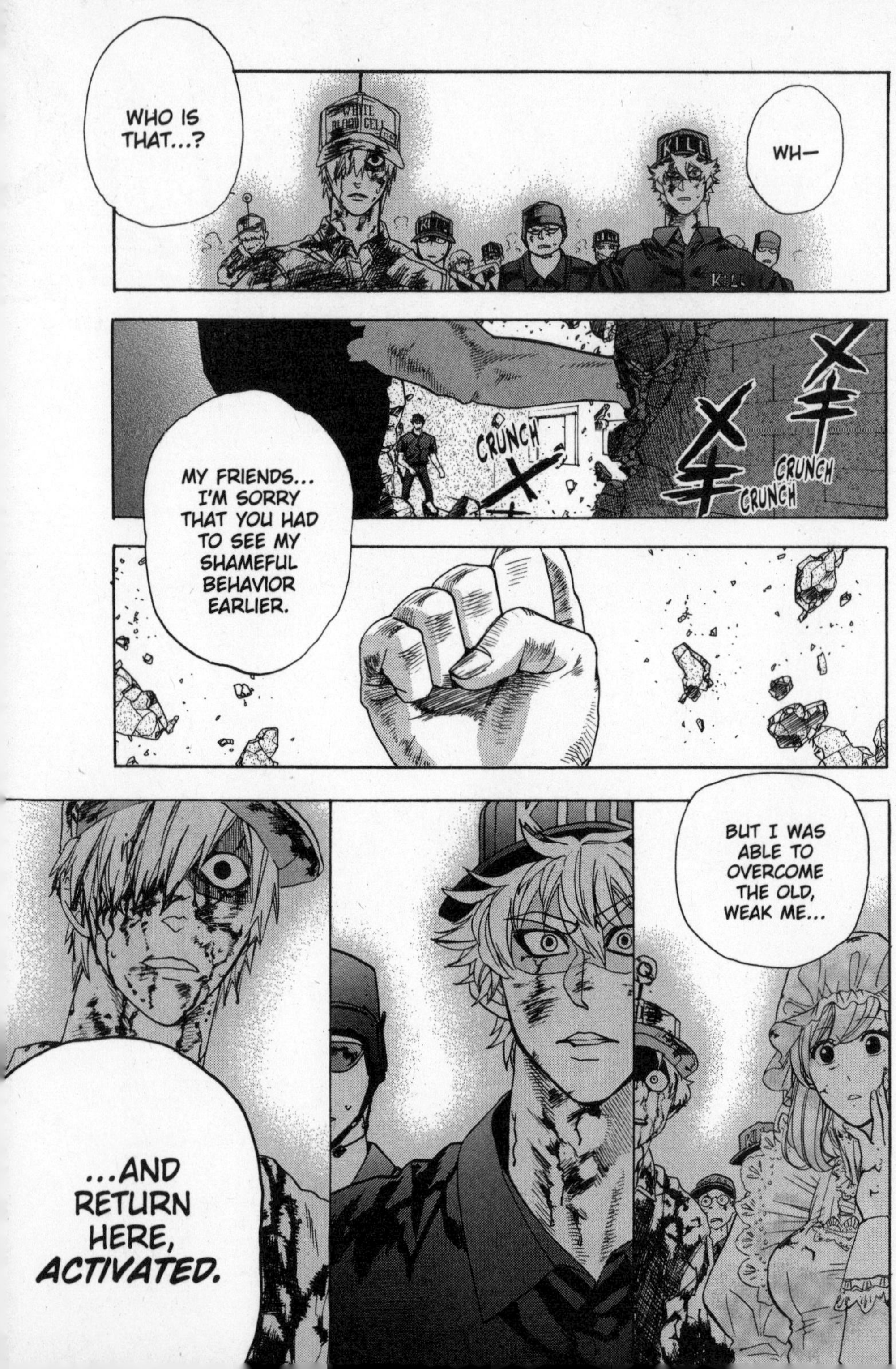
WH—
WHO IS THAT...?
CRUNCH
CRUNCH
CRUNCH
MY FRIENDS... I'M SORRY THAT YOU HAD TO SEE MY SHAMEFUL BEHAVIOR EARLIER.
BUT I WAS ABLE TO OVERCOME THE OLD, WEAK ME...
...AND RETURN HERE, ACTIVATED.

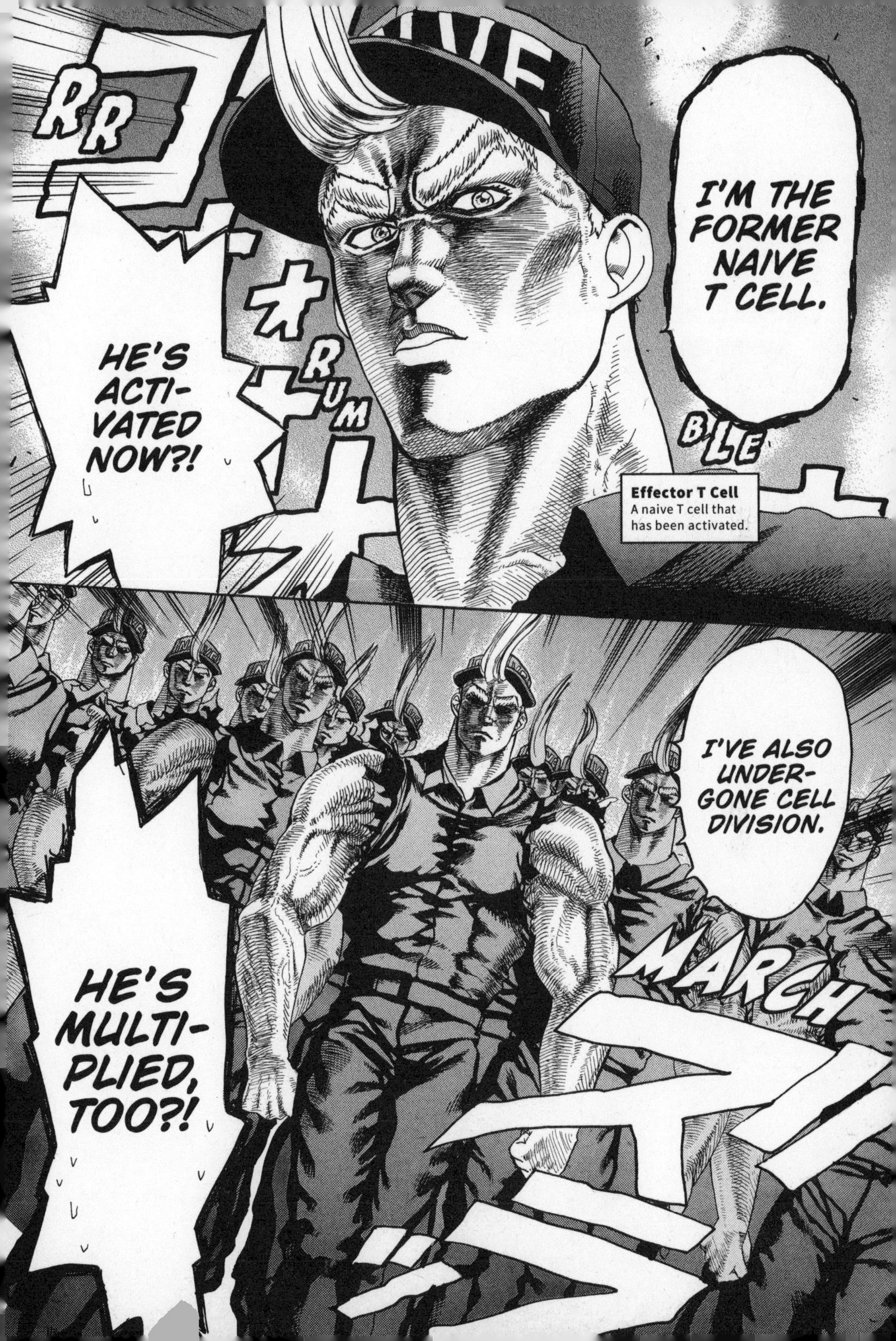

I'M THE FORMER NAIVE T CELL.
RR
RUM
BLE
HE'S ACTI-VATED NOW?!
Effector T Cell
A naive T cell that has been activated.
I'VE ALSO UNDER-GONE CELL DIVISION.
MARCH
HE'S MULTI-PLIED, TOO?!

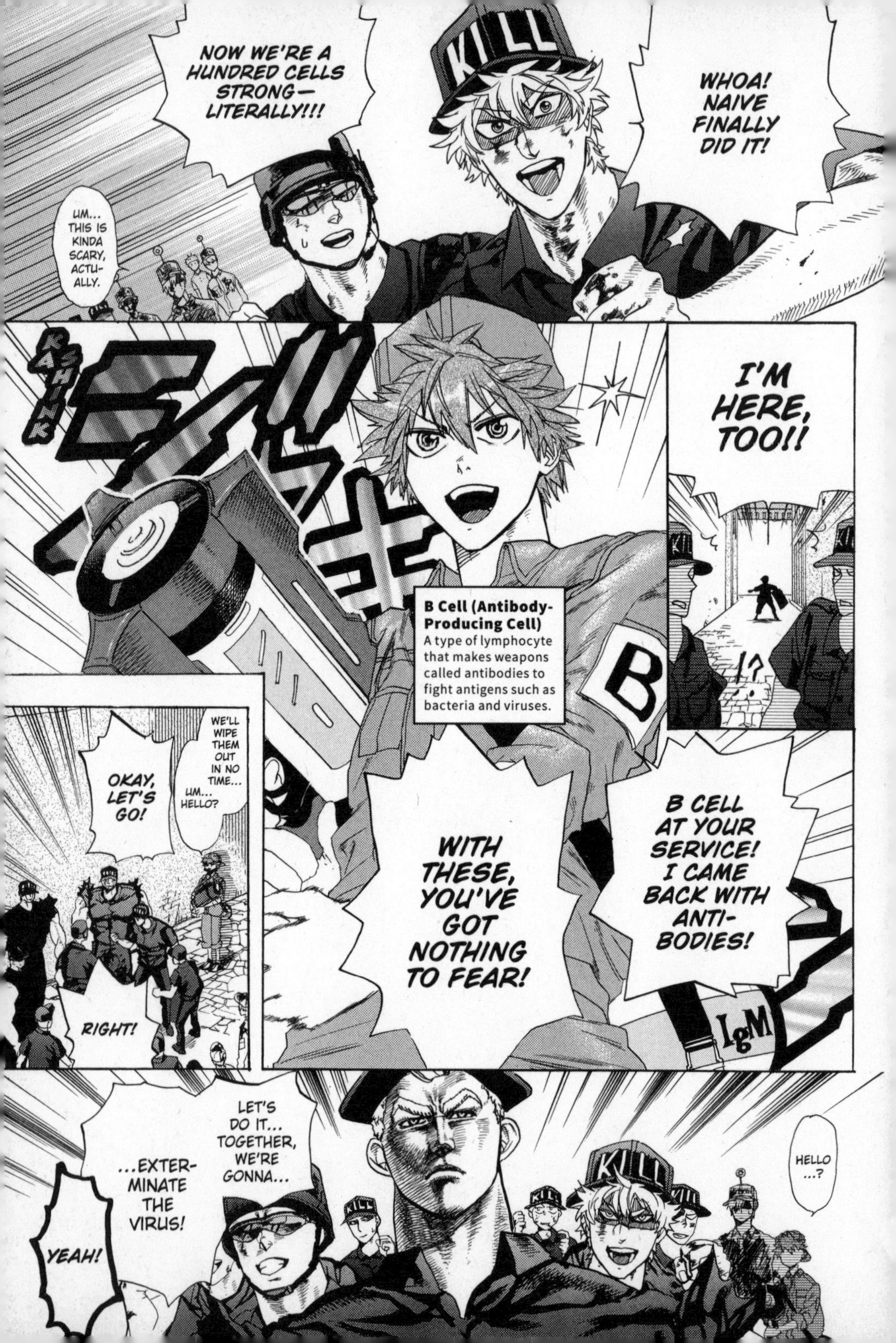
WHOA! NAIVE FINALLY DID IT!
NOW WE'RE A HUNDRED CELLS STRONG—LITERALLY!!!
KILL
UM... THIS IS KINDA SCARY, ACTUALLY.
I'M HERE, TOO!!
!?
B Cell (Antibody-Producing Cell)
A type of lymphocyte that makes weapons called antibodies to fight antigens such as bacteria and viruses.
B CELL AT YOUR SERVICE! I CAME BACK WITH ANTI-BODIES!
WITH THESE, YOU'VE GOT NOTHING TO FEAR!
IgM
WE'LL WIPE THEM OUT IN NO TIME...
UM... HELLO?
OKAY, LET'S GO!
RIGHT!
HELLO ...?
LET'S DO IT... TOGETHER, WE'RE GONNA...
...EXTER-MINATE THE VIRUS!
YEAH!

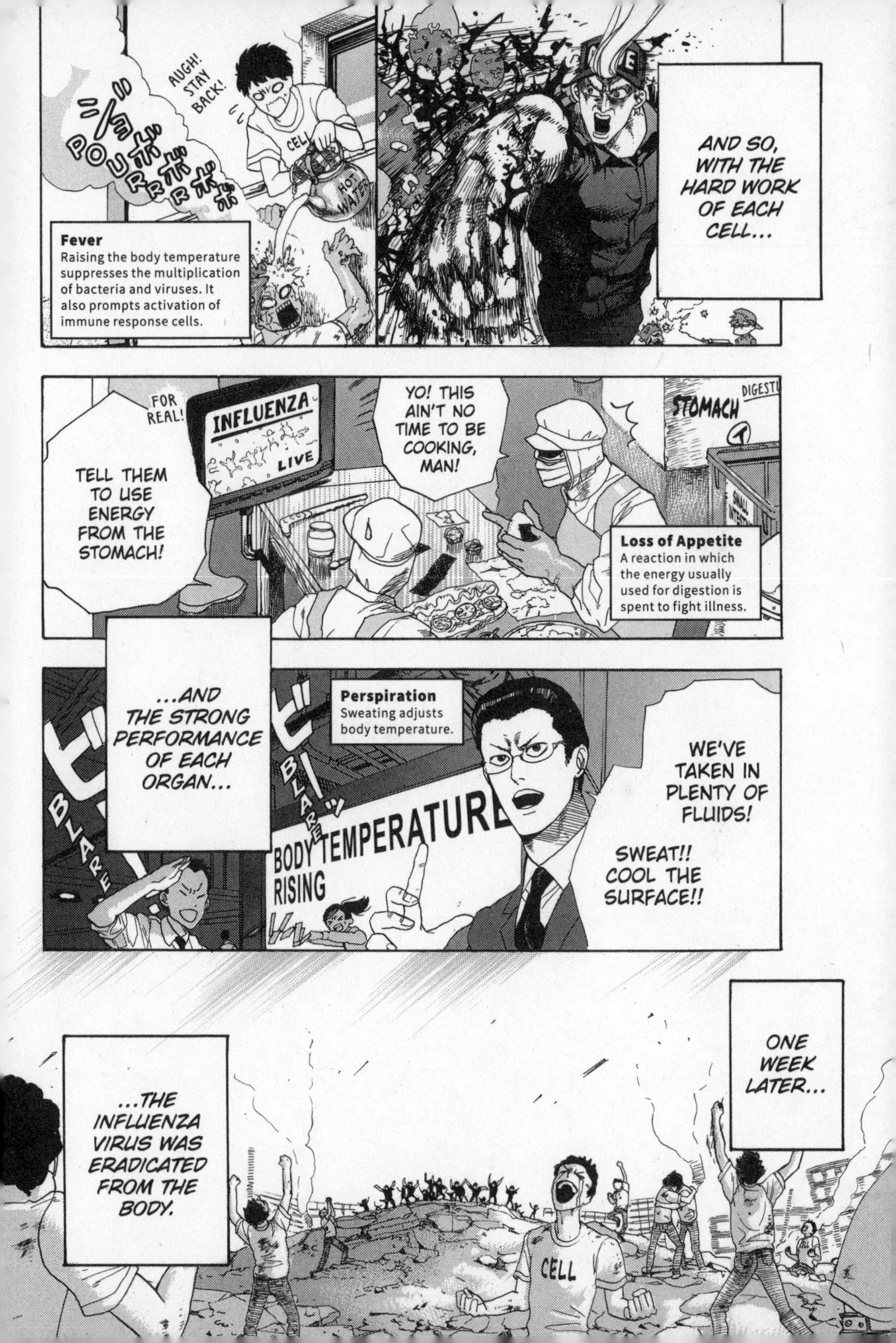
AND SO, WITH THE HARD WORK OF EACH CELL...
AUGH! STAY BACK!
POUR
CELL
HOT WATER
Fever
Raising the body temperature suppresses the multiplication of bacteria and viruses. It also prompts activation of immune response cells.
DIGESTI
STOMACH
YO! THIS AIN'T NO TIME TO BE COOKING, MAN!
INFLUENZA
LIVE
FOR REAL!
TELL THEM TO USE ENERGY FROM THE STOMACH!
SMALL INTESTI
Loss of Appetite
A reaction in which the energy usually used for digestion is spent to fight illness.
WE'VE TAKEN IN PLENTY OF FLUIDS!
SWEAT!! COOL THE SURFACE!!
Perspiration
Sweating adjusts body temperature.
BODY TEMPERATURE RISING
BLARE
BLARE
...AND THE STRONG PERFORMANCE OF EACH ORGAN...
ONE WEEK LATER...
...THE INFLUENZA VIRUS WAS ERADICATED FROM THE BODY.
CELL

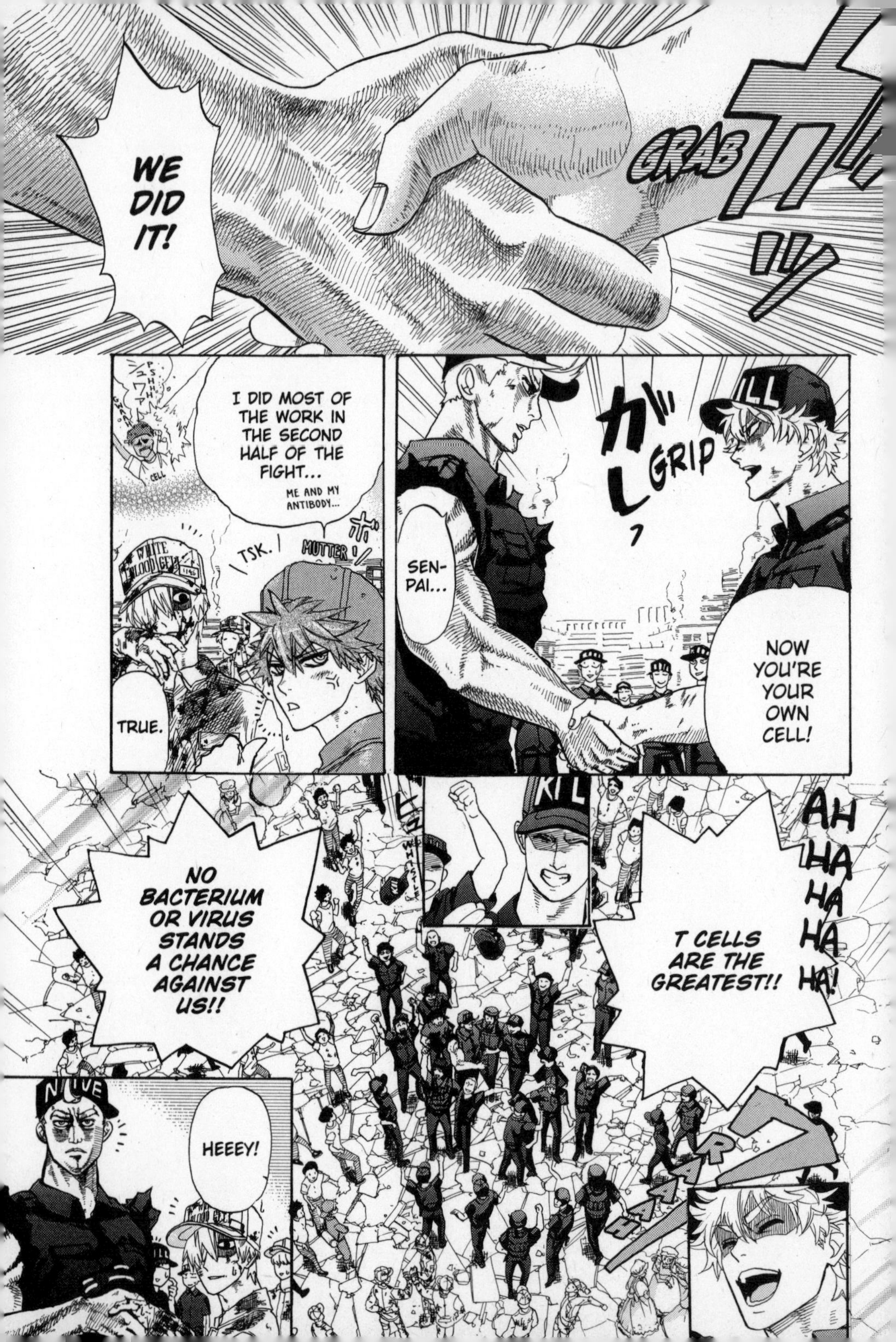
WE DID IT!
GRAB
GRIP
NOW YOU'RE YOUR OWN CELL!
SEN-PAI...
I DID MOST OF THE WORK IN THE SECOND HALF OF THE FIGHT...
ME AND MY ANTIBODY...
MUTTER
TSK.
PSHHH
TRUE.
AH HA HA HA HA!
T CELLS ARE THE GREATEST!!
WHISTLE
NO BACTERIUM OR VIRUS STANDS A CHANCE AGAINST US!!
HEEEY!

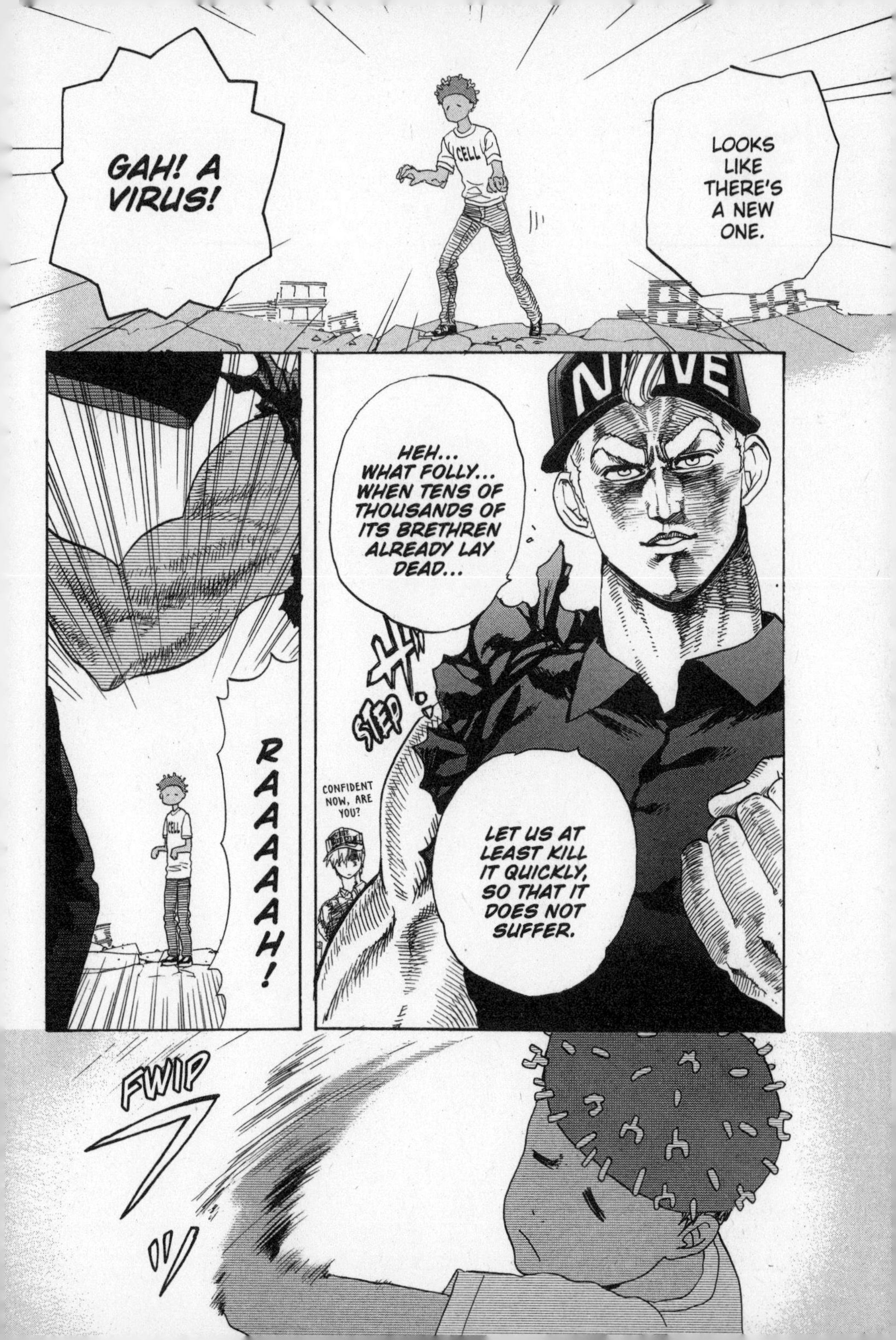
LOOKS LIKE THERE'S A NEW ONE.
GAH! A VIRUS!
HEH... WHAT FOLLY... WHEN TENS OF THOUSANDS OF ITS BRETHREN ALREADY LAY DEAD...
STEP
LET US AT LEAST KILL IT QUICKLY, SO THAT IT DOES NOT SUFFER.
CONFIDENT NOW, ARE YOU?
RAAAAAAH!
FWIP

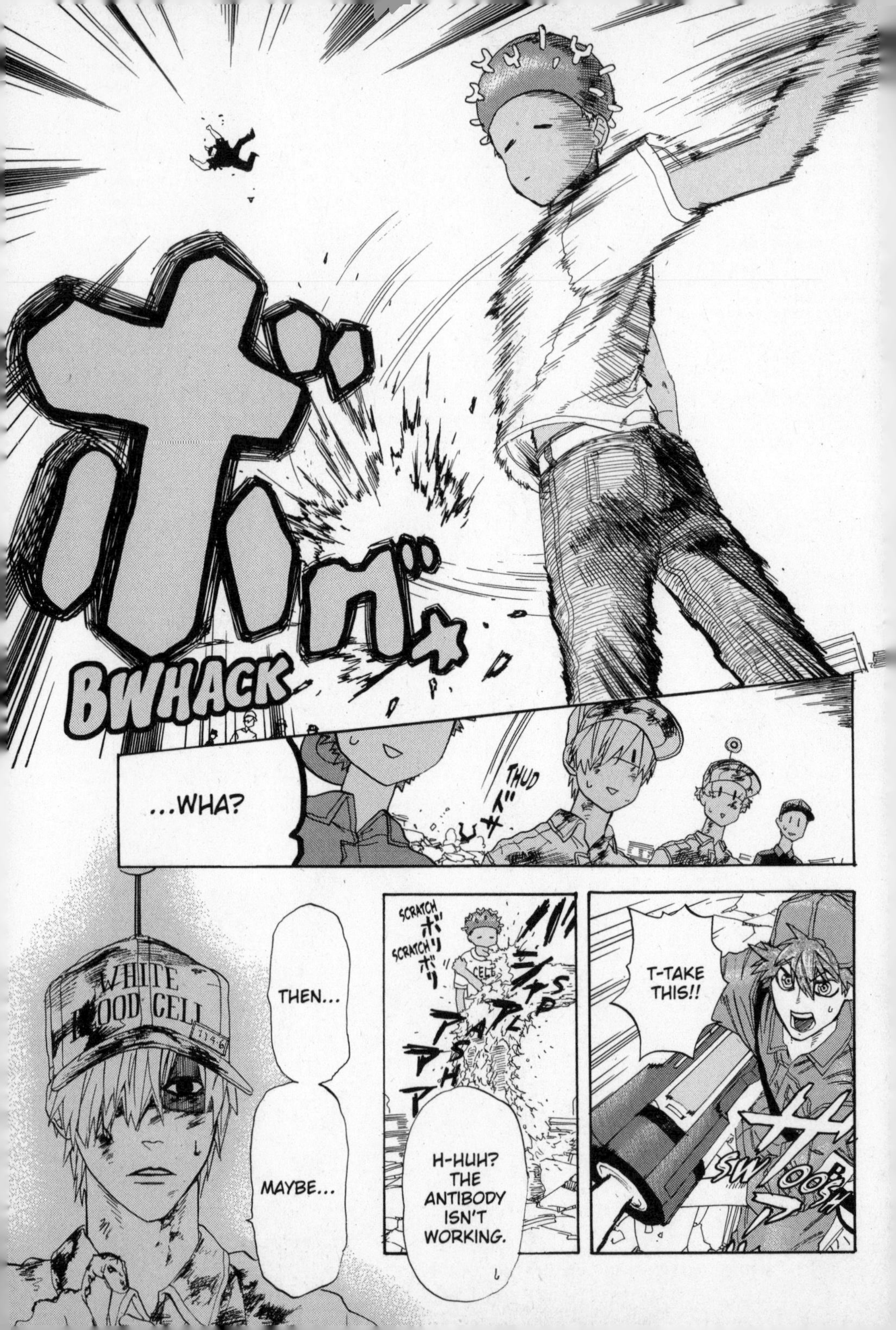

BWHACK
...WHA?
THUD
T-TAKE THIS!!
SWOOSH
SCRATCH
SCRATCH
SPLASH
H-HUH? THE ANTIBODY ISN'T WORKING.
THEN...
MAYBE...

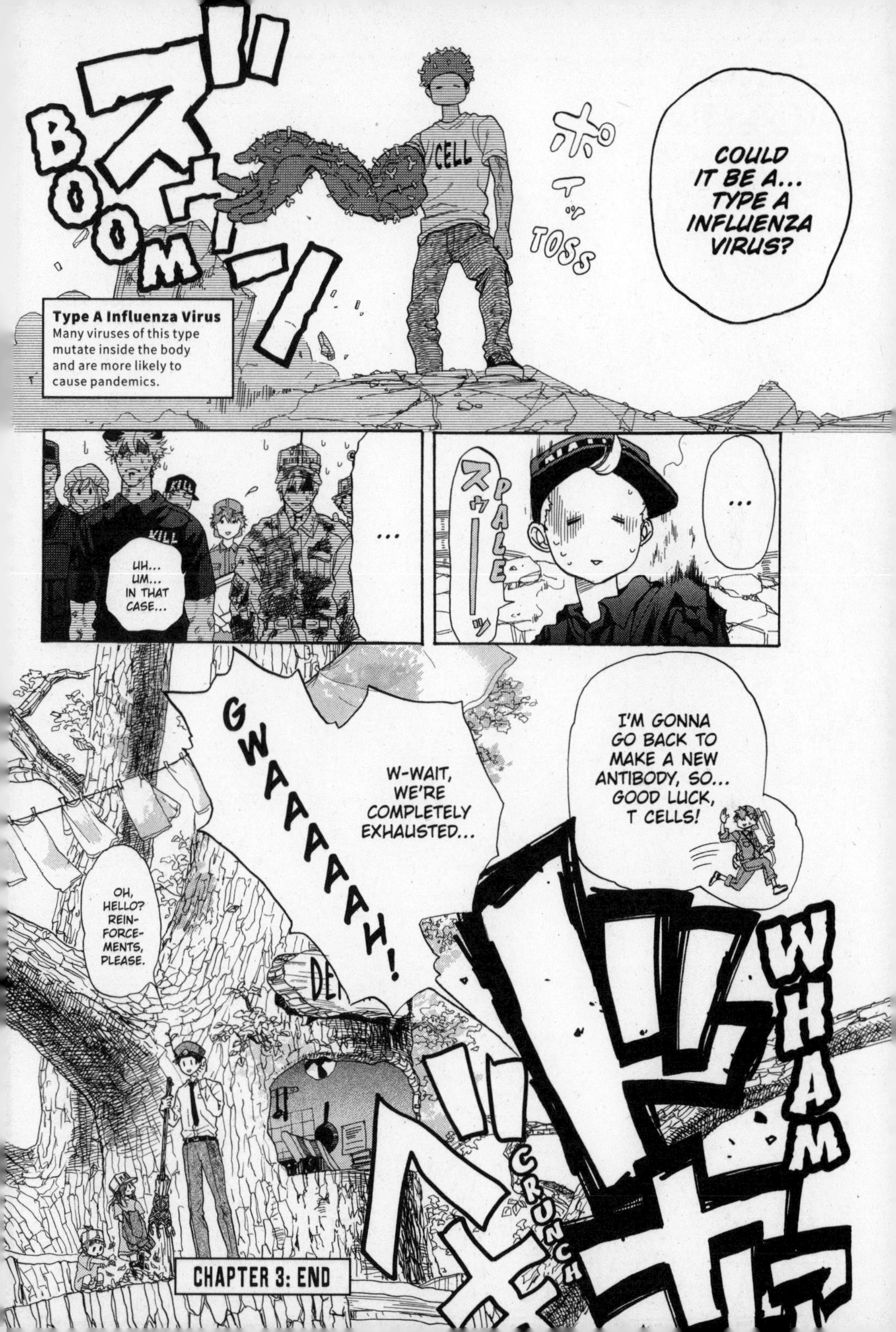
COULD IT BE A... TYPE A INFLUENZA VIRUS?
TOSS
BOOM
Type A Influenza Virus
Many viruses of this type mutate inside the body and are more likely to cause pandemics.
...
PALE
...
UH... UM... IN THAT CASE...
I'M GONNA GO BACK TO MAKE A NEW ANTIBODY, SO... GOOD LUCK, T CELLS!
WHAM
CRUNCH
W-WAIT, WE'RE COMPLETELY EXHAUSTED...
GWAAAAAAH!
OH, HELLO? REIN-FORCE-MENTS, PLEASE.
CHAPTER 3: END

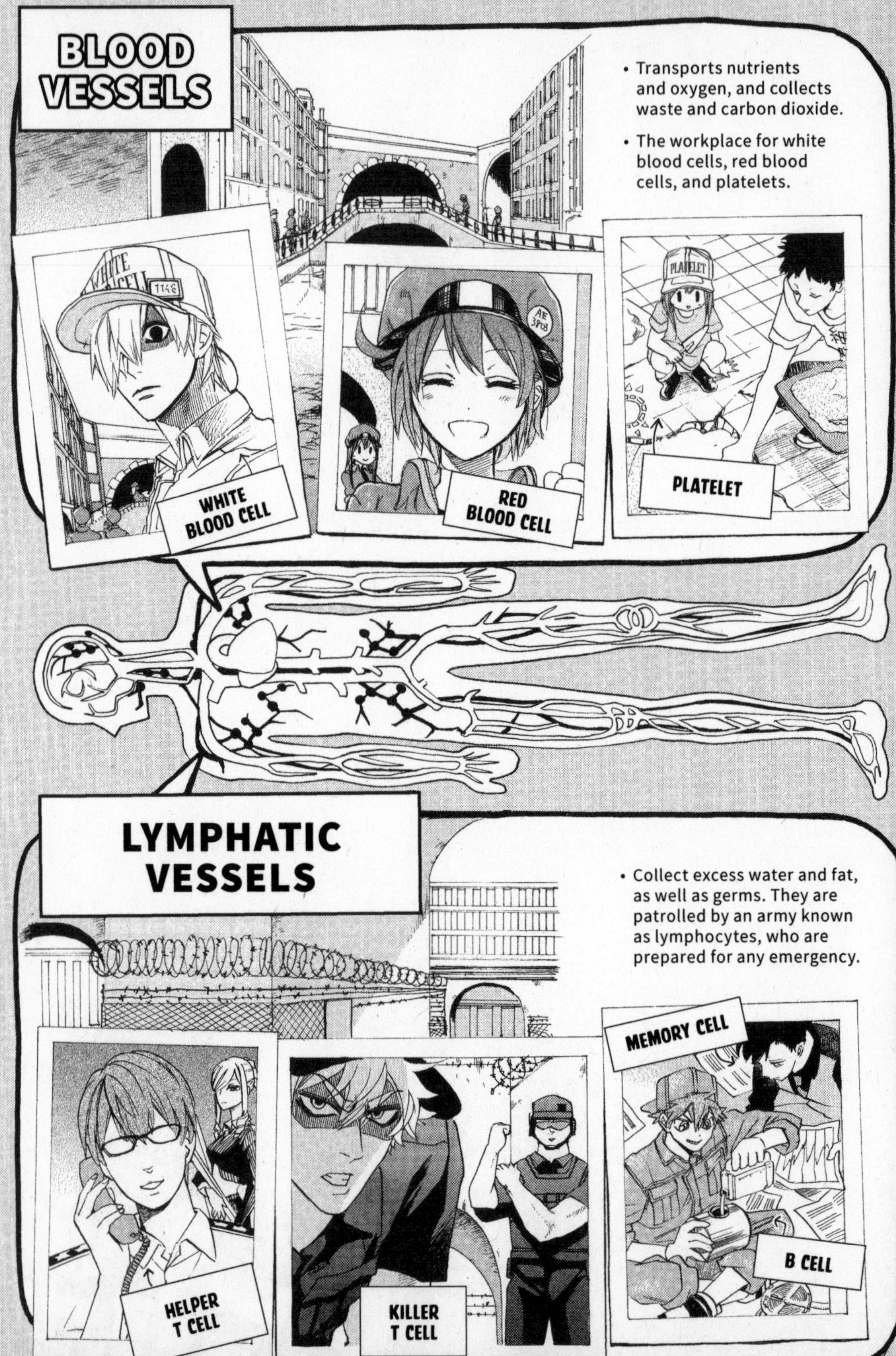
BLOOD VESSELS
• Transports nutrients and oxygen, and collects waste and carbon dioxide.
• The workplace for white blood cells, red blood cells, and platelets.
PLATELET
RED BLOOD CELL
WHITE BLOOD CELL
LYMPHATIC VESSELS
• Collect excess water and fat, as well as germs. They are patrolled by an army known as lymphocytes, who are prepared for any emergency.
MEMORY CELL
B CELL
KILLER T CELL
HELPER T CELL

Cells at Work!

はたらく細胞

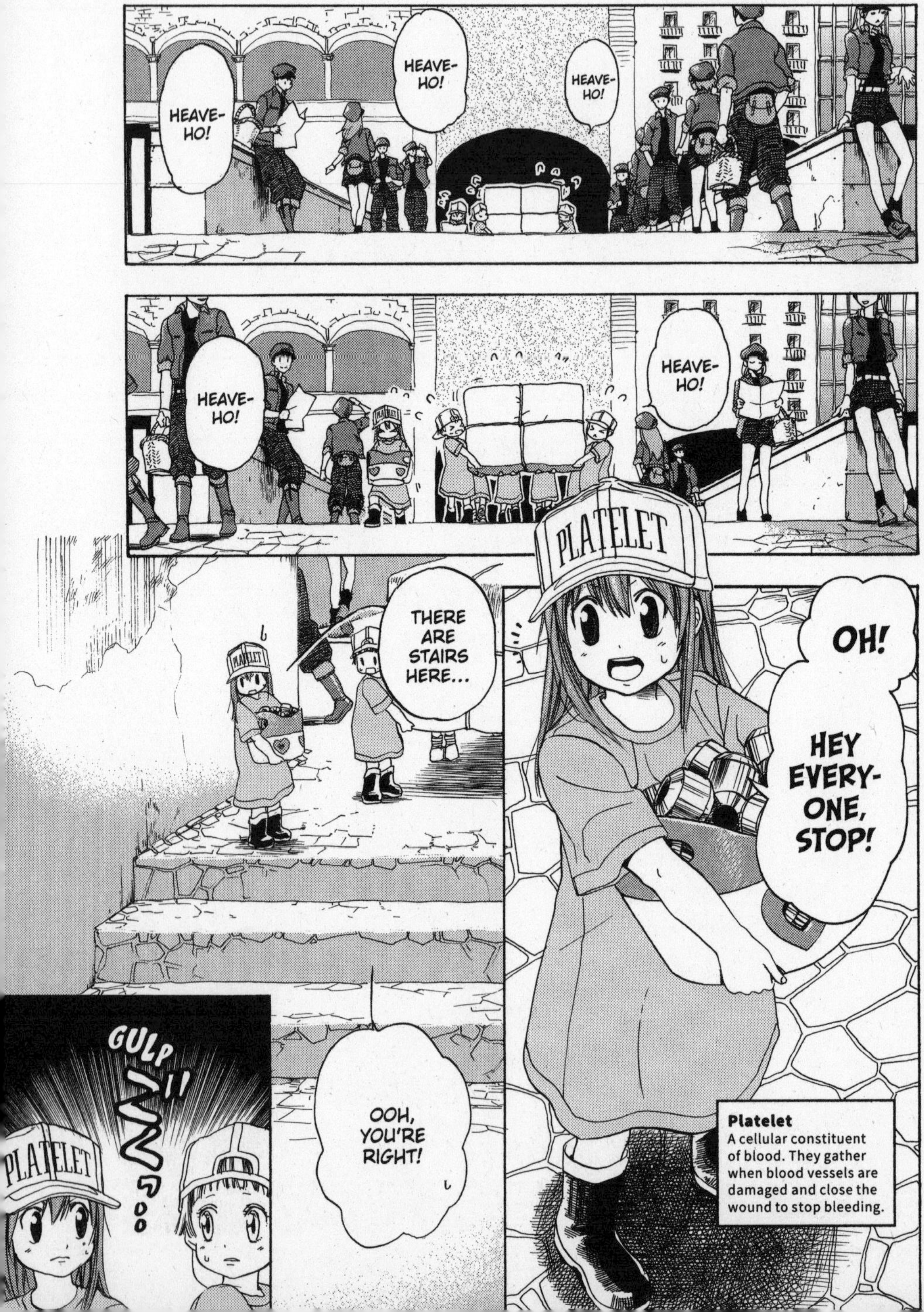
HEAVE-HO!
HEAVE-HO!
HEAVE-HO!
HEAVE-HO!
HEAVE-HO!
OH!
HEY EVERY-ONE, STOP!
Platelet
A cellular constituent of blood. They gather when blood vessels are damaged and close the wound to stop bleeding.
THERE ARE STAIRS HERE...
OOH, YOU'RE RIGHT!
GULP

CHAPTER 4: SCRAPE WOUND

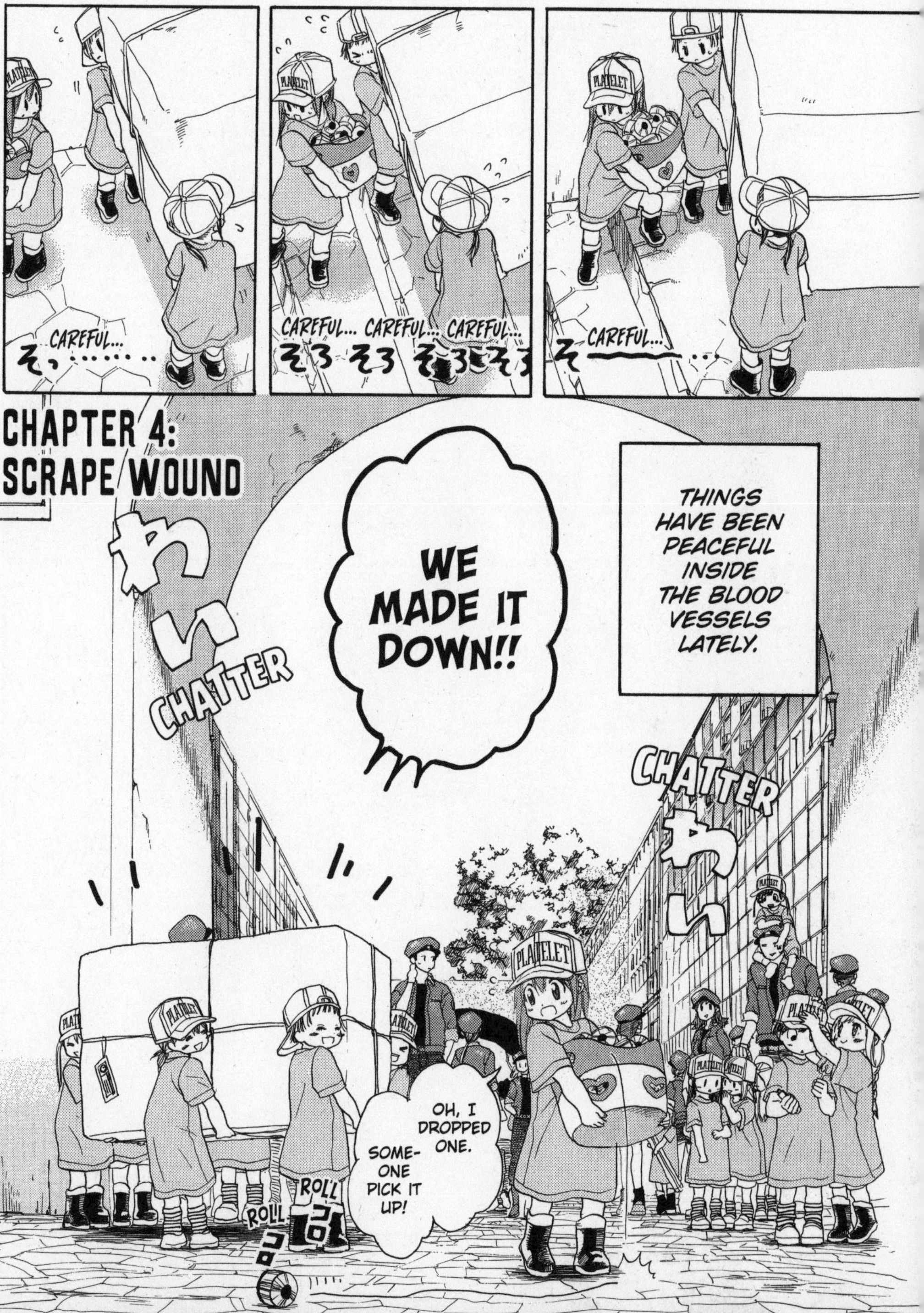

CAREFUL...
そ
CAREFUL... CAREFUL... CAREFUL...
そろ そろ そろ そろ
CAREFUL...
そっ
THINGS HAVE BEEN PEACEFUL INSIDE THE BLOOD VESSELS LATELY.
WE MADE IT DOWN!!
CHATTER
CHATTER
OH, I DROPPED ONE.
SOME-ONE PICK IT UP!
ROLL
ROLL

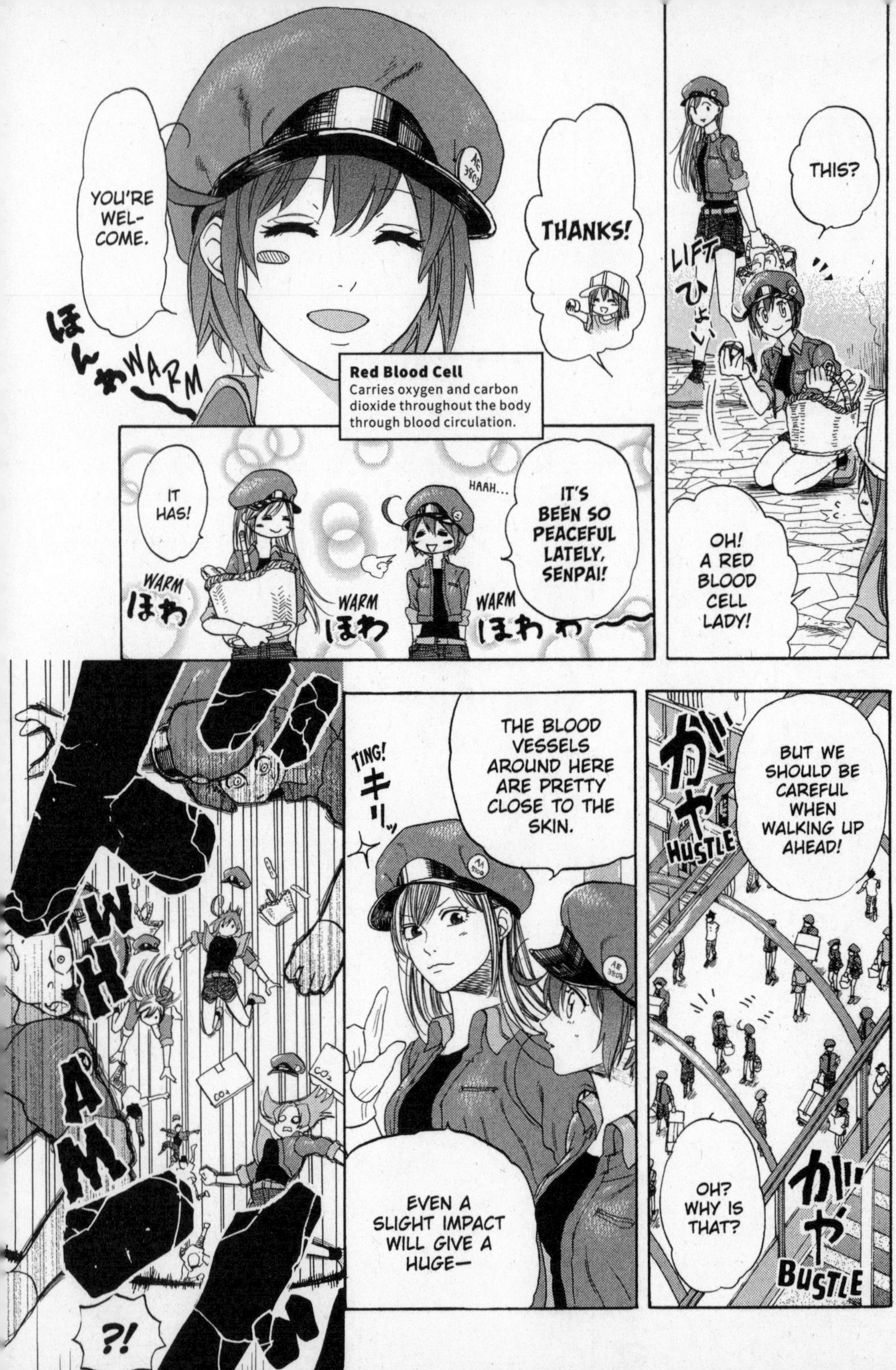
THIS?
LIFT
ひょい
OH! A RED BLOOD CELL LADY!
THANKS!
YOU'RE WEL-COME.
ほんわ WARM
Red Blood Cell
Carries oxygen and carbon dioxide throughout the body through blood circulation.
HAAH...
IT'S BEEN SO PEACEFUL LATELY, SENPAI!
IT HAS!
WARM ほわ
WARM ほわ
WARM ほわわ~~
がや HUSTLE
BUT WE SHOULD BE CAREFUL WHEN WALKING UP AHEAD!
OH? WHY IS THAT?
がや BUSTLE
THE BLOOD VESSELS AROUND HERE ARE PRETTY CLOSE TO THE SKIN.
TING! キリッ
EVEN A SLIGHT IMPACT WILL GIVE A HUGE—
WHAM
?!

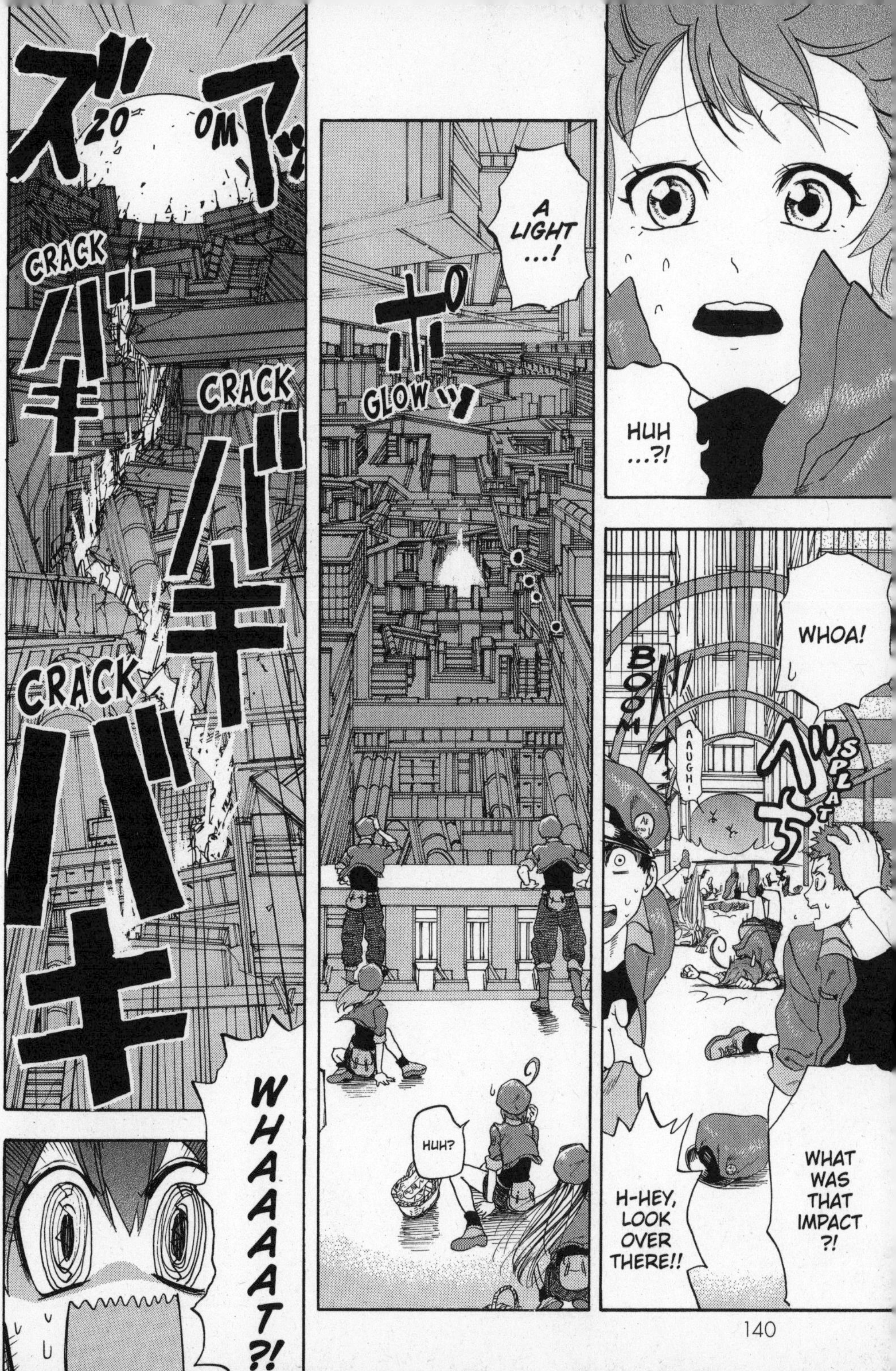
HUH ...?!
WHOA!
BOOM
AAUGH!
SPLAT
WHAT WAS THAT IMPACT ?!
H-HEY, LOOK OVER THERE!!
A LIGHT ...!
GLOW
HUH?
ZOOM
CRACK
CRACK
CRACK
WHAAAAAT?!

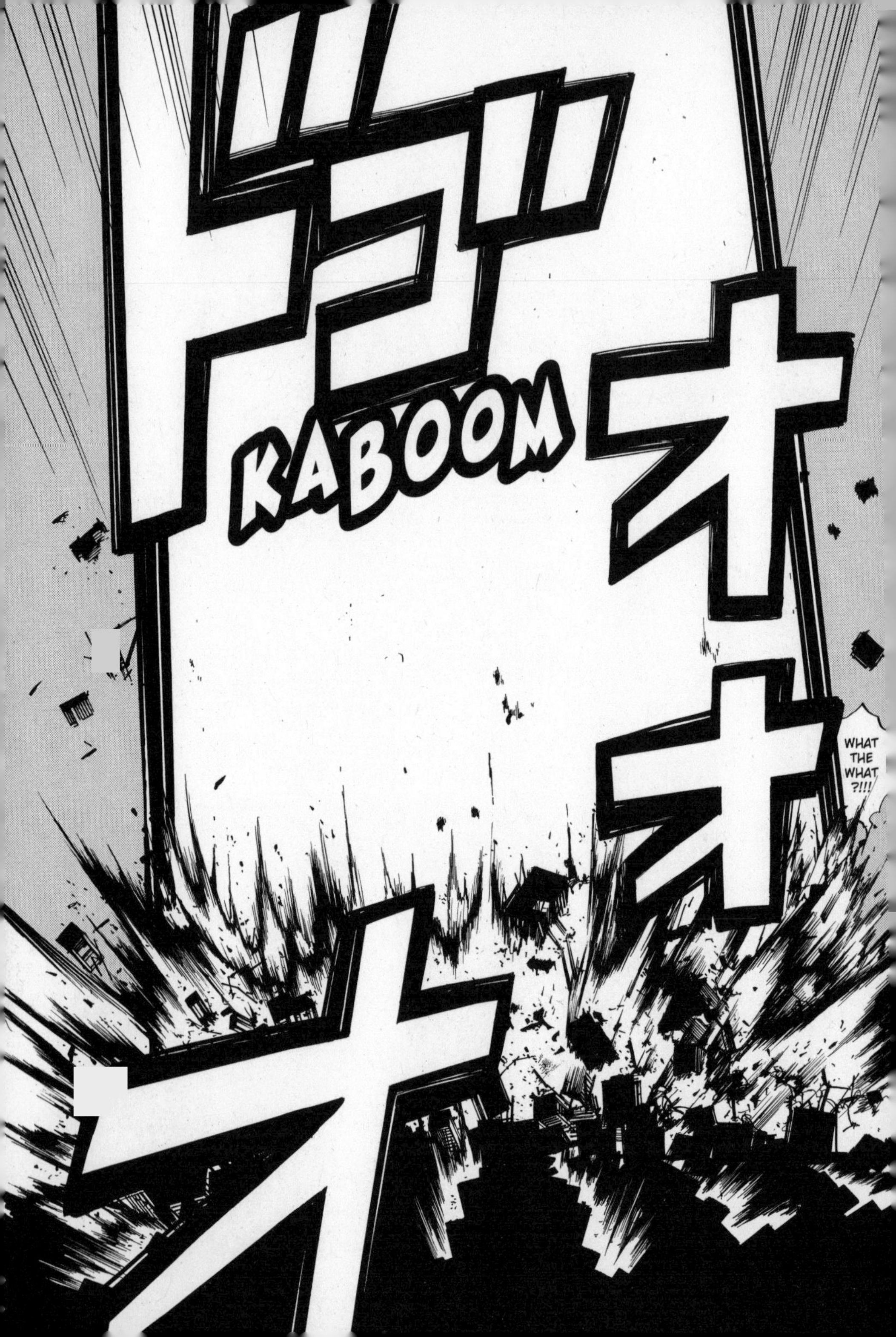
ドゴオオオ
KABOOM
WHAT THE WHAT ?!!!

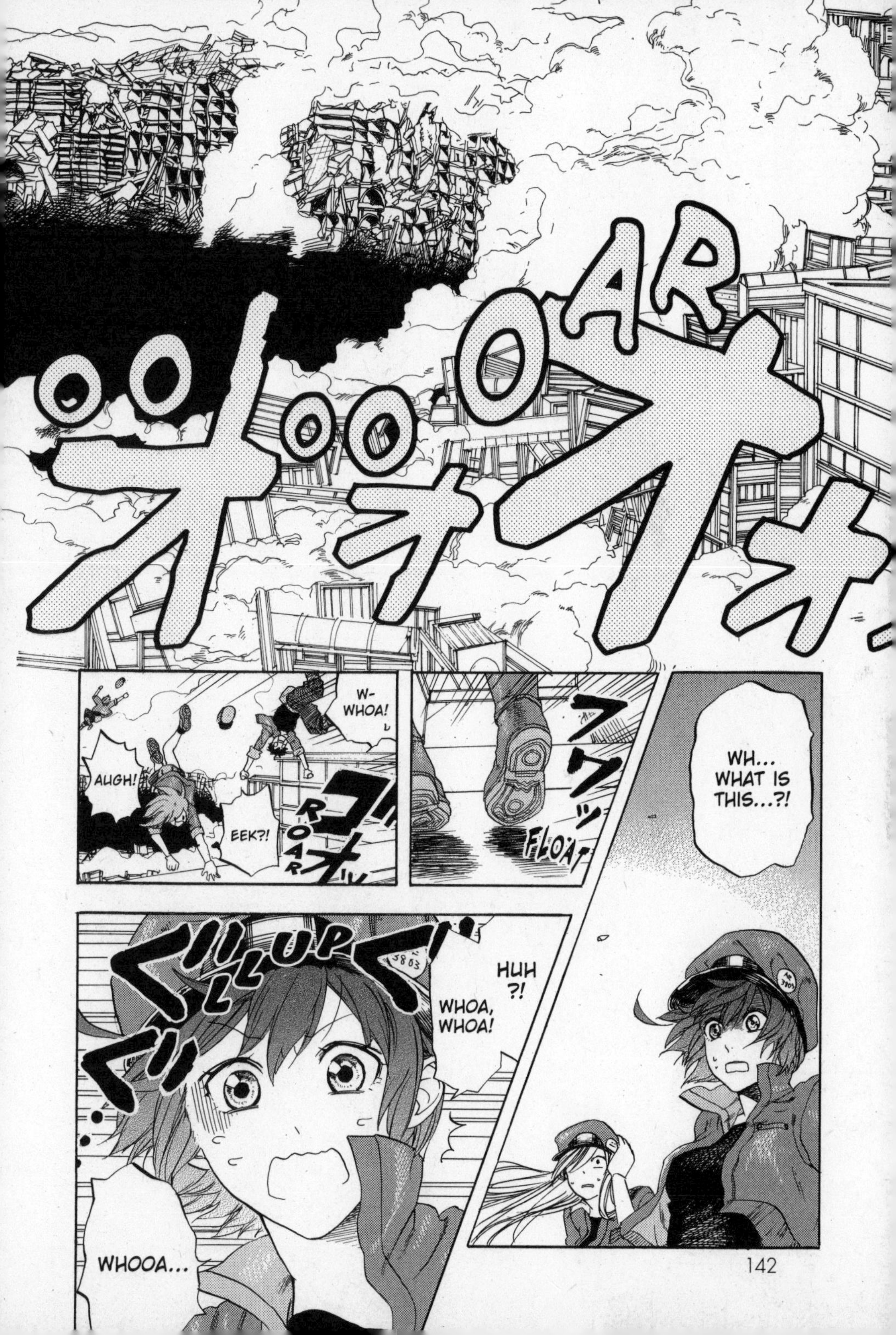
OOOOAR
WH... WHAT IS THIS...?!
FLOAT
W-WHOA!
AUGH!
EEK?!
ROAR
UP
HUH ?!
WHOA, WHOA!
WHOOA...

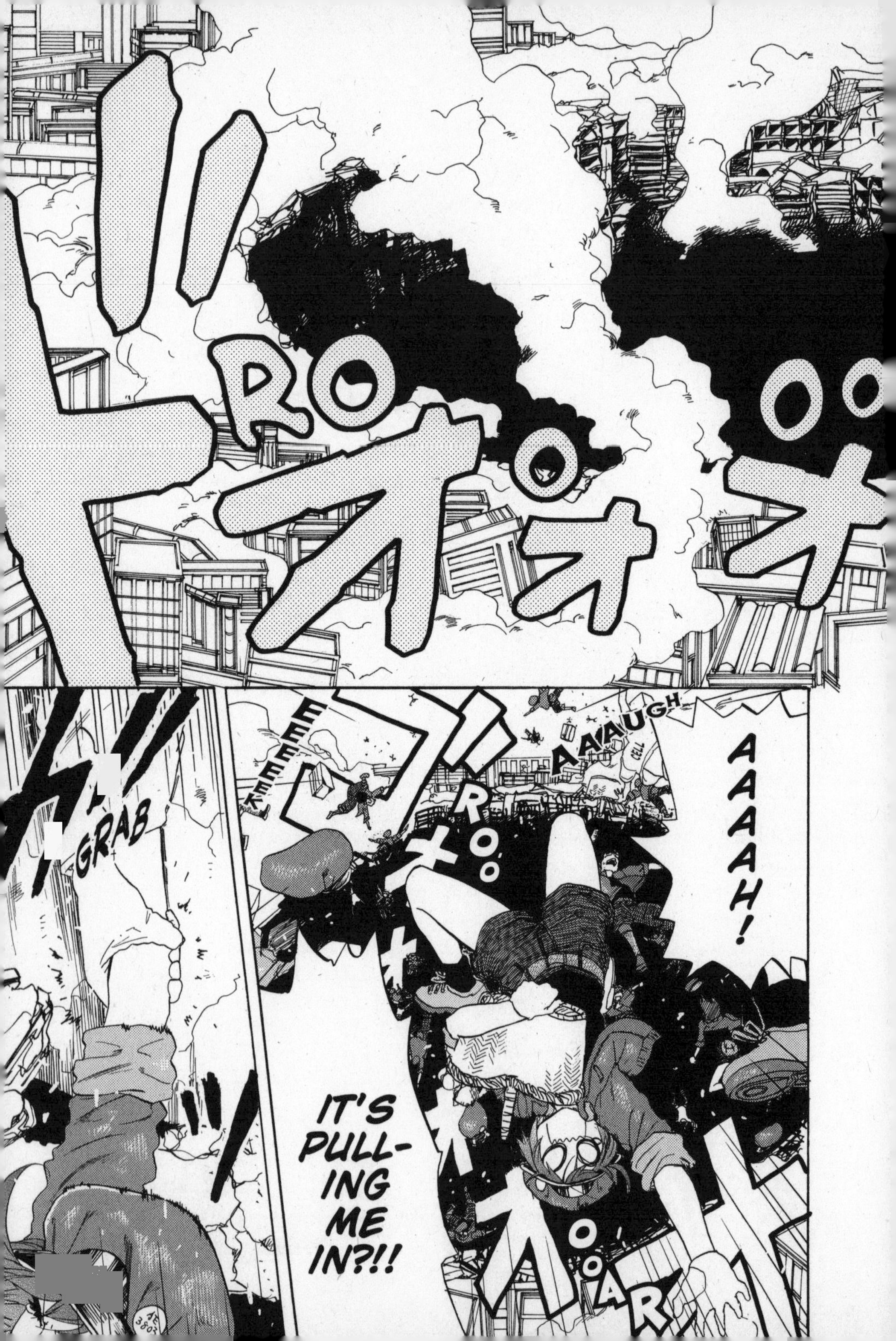
ROOO
AAAAAH!
AAAUGH
EEEEEEK
ROOO
IT'S PULL-ING ME IN?!!
OOAR
GRAB

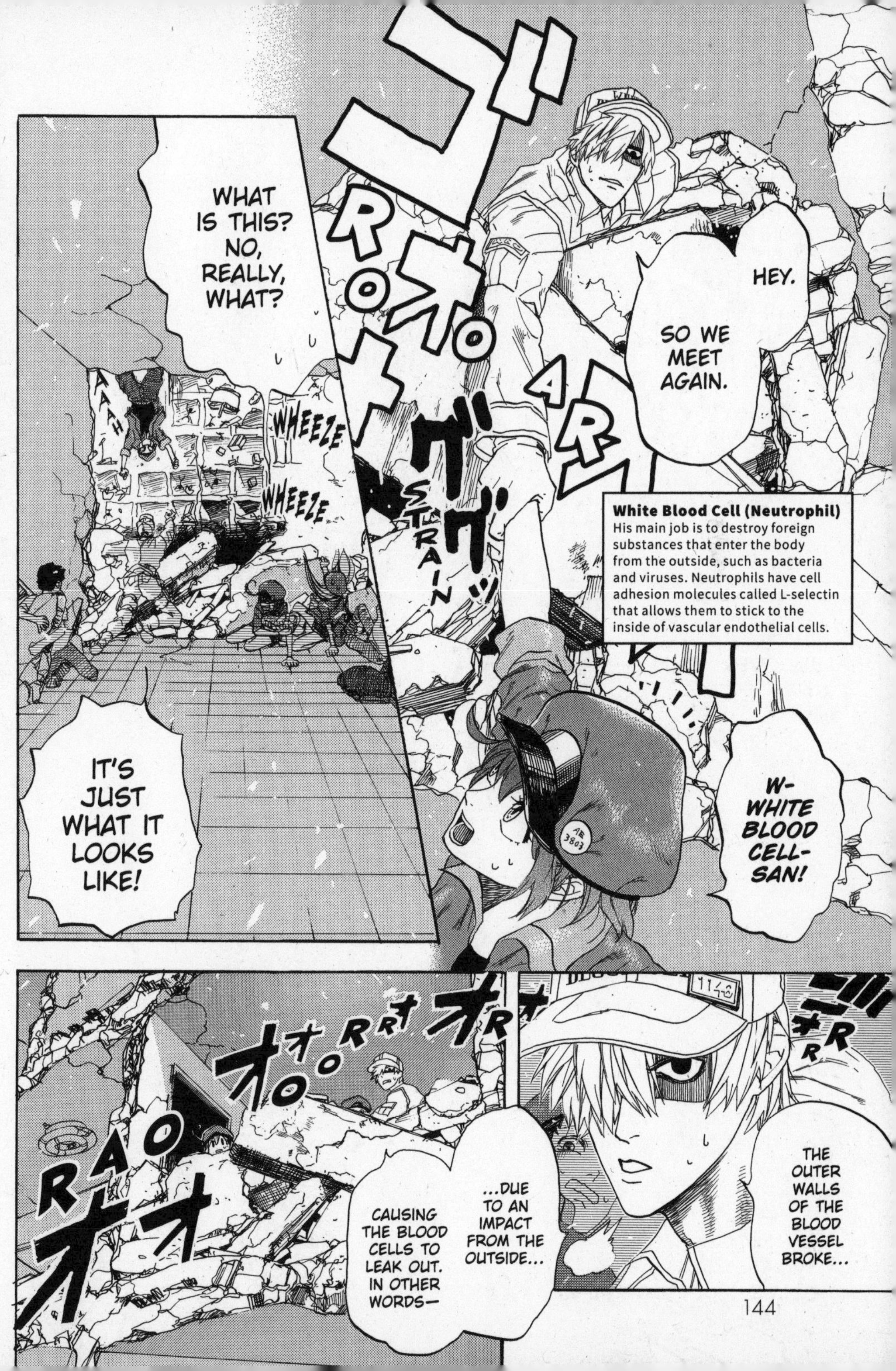
ROAR
STRAIN
HEY.
SO WE MEET AGAIN.
White Blood Cell (Neutrophil)
His main job is to destroy foreign substances that enter the body from the outside, such as bacteria and viruses. Neutrophils have cell adhesion molecules called L-selectin that allows them to stick to the inside of vascular endothelial cells.
W-WHITE BLOOD CELL-SAN!
WHAT IS THIS? NO, REALLY, WHAT?
AAAH
WHEEZE
WHEEZE
IT'S JUST WHAT IT LOOKS LIKE!
RRR
THE OUTER WALLS OF THE BLOOD VESSEL BROKE...
...DUE TO AN IMPACT FROM THE OUTSIDE...
CAUSING THE BLOOD CELLS TO LEAK OUT. IN OTHER WORDS—
ROAR
RAO

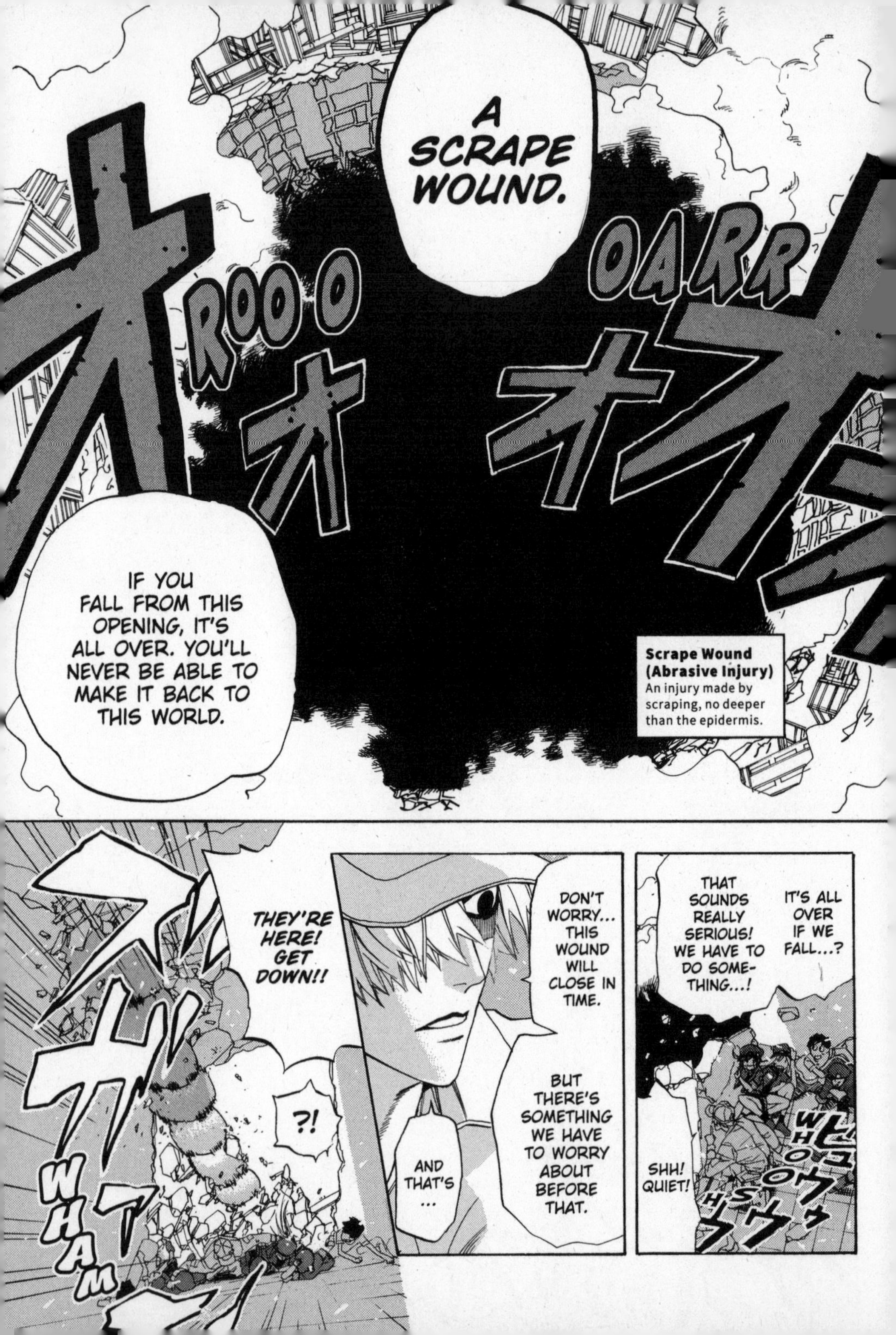
A SCRAPE WOUND.
ROO-O OARRR
IF YOU FALL FROM THIS OPENING, IT'S ALL OVER. YOU'LL NEVER BE ABLE TO MAKE IT BACK TO THIS WORLD.
Scrape Wound (Abrasive Injury) An injury made by scraping, no deeper than the epidermis.
IT'S ALL OVER IF WE FALL...?
THAT SOUNDS REALLY SERIOUS! WE HAVE TO DO SOME-THING...!
SHH! QUIET!
WHOOSH
DON'T WORRY... THIS WOUND WILL CLOSE IN TIME.
BUT THERE'S SOMETHING WE HAVE TO WORRY ABOUT BEFORE THAT.
AND THAT'S ...
THEY'RE HERE! GET DOWN!!
?!
WHAM

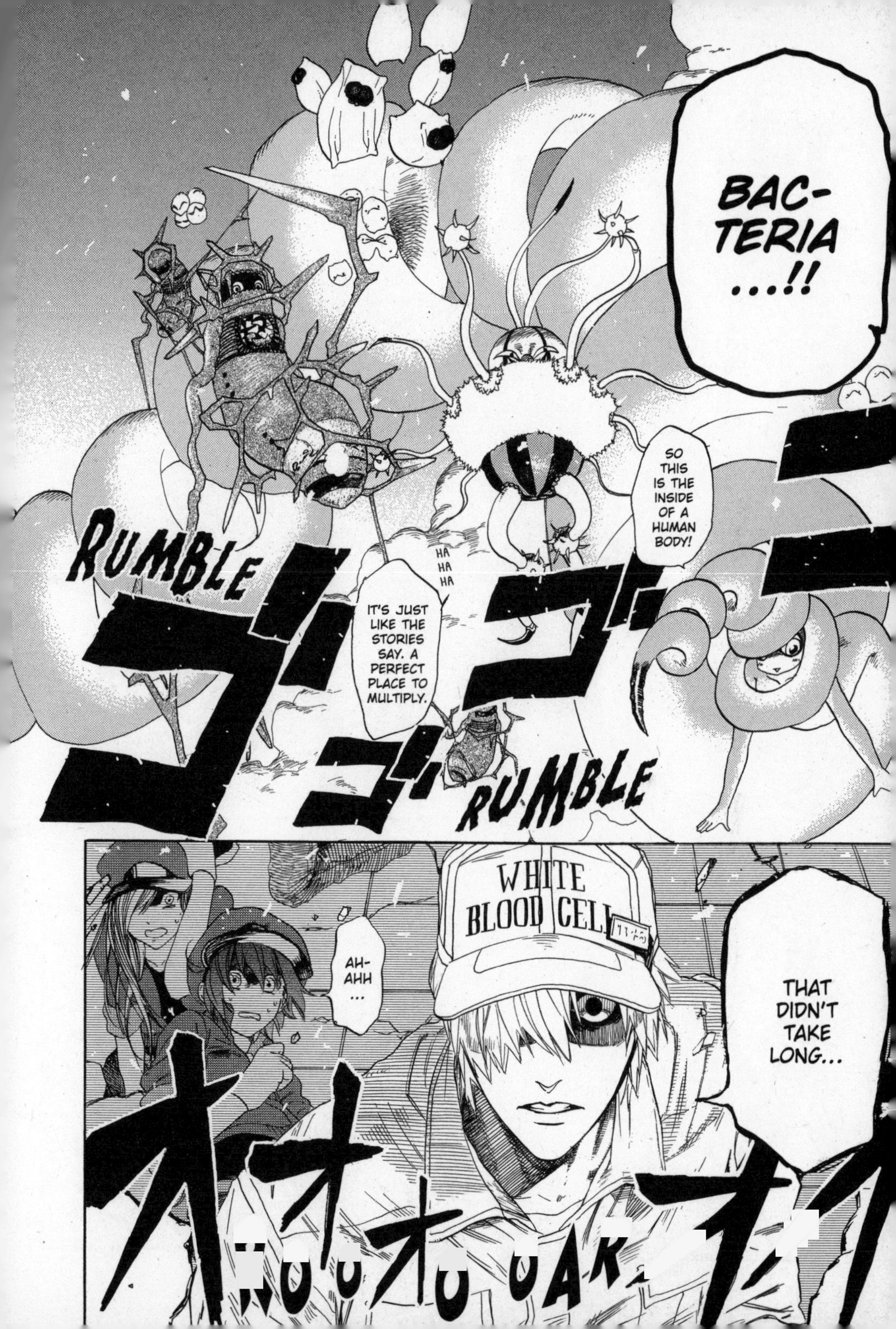
BAC-TERIA ...!!
SO THIS IS THE INSIDE OF A HUMAN BODY!
HA HA HA
IT'S JUST LIKE THE STORIES SAY. A PERFECT PLACE TO MULTIPLY.
RUMBLE
RUMBLE
THAT DIDN'T TAKE LONG...
WHITE BLOOD CELL
AH-AHH ...

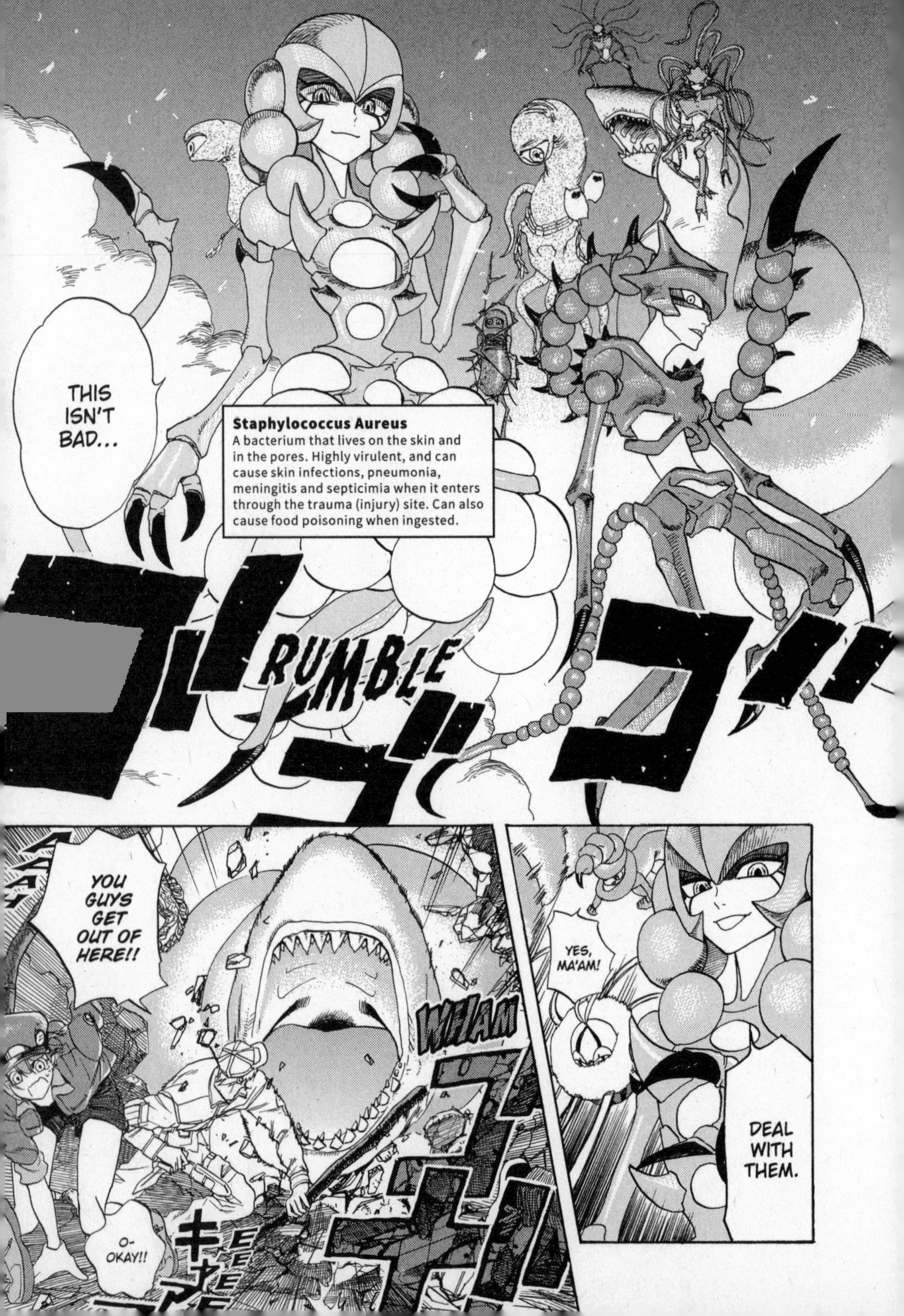
THIS ISN'T BAD...
Staphylococcus Aureus
A bacterium that lives on the skin and in the pores. Highly virulent, and can cause skin infections, pneumonia, meningitis and septicimia when it enters through the trauma (injury) site. Can also cause food poisoning when ingested.
RUMBLE
DEAL WITH THEM.
YES, MA'AM!
YOU GUYS GET OUT OF HERE!!
WHAM
O-OKAY!!

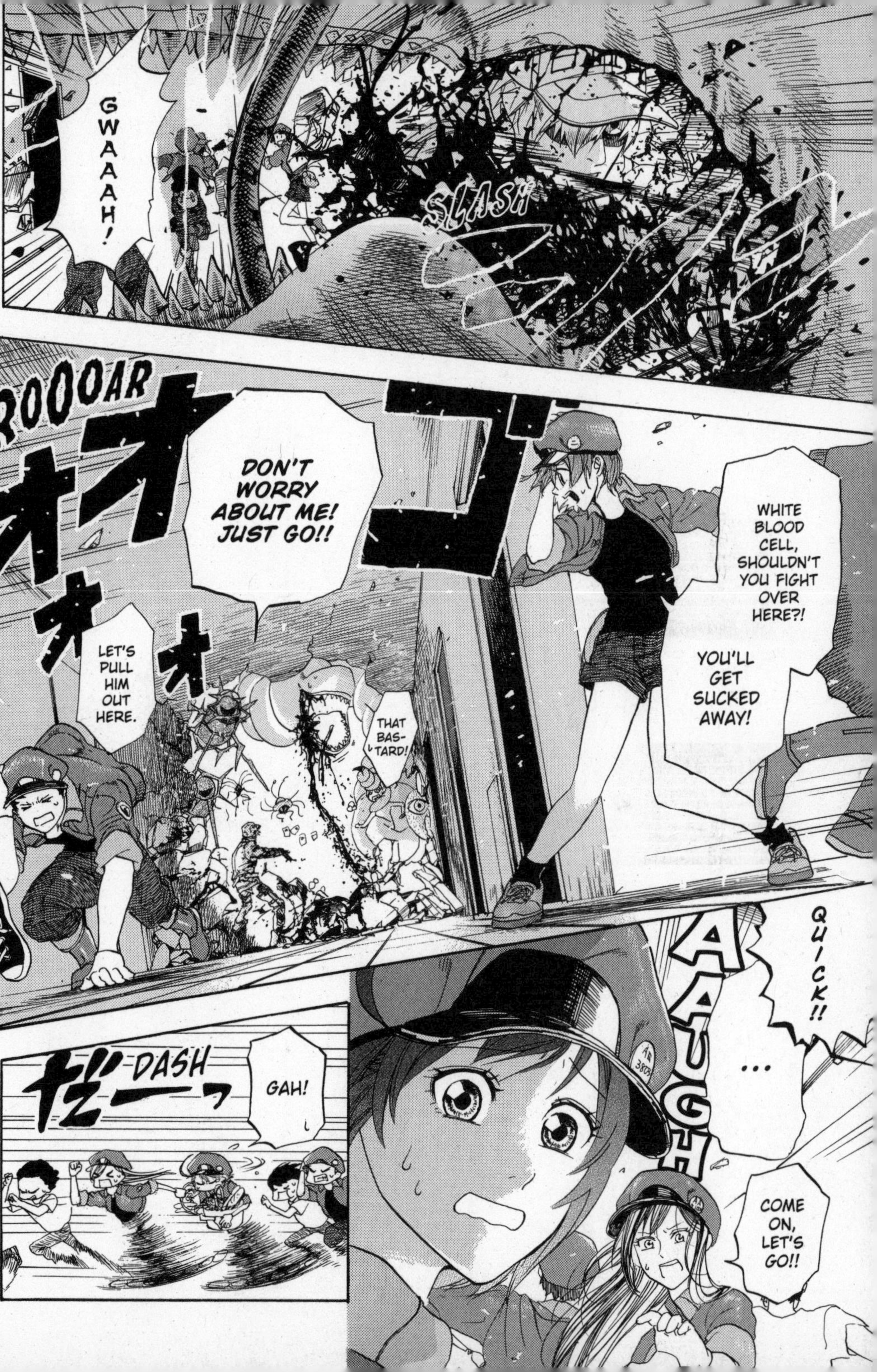
SLASH
GWAAAH!
WHITE BLOOD CELL, SHOULDN'T YOU FIGHT OVER HERE?!
YOU'LL GET SUCKED AWAY!
ROOOAR
DON'T WORRY ABOUT ME! JUST GO!!
THAT BAS- TARD!
LET'S PULL HIM OUT HERE.
QUICK!!
AAUGH
...
COME ON, LET'S GO!!
DASH
GAH!

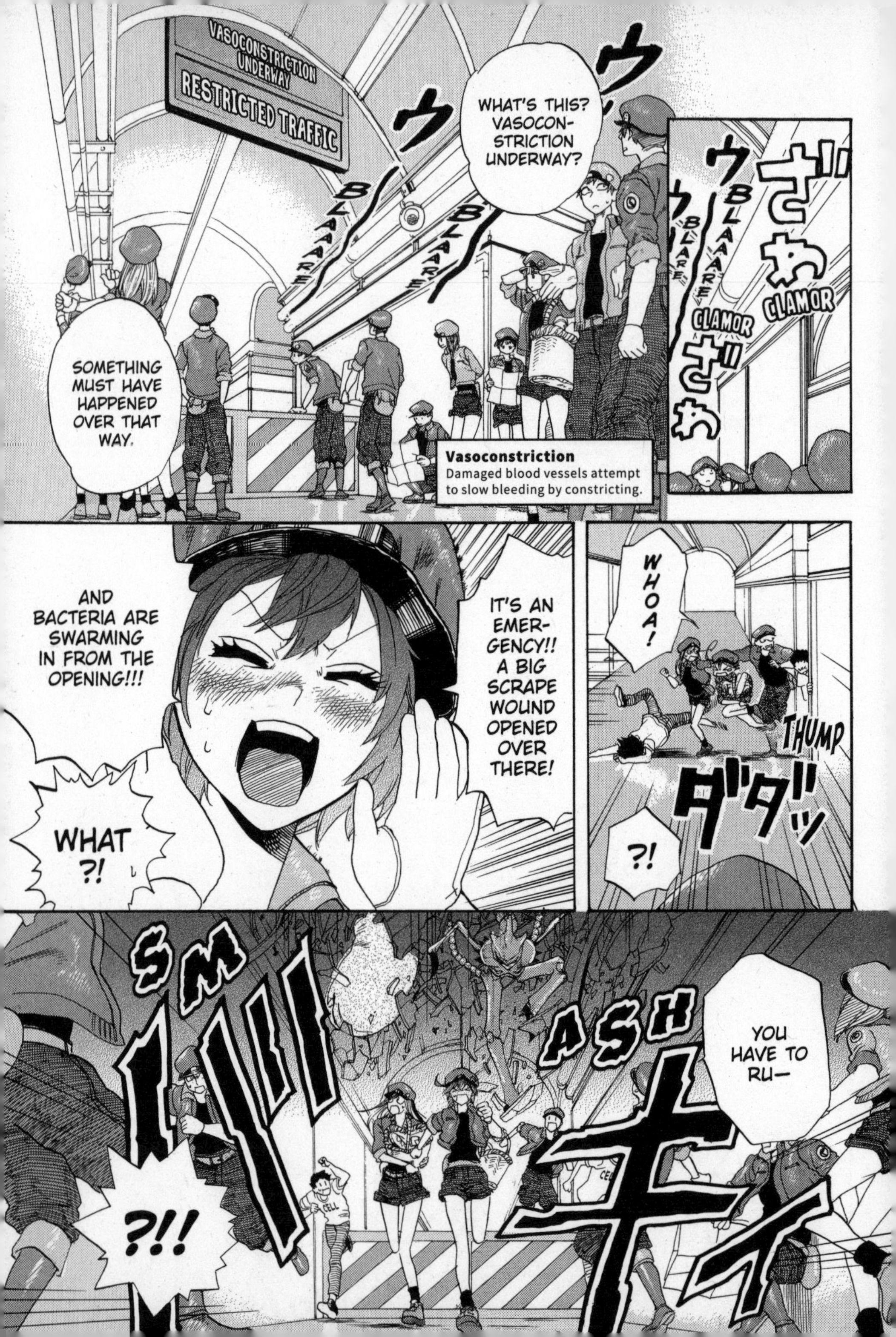
ざわ
CLAMOR
CLAMOR
ざわ
ウ
BLAAARE
ウ
BLARE
VASOCONSTRICTION UNDERWAY
RESTRICTED TRAFFIC
ウ
ウ
BLAAARE
BLAAARE
WHAT'S THIS? VASOCON-STRICTION UNDERWAY?
SOMETHING MUST HAVE HAPPENED OVER THAT WAY.
Vasoconstriction
Damaged blood vessels attempt to slow bleeding by constricting.
WHOA!
THUMP
ダダッ
?!
IT'S AN EMER-GENCY!! A BIG SCRAPE WOUND OPENED OVER THERE!
AND BACTERIA ARE SWARMING IN FROM THE OPENING!!!
WHAT?!
SMASH
バキ
YOU HAVE TO RU—
?!!

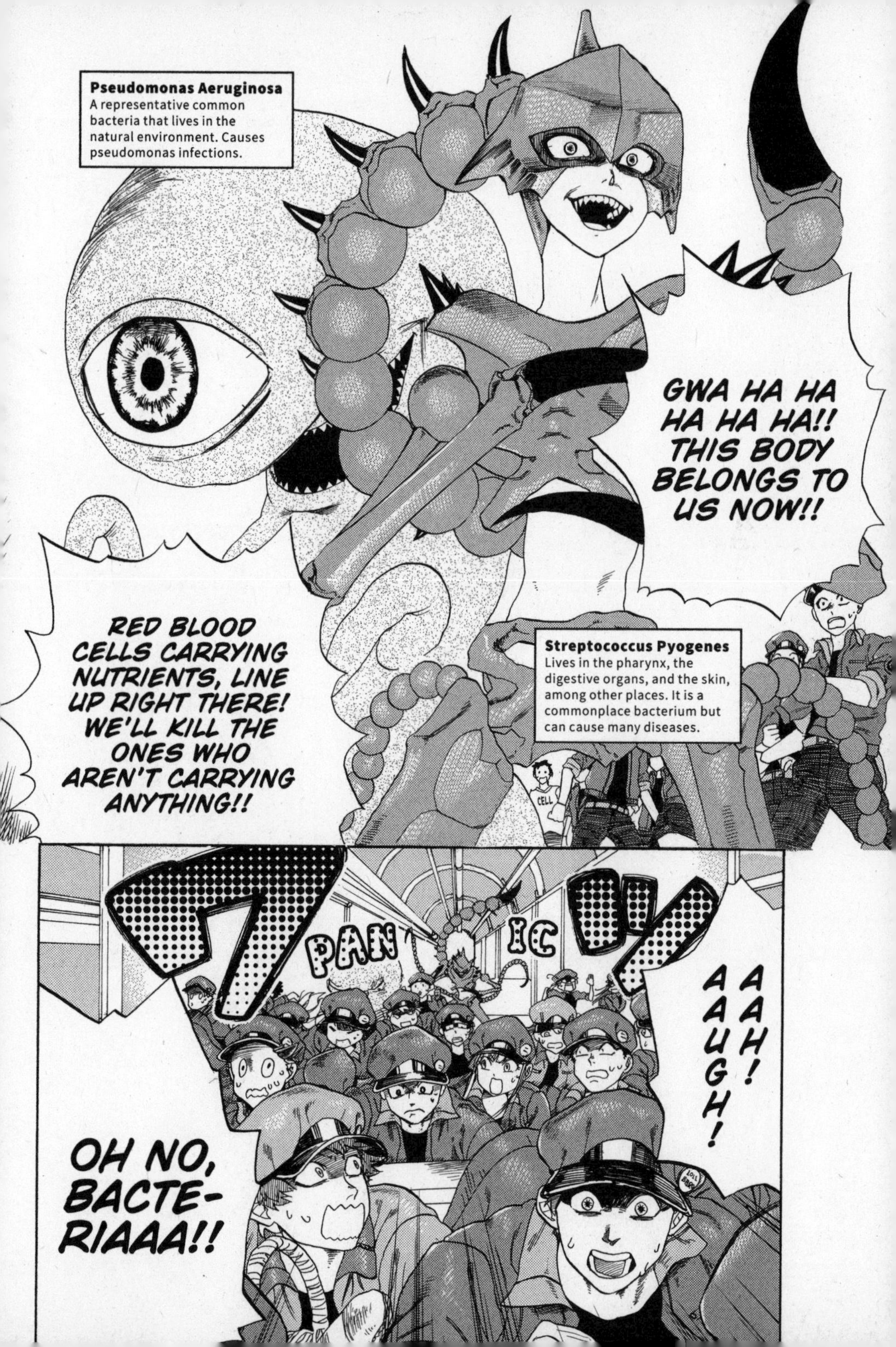
Pseudomonas Aeruginosa
A representative common bacteria that lives in the natural environment. Causes pseudomonas infections.
GWA HA HA HA HA HA!! THIS BODY BELONGS TO US NOW!!
Streptococcus Pyogenes
Lives in the pharynx, the digestive organs, and the skin, among other places. It is a commonplace bacterium but can cause many diseases.
RED BLOOD CELLS CARRYING NUTRIENTS, LINE UP RIGHT THERE! WE'LL KILL THE ONES WHO AREN'T CARRYING ANYTHING!!
PANIC
AAH!
AAUGH!
OH NO, BACTE-RIAAA!!

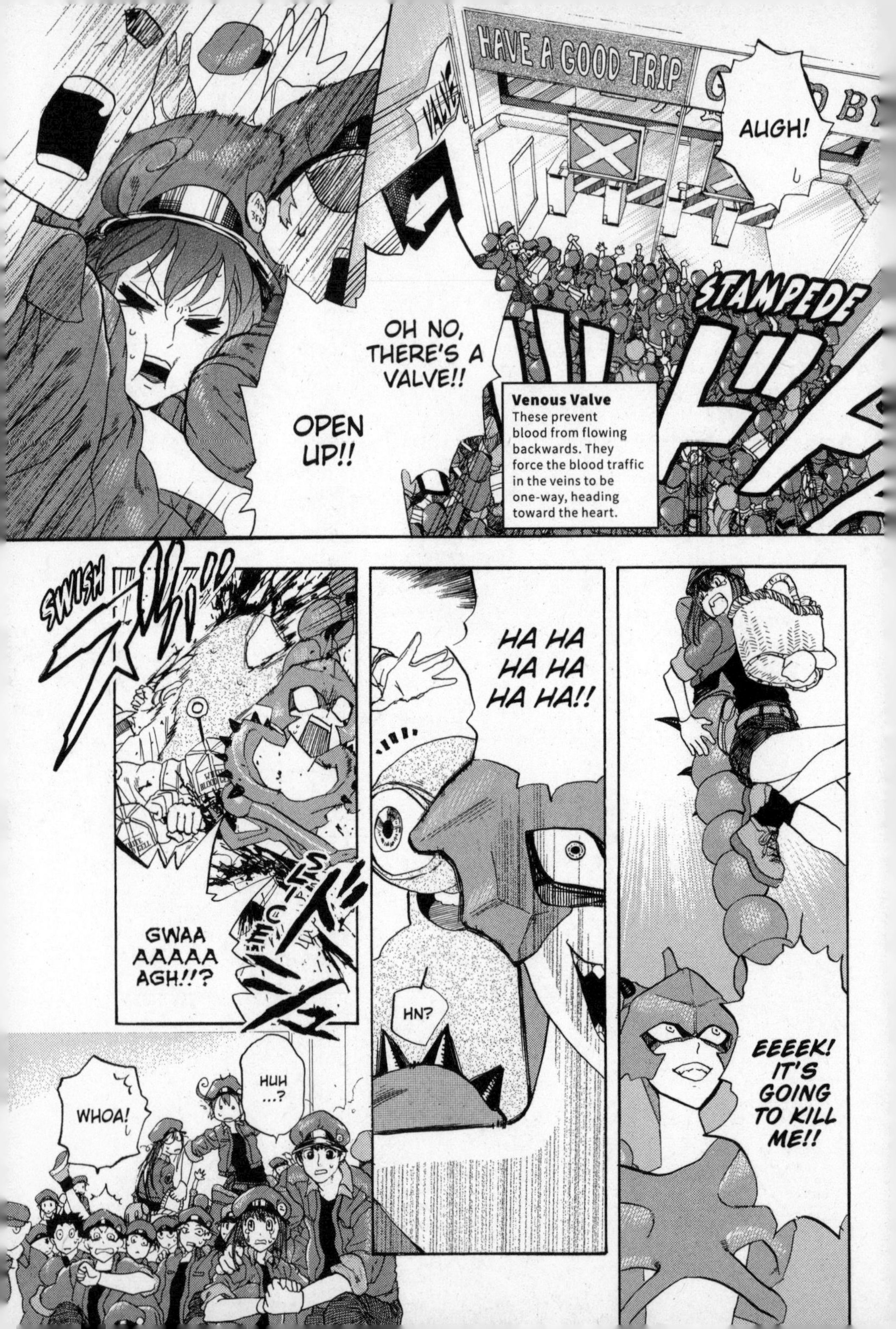
HAVE A GOOD TRIP
VALVE
AUGH!
STAMPEDE
Venous Valve
These prevent blood from flowing backwards. They force the blood traffic in the veins to be one-way, heading toward the heart.
OH NO, THERE'S A VALVE!!
OPEN UP!!
EEEEK! IT'S GOING TO KILL ME!!
HA HA HA HA HA HA!!
HN?
SWISH
SLICE
GWAA AAAAA AGH!!?
HUH ...?
WHOA!

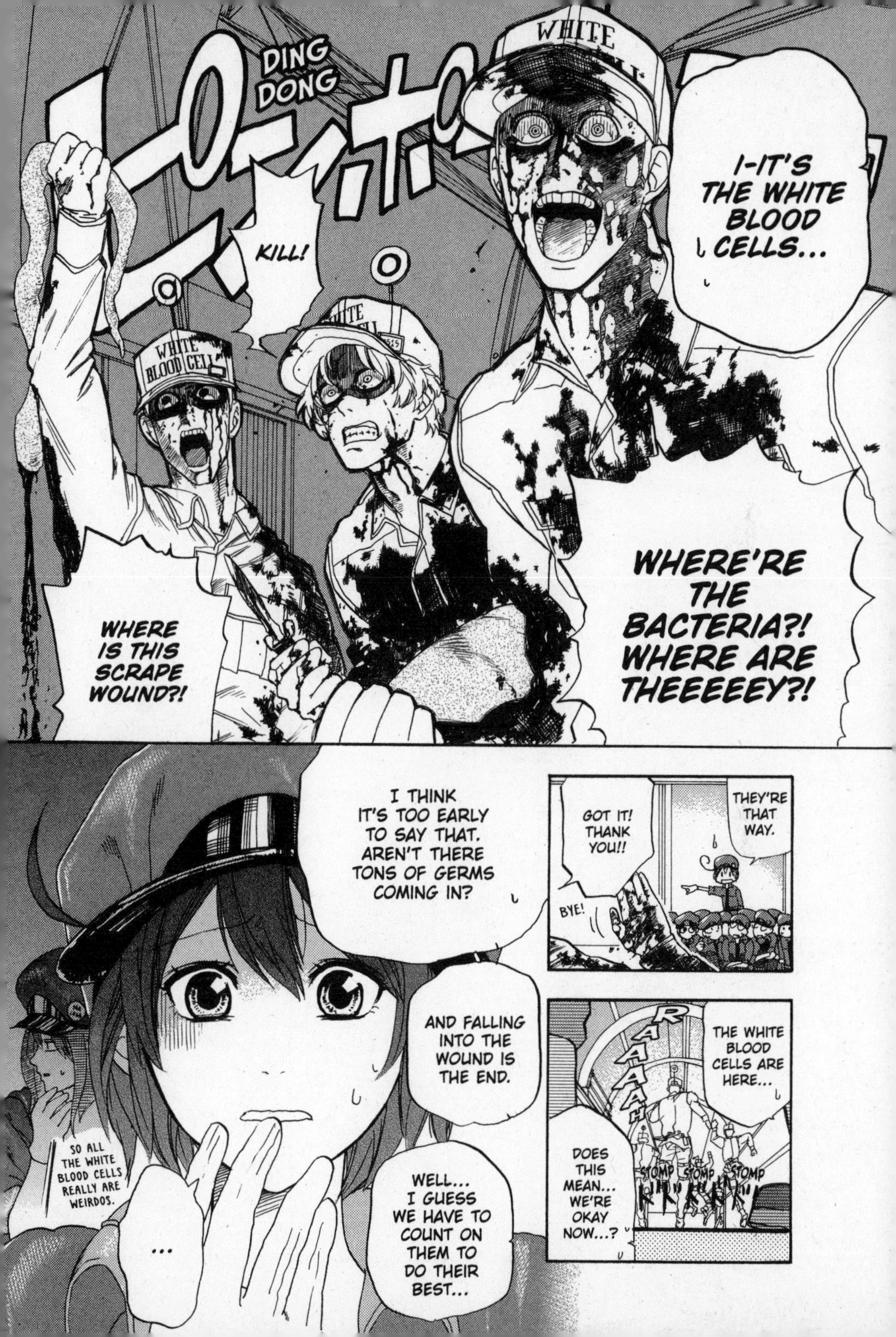
I-IT'S THE WHITE BLOOD CELLS...
DING DONG
KILL!
WHERE'RE THE BACTERIA?! WHERE ARE THEEEEEY?!
WHERE IS THIS SCRAPE WOUND?!
THEY'RE THAT WAY.
GOT IT! THANK YOU!!
BYE!
RAAAAH
THE WHITE BLOOD CELLS ARE HERE...
STOMP STOMP STOMP
DOES THIS MEAN... WE'RE OKAY NOW...?
I THINK IT'S TOO EARLY TO SAY THAT. AREN'T THERE TONS OF GERMS COMING IN?
AND FALLING INTO THE WOUND IS THE END.
WELL... I GUESS WE HAVE TO COUNT ON THEM TO DO THEIR BEST...
...
SO ALL THE WHITE BLOOD CELLS REALLY ARE WEIRDOS.

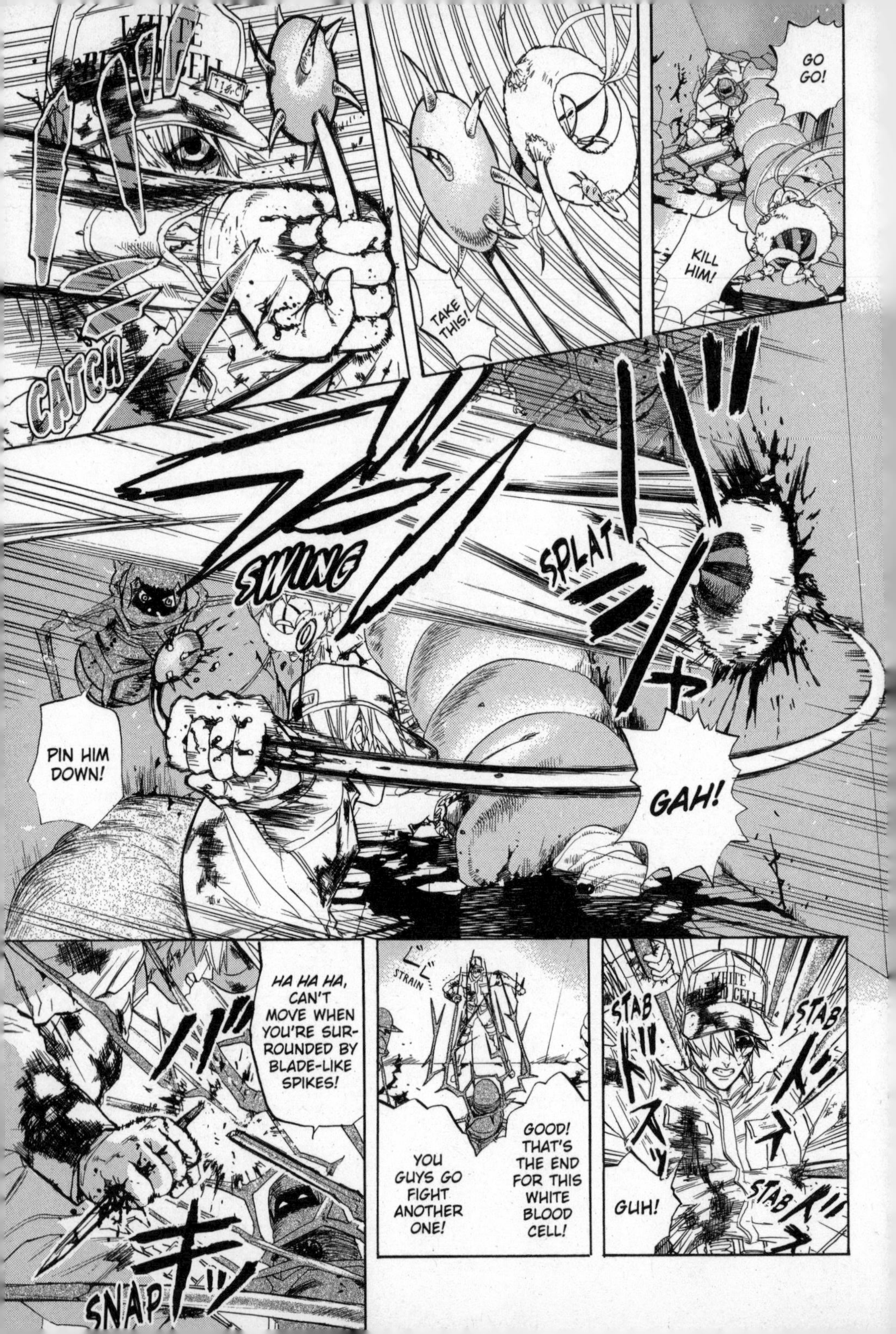
GO GO!
KILL HIM!
TAKE THIS!
CATCH
SPLAT
GAH!
SWING
PIN HIM DOWN!
STAB
STAB
GUH!
STAB
STRAIN
GOOD! THAT'S THE END FOR THIS WHITE BLOOD CELL!
YOU GUYS GO FIGHT ANOTHER ONE!
HA HA HA, CAN'T MOVE WHEN YOU'RE SUR-ROUNDED BY BLADE-LIKE SPIKES!
SNAP

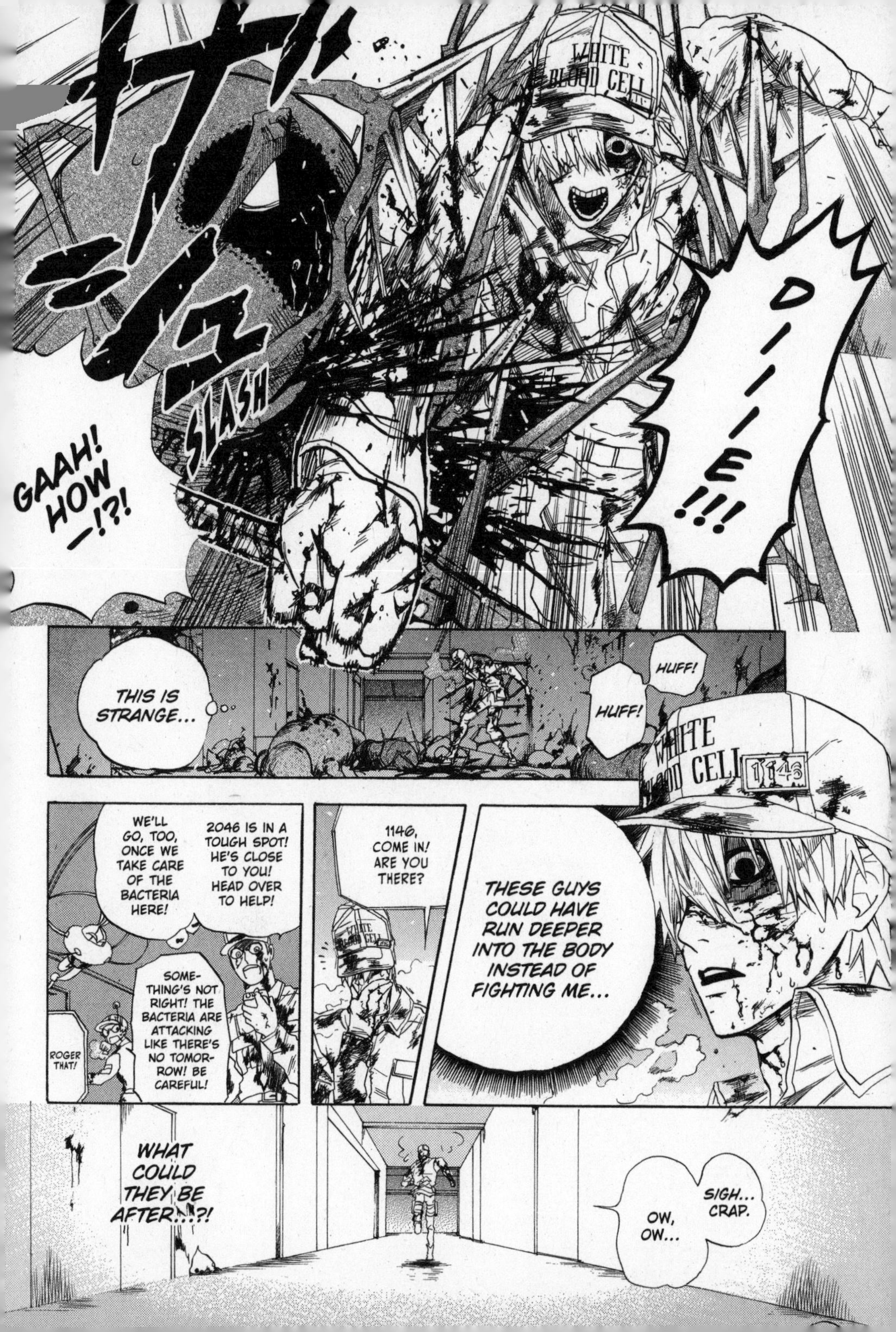
WHITE BLOOD CELL
D-I-I-I-E!!!
SLASH
GAAH! HOW—!?!
HUFF!
HUFF!
WHITE BLOOD CELL 1146
THIS IS STRANGE...
THESE GUYS COULD HAVE RUN DEEPER INTO THE BODY INSTEAD OF FIGHTING ME...
1146, COME IN! ARE YOU THERE?
2046 IS IN A TOUGH SPOT! HE'S CLOSE TO YOU! HEAD OVER TO HELP!
WE'LL GO, TOO, ONCE WE TAKE CARE OF THE BACTERIA HERE!
SOME-THING'S NOT RIGHT! THE BACTERIA ARE ATTACKING LIKE THERE'S NO TOMOR-ROW! BE CAREFUL!
ROGER THAT!
SIGH... CRAP.
OW, OW...
WHAT COULD THEY BE AFTER...?!

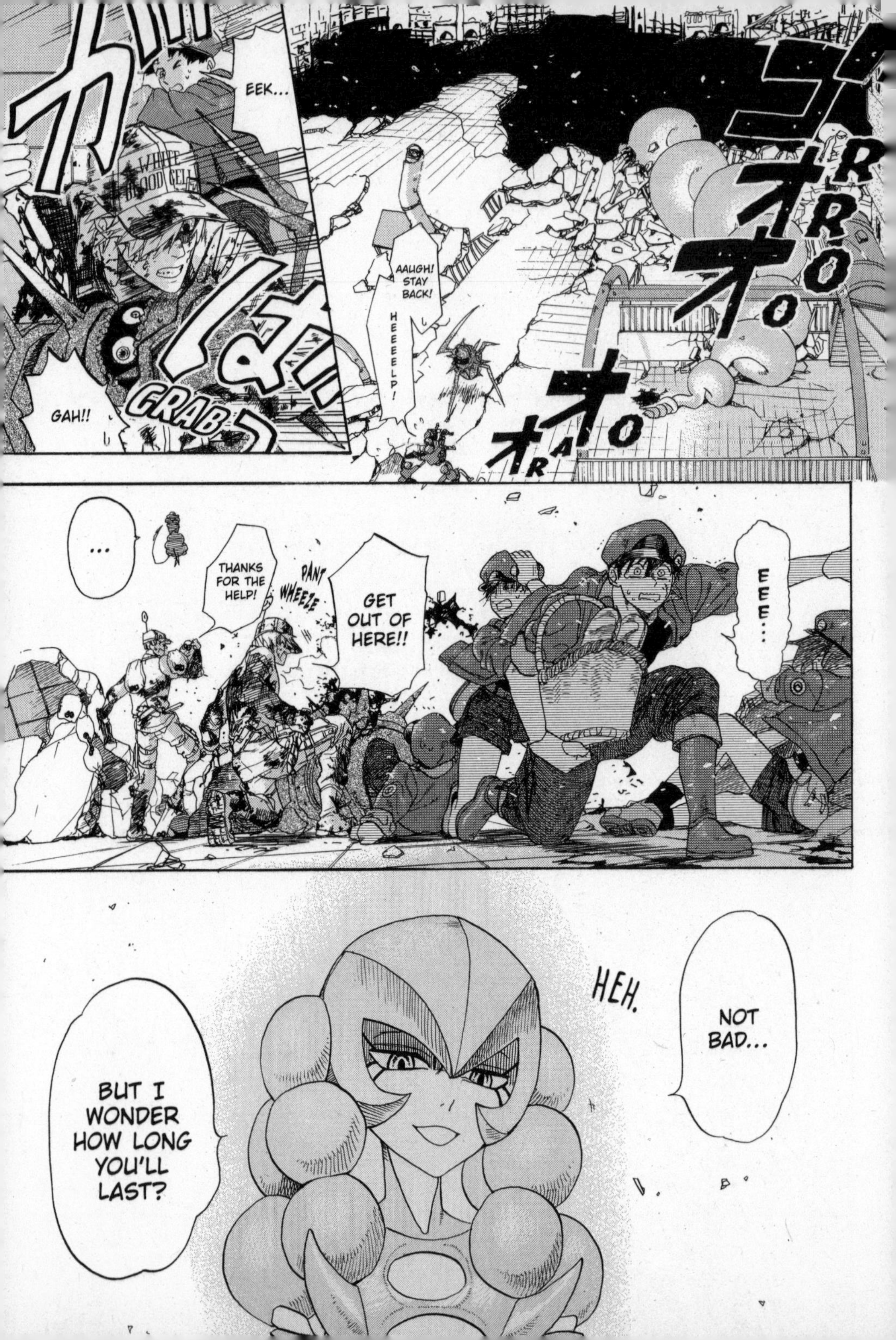

AAUGH! STAY BACK!
HEEEEELP!
EEK...
WHITE BLOOD CELL
GRAB
GAH!!
EEE...
GET OUT OF HERE!!
PANT
WHEEZE
THANKS FOR THE HELP!
...
HEH.
NOT BAD...
BUT I WONDER HOW LONG YOU'LL LAST?

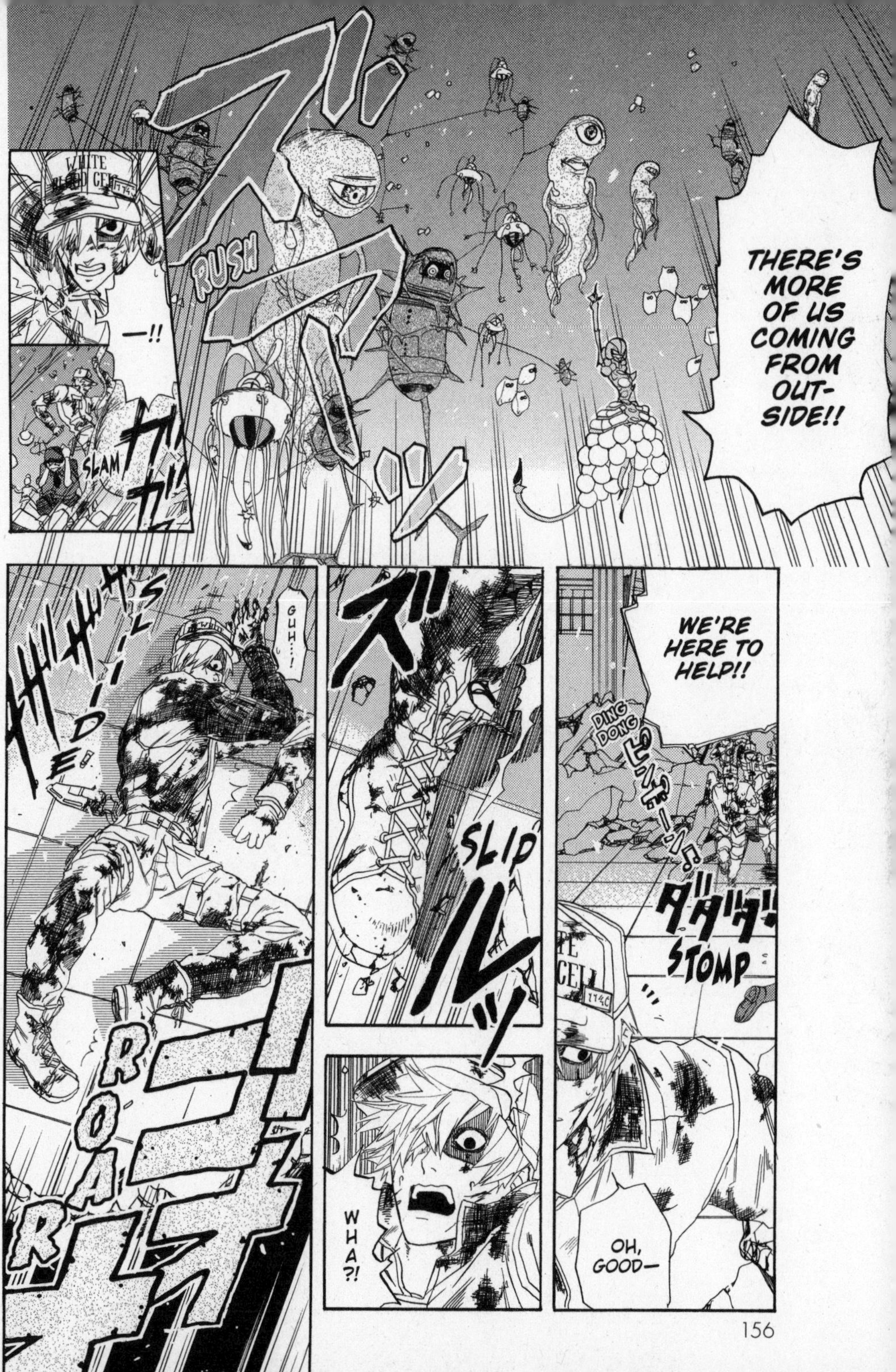
THERE'S MORE OF US COMING FROM OUT-SIDE!!
RUSH
—!!
SLAM
WE'RE HERE TO HELP!!
DING DONG
STOMP
SLIP
OH, GOOD—
WHA?!
GUH...!
SL-I-I-DE!
ROAR

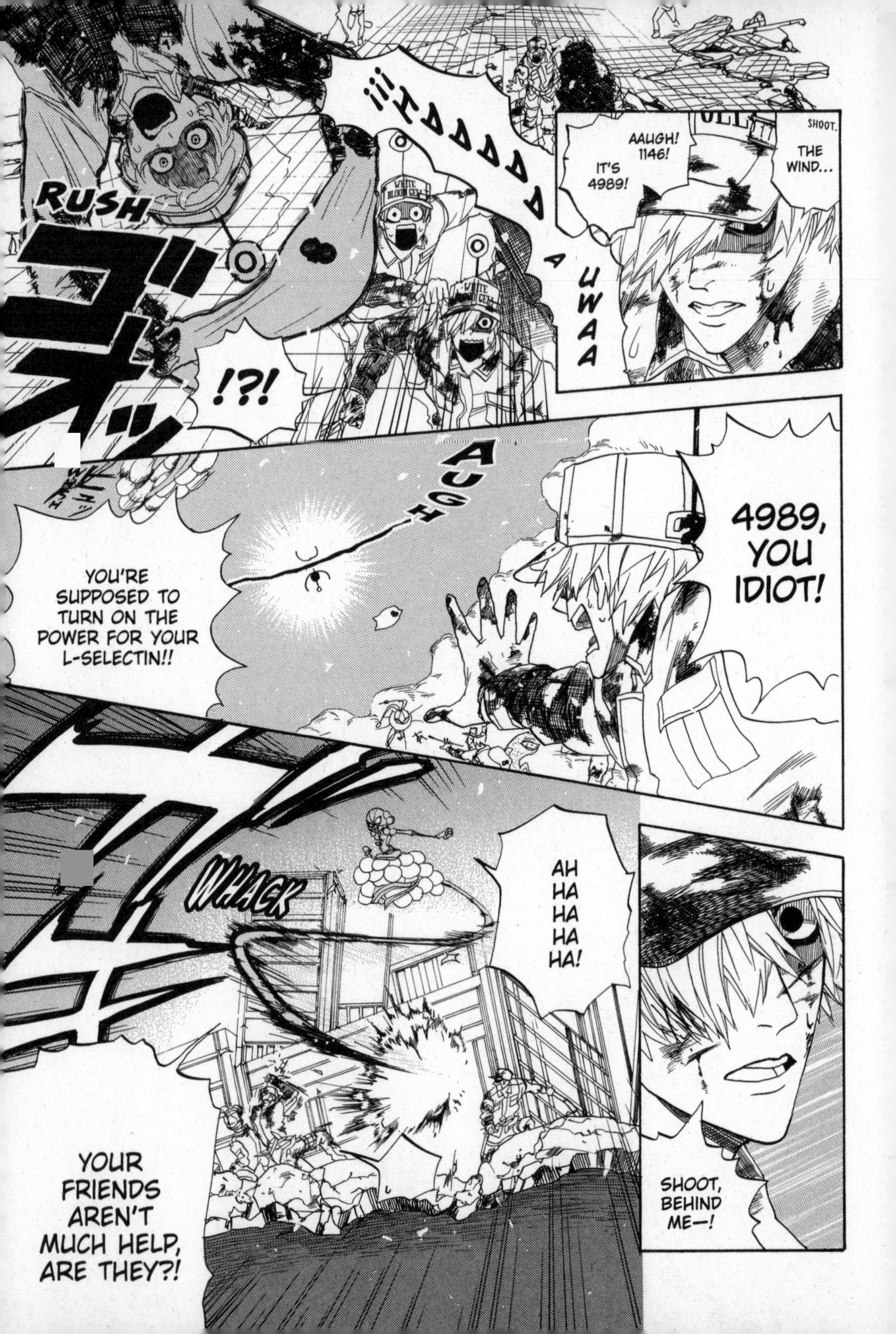
SHOOT.
THE WIND...
AAUGH! 1146! IT'S 4989!
UWAA
!?!
RUSH
4989, YOU IDIOT!
AUGH
YOU'RE SUPPOSED TO TURN ON THE POWER FOR YOUR L-SELECTIN!!
SHOOT, BEHIND ME—!
AH HA HA HA HA HA!
WHACK
YOUR FRIENDS AREN'T MUCH HELP, ARE THEY?!

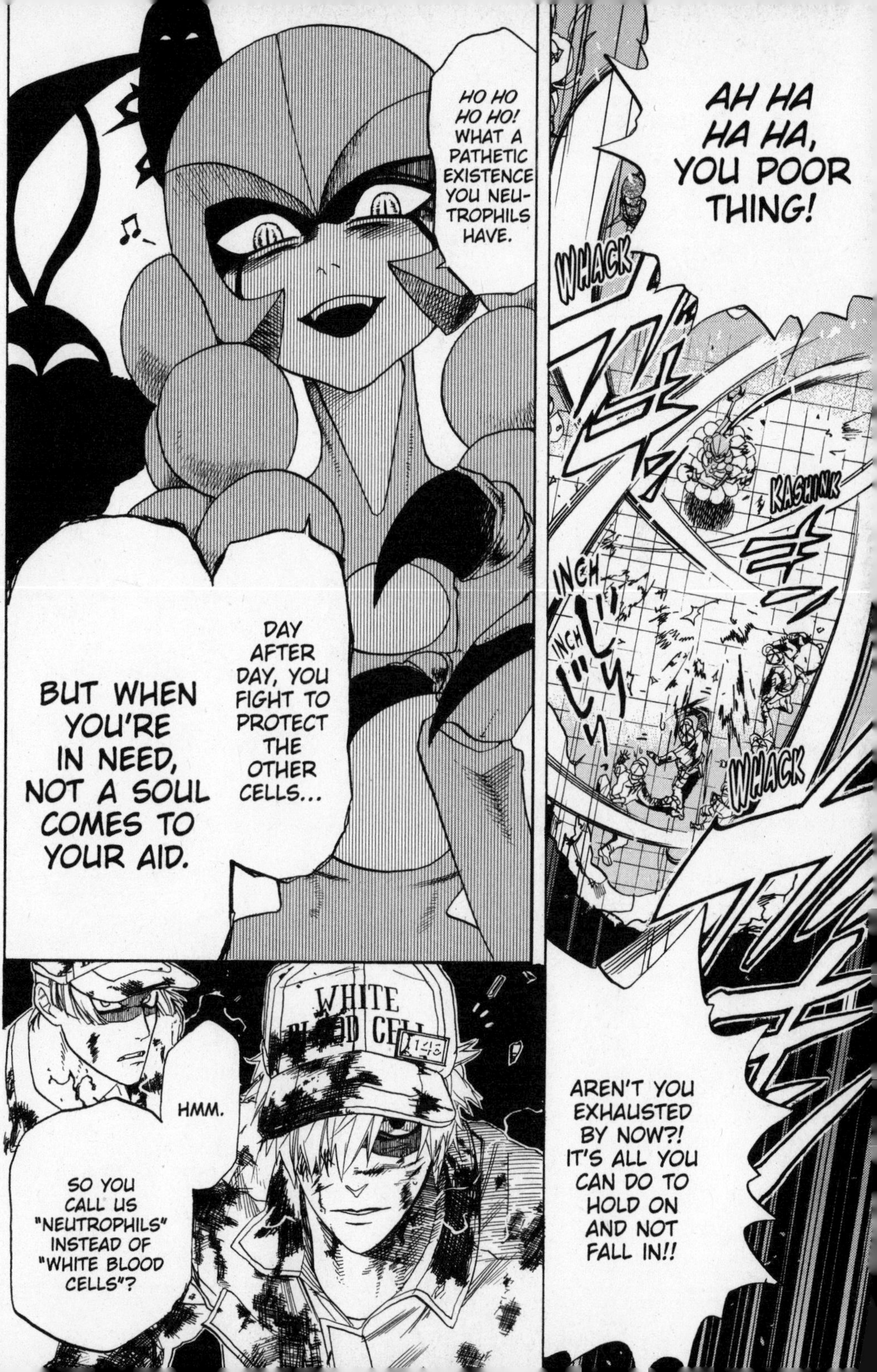
AH HA HA HA, YOU POOR THING!
WHACK
KASHINK
INCH
INCH
WHACK
AREN'T YOU EXHAUSTED BY NOW?! IT'S ALL YOU CAN DO TO HOLD ON AND NOT FALL IN!!
HO HO HO HO! WHAT A PATHETIC EXISTENCE YOU NEUTROPHILS HAVE.
DAY AFTER DAY, YOU FIGHT TO PROTECT THE OTHER CELLS...
BUT WHEN YOU'RE IN NEED, NOT A SOUL COMES TO YOUR AID.
HMM.
SO YOU CALL US "NEUTROPHILS" INSTEAD OF "WHITE BLOOD CELLS"?

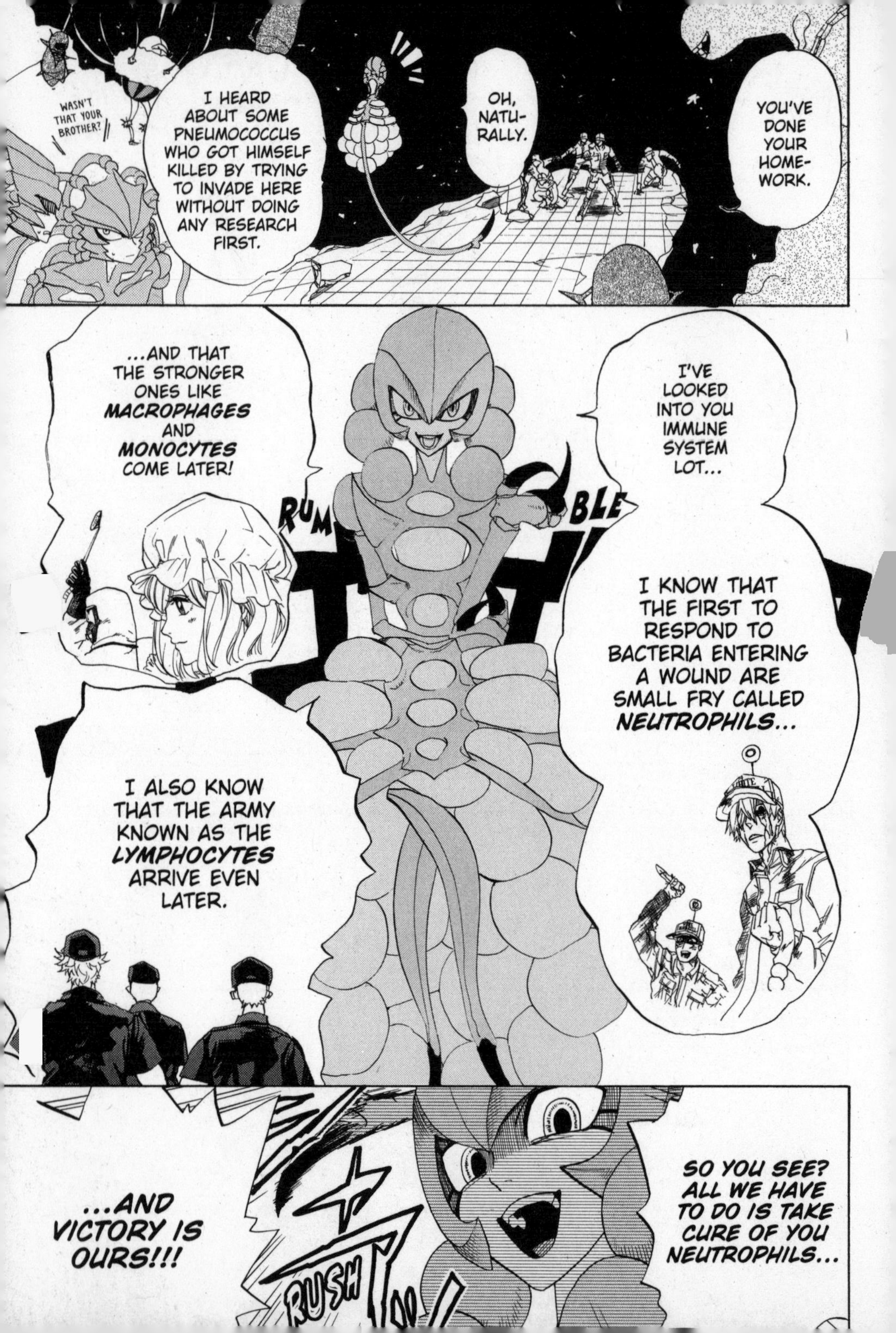

YOU'VE DONE YOUR HOME-WORK.
OH, NATU-RALLY.
I HEARD ABOUT SOME PNEUMOCOCCUS WHO GOT HIMSELF KILLED BY TRYING TO INVADE HERE WITHOUT DOING ANY RESEARCH FIRST.
WASN'T THAT YOUR BROTHER?
I'VE LOOKED INTO YOU IMMUNE SYSTEM LOT...
I KNOW THAT THE FIRST TO RESPOND TO BACTERIA ENTERING A WOUND ARE SMALL FRY CALLED NEUTROPHILS...
RUMBLE
...AND THAT THE STRONGER ONES LIKE MACROPHAGES AND MONOCYTES COME LATER!
I ALSO KNOW THAT THE ARMY KNOWN AS THE LYMPHOCYTES ARRIVE EVEN LATER.
SO YOU SEE? ALL WE HAVE TO DO IS TAKE CURE OF YOU NEUTROPHILS...
...AND VICTORY IS OURS!!!
RUSH

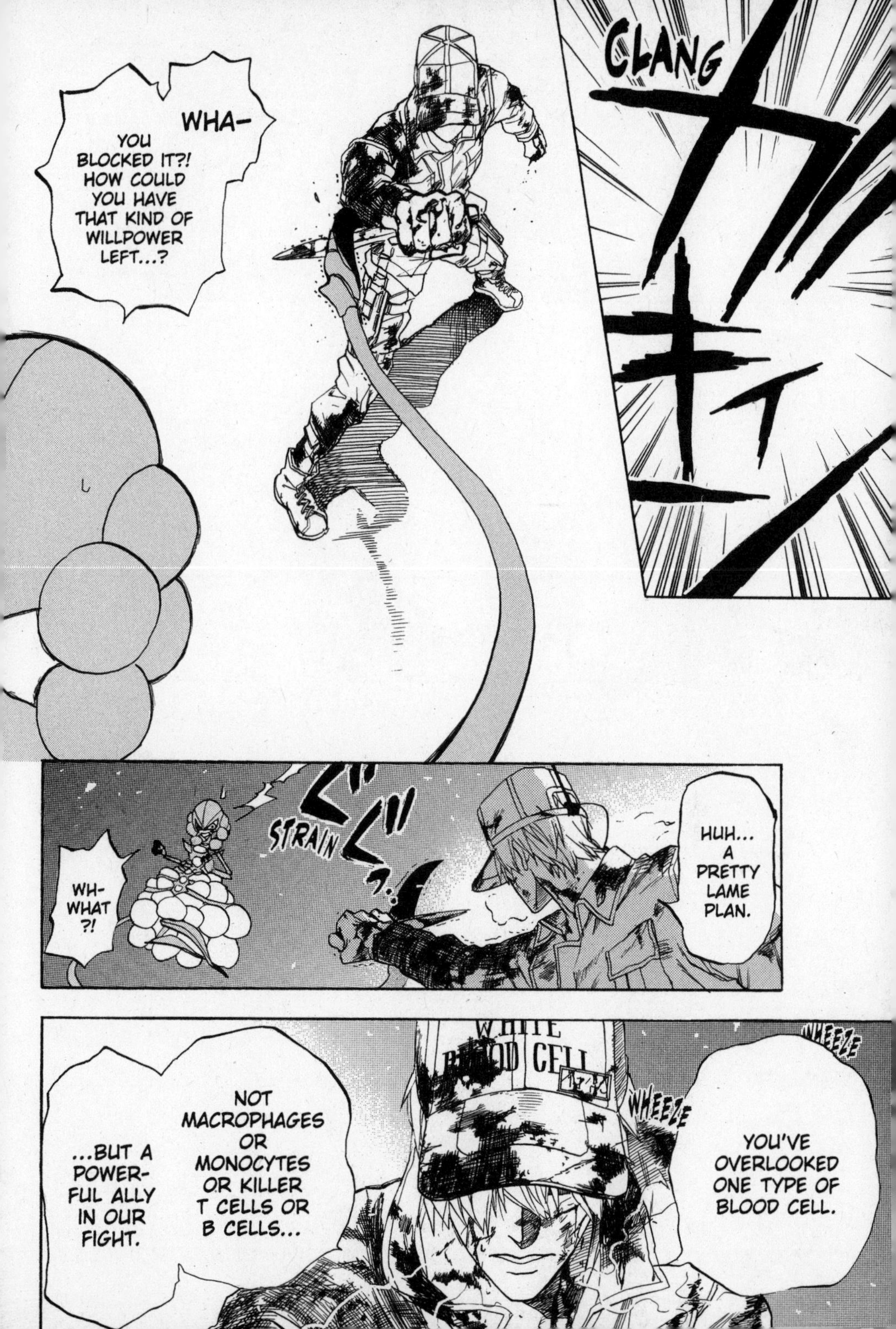
CLANG
WHA-
YOU BLOCKED IT?! HOW COULD YOU HAVE THAT KIND OF WILLPOWER LEFT...?
HUH... A PRETTY LAME PLAN.
STRAIN
WH-WHAT?!
WHEEZE
WHEEZE
YOU'VE OVERLOOKED ONE TYPE OF BLOOD CELL.
NOT MACROPHAGES OR MONOCYTES OR KILLER T CELLS OR B CELLS...
...BUT A POWER-FUL ALLY IN OUR FIGHT.
WHITE BLOOD CELL

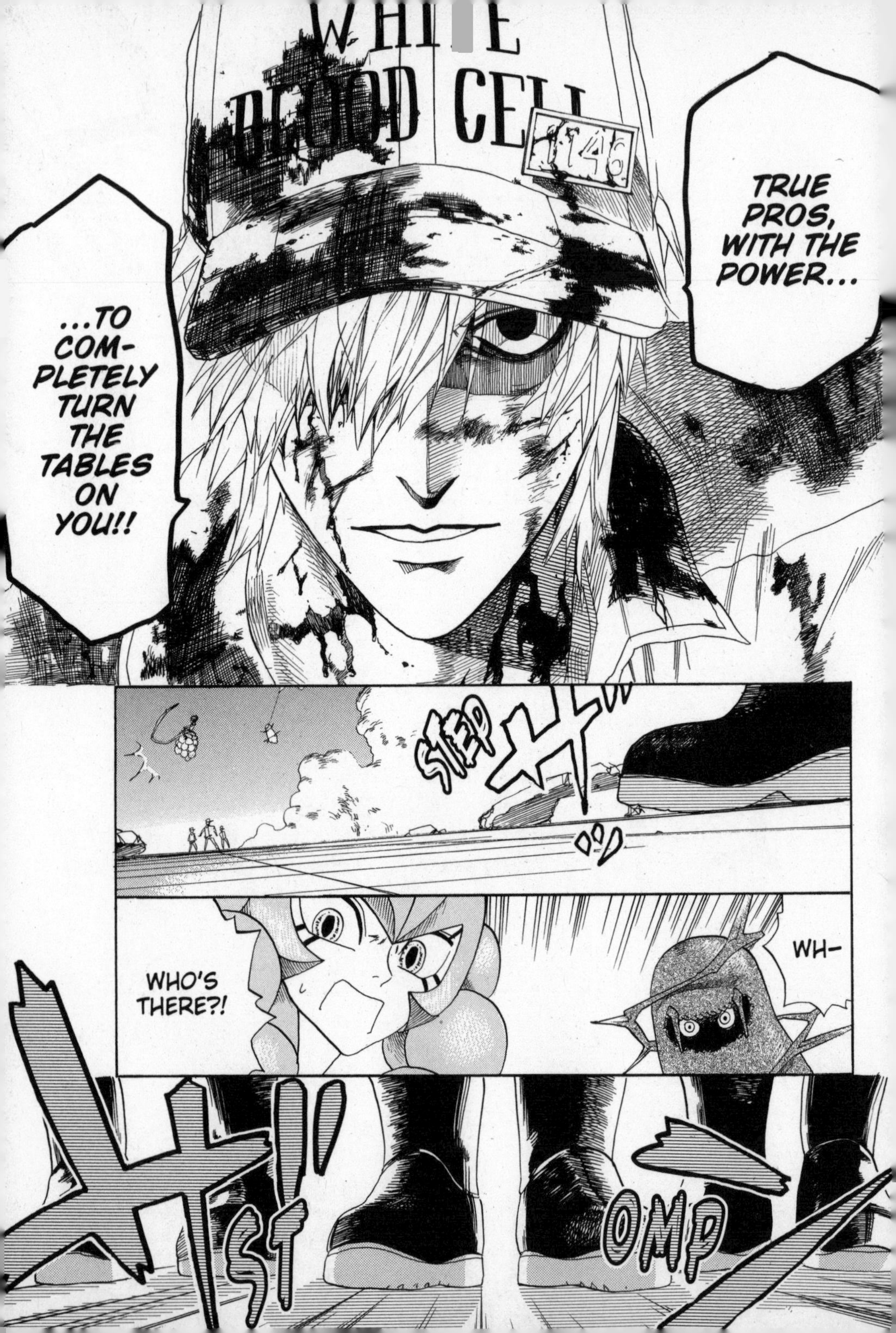
TRUE PROS, WITH THE POWER...
...TO COM-PLETELY TURN THE TABLES ON YOU!!
STEP
WH-
WHO'S THERE?!
ST
OMP

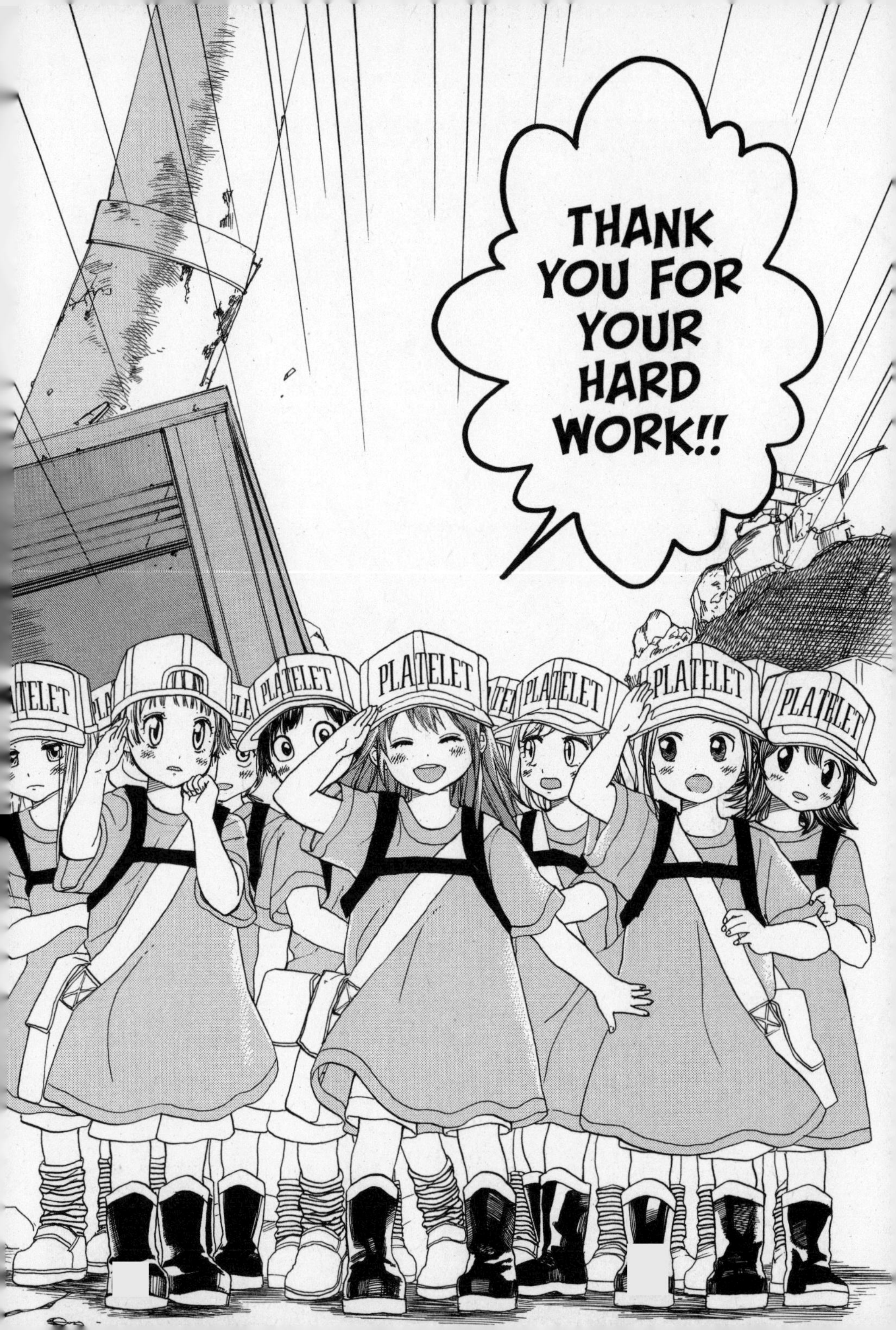
THANK YOU FOR YOUR HARD WORK!!
PLATELET

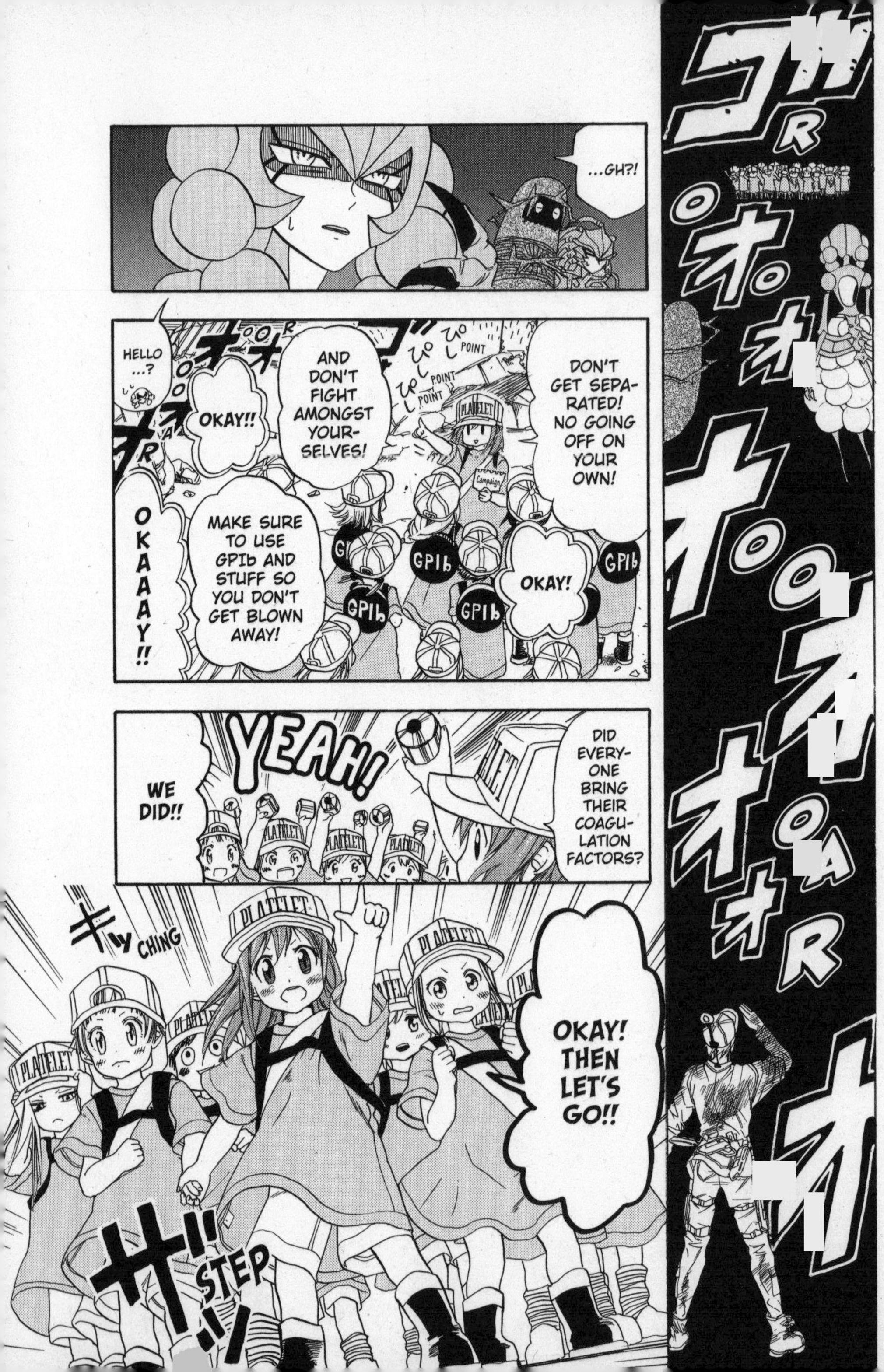
R
A
R
...GH?!
DON'T GET SEPA-RATED! NO GOING OFF ON YOUR OWN!
POINT
POINT
POINT
PLATELET
Campaign
AND DON'T FIGHT AMONGST YOUR-SELVES!
OKAY!
GPIb
MAKE SURE TO USE GPIb AND STUFF SO YOU DON'T GET BLOWN AWAY!
OKAY!!
HELLO ...?
OKAAAAY!!
DID EVERY-ONE BRING THEIR COAGU-LATION FACTORS?
YEAH!
WE DID!!
OKAY! THEN LET'S GO!!
PLATELET
CHING
STEP

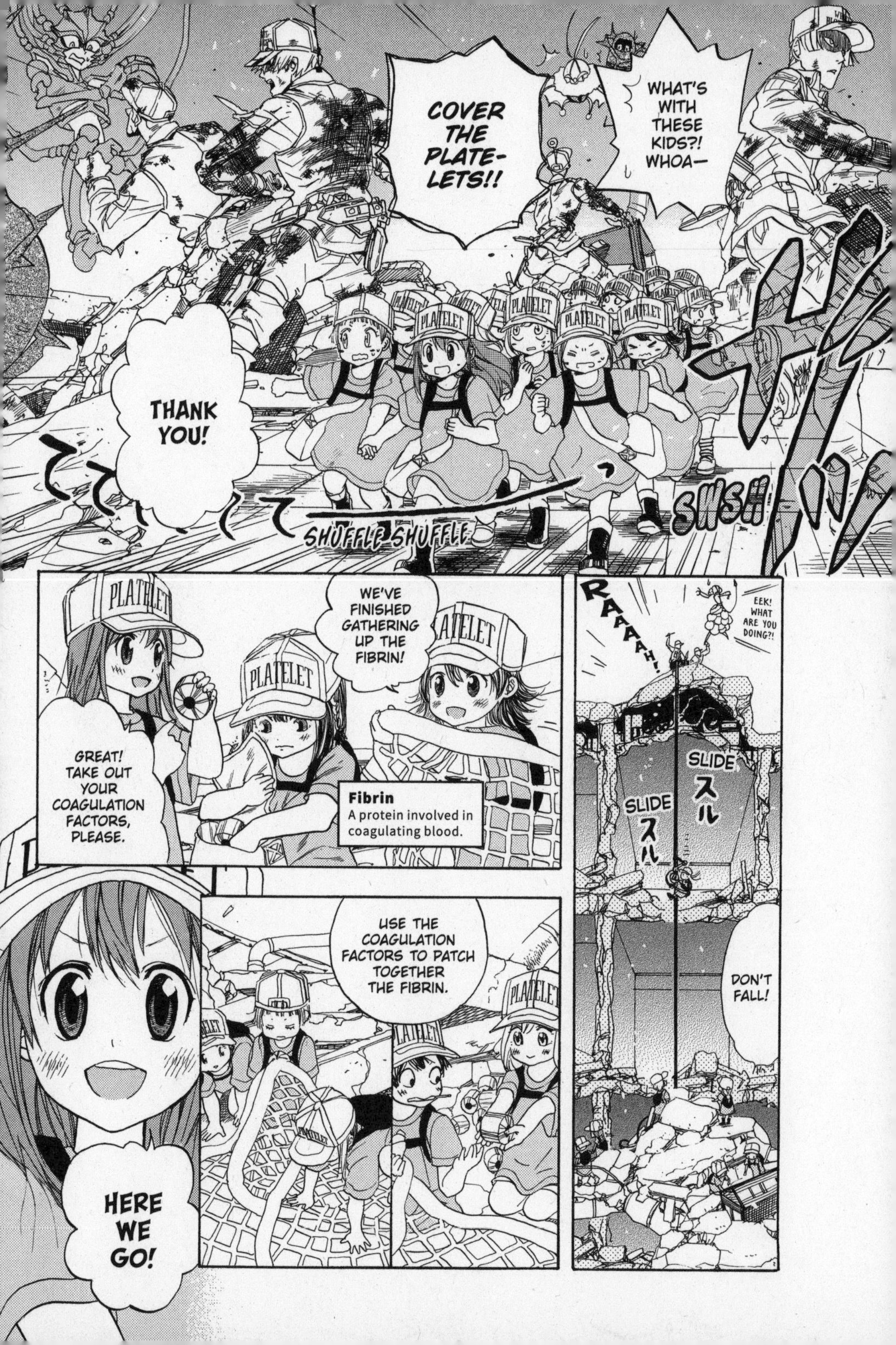
WHAT'S WITH THESE KIDS?! WHOA—
COVER THE PLATE-LETS!!
THANK YOU!
SWSH!!
SHUFFLE SHUFFLE
RAAAAH!
EEK! WHAT ARE YOU DOING?!
SLIDE スル
SLIDE スル
DON'T FALL!
WE'VE FINISHED GATHERING UP THE FIBRIN!
GREAT! TAKE OUT YOUR COAGULATION FACTORS, PLEASE.
Fibrin
A protein involved in coagulating blood.
USE THE COAGULATION FACTORS TO PATCH TOGETHER THE FIBRIN.
HERE WE GO!

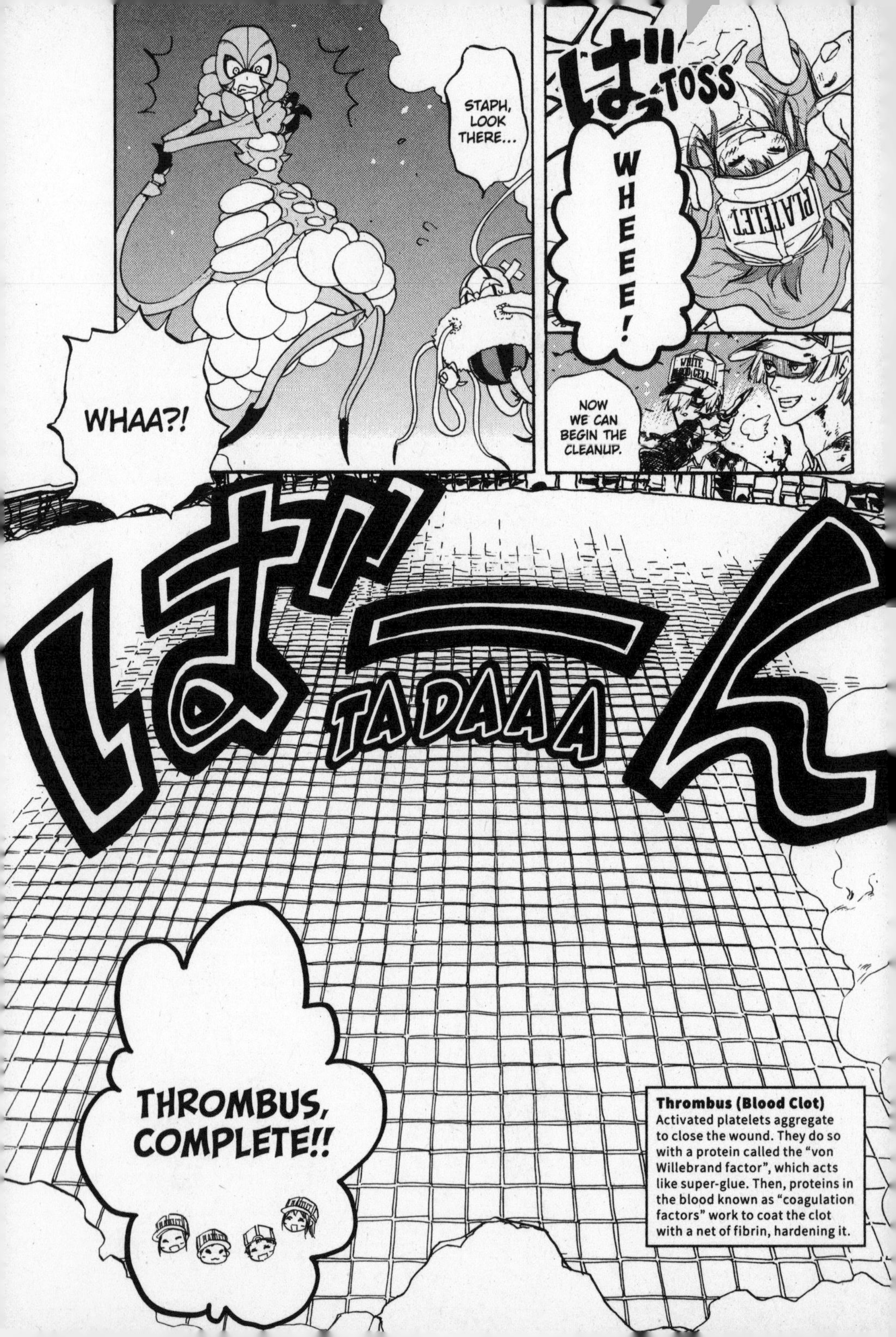

Thrombus (Blood Clot)
Activated platelets aggregate to close the wound. They do so with a protein called the "von Willebrand factor", which acts like super-glue. Then, proteins in the blood known as "coagulation factors" work to coat the clot with a net of fibrin, hardening it.

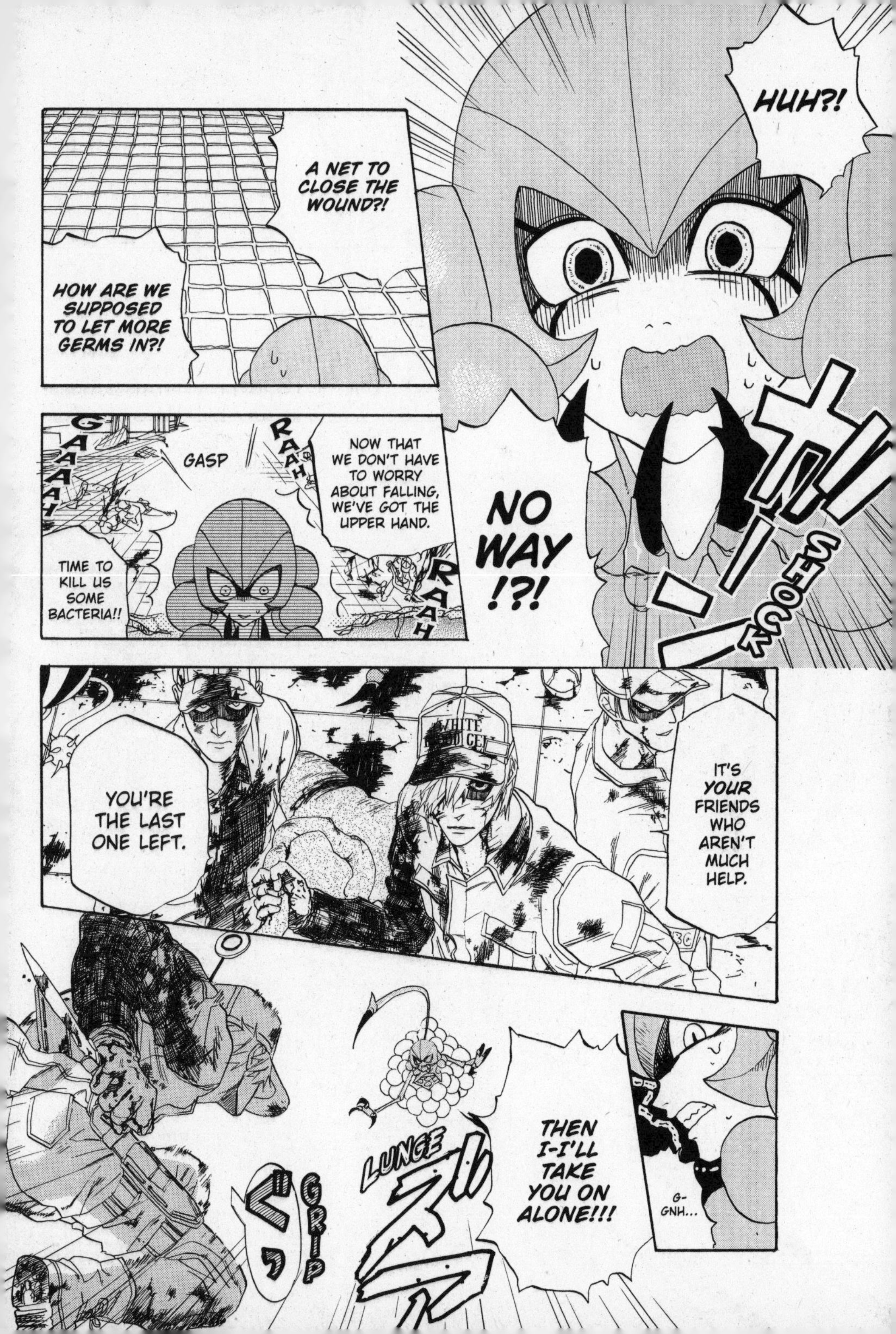
HUH?!
NO WAY!?!
SHOCK
A NET TO CLOSE THE WOUND?!
HOW ARE WE SUPPOSED TO LET MORE GERMS IN?!
RAAH
NOW THAT WE DON'T HAVE TO WORRY ABOUT FALLING, WE'VE GOT THE UPPER HAND.
GASP
GAAAAAH
RAAH
TIME TO KILL US SOME BACTERIA!!
IT'S YOUR FRIENDS WHO AREN'T MUCH HELP.
YOU'RE THE LAST ONE LEFT.
G-GNH...
THEN I-I'LL TAKE YOU ON ALONE!!!
LUNGE
GRIP

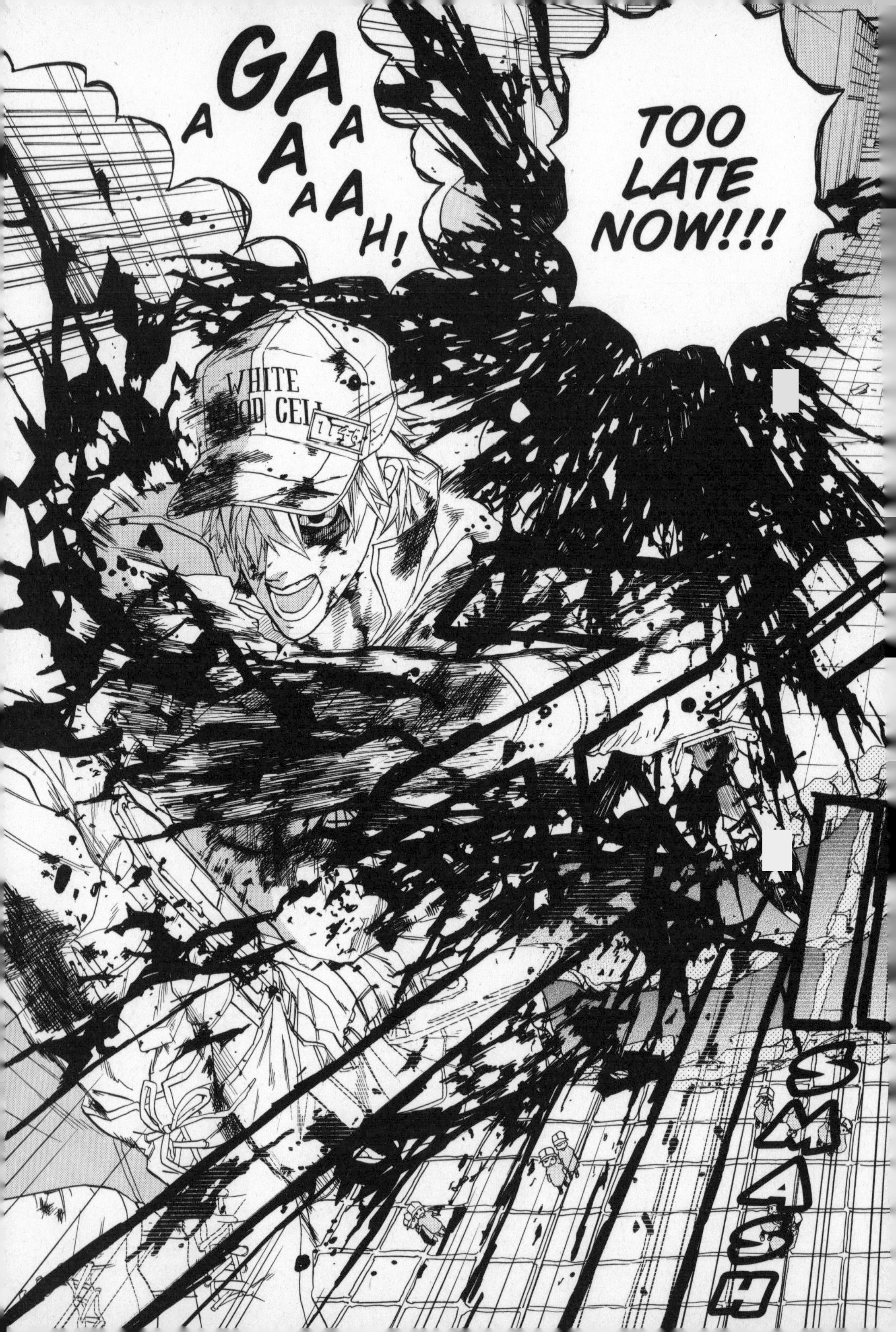
TOO LATE NOW!!!
AGAAAAAAH!
WHITE BLOOD CELL 1146
SMASH

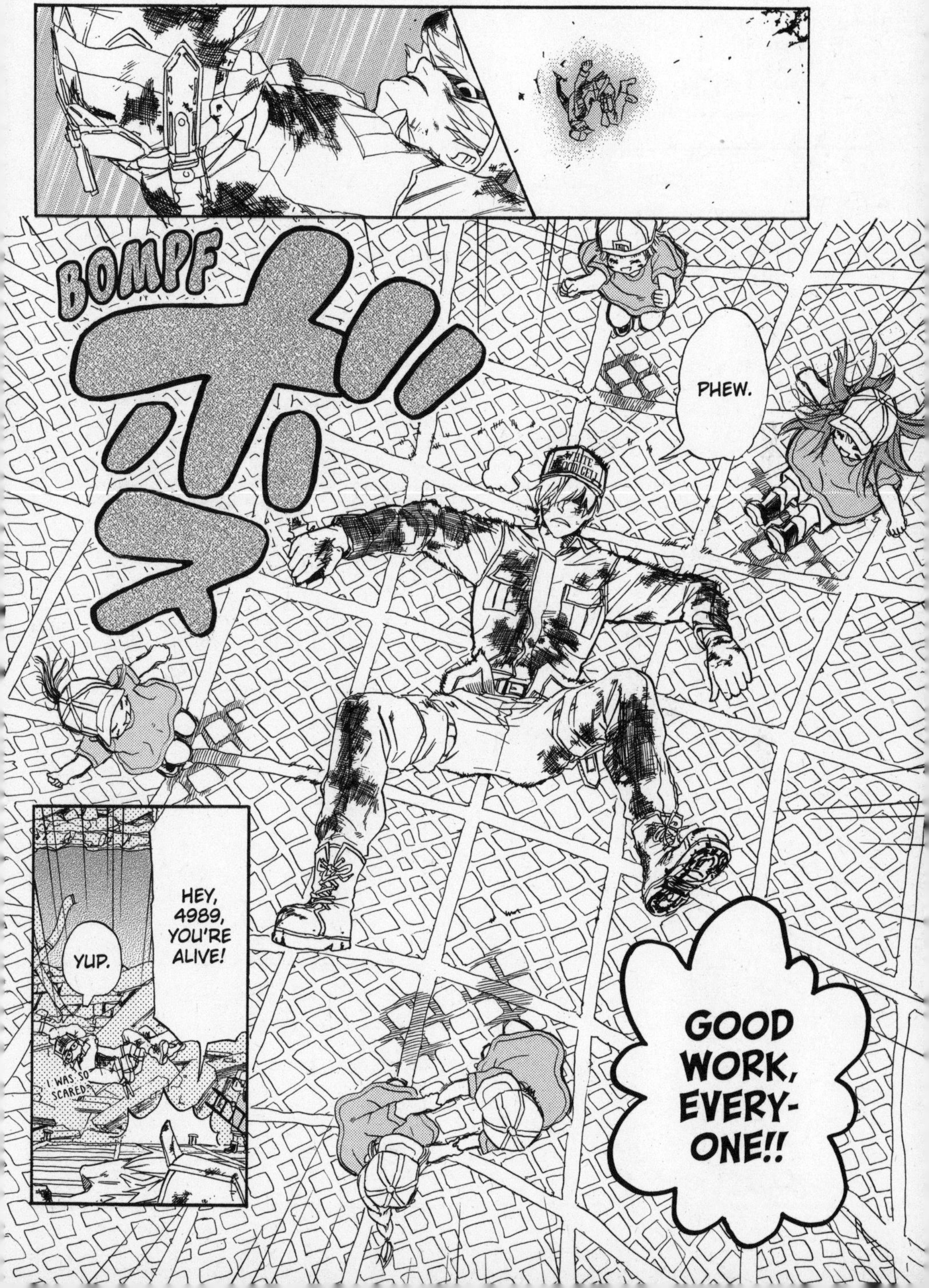
PHEW.
BOMPF
GOOD WORK, EVERY-ONE!!
HEY, 4989, YOU'RE ALIVE!
YUP.
I WAS SO SCARED

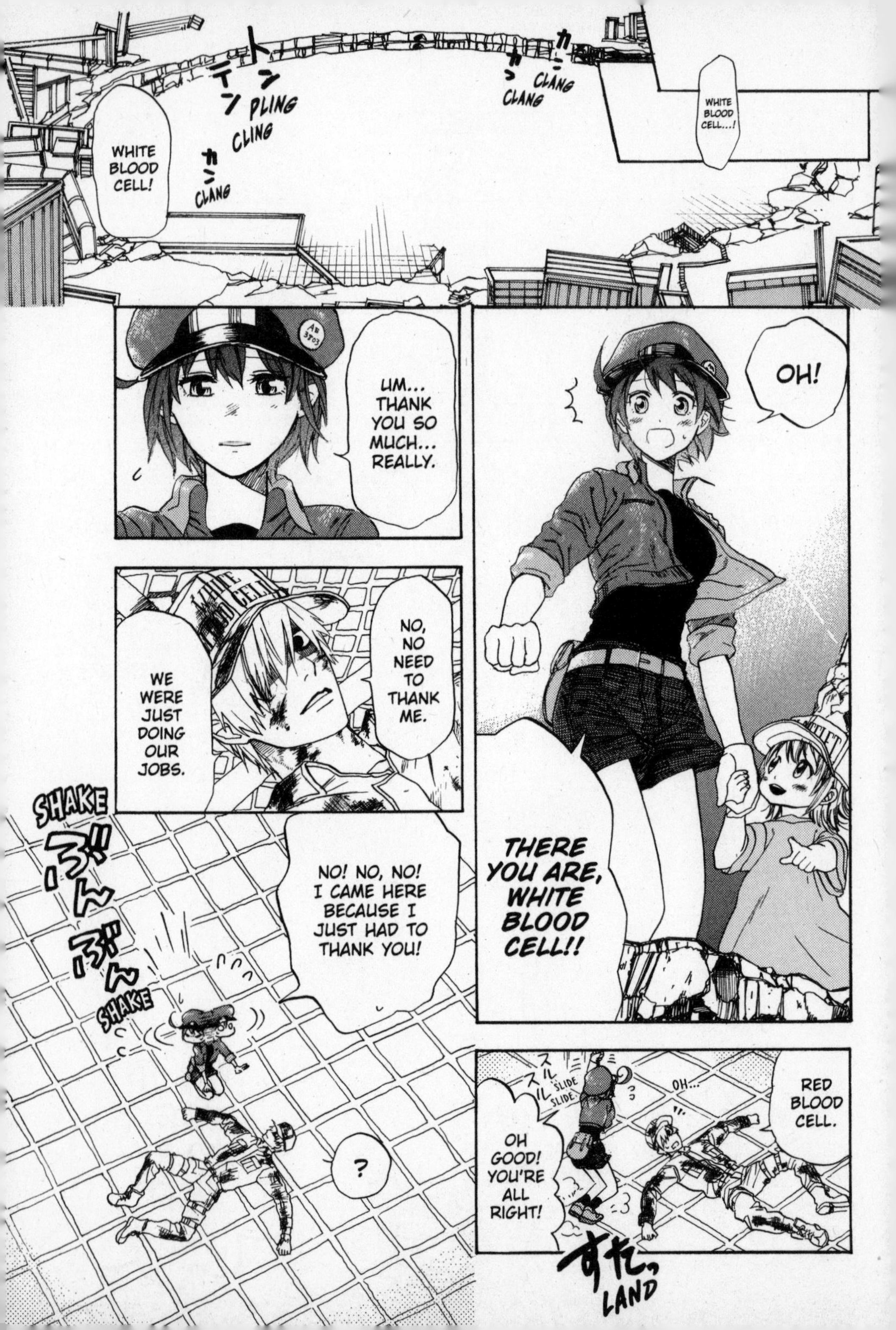
WHITE BLOOD CELL...!
カン CLANG
カン CLANG
テン PLING
テン CLING
カン CLANG
WHITE BLOOD CELL!
OH!
THERE YOU ARE, WHITE BLOOD CELL!!
UM... THANK YOU SO MUCH... REALLY.
NO, NO NEED TO THANK ME.
WE WERE JUST DOING OUR JOBS.
RED BLOOD CELL.
OH...
スル SLIDE
スル SLIDE
OH GOOD! YOU'RE ALL RIGHT!
すたっ LAND
NO! NO, NO! I CAME HERE BECAUSE I JUST HAD TO THANK YOU!
ぶん SHAKE
ぶん SHAKE
?

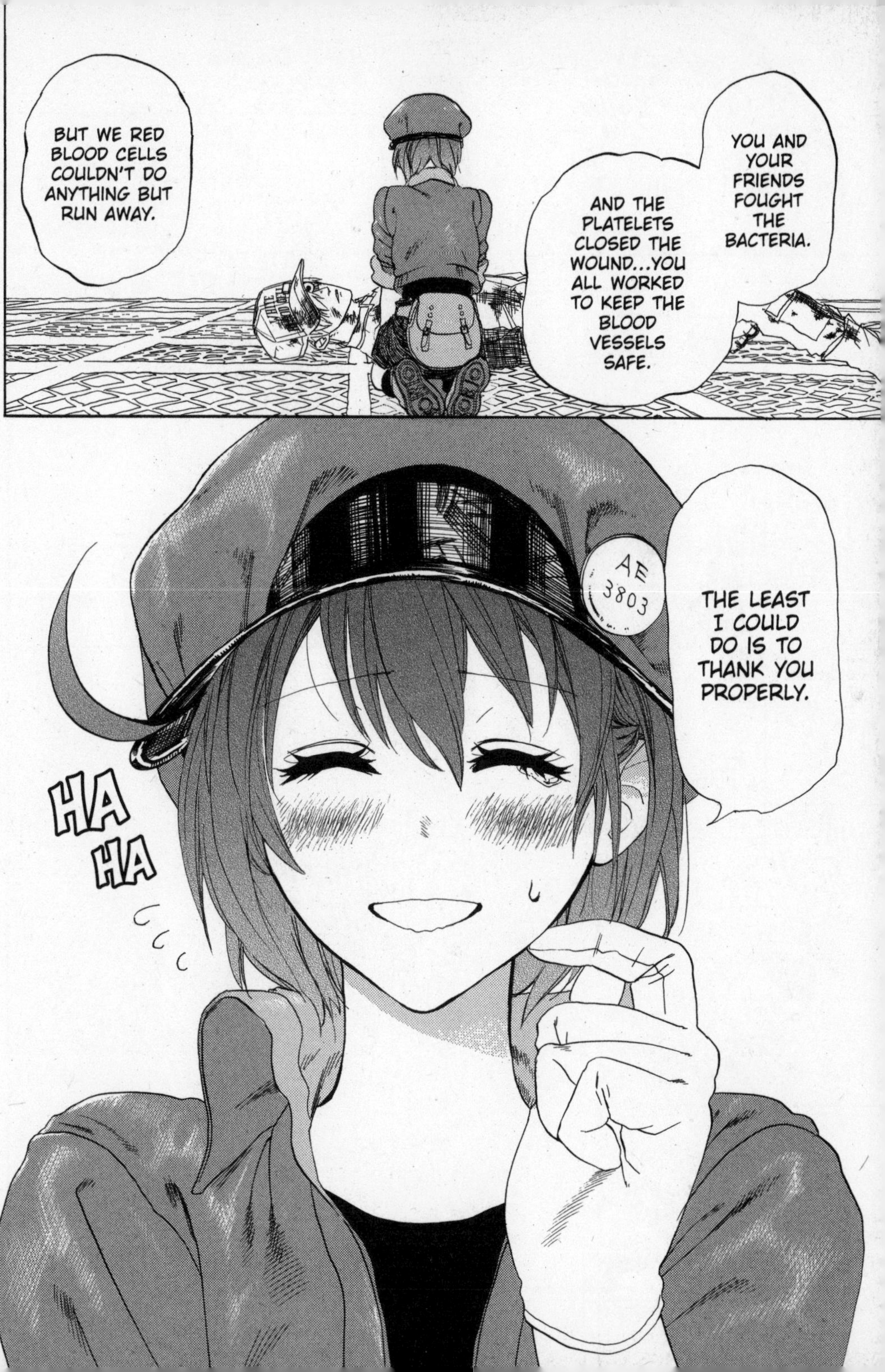
YOU AND YOUR FRIENDS FOUGHT THE BACTERIA.
AND THE PLATELETS CLOSED THE WOUND...YOU ALL WORKED TO KEEP THE BLOOD VESSELS SAFE.
BUT WE RED BLOOD CELLS COULDN'T DO ANYTHING BUT RUN AWAY.
THE LEAST I COULD DO IS TO THANK YOU PROPERLY.
AE 3803
HA HA

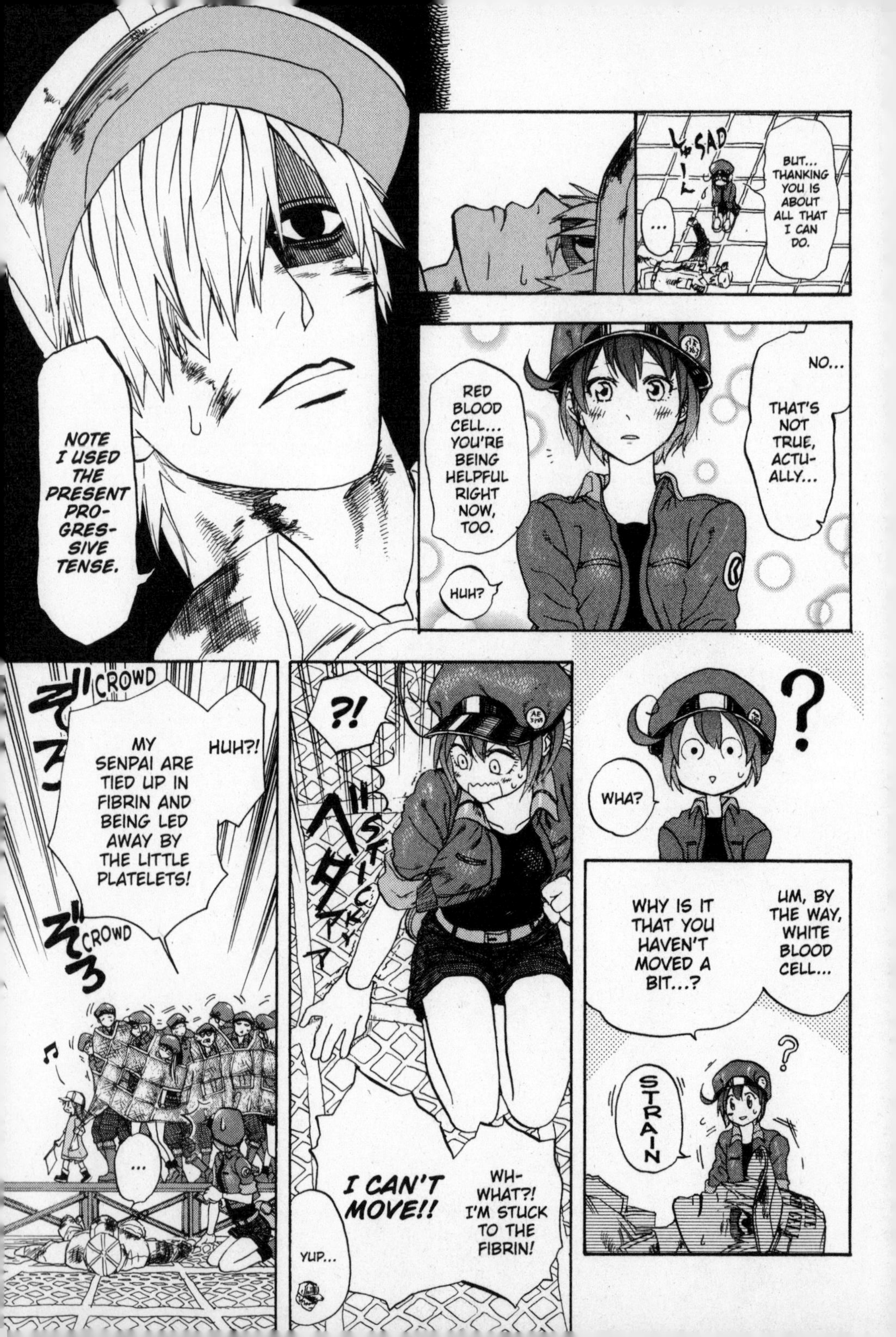
SAD
...
BUT... THANKING YOU IS ABOUT ALL THAT I CAN DO.
NO... THAT'S NOT TRUE, ACTUALLY...
RED BLOOD CELL... YOU'RE BEING HELPFUL RIGHT NOW, TOO.
HUH?
NOTE I USED THE PRESENT PROGRESSIVE TENSE.
?
WHA?
UM, BY THE WAY, WHITE BLOOD CELL...
WHY IS IT THAT YOU HAVEN'T MOVED A BIT...?
?
STRAIN
?!
STICKY
WH-WHAT?! I'M STUCK TO THE FIBRIN!
I CAN'T MOVE!!
YUP...
CROWD
HUH?!
MY SENPAI ARE TIED UP IN FIBRIN AND BEING LED AWAY BY THE LITTLE PLATELETS!
CROWD
...

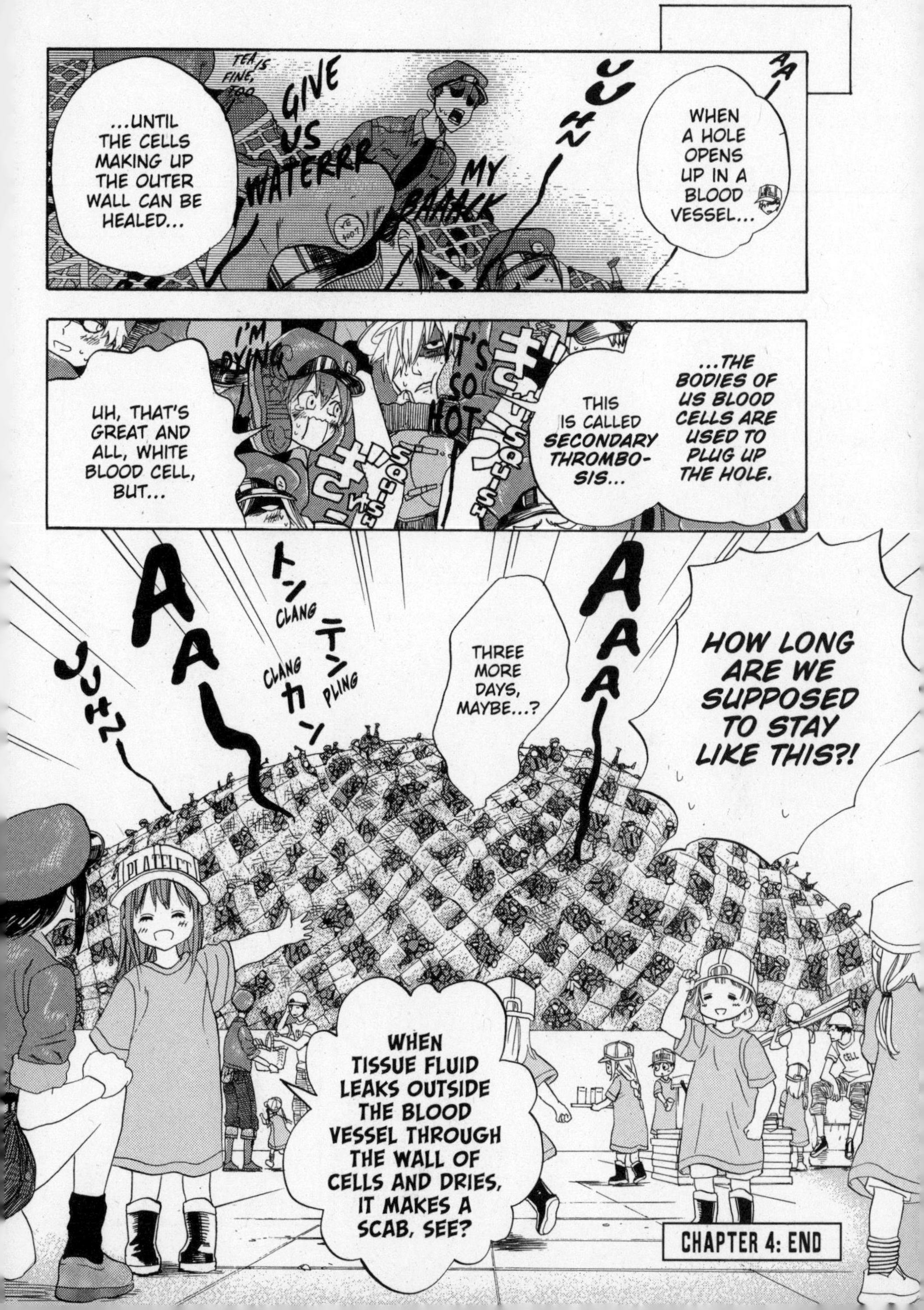
AA~
WHEN A HOLE OPENS UP IN A BLOOD VESSEL...
UUHN
MY BAAACK
GIVE US WATERRR
TEA IS FINE, TOO
...UNTIL THE CELLS MAKING UP THE OUTER WALL CAN BE HEALED...
...THE BODIES OF US BLOOD CELLS ARE USED TO PLUG UP THE HOLE.
THIS IS CALLED SECONDARY THROMBO- SIS...
SQUISH
SQUISH
IT'S SO HOT
I'M DYING
UH, THAT'S GREAT AND ALL, WHITE BLOOD CELL, BUT...
HOW LONG ARE WE SUPPOSED TO STAY LIKE THIS?!
AAA
THREE MORE DAYS, MAYBE...?
CLANG
PLING
CLANG
AA~
UUHN
WHEN TISSUE FLUID LEAKS OUTSIDE THE BLOOD VESSEL THROUGH THE WALL OF CELLS AND DRIES, IT MAKES A SCAB, SEE?
CHAPTER 4: END

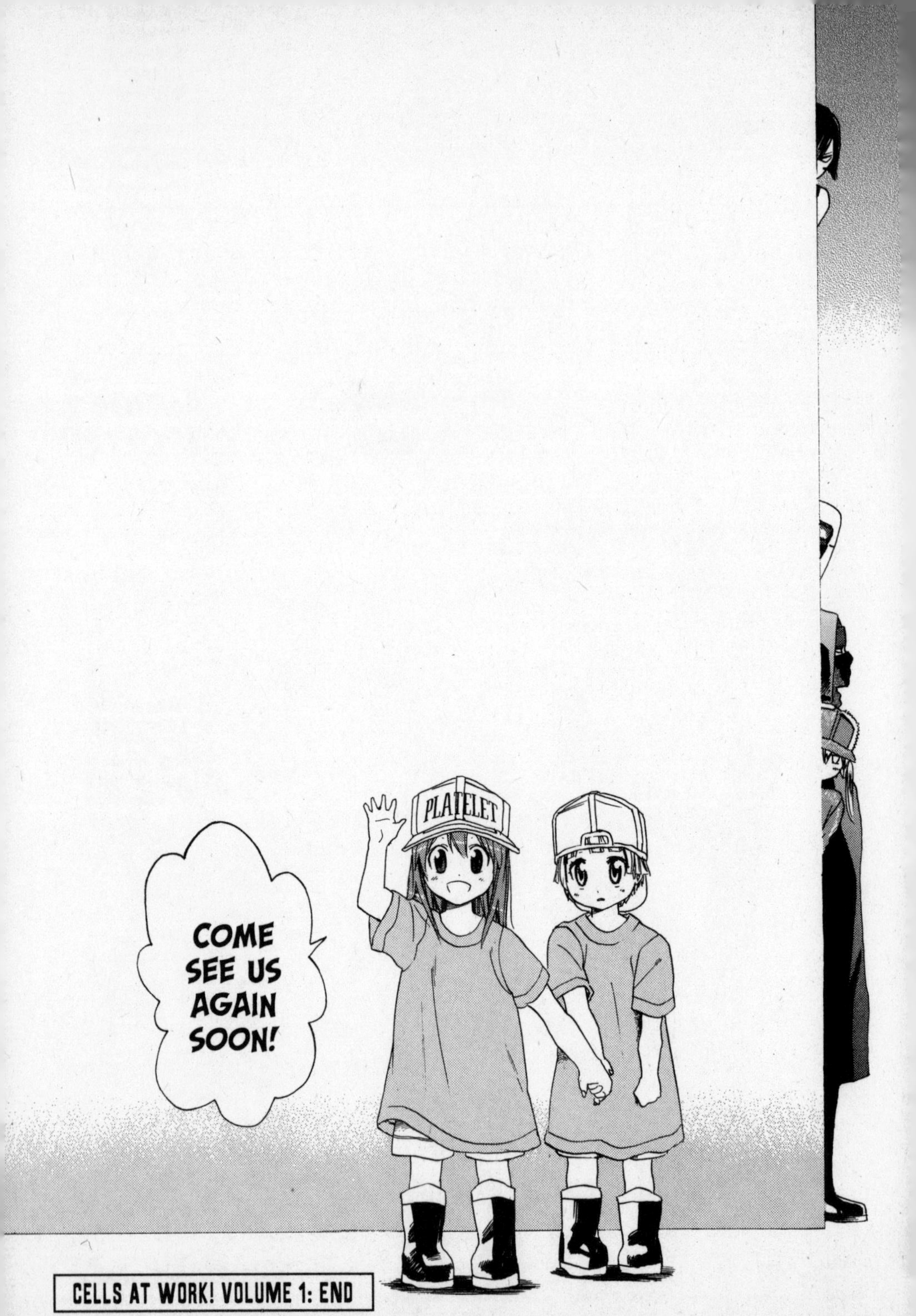
PLATELET
COME SEE US AGAIN SOON!

CELLS AT WORK! VOLUME 1: END

...AND HOW DO THEY REACH THEIR FULL POTENTIAL AS CELLS?

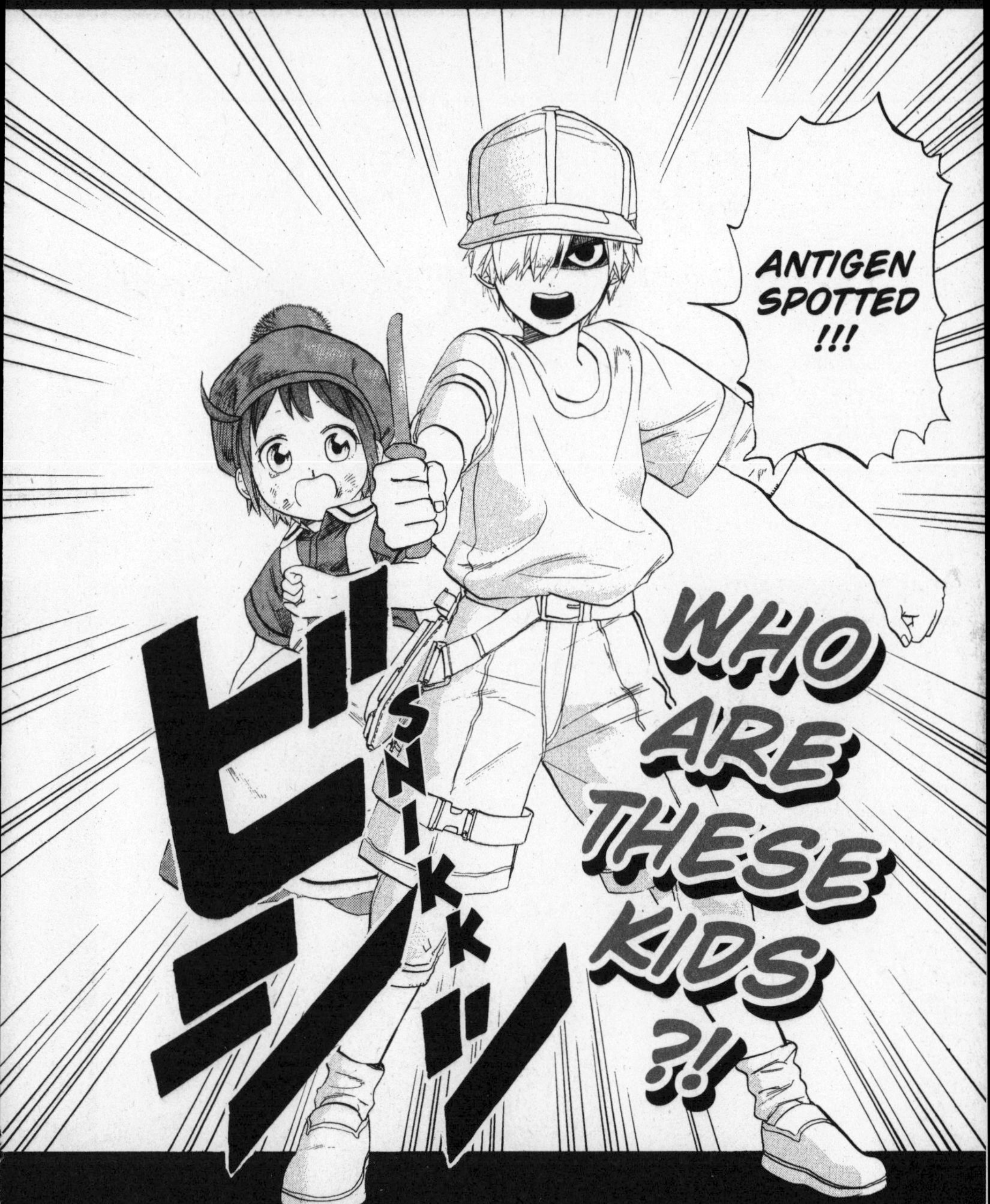
ANTIGEN SPOTTED !!!
WHO ARE THESE KIDS ?!
SHIKK

NEXT VOLUME!

WHITE BLOOD CELLS, RED BLOOD CELLS—WHERE ARE THEY BORN...

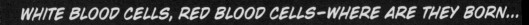

THEY HAVE A DREAM AND A DUTY!

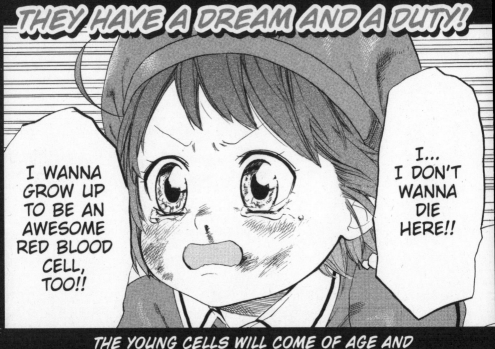

I... I DON'T WANNA DIE HERE!!
I WANNA GROW UP TO BE AN AWESOME RED BLOOD CELL, TOO!!

THE YOUNG CELLS WILL COME OF AGE AND FACE THEIR MYSTERIOUS DESTINY!!

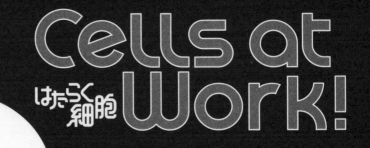

Cells at Work!

はたらく細胞

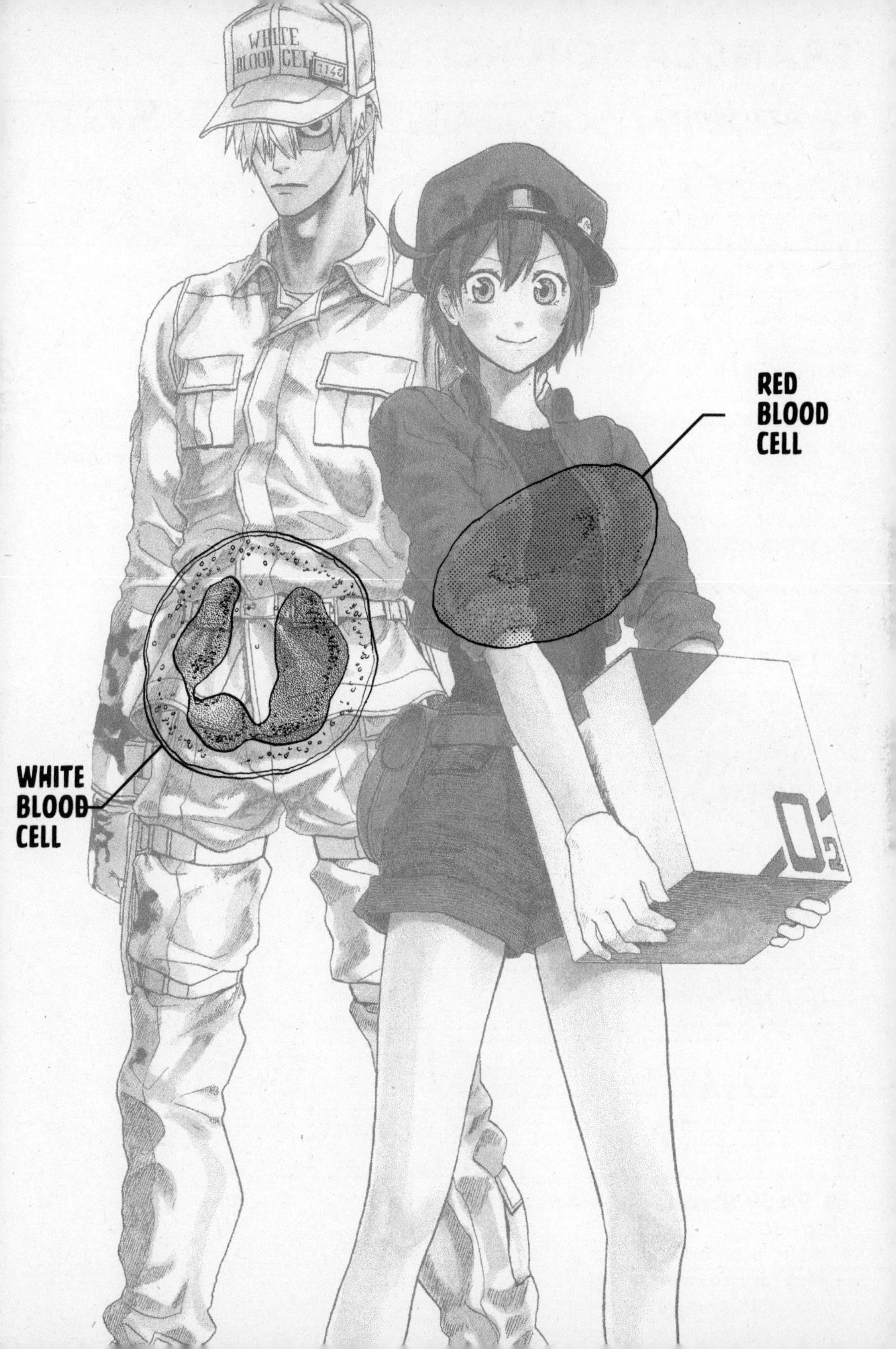
WHITE
BLOOD CELL
1146
RED
BLOOD
CELL
WHITE
BLOOD
CELL
O_2

TRANSLATION NOTES

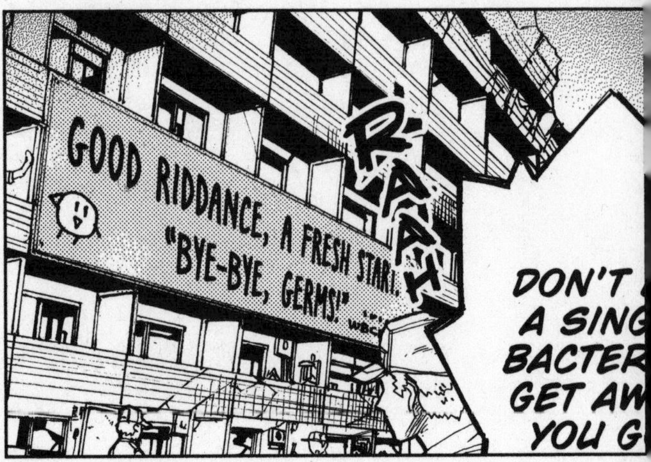
GOOD RIDDANCE, A FRESH START!
"BYE-BYE, GERMS!"

Bye-bye, Germs

Page 11

"Bye-bye, Germs," or "***Baibai-kin***" in the original Japanese, is the parting line of the main villain Baikin Man (Germ Man) from the popular, long-runnning children's cartoon ***Anpan Man***. It is a pun combining the English phrase "Bye-bye" and the Japanese word "***baikin***," meaning "germ." In the original Japanese, the sign is written in the 5-7-5 meter of a haiku poem, which is a common practice in educational messages for children as well as in public service slogans.

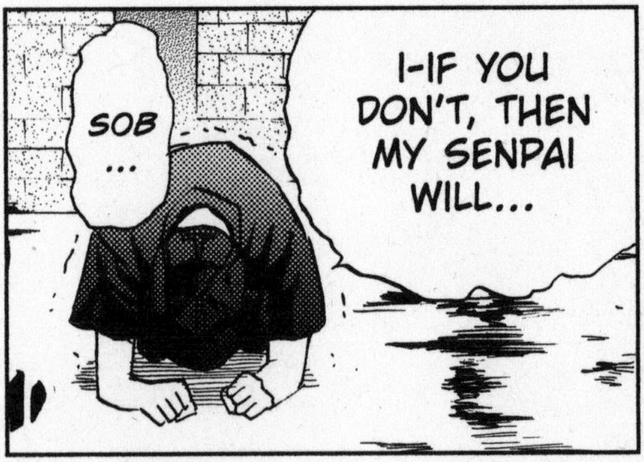
I-IF YOU DON'T, THEN MY SENPAI WILL...
SOB ...

Senpai

Page 115

The Japanese word "*senpai*" roughly translates to "upperclassman" or "senior." While it is used by students to refer to their older peers, it is not necessarily an academic term, and can be used to refer to anyone in a given situation who's more experienced than the speaker but not necessarily in a position of authority over them, as opposed to a teacher or a boss, who would not be considered a *senpai*. It often connotes respect and admiration.

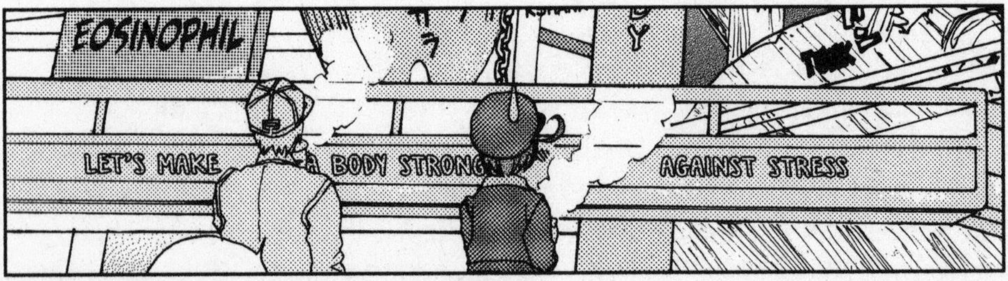
EOSINOPHIL
LET'S MAKE A BODY STRONG AGAINST STRESS

A Body Strong Against Stress

Page 50

This is a parody of popular municipal slogans—e.g. "A Town Strong Against Crime" for Yokohama City. The slogans usually seeks to promote a set of policies or infrastructure designed to combat a specific problem.

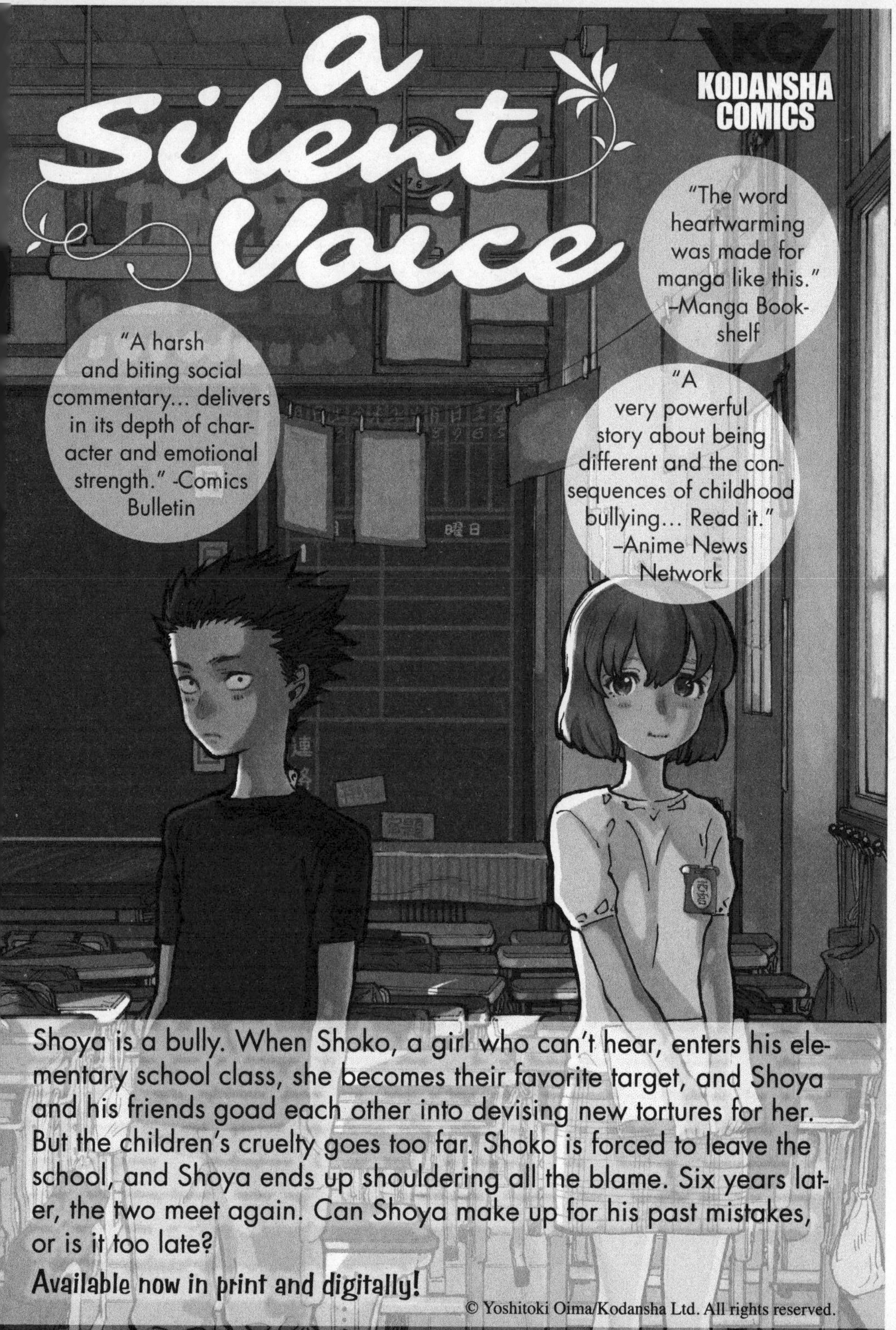
a Silent Voice
KODANSHA COMICS
"The word heartwarming was made for manga like this." –Manga Bookshelf
"A harsh and biting social commentary... delivers in its depth of character and emotional strength." -Comics Bulletin
"A very powerful story about being different and the consequences of childhood bullying... Read it." –Anime News Network
Shoya is a bully. When Shoko, a girl who can't hear, enters his elementary school class, she becomes their favorite target, and Shoya and his friends goad each other into devising new tortures for her. But the children's cruelty goes too far. Shoko is forced to leave the school, and Shoya ends up shouldering all the blame. Six years later, the two meet again. Can Shoya make up for his past mistakes, or is it too late?
Available now in print and digitally!
© Yoshitoki Oima/Kodansha Ltd. All rights reserved.

Yamada-kun AND THE Seven Witches

KODANSHA COMICS

SWAPPED WITH A KISS?!

Class troublemaker Ryu Yamada is already having a bad day when he stumbles down a staircase along with star student Urara Shiraishi. When he wakes up, he realizes they have switched bodies—and that Ryu has the power to trade places with anyone just by kissing them! Ryu and Urara take full advantage of the situation to improve their lives, but with such an oddly amazing power, just how long will they be able to keep their secret under wraps?

Available now in print and digitally!

DON'T MISS THE MOST ACCLAIMED ACTION MANGA OF 2013!

"Gripping doesn't begin to describe Vinland Saga. 5 stars."
—ICv2

"Deeply engrossing... If you have any interest at all in Vikings, the Medieval period, or pirates, this is not a series you want to miss."
—Anime News Network

"The art is gorgeous, a combination of beautiful cartooning and realistic backgrounds. Yukimura is also a master of pacing, both in frenetic battle scenes and charged emotional moments."
—Faith Erin Hicks, *Friends With Boys*

"For those who love Berserk, you'll love this too... Worth the long wait."
—A Case Suitable for Treatment

"It will be impossible to stop watching this story unfold."
—Japan Media Arts Awards jury

A VIKING EPIC FROM THE AUTHOR OF "PLANETES"

VINLAND SAGA

AVAILABLE NOW IN HARDCOVER

SHERLOCK BONES

KC KODANSHA COMICS

DEDUCTIVE DOG DETECTIVE

When Takeru adopts a new pet, he's in for a surprise—the dog is none other than the reincarnation of Sherlock Holmes. With no one else able to communicate with Holmes, Takeru is roped into becoming Sherdog's assistant, John Watson. Using his sleuthing skills, Holmes uncovers clues to solve the trickiest crimes.

Say I Love You.

Mei Tachibana has no friends — and says she doesn't need them!

But everything changes when she accidentally roundhouse kicks the most popular boy in school! However, Yamato Kurosawa isn't angry in the slightest— in fact, he thinks his ordinary life could use an unusual girl like Mei. But winning Mei's trust will be a tough task. How long will she refuse to say, "I love you"?

My Little Monster

OPPOSITES ATTRACT...MAYBE?

Haru Yoshida is feared as an unstable and violent "monster." Mizutani Shizuku is a grade-obsessed student with no friends. Fate brings these two together to form the most unlikely pair. Haru firmly believes he's in love with Mizutani and she firmly believes he's insane.

KC
KODANSHA
COMICS

SANKAREA

undying love

"I ONLY LIKE ZOMBIE GIRLS."

Chihiro has an unusual connection to zombie movies. He doesn't feel bad for the survivors – he wants to comfort the undead girls they slaughter! When his pet passes away, he brews a resurrection potion. He's discovered by local heiress Sanka Rea, and she serves as his first test subject!

KC
KODANSHA
COMICS

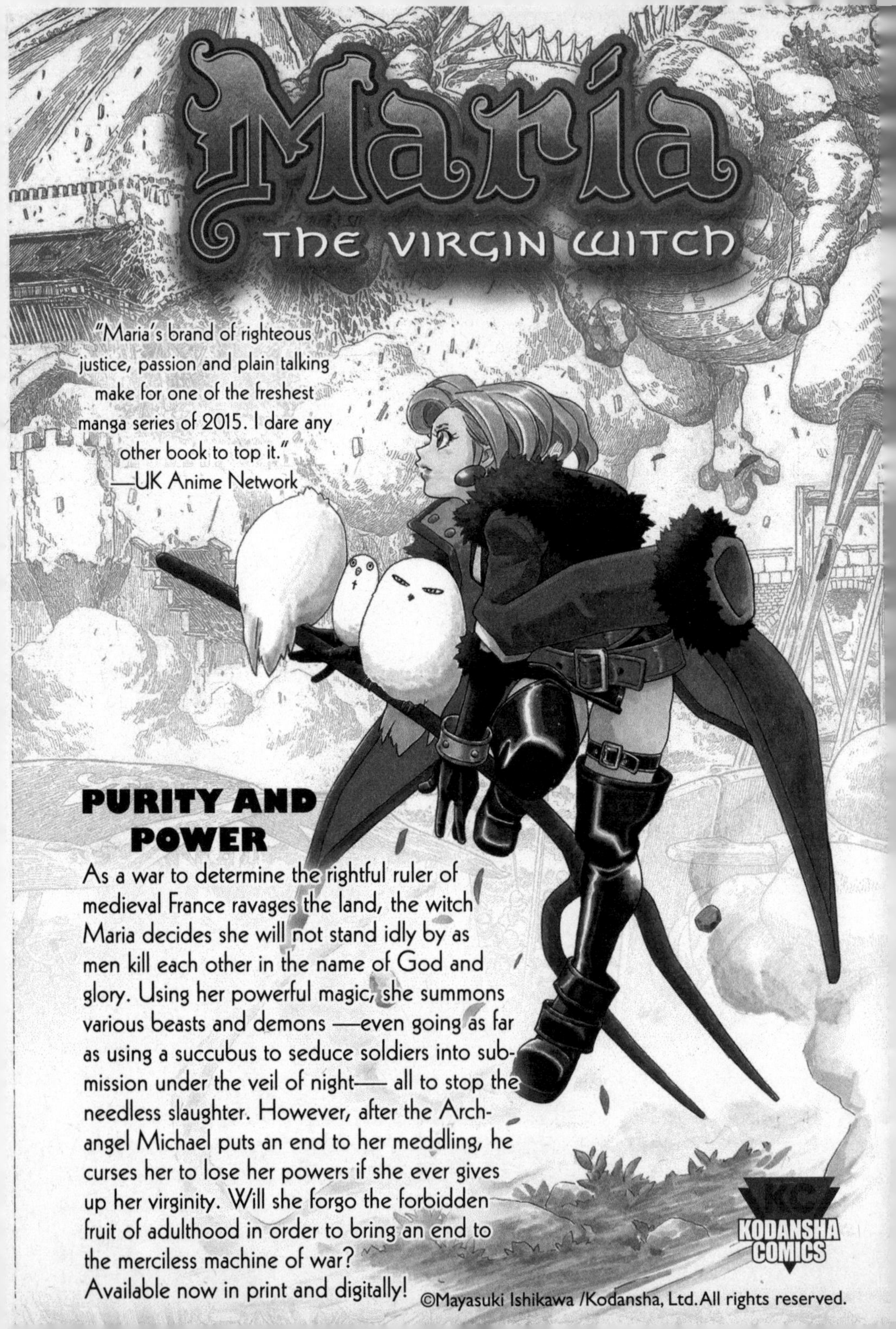
Maria
THE VIRGIN WITCH
"Maria's brand of righteous justice, passion and plain talking make for one of the freshest manga series of 2015. I dare any other book to top it."
—UK Anime Network
PURITY AND POWER
As a war to determine the rightful ruler of medieval France ravages the land, the witch Maria decides she will not stand idly by as men kill each other in the name of God and glory. Using her powerful magic, she summons various beasts and demons —even going as far as using a succubus to seduce soldiers into submission under the veil of night— all to stop the needless slaughter. However, after the Archangel Michael puts an end to her meddling, he curses her to lose her powers if she ever gives up her virginity. Will she forgo the forbidden fruit of adulthood in order to bring an end to the merciless machine of war?
Available now in print and digitally!
KC
KODANSHA COMICS
©Mayasuki Ishikawa /Kodansha, Ltd. All rights reserved.

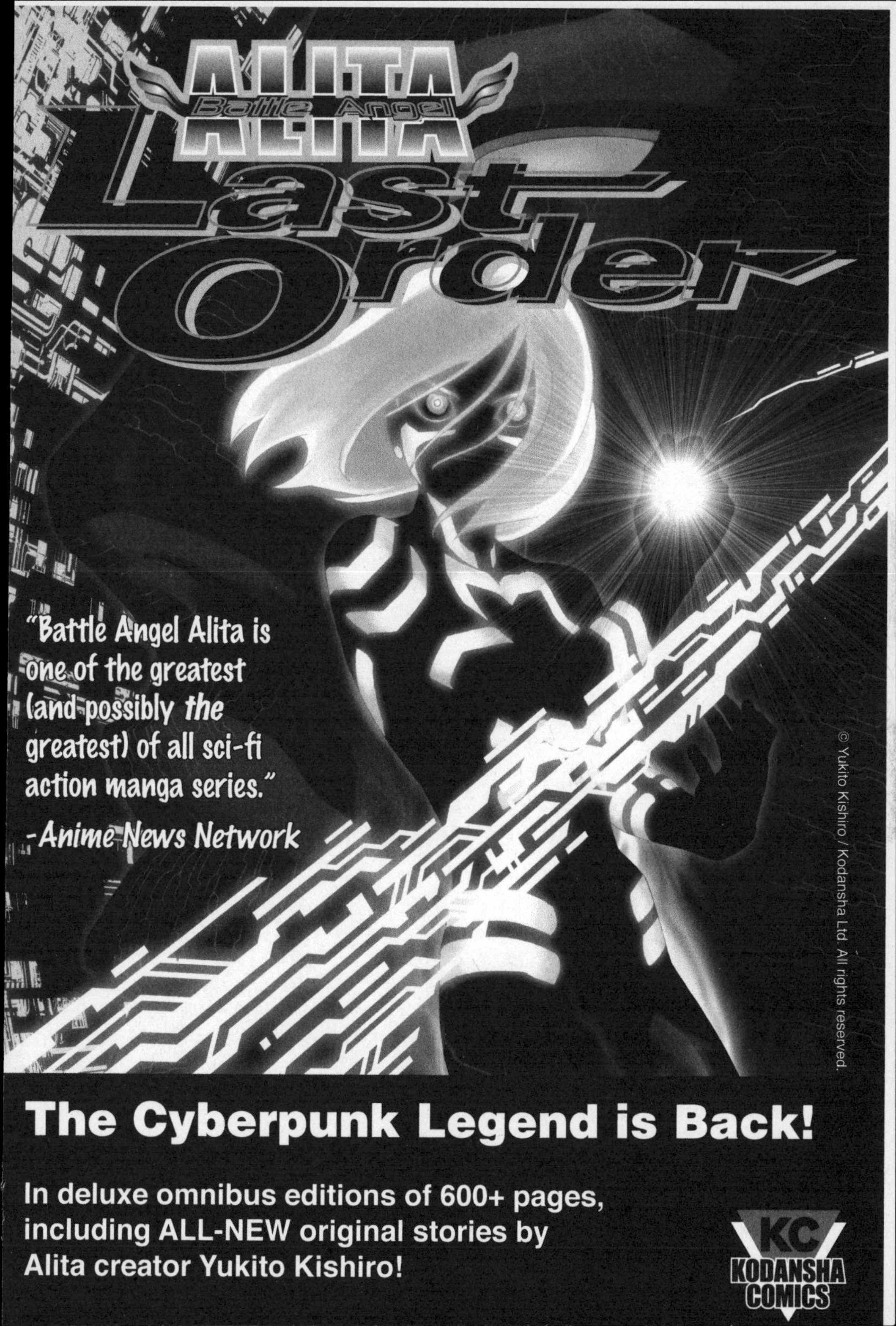
ALITA
Battle Angel
ALITA
Last Order
"Battle Angel Alita is one of the greatest (and possibly *the* greatest) of all sci-fi action manga series."
-Anime News Network
© Yukito Kishiro / Kodansha Ltd. All rights reserved.

INUYASHIKI

A superhero like none you've ever seen, from the creator of "Gantz"!

Ichiro Inuyashiki is down on his luck. He looks much older than his 58 years, his children despise him, and his wife thinks he's a useless coward. So when he's diagnosed with stomach cancer and given three months to live, it seems the only one who'll miss him is his dog.

Then a blinding light fills the sky, and the old man is killed... only to wake up later in a body he almost recognizes as his own. Can it be that Ichiro Inuyashiki is no longer human?

Comes in extra-large editions with color pages!

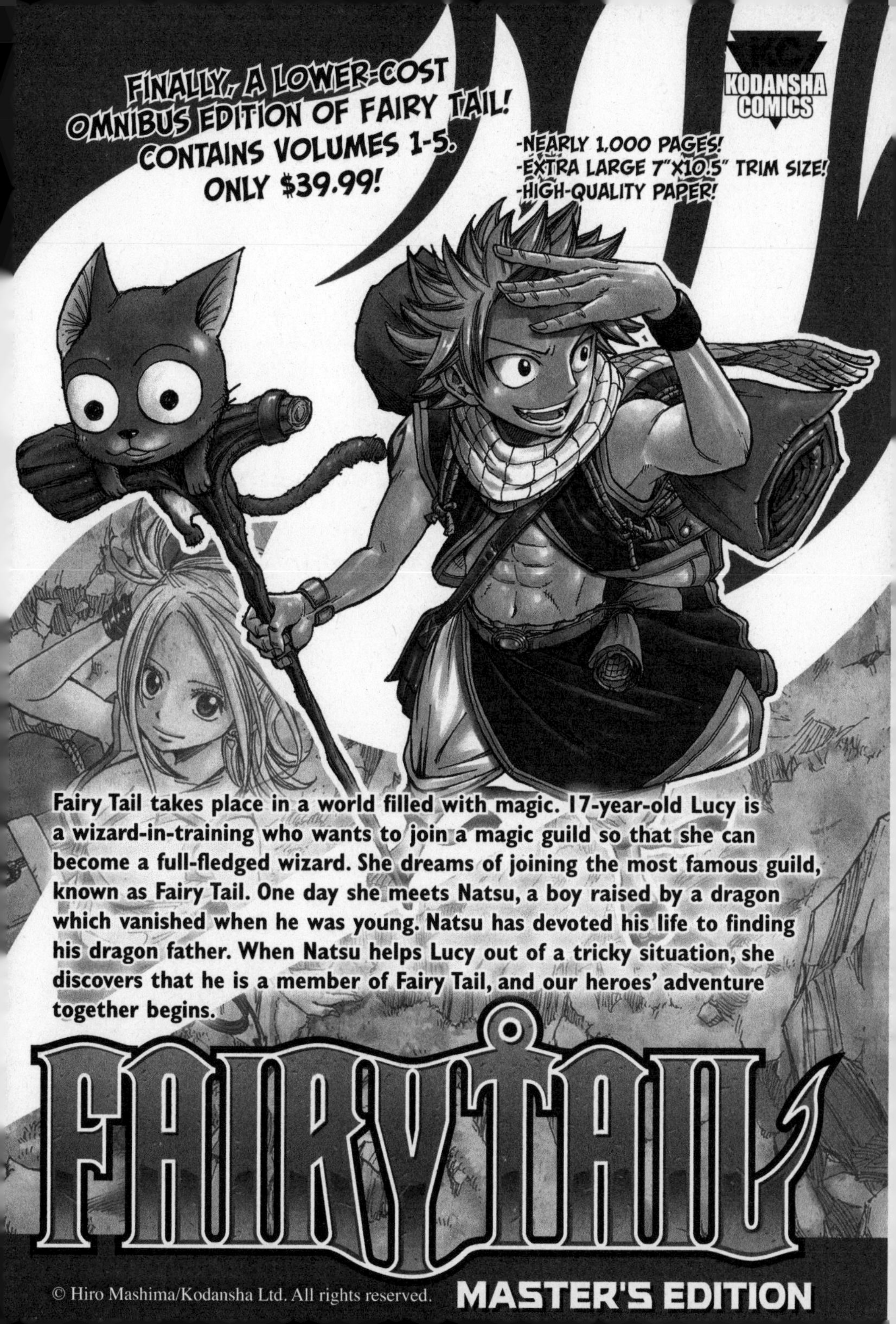
FINALLY, A LOWER-COST OMNIBUS EDITION OF FAIRY TAIL!
CONTAINS VOLUMES 1-5.
ONLY $39.99!
KODANSHA COMICS
-NEARLY 1,000 PAGES!
-EXTRA LARGE 7"X10.5" TRIM SIZE!
-HIGH-QUALITY PAPER!
Fairy Tail takes place in a world filled with magic. 17-year-old Lucy is a wizard-in-training who wants to join a magic guild so that she can become a full-fledged wizard. She dreams of joining the most famous guild, known as Fairy Tail. One day she meets Natsu, a boy raised by a dragon which vanished when he was young. Natsu has devoted his life to finding his dragon father. When Natsu helps Lucy out of a tricky situation, she discovers that he is a member of Fairy Tail, and our heroes' adventure together begins.
FAIRY TAIL
© Hiro Mashima/Kodansha Ltd. All rights reserved.
MASTER'S EDITION

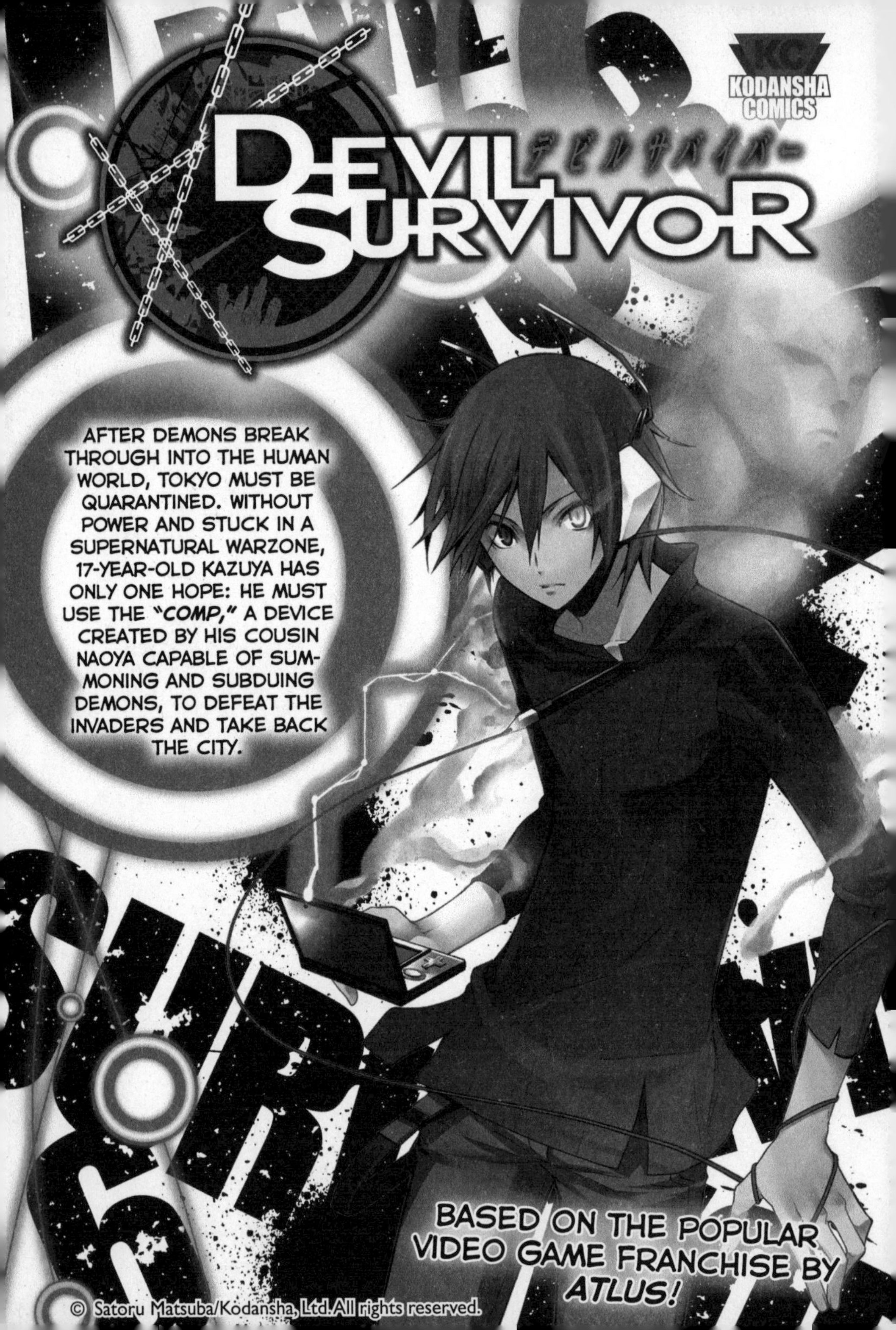
KC
KODANSHA COMICS
DEVIL SURVIVOR
AFTER DEMONS BREAK THROUGH INTO THE HUMAN WORLD, TOKYO MUST BE QUARANTINED. WITHOUT POWER AND STUCK IN A SUPERNATURAL WARZONE, 17-YEAR-OLD KAZUYA HAS ONLY ONE HOPE: HE MUST USE THE *"COMP,"* A DEVICE CREATED BY HIS COUSIN NAOYA CAPABLE OF SUMMONING AND SUBDUING DEMONS, TO DEFEAT THE INVADERS AND TAKE BACK THE CITY.
BASED ON THE POPULAR VIDEO GAME FRANCHISE BY *ATLUS!*
© Satoru Matsuba/Kodansha, Ltd. All rights reserved.

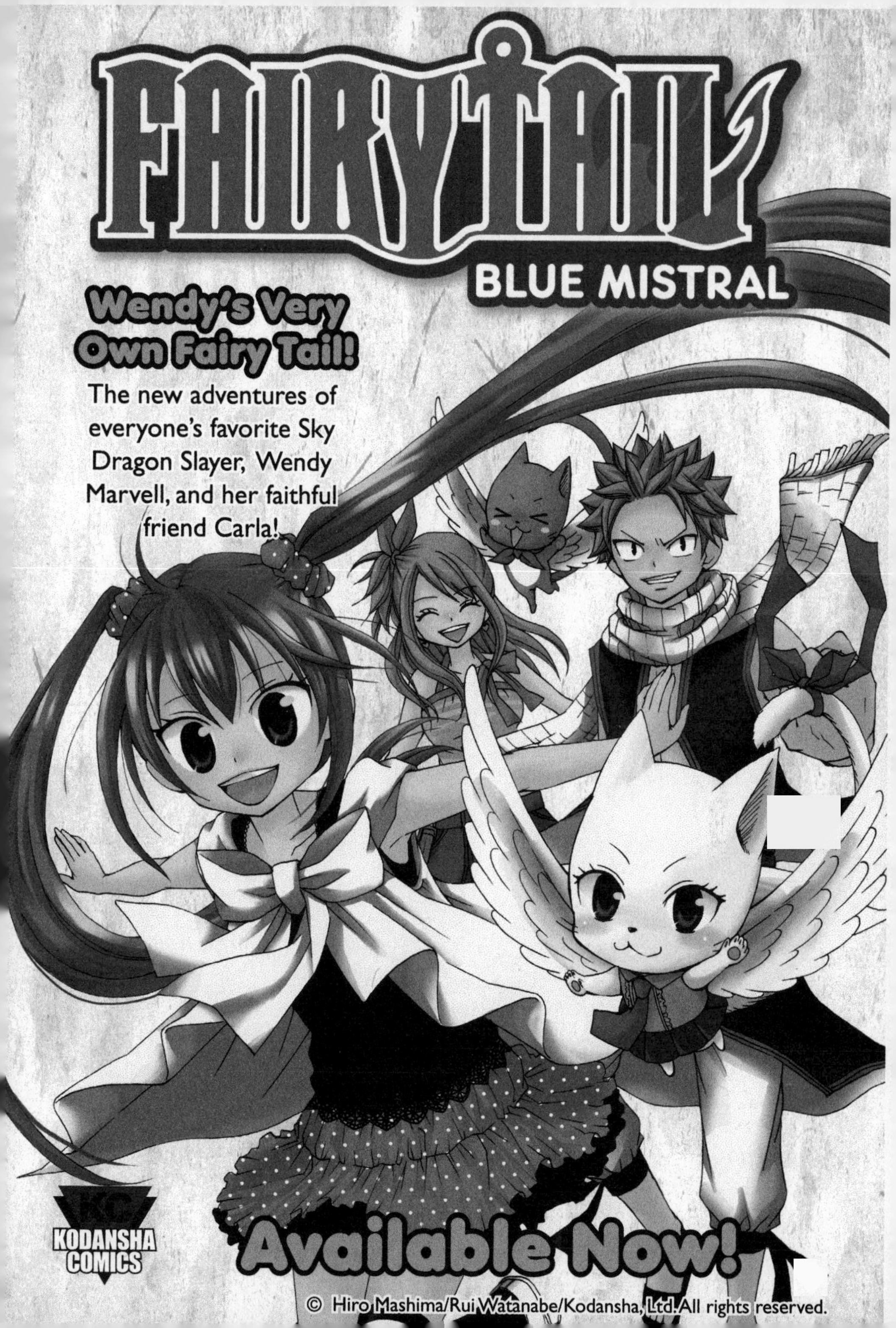
FAIRY TAIL
BLUE MISTRAL
Wendy's Very Own Fairy Tail!
The new adventures of everyone's favorite Sky Dragon Slayer, Wendy Marvell, and her faithful friend Carla!
KC
KODANSHA COMICS
Available Now!
© Hiro Mashima/Rui Watanabe/Kodansha, Ltd. All rights reserved.

Cells at Work! volume 1 is a work of fiction. Names, characters, places, and incidents are the products of the author's imagination or are used fictitiously. Any resemblance to actual events, locales, or persons, living or dead, is entirely coincidental.

A Kodansha Comics Trade Paperback Original.

Published in the United States by Kodansha Comics,
an imprint of Kodansha USA Publishing, LLC, New York.

Publication rights for this English edition arranged through Kodansha Ltd., Tokyo.

First published in Japan in 2016 by Kodansha Ltd., Tokyo, as *Hataraku Saibou* volume 1.

ISBN 978-1-63236-356-5

Printed in the United States of America.

www.kodanshacomics.com

9 8 7 6 5

Translation: Yamato Tanaka
Lettering: Abigail Blackman
Editing: Paul Starr
Kodansha Comics edition cover design: Phil Balsman

HOW TO READ MANGA

Japanese is written right to left and top to bottom. This means that for a reader accustomed to Western languages, Japanese books read "backwards." Since most manga published in English now keeps the Japanese page order, it can take a little getting used to—but once you learn how, it's a snap. Here's a handy guide!

Here you can see pages 10-11 from this book. The speech balloons have been numbered in the order you should read them in.

Start here, at the top right corner of the right hand page.

Page 10*—read this one first!*

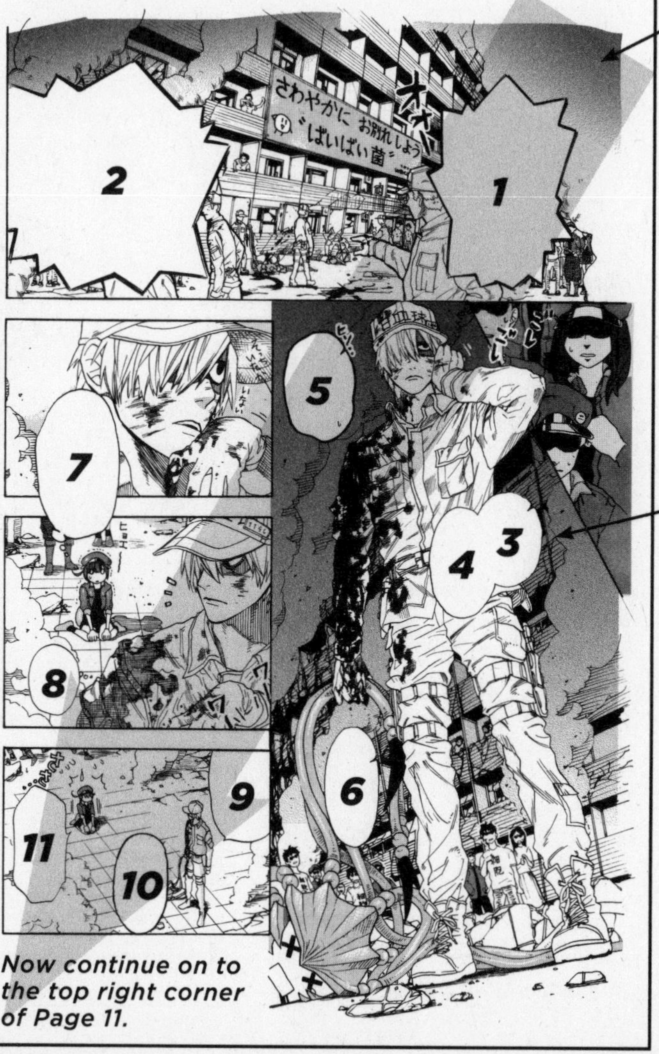
1
さわやかに お別れしよう
ばいばい菌
2
3
4
5
6
7
8
9
10
11

Read right to left, then top to bottom. In this panel, the leftmost speech balloon comes before the one in the top left corner.

Now continue on to the top right corner of Page 11.

Page 11

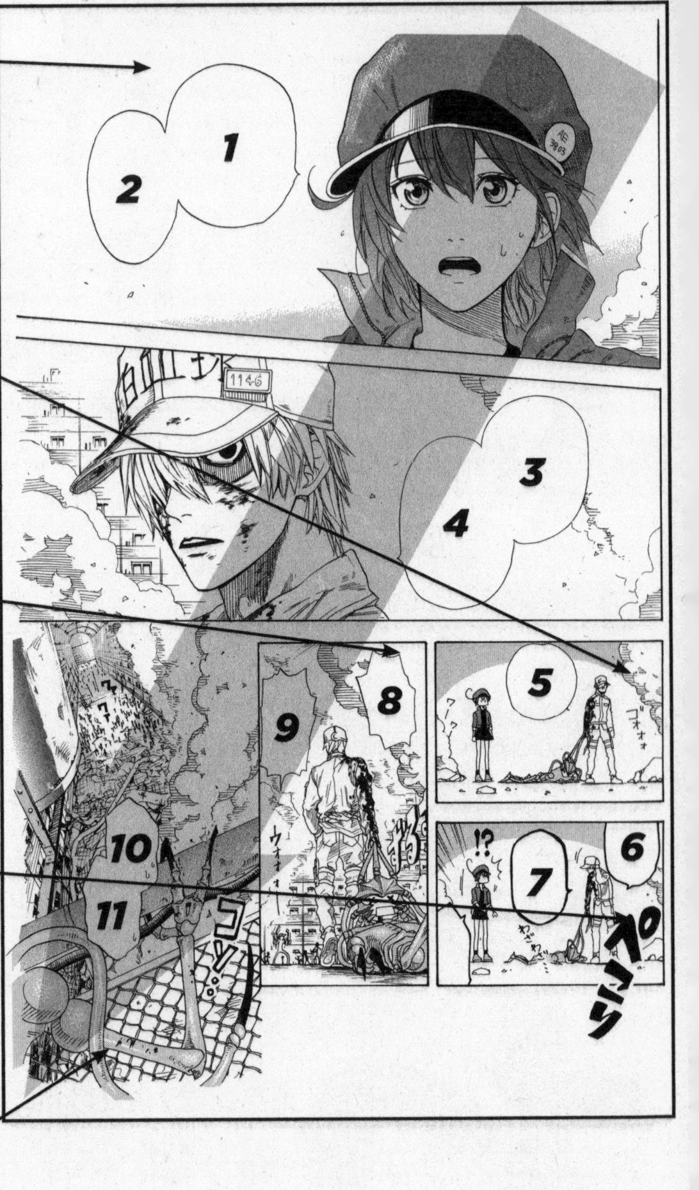
1
2
3
4
5
6
7
8
9
10
11

On this page, the top two panels are read first.

This panel is the top right-most after the first two, so it's next.

If you go to this panel next, you would have to move backwards (right) to read balloons 6 and 7.

Instead, after reading balloon 5, you move down to 6 and 7, then left...

...and then you arrive at the end of the page!

After a few pages, you'll be reading manga like a pro—*Japanese-style!*

止まれ

(That means STOP)

You're about to read a *manga*—a Japanese comic—presented in its original page order, which means you start at the other end of the book. If you need a quick guide on how to read manga the way it was meant to be read, flip to the next page—otherwise, turn the book over and enjoy!